# Strategic Marketing for Not-for-Profit Organizations

# Strategic Marketing for Not-for-Profit Organizations

## Program and Resource Development

**ARMAND LAUFFER**

THE FREE PRESS
*A Division of Macmillan, Inc.*
NEW YORK

Collier Macmillan Publishers
LONDON

The Free Press
A Division of Macmillan, Inc.
866 Third Avenue, New York, N.Y. 10022

Collier Macmillan Canada, Inc.

Printed in the United States of America

printing number

1 2 3 4 5 6 7 8 9 10


**Library of Congress Cataloging in Publication Data**

Lauffer, Armand.
    Strategic marketing for not-for-profit organizations.

    Includes index.
    1. Corporations, Nonprofit—Marketing.    2. Social
service—Marketing.    I. Title.
HD2741.L3154    1984        658.8        83-49509
ISBN 0-02-918260-3

# CONTENTS

# ACKNOWLEDGMENTS

THE RECOGNITION that many publics have an interest in an agency's programs and services is what distinguishes strategic marketing from other approaches to program design, development, and delivery. I learned this lesson early in my career from three master practitioners: David Macarov, Frank Loewenberg, and Jerry Bubis. Some years later I had the opportunity to test and refine the principles of marketing with a number of colleagues at The University of Michigan's Program for Continuing Education in the Human Services. Among them are Celeste Sturdevant-Reed, Carla Overberger, Tom Morton, George Mink, Marv Berman, Lynn Nybel, Larry Berlin, and Roy Gaunt.

For their forebearance, good will, and hard work, I want to thank Roxanne Loy, Pauline Bush, and the "fourth floor team."

The book is dedicated to my father, Georges Lauffer, from whom I learned that personal and professional integrity are at the core of most successful marketing strategies.

Armand Lauffer
*Jerusalem, 1984*

# LOOKING BACK AND LOOKING AHEAD: AN INTRODUCTION

"WHY WOULD YOU, a social worker, want to write a book on marketing?" I was challenged by a colleague who directs a large mental health center. She continued, "I'm familiar enough with your other work to know that your approach to planning pretty much parallels ours at the agency. And it doesn't include a hard sell. Our services are needed. And if they are any good, they sell themselves."

The occasion for this discussion was an informal meeting of I.E., a group of colleagues from practice and academia that met periodically for an *idea exchange*. We were exploring some of the concepts I hoped to include in this book. My ideas had been a long time in developing, and I was anxious to get feedback from people I respected. "You know Lauffer," another colleague added, "he's always looking for a new twist on things." But that's not the point at all, I thought to myself. "Why borrow from the business world?" asked another participant. "Haven't consumers been sufficiently exploited and manipulated by advertisers in the commercial world? Why apply the same practices to the social services?" That wasn't the point either.

We had met as a group many times before to explore a new idea or to help each other with a practice problem. Although we were accustomed to the criticism we offered each other, I felt this discussion was beginning to take on a merciless character. I wondered why. Was there really something offensive in my ideas or were my colleagues being overly defensive? Did they have something to protect themselves against? I suspected the answer to the last question was "yes," but not for the reasons they thought.

Before deciding to write this book, I had done a great deal of thinking about my experiences as a practitioner, a program manager, and a faculty member. Like a career in which the stages one passes through seem logical in retrospect, the evolution of an idea seems to make sense only at the point where one has recognized it.

My first professional job was to organize campus chapters of a minority rights organization. Convinced of the importance of my cause, I concentrated on the message that I had to sell and developed a way of packaging it: lunches or dinners at fraternity and sorority houses, guest lectureships in undergraduate psychology and sociology courses, ceremonial meetings with the president of the University, organizing sessions under the auspices of campus religious foundations, and so on. I finished the year with scores of articles and stories in the campus press or on campus radio and was convinced I had raised the "critical consciousness" (a term I didn't know at the time) of those who had been reached. Thirty-two or thirty-three chapters were in place.

Someone else took over the organizing responsibilities when I returned to graduate school. At the end of his first year, only seven chapters were left in operation. With the arrogance of youth and inexperience, I concluded the reason lay in my successor's lack of effectiveness. Still, I was troubled by a feeling that perhaps the real cause was, at least in part, the result of my own organizing efforts. Had my work with the members of each chapter provided enough meaning to sustain the chapter for more than a few months?

Some time later, I was employed as a camp director for a community center on the West Coast. "You'll never guess what happened," the agency's director chuckled one morning. "One of our senior citizens burst into my office a few minutes ago, still in her bathing suit and dripping on my carpet, enraged that she had to get out of the pool to allow the campers in. I explained that they were scheduled for instructional swim every morning at 11:00, and that adults would be able to use the pool again by 12:15. I told her that I hoped that it didn't inconvenience her too much and tried to explain how important it was for all of us, as members of the community, to share our facilities. And besides, wasn't it nice that our children were learning to swim? 'Mister,' she said, 'don't talk to me about children. I bought swimming!'"

Here we were, trying to convince her to behave like a good citizen, to share her membership benefits with others in the community. That is how we saw her, as a *member*, but that is not how she saw herself. As far as she was concerned, she was a paying *customer*. She *bought* swimming.

Many years later, as director of continuing education (C.E.) at the University of Michigan's School of Social Work, I was engaged in planning and managing summer workshops, and working with government and foundation sources on the development of more extensive programs and projects. As a rule of thumb, our faculty advisory committee had determined that the School should only engage in projects about whose success someone else cared as much as we did. The stakes had to be shared and the benefits, although they might vary for each of the parties involved (funders, providers, and consumers), would also have to be shared. In effect, we had decided that those who pay and those who consume had to have a share in the development of the product. The reasons for this decision may become clear if I describe one particular project. When the state office of Substance Abuse Services asked the School to design a training program, I thought I needed a bit of continuing education myself.

An ex-drug addict I knew invited me to observe some pushers, former buddies of his, working the street. He knew that I was in the midst of preparing a project proposal to train substance abuse counselors and thought I should have a first-hand view of the client population those counselors would be working with. I was fascinated. For 2 days I was submerged in an almost unknown world. I observed small-time pushers living precariously between the activities of the police and the norms of the street.

The pushers were addicts, dependent on other addicts to buy their products and on the suppliers to provide them with the necessary goods— heroin and cocaine. I remarked to my friend that the pushers seemed a sorry lot. "Yeah," he answered, "The pushers are being pushed. Consumer demand is up, but the supply is down and there are too many pushers around. Competition is fierce, not just for the customers' money, but also for the suppliers' goods."

"Incredible," I said to myself, "*I* am like those pushers." As a director of a continuing education program, I was just as dependent as a pusher on my suppliers, on my program's consumers, and the competitors of my program's operations. Unfortunately, demand for continuing education was neither high nor reliable. Our consumers weren't addicted to C.E.; nor were they limited to a single supplier. They weren't about to buy whatever the School would be willing or able to provide. They were only going to purchase something that they wanted.

Perhaps, in this case, they weren't buying "swimming." Neither were they about to be organized into chapters to achieve our organization's missions. They had missions and interests of their own. The question was whether those interests could be served through some form of exchange with the School's C.E. program. "Exchange" was the word I had been looking for in describing my ideas about marketing to the others in I.E. *That* is what the book would be about, the exchanges that take place between those in the business of developing and delivering programs and services and their competitors, collaborators, consumers, regulators, and auspice providers. Exchanges occur in a marketplace. A market is made up of these various publics. Those transactions that take place in a market shape and give meaning to the programs and services an organization provides. If the transactions themselves have little meaning to the participants—like those who joined campus chapters, the woman who bought swimming not membership, and some of the participants in C.E. activities—the programs or services an agency provides may be without much merit.

I forced myself out of my reverie and back to the meeting with my I.E. colleagues. "Back up a minute," I heard myself saying. "Let me tell you the story of a drug pusher." And I did.

Before you go on to read Chapter 1 and to begin your own examination of the strategic marketing approach to program planning and resource development, I thought it might make sense to dispense with the objection to marketing articulated by one of my colleagues, an objection heard too frequently in human service settings. I am referring to the disparaging remarks regarding experience or knowledge gleaned from the business community. It reminded me of a similar incident that occurred while I was teaching a course on the tools of planning at Berkeley back in 1969.

"These are nothing but tools of the military industrial complex," one of the students challenged. "Wasn't PERT designed for launching the first nuclear submarine?"

"And how about the origins of task analysis in the Air Force, or the development of Delphi by the Rand Corporation?" chimed in another.

Considering that this was the first session of the course, I thought these students were pretty well prepared. But so was I.

"Be right back," I said, slipping out the door. I ran down the stairs to my car, opened the trunk and took out a hammer, a badly chipped dish, and a disassembled picture frame. Back in the classroom, and somewhat out of breath, I proceeded to smash the dish. I then took a few nails out of my pocket and began to assemble the picture frame. They got the picture. Hammers are, in themselves, neither good nor bad. Only the use to which they are put can be subjected to moral interpretation.

Even if you do feel that the business world is exploitative and manipulative of the public—and so, by the way, are a number of social agencies—there is no reason why you can't learn from the experience of business. Nor is there a reason why you can't apply business concepts and practices where appropriate. Certainly we all do it in the areas of accounting, information management, and, interestingly, human relations training. So let's take off our blinders and look around us. As I think you will agree when you get deeper into this book, marketing concepts permit us to overcome a bias that many human service workers and administrators maintain.

Many of us tend to begin with the assumption that our products, the services that we provide, and the actions in which we engage are in the best interest of the public. We further assume that there is a need (even if sometimes there is no demand) for the services that we provide, simply because we are convinced that they are good for people. I remember working for a family service agency in which everyone's problems were defined in psychoanalytic terms the moment the client walked through the front door. It didn't matter what clients asked for—housing, guidance in coping with an aging parent, or help with a child who suffered from a learning disability. The agency's "products," its analytically oriented counseling services, were considered by the staff to be just what the client needed. Staff then set about shaping the client's perceptions about his or her needs according to the agency's definition of its services, and educating the client to make effective use of those services. Professionals, after all, were trained to look beneath the presenting problem, to the real problem and its underlying cause. At the time I *thought* this behavior was professionally irresponsible, even unethical; in retrospect I am *convinced* of it.

The marketing orientation could not be more different. It begins with an examination of the needs and interests of the consumers and other key publics. It then examines the range of programs or services that might accommodate to those needs or interests and seeks out a particular niche, a segment of the market that might be targeted for penetration. It considers the interests of various other publics in supplying needed resources for the operation of those services. It requires an understanding of various partners in the development and delivery of those services. It considers the cost of those services and the places where they might best be delivered. Then it considers ways of informing the relevant publics about those services. All of this is done within the context of resource development.

Far from being antithetical to the concerns of human services planning and program development, the strategic marketing approach increases the likelihood that professional activity will be responsive to consumer needs and societal concerns. These are sometimes in conflict with each other, just as they are often complementary. The marketing approach provides no guarantee that such conflicts will be reconciled, but it does increase the likelihood that they will be recognized as social workers and other human service practitioners build their program and resource development strategies on the *reconciliation* of interests between various publics—consumers, auspice providers, funders, and other potential partners in the service delivery system.

One of the reviewers of the first draft of this book, in fact, referred to it as a volume of "reconciliations." To reconcile means to bring (back) into harmony, to adjust, to settle, to make consistent or congruous. This is indeed my intent. I have attempted to bring into harmony the traditions of community organizing, social planning, and business marketing with some of the newest approaches to strategic planning. I have also attempted to draw upon practice concepts drawn from human ecology, role theory, and exchange and power theory and to make them consistent with one another. And in many of the examples I present in the text, I have attempted to emphasize the congruity between the "rational" and "transactive" approaches to planning and development. These efforts were essential to the presentation of an approach to practice that attempts to reconcile the interests of diverse publics—to adjust them to each other and to settle on programs and services that are at least satisfactory to the interested parties and that may, with good fortune, even achieve the optimal.

This recognition that many publics have an interest in an organization's programs and services is what distinguishes the strategic marketing approach from other approaches to program design, resource development, and service delivery. The actual services an organization performs for interested groups, both within the organization and outside, may very well be consistent with its *stated* goals. These services may, however, be in conflict with, or irrelevant to, other views of those goals. For example, an agency that provides rehabilitation and job training services may be expected to absorb part of the unemployed work force, to regulate the behavior of those unemployed who become its clients, and to provide resources (in the form of retrained personnel) for employers in the private sector. These are its actual goals, as expressed in activities and their functions. They may not be identical with the organization's officially stated goals of rehabilitation and placement of workers in stable and permanent jobs.

To the extent that achievement of those goals also articulates with the functions it is expected to perform on behalf of other publics, there is likely to be support for the agency. However, when the services that an agency provides to its primary consumers are perceived as irrelevant to other publics, the attainment of a particular goal may be immaterial to the organization's survival. Look around you. You'll see many human service organizations that do not rehabilitate, that do not cure, and that do not educate well. Nevertheless, they continue to operate with some degree of consistent support. Rather than attempt to reconcile the contradictory interests of various publics, they have chosen to respond to some while ignoring others. Perhaps this is another reason my colleagues were a bit uncomfortable with my decision to write a book on marketing.

There is a tendency on the part of some human service workers to complain that "We can't really do our job because the funders or some other public won't allow us to." That is a misperception of reality. To the contrary, it is just because these publics may expect something else from our agencies that we can get the resources we need to provide services. Our programs' stated goals legitimize the allocation of resources to them even if the functions of those programs have little to do with the goals. Providing needed health services to the elderly and to the poor are rationales for Medicare and Medicaid grants. The functions of those programs may be to support an ever-growing and expanding medical system and to regulate the ways in which segments of the population receive medical care. The interests of providers, consumers, legitimators, and funders cannot always be fully reconciled, but the strategic marketing approach described in these pages is one approach to the achievement of harmony and congruity.

## Organization of the Book

These dynamics will become clearer as you read the three chapters in Part I of the book. Chapter 1 zeroes in on the terminology that is central to program and resource development and shows how the marketing approach with its 5 P's—*p*roducts, *p*ublics, *p*rice, *p*lace, and *p*romotions—is distinguishable from other approaches to planning. Market conditions for the 1980s are analyzed. Exchange and other concepts that underlie strategic marketing are presented in Chapter 2, which I think you will find indispensable to your understanding of marketing and to your development of an effective marketing strategy.

Exchange, whether mandated or voluntary, is a process whereby individuals and/or organizations associate in order to achieve shared or complementary objectives. The exchange relationship has to be functional, or at least must be perceived as functional by each of the parties to it. Functionality is defined in terms of benefits, and those benefits must in some way outweigh the costs incurred through the exchange process.

All organizations respond to the needs and interests of throughput (staff, volunteers, and members), input (providers of resources and legitimacy), and output publics (those that receive or consume the organizations' products and other outputs). These make up an organization's markets, and those markets that are considered most relevant or desirable can be pinpointed for specific penetration. The extent to which an organization's programs and services are accepted by various publics determines the niche it will maintain in the market.

In addition to providing you with a conceptual foundation, these chapters also preview the structure of the remainder of the book. You will find that each chapter begins with an introductory vignette presenting real-life examples of both good and not-so-good practice. We learn from both our errors and our successes. In a number of vignettes, I will share with you my own experiences. In others (those in which the narrator's words are in quotation marks), I have permitted colleagues from a variety of human service occupations to speak for themselves. Other vignettes appear throughout the text.

Each chapter also includes one or more exercises. There is sometimes a tendency to skip over these with all good intentions of returning to them and completing them dutifully at some time in the future. This may be a mistake. I have purposely integrated them within the body of each chapter, instead of placing them at the chapter's end, to provide you with an opportunity to test the applicability of what you are reading to your own practice or areas of interest. The exercises also serve as integration devices. Subsequent portions of the chapter may build on the experience you gained through doing the exercise. In fact, by completing each exercise, you participate with me in writing the book, expanding it with your own experiences and insights.

The chapters in Parts II, III, and IV are intended to provide you with the "nuts and bolts" of the strategic marketing approach to program and resource development. Although they build on each other, they can be read out of sequence. Part II focuses on the processes involved in establishing and maintaining exchange relationships, particularly with the consumers of services and with other providers with whom the agency may be interdependent. Exchange relationships with funders and other resource providers are discussed more fully in Part IV. These are, I suppose, the "bread and butter" chapters. That would make Part III the "meat and potatoes." It is composed of six chapters that deal with almost all aspects of program development and design within the context of strategic marketing: assessment, design, location, pricing, budgeting, charting or scheduling, and evaluation. Chapter 16 places program evaluation within the context of evaluation of an organization's total marketing operation, thereby summarizing the integral connections between the needs and resources of the larger environment, program development, and marketing demonstrated throughout the book.

Those of you who may not be employed by a human service organization may have noticed that I make continual reference to "agencies" and frequently to "your agency." Although my own practice experience has been limited mainly to social agencies and many of the vignettes are drawn from human services like rehabilitation, family treatment, child welfare, and mental health, the concepts and methods discussed are much more generic. They are applicable to a wide variety of not-for-profit organizations, whether in the public, private, or voluntary sectors. I do, in fact, provide occasional examples of marketing approaches used by schools, libraries, and hospitals. Please consider the term "agency" in its most generic sense. Simply substitute the name of your association or organization for the word "agency," and you should have no difficulty in making the transition.

You can test the validity of the concepts in an atmosphere that is very real, but where decisions are not for keeps, by playing the gamed simulation in the Appendix. COMPACTS II will provide you and your colleagues with an opportunity to test out a variety of strategic marketing approaches through the *Co*llaborative *M*arketing, *P*lanning, and *A*ction Simulation. Try it before you get too far into this book. Try it again when you've completed it. How much have your actions changed on the basis of what you've learned?

# PART I

# The Framework of Strategic Marketing

# 1 THE STRATEGIC MARKETING APPROACH

STRATEGIC MARKETING IS a comprehensive approach to the management of internal and external environmental variables that often seem to control the behavior of our organizations. It focuses directly on the transactions between an organization and the various publics on which it is dependent. In profit-making organizations, the market is generally made up of those publics that are the actual or potential consumers of the organizations' products. If these publics "buy" what the organizations have to sell, management and investors are likely to evaluate the marketing strategy as being successful. This is not necessarily the case for not-for-profit organizations.

Because the consumer is not likely to be the only paying public for social agencies, libraries, and schools, the organization in question must develop a marketing strategy that will also address those other publics from which it recruits necessary resources—contributors to the United Way, government agencies, foundations, and so on. Moreover, because staff and consumers are generally involved as partners (albeit with different responsibilities) in the process of program development and delivery, an effective marketing strategy must account for what that staff and others may be willing or able to contribute to the enterprise.

Changes in market conditions throughout the 1980s and beyond are likely to require a new and more systematic approach to agency transactions with various publics. "Hard work, skill, and a little bit of luck," a colleague told me recently, "is what we attribute our success to in placing clients in community settings." Perhaps, but I discovered, on deeper probing, that hard work, skill, and luck were hardly sufficient. She, the administrator, also had a clearly thought-through marketing strategy. We'll examine that strategy and others as we progress through the chapters that follow. But first, I want to share with you an example of gambling and losing when we trust only to hard work and luck. We'll then examine some of the concepts that go into strategic marketing and itemize some of the market conditions that are likely to affect your organization throughout the rest of this decade.

### Gambling and Losing

"I guess you could say I gambled and lost. Only two years ago I was the darling of the board. Within a few months of being appointed director of the Citizens for Independence, I had managed to get us two state grants, and we were expecting to be designated a special demonstration agency by the Rehabilitation Service Administration in Washington. Voluntary contributions of money and materials were steady if not spectacular. Most of our staff and many of our Board members are disabled themselves and were committed to contributing to their own enterprise.

"Well, the economy turned sour and government financing for the disabled became incredibly scarce. My Board insisted we cut the budget by the amount we expected to lose in grants and gifts. But that meant we would have to cut our services by 50 percent or more. I refused. That kind of cut was not something I could face either staff or clients with. I insisted that we continue providing essential *services*, perhaps trimming a bit here or there or substituting some volunteer help for paid staff. But I would not permit any major cuts. I knew I was a pretty good fund-raiser, and I thought we had a salable *product*. If we could hold out for six months, I would be able to find the money we needed to continue for the second half of the year.

"And if the money wasn't forthcoming, I figured that there were other *resources* out there: people who could do more on their own behalf, family members and friends, civic-minded people who could volunteer to take on special jobs. It might mean some *program* redesign, but I was sure we could do it.

"I guess I did not fully anticipate what I would be up against. With the downturn of the economy, some of our disabled clients found themselves bereft of services which had been provided by other agencies. More people approached us for help with job training and job finding. The City Council reduced its funding support by $20,000, and the Community Mental Health Center was threatening an even larger cut. There didn't seem to be more volunteers available than before. My staff was overworked and grumbling. And demand for service was up. It looked like we would have to let staff go, borrow money to stay afloat, or else close down for the summer months. I got my dismissal notice last week. In some ways, I can't blame the Board. But I think Board members could have been out there hustling for resources just the way I was. Staff members were too harried, and I just could not ask them to do any more. Besides, they weren't really into resource development and I wanted to protect them.

"What hurt the most is that the staff did not stick up for me. Even the clients for whom I had worked so hard took my dismissal without any comment except to worry about whether this meant the end of the agency or not.

"Like I said, I gambled and lost."*

This is hardly an original story. We've heard it in one form or another from many talented human service professionals lately. In this case, the concerns with program design (or redesign), service delivery, and resource development were all important issues to address, but the way in which they were addressed left something to be desired: a strategy that would have been more likely to produce results. Consistent winners do not trust to luck, hard work, or good intentions. They have "win strategies" that reduce the likelihood of gambling and losing.

An awareness of what goes into strategic marketing combined with a more appropriate perspective and the requisite skills might have made a big difference to the agency, its board, its clients, and its staff—not to speak of the executive quoted. To understand what is meant by *strategic marketing* it might be helpful to begin with some definitions of the words used by the administrator: terms like *resources*, *program*, and *services*. We'll then move on to some terms more generally associated with what I call the five P's of marketing—*p*roducts, *p*ublics, *p*romotions, *p*rice, and *p*lace.

## Getting the Language Straight — Resources, Programs, and Services: Conceptions and Misconceptions

*Resources* refers to any means or commodities used to achieve a given end or objective. That end may be maintenance of an agency's program, delivery of a particular service, achievement of a political victory, or a change in the behavior or amelioration of a situation affecting the client. Resources include money and credit, facilities, equipment, professional expertise (often contained in books and journals), the people who can apply the aforementioned resources, and such ephemerals as political influence, legitimacy, and energy. Some of these resources are in short supply. Others are abundant, but so poorly orchestrated as to make them either unavailable or ineffective in use.

In the vignette, which resources were in apparent short supply? Which did the administrator seem unaware of? Could some of these resources have been used to substitute for those that were unavailable? Could some resources have been used to generate other needed resources?

*Many of the vignettes are reconstructions based on my interviews with practitioners. Persons and organizations have been disguised to preserve anonymity.

By *program*, I mean a sequence of events and activities that are at least potentially repeatable, in much the same order. A program has a beginning and an end, even when it is ongoing; that is, similar events and activities may occur over and over again. For example, a theater program may be described as a one-shot affair or one that exists over time regardless of how long a particular play may run. An agency's program may include all of its services and those other activities that reflect the purposes for which it has been established and for which it receives support. It may also specify a particular subset of activities such as a fund-raising campaign or a marketing program.

An agency's *services* are part of its overall program. I use the term services to refer to those activities of staff (and other personnel associated with a program) that are tended to benefit others. For example, counseling and placement are *services* offered to clients or trainees in a job training *program*. The way services are organized in relation to each other make up most or all of an organization's service program. Services assume a need on the part of a consumer population. An organization's capacity to deliver a service or services also assumes external support and internal capacity.

The delivery of the service requires (1) a system of delivery (the service program) and (2) sufficient resources to make that service program operable. These requirements might be thought of as the resource development, resource orchestration, and resource deployment program. In systems language, we would be talking about developing and orchestrating *inputs* (resources) that go through a transformation in the agency's *throughput system*, resulting in program *outputs*.

I have already discussed one of the five P's that is associated with marketing: the "product" which can be defined in output or program terms. The other four words that begin with the letter *P* are *publics*, *price*, *place*, and *promotion*; each of these contributes to strategic marketing. Marketing is "strategic" precisely when each of these P's is taken into account during efforts to achieve objectives.

By *publics*, I mean all those individuals, groups, and organizations external to an organization that either provide it with inputs or are the recipients of its outputs as well as those internal publics that carry on the organization's business. *Input* publics include the suppliers of resources (like money, knowledge, or facilities), the providers of auspice and legitimacy (like the board of directors), regulatory publics that make the rules or set the standards and pass the laws that govern what your agency can or cannot do (like legislators, or standard-setting professional associations). *Output* publics are those that receive some benefit from the service or activities of your organization. These are often the clients or consumers who are the direct beneficiaries of your agency's efforts and to a large extent the general public which may benefit indirectly.

A number of these external publics compete with your organization for resources, legitimacy, or clients. Often these very same organizations and groups are potential partners. It is not unusual for competitors also to be collaborators. At the University, I have engaged in a number of collaborative enterprises with faculty from the schools of Public Health, Education, Architecture, and Natural Resources. Each of these schools also competes for the scarce financial and other resources of the University's central administration. Our situation is similar to that of many organizations that are linked in some way to a common supplier. If you work for a United Way agency, you will know what I mean.

Finally, there are also a number of *internal* or "throughput" publics. These are the people who convert the resources or the legitimacy gained from input publics into services and programs. I am talking about the faculty, the caseworkers, the trustees, the librarians, the nurses, and the clerical staff in the organization. At any given time, representatives of one or another of these publics may be more powerful than others; that is, more likely to be influential in shaping your agency's programs or services. Such publics exist in a kind of ecological balance with each other, but it is a frequently volatile balance, easily upset and subject to modification in order to meet the needs of one or more of the publics involved.

Within any of these publics, there are likely to be some that are bona fide *partners* that interact in a variety of exchanges aimed at achieving the organization's objectives. In any organization that you may be affiliated with, your partners are those with whom you work for the purpose of achieving some mutual benefit, not necessarily for equal benefits. The same is true between organizations. For example, a state department of public welfare might purchase the services of a group home serving adolescents. Each of the partners in this exchange has its own particular objectives, defined in either service or survival terms. And each is likely to be able to achieve those objectives only in partnership with the other. Partners need not be on equal terms. If the state agency has many group home providers to choose from, it can call the shots. If few sources of supply are available, it may be willing to let the group home make policy.

The term *product* is generally used to refer to tangible programs, services, or activities conducted by the agency and offered to the consuming public. A product can be measured according to quality or utility and it can be described in terms of its various features, like styling and packaging. Some marketing specialists also speak about a "core" product. Essentially this is what the consumer wants from the agency service. In a family planning clinic, for example, the *tangible product* may be family counseling, but the *core product* that the consumer seeks is a more satisfying and gratifying family life, perhaps one that includes freedom from parenting. Most of us are accustomed to referring to this product as the "outcome" of an intervention program.

The term *price* throughout these pages will be used to refer to the costs that someone has to pay for the development, distribution, and utilization of the product. A client may have to pay a price in psychological dependency or in opportunities (to do other things) lost. An organization's consumers may also have to pay indirect costs for any benefits received: costs such as transportation to and from the agency, child care, or living up to a required dress code.

Part of the cost might also be paid by external resource suppliers, like the United Way, the Department of Housing and Urban Development, or the city council. A different kind of price might be paid by staff who are required to perform either dull or repetitive tasks, or to take on new and unaccustomed responsibilities.

The term *place* is sometimes used to refer to a geographic location where service delivery or action takes place. But we can also think about a place in time or in an individual's life space or in an agency or individual's career. A family life education program might be a good idea and there may be a real need for it. But the market may not be ready for it, in part because the targeted consumer public may be too young or too old to consider the content relevant. The content or format may not be in the right place in that particular public's life-stage development.

Finally, we get to the term *promotion*. Promotion refers to the persuasive communication that takes place on a purposive level between the producers of a service or the managers of an action program and their various publics. It includes personal contact, outreach, use of the media, advertising, and, as often as not, the use of a variety of incentives to get people to provide the necessary resources, utilize the services, or legitimize them.

Before moving on, complete Exercise 1-1. When you have clarified your own understanding of the five P's, you will be ready to focus on an organization's markets, perhaps one you are employed by or are studying in.

## EXERCISE 1-1

### Identifying the Five P's

1. Describe a program you have recently been involved in. If it requires that resource inputs be transformed into outputs, what are those resources? What are the outputs? Are these outputs synonymous with the program's goals? If not, how can they be brought into line with each other?

2. What are the program's input publics—those that provide needed resources and legitimacy?

3. Who makes up the program's throughput publics—those involved in the transformation of inputs into outputs, in the performance of program activities?

*continued*

**EXERCISE 1-1** *continued*

4. Who makes up the output publics—the recipients of a service, or the targets of change? Are these output publics transformed into input or throughput publics? Should they be? How?

5. What are the costs involved in the conduct of the program in financial, psychological, and social costs and in opportunities lost? Who pays these costs? Refer to your earlier designation of input, throughput, and output publics.

6. Where is the program located in time and space?

7. What kinds of promotional activities are associated with the program? Who conducts them? Do they emphasize the program itself, the organization that is responsible for it, the consumers of the service, targets of the program's intervention efforts, or a particular problem being addressed?

## Identifying Your Organization's Markets

Strategic marketing is an approach to the purposeful management of the flow of resources and products between your organization and its environment. That environment, or elements of it, compose the organization's "markets." We have seen that there is an output market composed of the actual and potential suppliers of resources, and an internal or through-put market composed of those who are involved in the transformation of inputs or outputs, of resources into services. Each of these markets can be designated as *primary* or *secondary*.

Primary markets are those considered central to the organization's achievement of its missions. The secondary markets are also important, though not as essential. For example, a university's primary *consumer* markets might include college-age students (the consumers of its educational outputs) and the industrial and government organizations that consume its research outputs. Its secondary market might be the consumers of other service programs like concerts and lecture series, that are not considered essential to achievement of the university's mission. For a community college, on the other hand, the consumers of such cultural and adult education services will tend to be much more central to its mission, as important as those who might potentially enroll in its degree and certificate programs. A rehabilitation agency might view as its primary market those area residents who suffer some form of disability. Its secondary consumer market might include the family or friends of those persons as well as their potential employers who might need consulting services in order to provide the disabled with work opportunities.

A private university's primary *supplier* market might include those publics (individuals and philanthropic organizations) that provide it with the necessary sources of funds to operate. The community college's primary supplier market might include such publics as the local citizenry that votes on the millages necessary to operate and the state board of education that provides it with annual appropriations. The rehabilitation agency's primary suppliers might be the state departments of social services and of public health. Secondary suppliers might include philanthropic foundations and a host of local organizations and individuals that contribute funds and other needed resources. Its internal markets would include paid staff, volunteers, and lay people involved in policy boards and committees. Which of these are primary and which are secondary?

At the university, such publics as faculty and trustees might be considered to make up the primary internal market whereas clerical staff, research assistants, maintenance personnel, and others might be considered of secondary importance to the institution's operations. If the rehabilitation agency is heavily dependent upon contributions by volunteers, they might be included in the primary market together with the paid professional staff.

## Market Conditions for the 1980s

Whatever the position of key publics regarding the agency's appropriate place in the market, its programs and services are also likely to be shaped by forces in the larger societal environment. These forces are often beyond the agency's control. For example, consumer demand for retraining services is likely to be higher in times of high unemployment, but an organization's capacity to provide the desired service will depend upon its ability to secure necessary financing from government and other sources. Public awareness and sensitivity to the needs of minority children may create an atmosphere in which extensive services may be possible. Public perceptions that these populations are unworthy, or that previous programs have proved themselves unproductive, are likely to create just the opposite atmosphere.

Although your agency may not be able to control such events or effect substantial changes in public sentiment, it can learn to respond to changing market conditions. Such conditions are likely to differ for various sectors of the human services and for different sections of the country. They are also bound to differ over time.

Prognostications about the future are always somewhat dangerous. Nevertheless, an examination of trends during the previous decade make it possible to anticipate developments that are likely to occur in the 1980s and beyond. These developments include (1) a restructuring of the human services industry, (2) a shift of power in favor of the consumer, (3) a temporary shift in the locus of decision making to smaller and more immediate units, and (4) the increasing impact of technology on the delivery of services.

## Restructuring the Human Services Industry

Large-scale budget cuts in every sector of the human services industry are only one manifestation of the many changes that are likely to take place in that industry. Toward the latter half of the 1980s, many of the cuts experienced in the first half of the decade are likely to be restored, but the industry itself will look different. Some may object to my use of the word "industry." But like it or not, we do, to a large extent, follow a factory model. Many of our social and educational services are manufactured and distributed through plants and factory outlets. Like other industries, their operations are characterized by (1) standardization, (2) specialization, (3) centralization, and (4) coordination. *Standardized* products and services, like Medicare and Medicaid, require identical procedures, benefits, fee scales and so on. Earlier efforts to standardize services through the establishment of categorical programs at the national level have come increasingly under attack, as part of a general disenchantment with regulatory practices. But questions continue to be raised in other quarters as well. Even those practice standards established by professional associations like the Child Welfare League or the American Hospital Association have come to be challenged by some providers of services and by their consumers at the local level.

The complexities of the tasks to be performed and the diversity of the services offered have required increased *specialization*. But specialization, too, has come under fire for focusing on parts of a human being rather than on the person as a whole. Specialists tend to examine only the aspects of a problem or a social system for which they're trained, rather than examine the system as a whole.

Specialization also requires the coordination of the efforts of various providers. Such coordination requires *centralized* or delegated authority. But centralization has to generate sufficient payoffs to those giving up some autonomy, if they are to be willing to be coordinated. The concentration of decision making and goal setting at more central levels is virtually always under attack by one party or another. For example, as categorical programs become partially decategorized in the early 1980s, new forces emerged to compete for control over those programs.

Although arguments are frequently heard in favor of greater comprehensiveness and *coordination* at the local level, there seems to be little consensus on the notion of the coordinating mechanisms that should be used. As programs diversify and as a relationship between them gets played out at the local level, new mechanisms for coordinating and orchestrating programs are likely to emerge. Many of these are likely to require carefully tested exchange relationships between providers and suppliers, and between providers and consumers.

## Let the Consumer Decide

What some observers have called a "shift of power" in favor of the consumer is the direct result of the consumer's disenchantment with the factory-built product. For example, the growth of self-help groups and the increasing importance of other elements in the natural helping system have resulted in the development of "grass-roots social agencies" like the Citizens for Independence described at the beginning of this chapter. Whether these deal with the needs of particular populations (e.g., disabled people, the victims of domestic violence, retarded children) or set out to change public education and the social services, such groups share a number of characteristics.

First, they are fiercely consumer-oriented and often consumer-dominated in their policy making, in their staffing, and in their service provisions. Often strongly ideological, they build on the commitments of volunteers. The division of responsibility between professionally trained and lay volunteers is sometimes hard to distinguish. Not infrequently, volunteers are more professionally trained than are the paid staff.

The shift in favor of the consumer as decision maker is also in evidence in more traditional social agencies. Recent events suggest that producers may be less able to control the nature of the services provided than has been the case in the past. This is so even when services are intended to be in the "best interests of the client." The paternalistic and maternalistic orientations of many professions and professional providers may have to give way to the demands of more educated and assertive consumers, many of whom are quite ready to take the provision of services into their own hands.

Consumers, in fact, seem to be discovering that producers, no matter the sincerity of their rhetoric, or competence and sophistication of their methods, seem to have more in common with other producers than with consumers. Thus, for example, rewards for effective work in an agency or school setting rarely have anything to do with improving the conditions of those who are the recipients or consumers of service. Recognition or other rewards is given for team work, efficiency, and enhancing the prestige of the institution (by publishing, for example), securing funds and other resources, or following the correct therapeutic procedures (i.e., maintaining professional standards). These rewards are rarely in the hands of consumers who have little to do with awarding or withholding them.

Employees of service industries cannot easily escape identification with sponsors in government that may be perceived by many as being unresponsive if not downright oppressive. The realization that Chrysler employees have more in common with Chrysler management than with the American buying public is slowly entering the public psyche and the implications for other industries are increasingly clear. Some of the consuming public, at least, will balk at buying inferior products that put big bucks in the pockets of union labor and even bigger bucks in the pockets of management and stockholders. The social worker, health worker, educator, and other human service producer-providers will be under similar challenges to respond with quality and safe products—their services and the outcomes intended.

## Doing Better Closer to Home

These developments have at least temporary, if not long-term, implications for shifts in the locus of decision-making power from the central to the more local level. That shift is also likely to result in smaller and more immediate organizational units. In some ways, this seems an anachronism in the age of the multinational corporation, and at a time when most of the problems that are manifested at the local level clearly do not originate there. Nevertheless, there exists a sentiment in favor of increased state, substate, and local decision making that supports various interpretations of the "New Federalist" orientation, whether articulated by Republicans or Democrats.

Each party has had its own program for sharing authority and responsibility with state or local units. Rather than reflect nineteenth-century thinking, as the critics of the New Federalism sometimes argue, it may well reflect a twenty-first-century orientation in its recognition of the complexity of social reality. At least part of that complexity may be best understood and confronted at the more approximate levels of social organization: the primary group, the neighborhood, the community, and the state.

The more local the locus of decision making, it is often argued, the more likely the decisions are going to be relevant and responsive to local needs and interests. If "smaller is better," it is because it is close to home, more manageable, more personal, and possibly less wasteful of resources. The greater the diversity of local responses to locally felt needs, the greater the freedom of choice. Getting "big government off our backs," although clearly endangering the security of some minorities, restores responsibility to the individual and to the locale where many Americans feel it truly belongs. In effect, then, what is being proposed is a redistribution of responsibility for both decision making and action.

Such redistribution is not likely to take place without considerable conflict and without danger to the populations that human service professionals have traditionally been concerned about or involved with. It is likely to result in new and unaccustomed alliances between professionals, consumers, policy makers, and other publics. It challenges the ways in which we view our work and our relations to targets of intervention and to consumers. It puts serious strains on our commitments to such cherished notions as social justice and social equity.

## Newer Is Better, or at Least More Powerful

The very ways in which services are provided and organized are being further challenged by new technology. Jerome Wiesner, formerly Chancellor of MIT, once remarked that the half-life of an engineering education at his institution was only 5½ years. By this, he implied that changes in technology are so rapid that without continuing education a graduate out of school for 5½ years would be likely to know half as much as a more recent graduate.

The half-life of a social work degree may be even shorter. New information processing methods made possible through computer technology have implications not only for the management and coordination of service programs but for increasing the access of information to consumer populations. The very way in which the information is processed defines what is considered important and what is to be shared with others. It has direct implications for the interventions used.

Information technology is just the "new kid on the block" of technological remedies for social and other problems. Advances in biochemistry have already made possible the return of millions of former mental patients and substance abusers to the community. Other advances in biochemistry (and in research on the brain and nervous system or genetic engineering) may have even greater impact. In the same way, changes in budgeting and accounting systems have affected supervisory and management practice.

At this point, do Exercise 1–2 and then proceed to the Review.

---

**EXERCISE 1-2**

### Assessing Market Conditions

1. Review the vignette at the beginning of this chapter. Which of the market conditions discussed (restructuring of the human service industry, consumer activism, local decision making, and changes in technology) was the agency director clearly aware of? Which others do you think also affected the agency?

2. Had the agency director focused on those conditions more fully, could he or she have avoided the severe budget cuts to the program and perhaps avoided getting fired? How? Think back to your responses when you answer the questions in Exercises 3–1 and 3–2.

## Review

Market conditions during the 1980s are likely to be turbulent for social agencies. Large-scale budget cuts have already induced considerable restructuring of the human service system. Activism is likely to shift many consumers from the role of recipient to that of partner in service development and delivery. A greater emphasis on local decision making will in turn create the context for new partnerships between agencies and their various publics. These conditions are further affected by the growth of technology that makes new services to formerly underserved or unserved populations possible.

This situation makes it all the more important for agencies and other human service organizations to position themselves properly within the market, to find the niches that afford the greatest opportunity to achieve their missions while attending to the problems of organizational survival and growth.

The marketing process requires attention to five *P's*: *publics, place, price, promotion,* and *programs* or *products*. A sixth P refers to *partners*, the specific publics with whom the organization engages in planned and cooperative exchanges.

*Publics* are those segments of the market upon whom the organization is dependent for inputs of legitimacy and resources, those that are responsible for transforming resources into programs and services, and those who consume the organization's outputs. These outputs can be defined as the services the organization provides (e.g., counseling, education, or social action). They may also be defined in terms of the outcomes or intended results of those programs and services (e.g., independent behavior, knowledge, or social change).

*Programs* are all those sequences of activities and events in which an organization engages purposefully. *Promotions* are those activities aimed at increasing awareness and support for a particular program, organization, public, or problem to be addressed.

*Place* refers to the distribution or location of programs in time and space. *Price* refers to the costs of such distribution and of the development of programs. It also refers to the costs incurred by various participants, including consumers. Price can be financial, psychological, or social; it can also be measured in opportunities lost and gained. In summary, strategic marketing is a process that accounts for the needs and interests of an organization's various publics in the development, promotion, distribution, and pricing of the organization's program.

# 2 "EXCHANGE" AND OTHER CONCEPTS THAT UNDERLIE STRATEGIC MARKETING

MOST INTERVENTION STRATEGIES are built on a set of concepts, beliefs, and perspectives that provide them with guidance and consistency. Strategic marketing is no exception, being built on a number of conceptual frameworks that both support and complement each other. Foremost among these concepts is what is sometimes referred to as *exchange theory*.

### It's Costing You Plenty!

It is costing you plenty to read this book! The biggest cost of all is the time you are investing in it: time that might well be allocated to other literature, to social activities, or to satisfying other demands at work or at school. Not inconsequential is the 20 dollars or more, plus tax, you may have paid for it. Perhaps you decided to save the price by borrowing the book from a friend, someone with whom you have exchanged books and other commodities in the past. Conversely, you may have just decided against borrowing it. You know well that the loan would set you up for a similar request, and you just don't trust the friend in question. Of the seven or eight books you've lent during the past year, four were returned with coffee stains and pencil marks and three will probably never be seen again. The exchange of books, you fear, is likely to jeopardize rather than reinforce your friendship.

Let's explore the reasons you decided to buy or borrow the book in the first place. You may be involved in a marketing or program-design process and in need of a "quick study" that will provide you with an overview of how that process works. Or you may be interested in more limited and specific aspects of marketing, like fund-raising or budgeting. Perhaps you are responsible for presenting some new ideas at a staff meeting. Strategic marketing may be just the approach that will impress your colleagues with your ability to find new ways of looking at old problems. If you are a student, you may be reading this book for a course assignment, with virtually no interest in the subject matter, but you are interested in getting a decent grade and applying the course credits toward your degree.

As long as we are being honest about things, I might as well tell you why I wrote this book. First of all, I get a kick out of playing with ideas and organizing them in some coherent framework. Second, I've had an interest in program design and marketing for a long time and wanted to share my insights and methods with others who might find them useful. I like to teach, and writing gives me an opportunity to interact, at least indirectly, with many people with whom I might otherwise not be able to relate. And not inconsequential is my interest in earning the royalties that accompany publication. At an earlier stage of my career publishing might also have had some impact on my academic promotion or tenure and on my marketability as a teacher and a consultant. There is, after all, some prestige associated with being in print. Even tenured professors perish if they don't publish.

## Economic and Social Exchanges

In each of these considerations, your behavior and mine have been shaped by the anticipation of rewards for which we were willing to engage in some form of exchange relationship with others. Exchanges are activities that people and organizations engage in as means of achieving goals. Such activities entail both costs and benefits to the partners in the exchange. Exchanges can be simple or complex, direct or indirect, economic or social. Most economic exchanges are relatively simple or straightforward.

If you paid a bookseller with a 20 dollar check, your only obligation was to make good on the check. The bookseller's only obligation was to sell you the book you ordered, in good condition, at the agreed-upon price. These obligations are generally understood and require no extensive explication. The economic exchange I engaged in with The Free Press was somewhat more complicated and, for this reason, we spelled out our mutual obligations in a written contract.

Among other things, the contract stated that I promised to deliver a manuscript roughly 550 pages long on an agreed-upon subject matter by a given date. On the assumption that the final product would be acceptable, The Free Press in turn obligated itself to paying me royalties and to a distribution effort which I thought was a fair remuneration for my efforts.

But there is more to it than this. You and I are also engaging in a form of exchange, albeit indirect and perhaps one-sided. Although I may feel some obligation to provide you, as part of my reading public, with useful information, you have no obligation to me. But you may feel obligated to report on what you have learned to others or to utilize that knowledge in your practice. In this case, your reading the book may lead to new exchanges with other partners. Even if you are reading this book as part of a course assignment, the very act of reading may be the fulfillment of an obligation, a requirement that leads to achievement of a desired reward: a passing grade.

Exchange processes may thus become rather complicated, involving several parties directly and indirectly. I will give you another example. When you make a contribution to the United Way, you do not expect thanks from the agencies that are to be recipients of the funds raised or from their clients who are the ultimate beneficiaries. You may, however, experience a sense of wellbeing at having met a social obligation. The size of your donation may be related to the extent to which you feel that obligation or the extent to which it generates recognition from peers. "Big givers," after all, tend to be prestigious people, and at least some of that prestige relates to the size of their gift.

For a simpler example, consider a person you know who has the reputation of being a big tipper. That tip may have an instrumental purpose. It may net your acquaintance special consideration every time he or she enters a particular restaurant. It may also have expressive purposes. The big tipper may be more interested in impressing the others with whom he or she is sharing the meal than in impressing the waiter. I suppose it is even more complicated than that. Some big tippers even feel good about being generous!

We are now exploring some of the similarities and differences between social and economic exchanges. Social exchanges tend to be intrinsically rewarding, that is, the rewards are internal to the activity itself. These rewards, however, also tend to be more ambiguous, not nearly as clearly spelled out or understood as in economic exchanges. The obligations involved in buying or selling a book or a manuscript include mutual obligations that are both straightforward and objective. The exchange is primarily economic.

The rewards and costs involved in social exchanges are rarely that clear. Social benefits do not have an exact price, since the utility of a given benefit cannot be clearly separated from that of other rewards derived from a given relationship: sharing a sense of comradeship or gaining status through association with prestigious people.

The marketing of human service programs is greatly influenced by what transpires in both economic and social exchange. To understand the operation of the exchange process as well as its implications for strategic marketing, let's investigate how the process is initiated.

## Attraction in Exchange Relationships

The concept of *attraction* is generally used to explain the first stages of an exchange relationship. A book or dress, or what they can be used for, may be attractive. Attractive associates are persons who have impressed others as being rewarding to associate with. Rewards can be extrinsic, intrinsic, or both. Extrinsic rewards lead to some benefit outside the relationship, like prestige which can be used for purposes of social climbing. Intrinsic rewards, on the other hand, come from the association itself. Dating can be intrinsically rewarding if both parties genuinely enjoy each other's company and their relationship. It can be also extrinsically rewarding to both if one party to the exchange is "out for a good time" and the other is out to impress his or her friends.

The satisfaction that staff in your agency (or some other organization with which you may be familiar) may derive from participating in joint endeavors is intrinsic, whereas the results of those endeavors, benefits like recognition or promotion, are extrinsic rewards. Working together on a fund-raising campaign may be its own reward because it generates a sense of well-being, of belonging, and of contributing to a worthwhile enterprise. These rewards are sufficient motivators for many of those involved. For others, however, the payoffs will have to be measured in dollars raised.

The initial attraction of individuals to each other tends to rest more on extrinsic than intrinsic factors. Let's go back to the dating example. An interest in dating someone may be stimulated by how the other person looks and by assumptions about impressing one's friends by "having scored" with an attractive person. But to get a date, the interested party has to make himself or herself attractive as well. To make themselves attractive, people try to display those distinctive traits that are likely to impress others with the qualities that command admiration and respect.

Consider the experience you may have had in working on a committee or an interagency task force. At least some members tend to try to impress others with their superior intellect, their previous accomplishments, the extent that they care about the missions or tasks of the committee, or simply with their hard work. It stands to reason that by making oneself more attractive to others, one is likely to attract them.

Nevertheless, people are frequently reluctant to appear overly attractive. Those impressive qualities that make a person particularly attractive may constitute a status threat to the rest of the group. It is not unusual for those other people to develop defensive postures, not allowing themselves to become too easily impressed. After all, when someone in the group becomes too attractive, others may become dependent on that person for approval or some other reward. Sometimes, appearing too attractive may be taken as promising too much. Not everyone can live up to promises that may be implied by their looks or by their actions. What is true of individuals and of those with whom they interact is largely true of organizations and their publics.

## Organizations in Association with Their Publics

Let's explore some of these similarities. To what extent does your agency or organization attempt to impress actual or potential client populations with its capability to perform a needed service? By implying certain competencies, does it obligate itself beyond its capacity? How do clients, in return, impress the organization with those characteristics that would make them attractive as consumers? Do they sometimes redefine their needs or their problems in such a way that the agency is more likely to be responsive and more willing to provide them with the benefits they seek? To what extent are consumers likely to misrepresent themselves in hopes of achieving such benefits despite the risks that come with exposure?

Whatever the anticipated benefits, costs are also likely to be incurred in receiving service. Dollar costs, like those required for the payment of tuition, agency fees, transportation, and child care, are relatively assessable. Consumers may attempt to weigh these costs against presumed benefits, which, unfortunately, may not be so easy to calculate. Other costs may be equally difficult to assess. What are the "psychic" costs of admitting one's inadequacy, the presumed reason for seeking help? What are the "social" costs incurred when asking a relative or neighbor to provide child care service or a ride to the agency on the day of the client's appointment? What are the "opportunity" costs of seeking help from one source instead of help from other providers?

Rewards may be even more difficult to measure. Sometimes, the intrinsic rewards of association take precedence over the stated or instrumental reasons for that association. The feeling of acceptance in a treatment relationship may be sufficient reward to overcome the real costs incurred. It may even substitute for the stated purpose of the relationship—getting better. Clearly, neither the costs nor the benefits of association and exchange are easy to calculate. What seems to be the key to maintaining a successful relationship is the perception, on the part of all parties to the exchange, that the relationship does or will generate some benefit, and that the benefit is likely to outweigh the costs.

It is not necessary for both parties to achieve similar benefits or even to be rewarded during the course of interaction itself. An agency that refers clients to another organization does not expect to receive the same benefit as the second organization. Neither benefits nor costs must be equal. Nor does the nature of the dependence between exchange partners have to be the same or of equal weight.

Suppose a school has no organization other than a child guidance clinic to which it can refer children with learning-related problems. The clinic, on the other hand, may already be overloaded with referrals from other schools and social agencies. One can easily imagine that the clinic's intake department may become very selective about which clients it will accept for treatment. It may establish complicated referral procedures that put considerable demands on those organizations from which it will accept referrals. In this situation, the child guidance clinic is in a relatively powerful position. It has an overabundance of demand for its limited supply of service. The school, on the other hand, has no alternative sources of supply for the services needed by its clients. It is, therefore, dependent upon the clinic.

In this situation, the school must present itself in such a way as to make itself attractive to the clinic. It might consider the following alternatives: (1) covering some of the costs of the clinic or locating a civic association (like the PTA [Parent–Teacher Association]) willing to "sponsor" the referral clients; (2) using procedures that integrate well with those of the child guidance clinic, including the screening of all referrals in such a way as will most closely fit the clinic's interests; and (3) establishing an after-school program for children with learning difficulties to which the clinic might refer its own clients. Clearly, the costs of some alternatives may be perceived by the school to be too high. Nevertheless, the point is clear; the more attractive an agency can make itself to others, the less dependent it will be on those others.

The same dynamics hold true between agencies and their suppliers. Some years ago, the School of Social Work where I teach was approached by a philanthropic foundation interested in promoting adoption services to children with special needs, those commonly referred to as being "hard to place." There was no question about our interest in the grant. Many of the faculty had long-term commitments to the child welfare field. Getting grants is the name of the game in many academic departments, and we were no strangers to that game. The grant was likely to increase the prestige of our institution among some publics that were important to us, and it was likely to provide at least some faculty with opportunities for career development as well as for national recognition for their research, teaching activities, and publications. Clearly, the foundation and its interests were attractive to us.

But we were attractive to the foundation too. First of all, we had some of the practical expertise needed to make the project work. Second, the University of Michigan is an institution with a national reputation. Its involvement would confer a certain amount of prestige on the foundation, which, still relatively new to this kind of project, was only just beginning to move into the child welfare arena.

In negotiating the contract with each other, these considerations were implicitly understood, if never fully or explicitly verbalized. They formed the basis for some of the intrinsic as well as some of the extrinsic rewards both sides anticipated from the association. Thus, what might have seemed on the surface to be strictly an economic exchange—providing a given service for a given sum of money—included many of the dynamics associated with social exchanges. As members of the University and the foundation staff interacted with each other over a period of years, they came to value those relationships, sometimes finding it difficult to separate the intrinsic rewards from the extrinsic and more measurable benefits of association.

The partnership served many of the ends of the foundation just as it served many of the University's. Both institutions were in relatively equal power relationships to each other. Both could have gone their own separate ways if they perceived the costs of association to outweigh the benefits. The foundation could have gone to other universities. Neither the University nor the School's faculty was dependent on the foundation for its economic survival. Now see what you can do with Exercise 2–1.

---

### EXERCISE 2–1
### Analyzing an Exchange Relationship

Stop and think for a moment about an exchange relationship in which you are currently participating. The relationship you select may be ad hoc or ongoing, in your personal life or at work.

1. Describe it briefly. Indicate who the parties to the exchange are and what is being exchanged.
2. Is the relationship intrinsically or extrinsically rewarding or both? Are the actual or anticipated rewards worth the actual or anticipated costs to you? To the other parties to the exchange?
3. Is it a simple exchange, building on mutual obligations between the parties directly involved? Or is it more complex? Remember the example of the big tipper. Who is directly or indirectly involved and who is likely to be in the future?
4. Have there been any expectations imposed on you regarding the way in which you behave in the exchange relationship? Are these expectations appropriate? Can you live up to them? If not, what are the consequences for your behavior and for the future of the exchange relationship?
5. What of the other partners to the exchange; are they living up to your expectations? If not, what are the consequences for your behavior?

Take a few more minutes to think about an interorganizational exchange relationship your agency or an association you are affiliated with may be involved in. The exchange may occur between the organization and one of its publics (funders, auspice providers, and others) or one of its output publics (consumers, organizations to which it refers clients) or one of its throughput publics (paid and volunteer staff). Answer questions 1 through 4 in reference to interorganizational exchange. Refer to the exercises you completed in Chapter 1. In what ways would the use of exchange concepts modify your earlier responses to those exercises?

## Role-related Relationships, Conflicts, and Strains

As exchange relationships become more complex, the performance of various tasks is required in order to maintain the association. Over time these tasks may be routinely assigned to one or more of the persons participating in the exchange. As tasks are grouped by function, they come to constitute the role performed by a given participant. The ways that these tasks are performed are influenced by the expectations held about that role by its incumbent and by others who interact with the role occupant.

Many social roles are clearly defined and relatively well understood by all members in society, not only the actual participants in an exchange association. Supervisors, for example, may be expected to interact in given ways with their subordinates. The rules of conduct may be specified in agency procedures and in union contracts, but they may also emerge informally out of employee experience in the agency setting and in other work settings.

In order to perform a given role, the role performer must interact with members of his or her *role-set*. Efforts to perform a role without relating directly or indirectly to members of the role-set are likely to yield rather strange results. Let me give you a graphic example.

Think for a moment about a goalie in a soccer game. Imagine the goalie standing on a field all alone. There are no other members of the team present, nor are there any opponents on the field, but the goalie is performing all the tasks normally associated with his or her role. How would you define that person's behavior? Wacky? Psychotic?

Role-related behavior unconnected with members of a role-set is bizarre. Role-related behavior "out of sync" with members of a role-set creates all kinds of stresses and strains. That is why co-workers at an agency often put pressure on a colleague to conform to their expectations. This is true in all situations in which people interact in patterned ways and in which those patterns exist over time.

Whatever the nature of these interactions, many roles endure over time regardless of their occupants. The job of executive, or of fund-raiser in an agency may exist beyond the period of any particular incumbency in that role. While this is a major stabilizing factor for the organization, each occupant of that role modifies the way he or she chooses to perform that role. Nevertheless, people frequently perform a given role according to accepted norms and/or to clearly defined expectations.

Some observers suggest that when someone new is placed in an existing role, he or she is more likely to act very much like the person who previously held that role than like the way in which he or she acted in a previous role. The new role occupant's actions, of course, depend upon the strength of the reference group the person brings along to the new position. They also depend on the talents, experience, charisma, and skill of the new role incumbent.

To understand, think about the actors in a play. Roles are generally established and defined in the script, but different actors will bring different styles, interpretations, and experiences to the same role. No role will ever be portrayed by two performers in exactly the same way. What one actor does with the role may also be affected by how other actors play their roles or how the director wants the script interpreted. Change the director or any of the other key performers and one is likely to see considerable changes in performance of the role we are focusing on. Nevertheless, the role continues to exist beyond the incumbency of any particular player or director.

Now consider the tasks assigned to a staff member recently given responsibility for fund raising or for promoting agency programs. Had there been a former incumbent in that role, and had that person's performance been deemed satisfactory, the expectations imposed on the new staffer might be quite clear. But if this is a new position, or if a previous staffer's performance had been unsatisfactory, the new incumbent might find a great deal of ambiguity in the definition of his or her role. Even in stable and well-institutionalized roles, a new person who is energetic, intelligent, and innovative may in time shape the expectations of others such that they will be brought into line with his or her own perceptions of how the role should be performed.

You may find this ambiguity exhilarating if you should be the first person in your organization to try to put strategic marketing into practice. You may also find that there are considerably different expectations about how that role should be played or whether it should be played at all. These expectations are likely to differ with each actor in each of your role-sets. Funders and other resource suppliers may have certain expectations; providers of auspice may have others. Active members may have perceptions that complement those of the other two groups, but which conflict with those of professional colleagues within your agency or in other service organizations with which the agency maintains ongoing exchanges.

Role conflict occurs when contradictory expectations of how a role should be played exist and when compliance with one expectation makes compliance with another difficult if not impossible. Role strain is the discomfort experienced with role conflict. Persons can and do occupy more than one role at a given time, and different roles may not always be compatible. For example, being a caseworker and a fund-raiser in the same organization may be incompatible roles for some people.

Sources of conflict include contradictory messages from two sources about each of the roles performed; lack of knowledge, skill, or resources to fulfill a required role; lack of clarity about expected behavior; lack of time or energy to perform one or more roles as expected; and conflicts emerging from personality traits that become associated with, or that interfere with, role performance.

Staff members most likely to experience role strain are those who must satisfy many publics, some of them inside and others outside the organization. These often include (1) direct service workers who are caught between the employing organization's expectations and those of clients; (2) supervisors who must satisfy management and workers; and (3) those in middle management positions who must respond to both supervisors and to subordinates. In fact, anyone whose job puts one "in the middle" is likely to feel some strain in trying to respond to the expectations of different publics: clients, board members, suppliers, competitors, and collaborators. The perceptive reader will recognize that getting caught in the middle may be an occupational hazard for many people assigned marketing tasks.

Those engaging in marketing are often particularly sensitive to the interdependence of organizations and individuals. This interdependence may best be understood by examining some of the concepts associated with the study of "human ecology." Before moving on, however, this might be another good point to stop and think. Complete Exercise 2–2, then continue.

---

### EXERCISE 2-2
### Analyzing Role/Role-Set Relationships

This is another good point to stop and think and to relate what you have just read to your concerns with the development of a strategic marketing approach.

1. Describe a situation in which you stepped into an existing role. To what extent were your actions circumscribed by the expectations, formal and informal, imposed on that role? How were you able to shape those expectations and in the process redefine them in ways you found more functional or compatible?
2. Describe another situation in which you were the first incumbent in a role new to an organization or association in which it was performed. How did your expectations and those of others get expressed?
3. What kinds of role conflict or role strain accompanied either of these situations? How were they resolved, if at all? What were the consequences of these conflicts or strains?
4. As your organization moves toward development of or expansion of a strategic marketing approach, what kinds of new

*continued*

## EXERCISE 2-2 continued

> roles will it have to develop? Who will perform those roles? What kinds of stresses or strains are likely to occur as the ambiguities associated with new roles are clarified? Are strains likely to be expressed more strongly within the organization (i.e., between staff internal to the organization), or in those relationships that develop between your organization's representatives and those who represent other organizations?

## Human Ecology

Human ecologists talk about *symbiotic* and *commensalistic* interdependence. Symbiosis presumes difference in both characteristics and goals among actors; yet their differences are essential for them to interact. Using systems terminology, one actor's output becomes the other's input. The school that refers its learning-disabled pupils to the child guidance clinic is in a symbiotic relationship to that clinic. Symbiotic relationships describe many of the relationships between organizations and within them as well. Think of a familiar school, public welfare department, or hospital. Which individual departments and work units are involved in symbiotic exchange relationships with others?

In contrast to symbiotic relationships, commensalistic interdependence is based on common characteristics or interests (behavior and goals). A union, an environmental protection group, a Monday night poker club, or a church are typical examples of commensalistic associations.

On a societal level, certain organizational forms can be viewed as the result of environmental forces as mediated by the development of technology. The mental health system, including the mental hospital, is a good example. Mental hospitals can be viewed as the product of centuries of effort to control the threatening behavior of some members of society in such a way as to protect the dominant populations while providing at least minimal care for the deviant. Although the technologies used in providing care or imposing control have changed over time, they continue to include certain modalities: physical restraints, planned social organization, drugs, and psychotherapies. As perceptions of mental illness and health change, as new technologies are developed and prove themselves and as economic conditions change, the mental hospital and the system of which it is a part also change.

For our purposes, it may be useful to explore some of those changes and their environmental causes and consequences. Let's consider the hospital and its environment as we might any other ecosystem. All ecosystems tend toward the maintenance of equilibrium. Because the systems are complex, however, they tend to change as one (or more) elements in the system change in response to some other element or elements in the environment.

Ecosystems tend to be more or less open or closed. So long as persons defined as mentally ill were committed to mental hospitals and those hospitals included all the services that were either needed by or provided to mental patients, they operated as relatively closed systems. But when the preferred treatment plan shifted to community care, mental hospitals found themselves involved in many new symbiotic and commensalistic relationships with external organizations.

At one time, only the superintendent or medical director may have had extensive responsibility for relating to elements in the hospital's environment; today, staff at all levels of the organization must take responsibility for exchange activities that are directly related to achievement of the hospital's objectives. The hospital's success in rehabilitating patients depends on the availability of community support systems, the readiness of the general community to accept ex-patients, and the availability of jobs and other resources.

The sheer number of needed external relationships, their complexity and variety, require that many actors within the hospital develop and maintain relationships with suppliers and collaborators in the organization's environment. In ecological terms, then, the hospital becomes a relatively open institution with permeable boundaries. Because clients receive services from many sources rather than the hospital alone, the boundaries between service organizations become relatively diffuse.

The more open an organization, the less importance is placed on its boundaries, and the more interest there is in expanding functional interactions with key elements in that organization's environment. Sometimes, in fact, it becomes difficult to determine where one agency ends and the outside world begins. An agency's services may be *so* interdependent with those of other organizations that boundary lines must be redrawn continuously.

Consider your organization's relationship to its publics: those that provide it with the resources it needs to survive and to achieve its mission; those with whom it competes for resources or for consumers; those with which it collaborates along symbiotic or commensalistic lines; and those to which it supplies its services or outputs. How many of your agency's staff and board members are involved in the management of environmental relationships? Has your organization moved toward greater openness or toward greater closure during the past 5 years?

Consider, also, our earlier discussion of role and role-set relationships. Sociologists speak about similar relationships between an organization and its *organization-set*, sometimes referred to as elements of the *task environment*. Just as individual roles are shaped through interaction with members of their role-set and by expectations about role behavior inferred from those interactions, so are the functions performed by organizations influenced by their organization-set interactions. For this reason, the most important actors in your organization may be those who have sole or shared responsibility for developing and maintaining relationships with key elements in the environment. This is particularly so for those who are able to secure the resources necessary for the organization to perform and to survive.

These persons are sometimes known as *boundary personnel* whose influence within their own organizations is to a large extent the result of their ability to maintain effective exchanges with key elements in the environment. Their success in maintaining effective external relationships consolidates their power or influence on others within the organization. At this point, try Exercise 2–3.

---

**EXERCISE 2-3**

**Analyzing Ecological Relationships**

Take a few moments for reflection before moving on to the remaining sections of Chapter 2.

1. Identify three examples each of symbiotic and commensalistic relationships that your agency engages in with key elements in its environment.

2. Over the past 5 years, has your organization become more closed or more open (i.e., with more permeable boundaries)? To what would you ascribe these changes? If there has been no significant change, how would you account for maintenance of the status quo?

3. Over the next 5 years, do you think the direction will be toward more openness and greater interdependence between various components of your organization and elements in the task environment of each? Or do you think that the organization will have sufficient resources to be able to draw tighter boundaries around itself, thereby being in the position of exerting greater control over its various operations?

4. What are the implications of these changes for strategic marketing? How are these implications influenced by the role/role-set relationships you described in Exercise 2–2?

---

## Organizations and Their Task Environments

This will become clearer when we examine the relationship between an organization and key elements in its environment. You will recall that in the previous chapter we discussed input, output, and throughput publics. *Input publics* are those from which we secure the necessary resources and the legitimacy to survive and provide services. *Output publics* are perceived as the consumers of our services or products. The term *throughput publics* refers to all those personnel, volunteers, paid staff, board members, and others who are involved in the process of turning *resources* (raw material like money or expert knowledge) into *products* (services and outcomes available to our output publics). An effective marketing strategy must accommodate the needs and interests of each public.

Programs and the organizations from which they evolve exist in ecological balance with those elements in their environments upon which they are dependent or with which they are interdependent symbiotically or commensally. Many of the individuals gathered together in advisory groups to the School of Social Work's Continuing Education Program, with which I was affiliated, were involved in commensalistic relationships with each other. They had similar objectives. Many of the School's collaborative efforts with state and local agencies might also have been identified as commensalistic. A number, however, were symbiotic; that is, the School's output become the input of its consumer publics.

If we use the role/role-set concepts discussed earlier, we can begin to construct a map of the relationship between an organization and its key publics. Those are the publics we identified as part of the organization-set. Some sociologists prefer to refer to all those in the organization-set as composing an organization's task environment.

The task environment is composed of all those elements in the organization's set which most directly impinge on its ability to accomplish its objectives. These include the suppliers of resources, the consumers of services, the competitors from both resource and service markets, the collaborators in resource development or service delivery, and those regulatory groups that provide auspices and legitimacy or which set the rules and procedures that govern the organization's operations.

*Suppliers*, you will recall, are those organizations, groups, and individuals who provide the organization with the resources necessary to produce its product, provide its service, or maintain itself. For example, a state mental health department might be the supplier of funds to a local community mental health center through an annual appropriation, and to a group home for the aged through a purchase-of-services agreement. The same local service agency might also receive additional funds from the United Way, from local foundations, or from civic associations that raise funds specifically for that agency or for the provision of services to one of its client populations.

However, suppliers need not limit themselves to funds. A nearby university might provide a mental health center with the necessary expertise to assess a need, evaluate a program, or design a new service approach. Churches in the area might provide the center with the facilities in which its services might be delivered to the public or where community groups might meet to discuss needs and share ideas for expanded services. One of those churches might organize a group of volunteers who collaborate with agency's staff on special tasks: e.g., recruiting clients, visiting them at home, or providing transportation to and from needed services.

The more dependent an organization is on a single source of supply, the less likely that it will be able to respond flexibly to changes in demand for its services unless the supplier is willing and able to respond as well. This same holds true if an organization depends exclusively on one or two types of resources, like money or paid staff. An organization that can shift its programs to accommodate ups and downs in financial support by increasing or decreasing volunteer and consumer inputs is likely to accommodate a new challenge and respond to new opportunities more effectively. An agency that can absorb a budget cut from one funder, because it has other sources of financial supply, is likely to be in a stronger position to maintain its ongoing operations and to negotiate with each of its funding sources.

Look at your own organization. Which resources might be substituted for others? To what extent is your organization capable of accommodating to or developing new sources of supply, or of utilizing alternative resources?

To a large extent this capacity may correlate with how the organization perceives its *consumers*. Consumers, we know, are generally defined as output publics: those who are the recipients of an organization's service. They can also be defined as "input" publics, without whose contributions the agency's services would not be possible. Agencies that charge sizable fees (like private universities), are dependent on consumers for their operating budgets. When an agency organizes its clients into self-help groups, or utilizes them as volunteers and aides with other more dependent clients, it has redefined at least some of its consumers from output into input constituents who become partners with agency staff in the provision of at least some services. They also are redefined as input publics when they participate in committees, task groups, or other decision-making bodies that influence the nature of the organization's programs or services.

Generally, however, consumers are likely to be relatively powerless in their exchanges with the organization. So long as the agency holds a monopoly over services, or there are more consumers than available services (higher demand than supply) and so long as the organization can shift its services to new and different consumers, the current consumer population is not likely to be very influential. To understand this, let's examine a fairly typical symbiotic exchange between two providers of service. Think back a moment to the example of the school that referred its clients to the child guidance clinic. As long as the clinic received more referrals than it could accommodate, it was in a strong position to dictate the terms of the exchange with other service organizations in its task environment. The school, having no other place to refer families of children with learning-related problems, was in a relatively powerless position. If it wanted its clients to be accepted by the clinic, it had to comply with the clinic's regulations and find ways in which to make itself and its referrals attractive to the child guidance clinic staff. The tables would have been reversed, however, if the child guidance clinic found itself with consumers in short supply. It would then have had to find ways to make itself more attractive to the school and to other potential suppliers of referrals.

In any situation in which there is a scarcity of resources, there is also likely to be competition for those resources. A limited supply of volunteers or funds for services to a given population may cause competition among service providers for those resources. Conversely, when services are in an abundant supply and there is insufficient demand, agencies may compete for consumers. In some communities, nursing homes with high standards of care may be rare; and they rarely have an available bed. In other communities, however, they have to compete for patients.

Some human resource training agencies have been known to compete for trainees who have the greatest potential for rehabilitation and job placement. At times, agencies compete for a particular clientele with certain attributes based on racial, ethnic, or socioeconomic characteristics as well as the psychographic characteristics that we discussed earlier. Universities are good examples. Not all universities compete for the brightest students. They might have some other mix in mind in terms of the qualities by which they wish to have their student bodies characterized. Sometimes that mix is determined on the basis of what they "think they can get," in a highly competitive market. A small, not very well known, private college is not likely to compete with Harvard or Michigan for either faculty or students. It may, instead, choose to aim for a particular niche in the market by specializing in music or in computer technology, for example.

It is not unusual for competitors also to be collaborators. Agencies that compete for scarce resources, such as highly trained staff, might find it beneficial to try a number of collaborative staffing arrangements. For example, one agency might lend a staff member expert in family diagnosis to a second agency that has neither the financial resources nor the experience to perform that kind of service. The staff member "on loan" would then operate as a member of the second staff for an agreed-upon time period. The second agency might reciprocate by making its facilities available for special events conducted by the first agency.

Joint efforts to initiate a new service, or to generate new sources of funding to be shared at the community level, are examples of commensalistic—cooperative and collaborative—efforts. It is not unusual for agencies to be engaged in both collaborative and competitive activities with each other, as when two agencies cooperate on a public information campaign, but compete for allocations from the United Fund.

Just as organizations are interdependent with suppliers, competitors, collaborators, and consumers, they are also interdependent with *regulatory* authorities. Most organizations are responsible to boards of directors, legislative bodies, governmental agencies, or other bodies under whose auspices they operate. At the local level, an agency's board of directors may provide both auspice and legitimacy. Some local agencies are also regulated at the state or national level. For example, family service agencies are certified and legitimized through voluntary affiliation with the Family Service Association of America which also imposes certain regulatory constraints on its member agencies. Many other voluntary agencies, such as Jewish Community Centers, YMCAs, settlement houses and child welfare agencies, are also affected by national bodies with which they are affiliated and which impose standards or regulations on their local affiliates. It is not unusual for such organizations to be further regulated by local United Way organizations or sectarian associations to which they may belong.

All agencies under government auspices, as well as many private agencies that receive government grants or contracts, must also meet governmental standards in order to continue to operate. Even those that receive no government funds may be regulated by a government agency. Nursing homes, convalescent centers, and day-care centers, for example, are periodically inspected by state agencies which license them. Medium-sized or larger hospitals, in order to operate, must be accredited by the American Hospital Association, certified by the state board of health, and may find many of their departments subject to standards and regulations imposed by various academies of the American Medical Association (A.M.A.). The pathology department, for example, will have to be certified by the A.M.A.'s Academy of Pathology. Insurance companies, generally thought of as "third-party" suppliers, may also perform regulatory functions when they specify how certain procedures are to be performed or reported for reimbursement purposes.

Employee associations and unions can also perform regulatory functions as when they specify the conditions under which staff are permitted to perform certain duties. Generally, however, employees are thought of as *throughput* publics. The extent to which agency personnel are able or willing to become involved in new services or programs will greatly influence an organization's capability to provide them. Before examining the anatomy of influence more explicitly, complete Exercise 2–4, an eco-mapping approach to analysis of the task environment.

---

### EXERCISE 2-4
### Analyzing the Task Environment: An Eco-Mapping Assessment Technique

1. Draw up separate lists of your organization's major suppliers, consumers, providers of auspices, competitors, and collaborators. If you are not currently employed or working in an orga-

*continued*

**EXERCISE 2-4** *continued*

> nization, pick an organization you are familiar with. Which
> of these might be placed under more than one category?
> 2. Draw up a similar list of the internal publics in that organiza-
>    tion. You might include various departments, professional
>    groups, informal groups, key individuals, and so on.

These are your actual or potential markets. If you were to pinpoint
some of those markets that should be influenced, which ones should
they be? How might you want to influence them? You will have the
opportunity to make these decisions as you complete the exercise.
You are now engaged in a form of eco-mapping. You may wish to
complete the exercise alone or to collaborate with colleagues from
your organization and from other organizations with which it is involved.

> 3. Look at Figure 2-1. Use it as a guide for listing all the key ele-
>    ments of the organization's task environment. Put the organi-

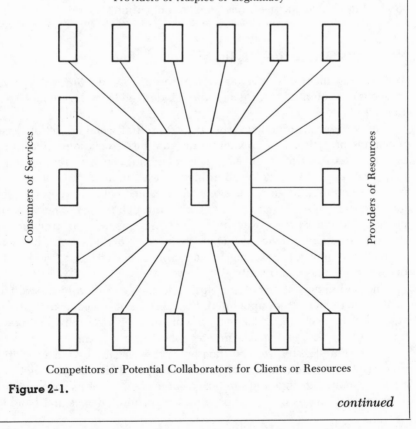

Figure 2-1.

*continued*

---

**EXERCISE 2-4** *continued*

zation's name in the central box. You will note that there is a
larger box that surrounds it. List the internal publics in that
box, fill in the other boxes in the task environment. You may
need more or fewer boxes than are indicated on the sample.
Since most competitors are also potential collaborators, you
might list all of these on the same side.

4. Now use a pen or pencil of different color to star or check those
elements in the internal or the external environment that you
have targeted for change.

---

You have now completed the beginning of an assessment exercise aimed
at designing a market structure analysis. What kind of exchanges currently
take place between the organization or representatives of its internal publics and the other organizations and the other elements in its task environment? Which of those exchanges are satisfactory from the organization's
perspective? Which of those exchanges might be modified? How? What
kinds of influences are needed for such modification?

## Power: Its Origins and Its Uses

When we speak of influence, as we have been, we are referring to power.
Power is the potential to influence and it is derived from the exchange relationship.

You will recall from our earlier discussion that social attraction occurs
when one party is drawn to another because the association is likely to be
perceived as rewarding. If one needs something, such as recognition or
help, one may be willing to subordinate oneself to another in order to receive the required service. Once one has accepted help, one becomes obligated to the helper. By obligating another through the act of helping, one
can increase one's power over the other. This sequence holds true for both
organizations and individuals. That is why some organizations, like some
individuals, may resist exchange relationships. Nevertheless, the benefits
of association may clearly outweigh the costs.

The willingness of some participants in an association to subordinate
themselves to an elected, appointed, or otherwise accepted leadership suggests that they are willing to give up some of their own individual power
for something else, perhaps the greater collective power that is the result of
concentration. This power can then be used externally by the association
in its relationship to elements of its environment. Think about a motorcy-
cle gang. Without implying similarity in purpose, is not its concentration
of power similar to an association of independent clinicians that band to-

gether in order to contract for services with a state mental health system? The pooled effort by a foundation and the School of Social Work in a project aimed at increasing placements for the hard-to-place child is another example.

Although it can be shared, power is always unevenly distributed. Some members of an organization or of an ecosystem tend to exercise greater power over others than is exercised over them in return. This sometimes creates imbalances that require adjustment. Power takes on the quality of *legitimacy*, so long as subordinates agree that more powerful individuals and organizations should hold power and are using that power in a fair and equitable manner. Both the delegation of power and the acceptance of a subordinate position must be seen as more beneficial than some other arrangement; otherwise legitimacy will be brought into question.

A person's or an organization's power can be maintained through the use of coercive, reward, expert, referent, or positional tactics. *Coercive* tactics imply threatening the use of, or actually applying, negative sanctions. These might include strikes by employees (for better working conditions), sit-downs by clients (until their demands for benefits are met), a threat of reduction in an annual allocation by the United Way (unless the recipient agency agrees to modify its service in some desired direction), or refusal by a worker to permit a client some desired activity (until his or her behavior is modified).

*Reward* tactics are just the opposite. They reflect the ability of one party to enable another to achieve some form of gratification, to acquire desired benefits. Such benefits might be in the form of recognition, salary raises, the allocation of time to a relationship, or access to other resources. The ability to withhold a reward implies the ability to coerce or to threaten coercive action, particularly where rewards have come to be expected as automatic. Examples include the expectation of ongoing financial support from the Area Agency on Aging, or automatic salary increments each year.

Using *expert* tactics refers to the ability to get someone or some organization to do something based on their belief in one's expertise. Such expertise may be reputational. For example, an outside consultant might have disproportionate influence on the behavior of an organization's management because of his or her presumed expertise—influence that is disproportionate to the time and energy expended. In 2 or 3 hours of consultation with top management he/she may be able to induce organizational decision makers to move from positions that lower-level staff, having invested countless hours and days, were unable to budge them from. Would consumers come voluntarily to our organizations if they did not expect we had the required expertise? Would funders provide us with needed resources if we could not convince them of our organizational competence?

The use of *referent* tactics depends on the kinds of relationships that exist between persons or organizations. Referent power is based on mutual trust. One permits oneself to be influenced or induced to act in certain ways by another if one knows one can depend on the other. It is not necessary to be repaid on the spot. One is secure in the knowledge that one can always call in one's cards at a future date. Trust grows with each successive successful exchange. Previous exchanges need not have taken place between the parties to the current exchange. Thus you may be willing to take a risk on parting with your 20 dollars because you trust a teacher or colleague who suggested this book, or because you know The Free Press and its reputation. A person in need of family counseling may risk exposure because a friend had a successful experience at the Davidson Clinic. A foundation will be willing to fund a new service because it is aware of the reputation of the project director or is willing to trust the judgment of one of its referees that the proposal is worth funding.

Power is also related to *position*. This refers to a formal arrangement, a delegation of authority to persons or to organizations performing designated and agreed-upon roles. For example, the executive director is generally presumed to have more authority and thereby more power than a line supervisor. An agency that has the authority to coordinate other agencies may have greater power than those others. By putting a person or organization in a particular position vis à vis others, one can increase its relative power. Run through Exercise 2–5.

---

**EXERCISE 2-5**

**Analyzing Power Relationships**

By now you may be making connections between the concepts described in this chapter and strategic marketing.

1. Think of several situations in which you had power over others because of your position, your ability to reward or to coerce them, your expertise, or the mutual obligations that you and the other parties built up over time. Jot them down on a piece of paper.
2. Now examine any one of these. Could the objectives of your involvement in these situations have been optimized by using a different power tactic or by using a different mix of tactics? How?
3. Think of a similar situation in which the organization exerted influence on others or was influenced by them. What power tactics did each of the parties to the exchange use or imply it would be using with reference to the other parties?
4. To what extent are these power relationships legitimized as a result of expectations by all parties to the exchange? To what

*continued*

**EXERCISE 2-5** *continued*

> extent are they considered illegitimate by one or another of the
> parties, because the tactics used are considered inappropriate?
> Do differences in expectation impact on role/role-set strains or
> conflicts? On the perceptions by one or more parties to the ex-
> change about net benefit (the benefit minus the cost)?

## Review

Exchanges are activities that people and organizations engage in in order
to achieve personal or organizational goals. Exchanges may be in the form
of commodities (like money and books) or services (like counseling or referral). Positive exchanges generally result in "rewards" to one or more of the
parties involved. If an exchange relationship is to be established and maintained, all parties to it must perceive the net gain (reward minus cost) to be
in their favor, now or sometime in the future.

Exchange relationships lead to role differentiation and to power imbalances. Role incumbents are often required to shape their behaviors to
the expectations of members of the role-set, without which it would be impossible to perform the role. It makes no difference if the actor is an individual, a group, an organization, or a larger system. They all operate in a
balanced relationship to the elements in their environment upon which
they are dependent for survival or for goal achievement. These dependen-
cies may result in one unit having greater or lesser authority or power over
another unit. Power, the potential to influence, can be increased through
the right mix of position, coercion, reward, referent, or expert tactics.

Environmental factors, including both expectations and the availability of needed resources, may influence the extent to which an organization
will be closed or open. Open systems tend to have more permeable boundaries and are more interdependent with a larger number of elements in the
organization's environment.

Those elements which can shape the direction of an organization's mission and its activities or its growth and decline are part of its task environment. This environment is composed of resource suppliers, legitimators,
consumers, competitors, and collaborators.

# 3 FINDING YOUR PROGRAM'S NICHE IN THE MARKET

ALL HUMAN SERVICE organizations respond to a variety of input, output, and throughput publics. These make up its markets: the elements in each organization's environment from which it draws resources and through which it develops its products and finds outlets for its products. But for every market, there is at least potentially a wider market that might be reached. Organizations limit the markets to which they pay attention. "We can't be all things to all people" is heard all too often—perhaps as a cop-out, perhaps as a statement of reality. A converse of that statement is, "Your organization does not respond to our interests." No organization can respond to all interests and none can be all things to all people. Every organization finds a place for itself within several markets, a niche for itself, a domain it lays claim to. Finding an appropriate niche is the focus of this chapter. I'll share some of my own experiences with you.

### What Kind of Continuing Education and for Whom

Some years back, I undertook an assignment to develop a continuing education (C.E.) program at the University of Michigan School of Social Work. At that time, few social work schools were heavily into C.E. programs. The University of Chicago's School of Social Service Administration had the only well-established program in the Midwest, a summer school in which seasoned practitioners could enroll for 2 weeks or more for postgraduate academic credit.

Most Michigan social workers, I found, continued their educations through agency-based in-service activities or by finding courses and workshops conducted under such auspices as business schools, professional associations, and private training firms. The occasion of our entry into what looked like a relatively open market was a grant by the National Institute of Mental Health (NIMH). NIMH had recently established the Mental Health Continuing Education Branch. Its aim was to increase the capacities of universities, state mental health agencies, professional associations, and local community mental health centers to provide ongoing educational opportunities to mental health professionals: physicians, psychiatric nurses, psychologists, and social workers.

I was a new faculty member, and one of my first tasks was to find out in what kinds of continuing education and consultation activities my colleagues were engaged or might be interested in becoming involved. I needed to get a line on the School's internal capacity to do C.E. and what the faculty thought were high-priority areas. I also conducted a survey of social workers, drawn from a random sample of National Association of Social Workers (NASW) members throughout Michigan and contacted the other schools of social work to find out what kinds of C.E. activities they were involved in. Later, I met with those in charge of C.E. at the University's Schools of Medicine, Public Health, Nursing, Business, and Law in order to find out whether any of their activities reached social workers or if they might be interested in collaborating with the School of Social Work. All the findings were shared with a faculty committee charged with overseeing the C.E. program and providing it with policy directives.

The next step was to meet with social workers and human service agency administrators around the state. What kinds of collaborative activities between the School and local agencies were possible and desirable? I learned a great deal. I also found myself stimulating demand from a constituency the School had not paid consistent attention to in the past. We would have to respond to that demand. As long as the demand was diffuse, however, there was no guarantee that social workers would attend any courses or workshops that we might offer. It was important to target our offerings to the specific interest of key consumer populations. Accordingly, I set up a number of advisory committees throughout the state. In each locale, I asked the executive officer of the local welfare fund or the community mental health center, a respected local social worker, to convene an advisory group. On the basis of the recommendations made by those advisory groups, the School's faculty committee for C.E. designed a series of short courses and workshops to be offered in Ann Arbor as well as others to be "parachuted" into local communities throughout the state. This clearly differentiated Michigan's approach from the University of Chicago model, with which we did not think we could compete effectively.

For several years, we continued what some people might call a "smörgåsbord" or "cafeteria" approach to C.E. Courses and workshops were generally well attended and enthusiastically received by their participants.

However, two of the local advisory committees had other ideas in mind. Each wanted to see the School provide more service at the local level. One submitted a plan whereby the School would undertake major responsibility for planning and conducting staff development and in-service training to all agencies in its locale. The second proposed that the School offer a full range of credit courses in its community, all applicable to the MSW degree—in effect, proposing a "branch campus."

Neither of these proposals was received with much enthusiasm by the School's faculty committee for C.E. or its administrative officers. Either one of them might have had considerable impact on the way in which the School allocated its resources and would have substantially affected its sense of mission and its image of itself. From my perspective, I began to see the local advisory groups as no longer functional. In part this was because as they took on lives of their own, they were beginning to place demands on the School to which it was neither willing nor able to respond. There were other reasons, however.

By now, the C.E. program had established a positive image. Large numbers of social workers and others continued to attend activities based in Ann Arbor, and the early legitimacy conferred by local committees was no longer a necessity. The local committees might better attend to local needs, I reasoned. For the next several months, I worked to redirect their efforts toward greater assumption of local responsibility for C.E. and toward less dependency on the School.

Something else was wrong, however. Although demand increased each year, and the level of participation in our activities rose by 20 or 30 percent annually, I was bothered by the feeling that participation in C.E. activities had little impact on practice or on improving the quality of social work and mental health services for client populations. It became increasingly evident that unless the agencies in which our consumers were employed showed interest in changing their intervention methods or in expanding services to populations in need, few changes were likely to occur in practice as the result of the School's C.E. activities. It seemed logical, therefore, to approach employers and others who might be concerned with services in various sectors—child welfare, aging, mental health, etc.—for purposes of developing the goals and activities of the C.E. program.

Together with other faculty members, I set out to establish collaborative relationships with the state's departments of mental health and of social services, and with the heads of major local agencies in sections of the state where we already had extensive relationships. We also approached professional associations and advocacy groups. We identified new program directions that those organizations were interested in and specified the capacities that their staff would need in order to effectively provide the services needed. We then explored ways in which each organization and the University might collaborate in preparing those staff members for the tasks identified. The result was a dozen or more contracts and grants from those organizations over the next few years.

We had now established a new pattern that we were to use in our relationships with federal funders and with philanthropic foundations in the future. It was to be a partnership relationship. In each partnership, we decided, the sponsor would have to be at least as interested in the success of the program as we were. The program would also have to be designed to affect service delivery, not merely to respond to the career or occupational interests of individual practitioners. Payoffs would have to be measurable in terms of improved service to clients.

I wasn't quite aware of it at the time, but in retrospect it is clear I had been engaged in marketing activities. The School had developed not only a product but a relatively extensive product line. Moreover, the School had also begun to identify its peculiar niches in several markets. Each niche was based in part on our capacity, in part on expressed or stimulated demand, and to a large extent on the anticipation of rewards by individual and organizational consumers. Many of these consumers had also become suppliers and full partners in the enterprise.

## Needs, Demands, and Interests

Marketing is in part an effort to respond to or to generate demand. Demand is based on perceived need or interest. Neither are static properties. Several years ago, a "hot" topic in C.E. was "staff burnout." People were concerned about not only the stresses that led to fatigue and dissatisfaction at work but also the lack of opportunities about which many workers complained. I'm referring not to opportunities for advancement, but for self-development, personal growth, and self-actualization. These are what Maslow called "higher-order" needs. They are hardly the needs I hear discussed by agency workers today.

Today's needs are more likely to be expressed in terms of survival and safety. Social workers are as prone to be concerned with keeping their jobs as with finding fulfillment within them. Social agencies may be just as interested in survival, focusing their energies on maintaining the necessary level of resource input to assure that survival, perhaps to the exclusion of focusing on work environments that are fulfilling to the employees. Thus, what we described in Chapter 1 as "changes in market conditions," are likely to influence perceptions of need. To a large extent, these perceptions are likely to be influenced by objective market conditions. They are also likely to be influenced by public awareness and public opinion around any given issue.

For example, if people are unwilling to face the fact that a drug problem exists in a community high school, it will be impossible for school officials to develop strategies to deal with that problem. The important suppliers of resource and legitimacy (boards of education or parent–teacher associations) for any intervention effort may be indifferent to the issue or unwilling to deal with it. Sometimes, recognition of an issue is insufficient if people don't feel that it presents a problem that affects them directly. The issue of teenage motherhood didn't seem to be a problem of epidemic proportions until middle- and upper-income parents were forced to face it in their own homes. In the drug example, parents and officials may refuse to recognize or accept a reality. In the case of teenage pregnancy, they may be indifferent to it until it is deposited on their doorsteps.

The characteristics of what we might call the "acceptance environment" will tend to have signficant implications for any product or product line your organization intends to promote. Let's explore what is meant by the term "acceptance environment."

On any issue there will tend to be consensus, indifference, or disagreement. Research by Roland Warren on community intervention programs suggests that it is quite appropriate to use a collaborative strategy when there is consensus that a problem exists or consensus around a proposed solution. The program designer or planner might play an enabling or facilitating role, serving as a guide or catalyst, a convener, a mediator, a consultant, and perhaps even a coordinator of those willing to fund or support a program and those willing to collaborate in its development or management. The presumption is that good will exists between the parties and that their objectives, if not identical, are at least complementary.

Under such circumstances, those in accord might be brought together in some structured relationships like a planning or advisory committee. This structure, whether formal or informal, would assume responsibility for arriving at a mutually desired outcome. This is pretty much the situation I had described in my reflections on the development of the University of Michigan School of Social Work's Continuing Education Program. The program planner, in this case, performs most effectively as an orchestrator of consensus.

But a very different role would be required in an environment characterized by indifference. One would hardly be able to convene the interested parties if they were uninterested. The Continuing Education Program would hardly have considered itself successful had it produced a series of well-designed workshops only to find that nobody came. Where no one seems to care, or at least care very much, program planners must engage in promotional activities.

These entail heightening public sensitivity and awareness, animating those who are most likely to be directly affected by the problem (for example, parents of kids with drug problems) or those who can afford to take risks (i.e., committed clergy rather than school officials). Such persons might gain personal or institutional objectives (e.g., public recognition) through support for the program or service in question. Here the planner, as marketer, would aim at moving key publics from indifference toward consensus. Such consensus would be used to activate newly interested parties to work in collaboration toward a given end or ends. The exchange concepts we discussed in Chapter 2 have a great deal of bearing on this process. How might one attract others to associate with them in dealing with a particular issue or problem? What transactions must take place in order to induce people to participate in the development or expansion of a program, if they do not feel a personal need for it or are not sure of the benefits that might accrue through their involvement?

A third possibility exists: one in which there is no acceptance whatsoever of the existence of a problem or of the legitimacy of a proposed solution. Or perhaps there is considerable disagreement about either the problem or the solution for it. This might be called a "dissensus environment" in which disagreements over means and ends are likely to impede the successful development of a program.

Under these circumstances, promotional efforts aiming to persuade those in disagreement, or even efforts to bring the competing sides together, are not likely to prove successful. Ignoring a conflict that represents real differences, one in which none of the parties see any advantages to accommodation, may prove counterproductive. More appropriate are efforts to overcome or nullify resistance. One might attempt to increase the coercive or reward power of those parties in agreement that something needs doing, increasing their capacities to "win" on an issue, even if someone else loses. Although in some cases the best approach might be to ignore the opposition, at other times efforts may have to be put forth to box it in. Initially, at least, those who oppose the program should not be viewed as potential collaborators. Indeed, their opposition will have to be overcome through political action, education, persuasion, and other tactics before they can be involved in collaborative efforts.

The fact that indifference or disagreement exists need not discourage you from starting a new service or developing a new product line. Despite differences, or indifference, it is frequently possible to find your own niche in the market. There may be a strong anti-abortion sentiment in a particular community, but that does not mean your agency should not provide abortions or abortion counseling services to those in need. You won't find a niche among those opposed to abortions but you may find it among those who desire such service regardless of the opposition.

Indifference to the needs of the disabled on the part of the general public need not inhibit your organization from trying either to change that indifference to concern, or to serve the disabled who seek help with whatever resources you can muster. Your organization's ability to find its niche in the market (or niches if it has more than a single product) will depend a great deal on the kinds of relationships it establishes with its key publics.

## Segmenting the Market

When the market is divided into various publics, each of which is to be treated differently, we call the process *market segmentation*. Market segmentation refers to dividing the market into fairly homogeneous parts such that any one or more of these parts can be targeted for special attention. These are the publics we have been discussing. The segmentation process might result in clusters based on geography, function, demographics, or psychographics. Segmenting your market makes it possible to customize your marketing activity and to target it purposefully.

The organization's *geographic market* refers to the locale in which it provides services and from which it recruits much of its resources. The geographic market can be drawn up on the basis of size, density, or both. For example, a state department of aging might designate certain regions for the establishment of Area Agencies on Aging. Because of the population density of a metropolitan area, it might choose to establish two or three Area Agencies there even though the geographic size is very small, perhaps no more than 50 or 60 square miles. In other sections of the state, an Area Agency on Aging might serve a five- or six-county rural area, covering more than 50,000 square miles.

Within those geographic areas, certain subregions might be designated as primary markets, perhaps on the basis of demographic characteristics like income or minority composition. A state university might draw from a national or even an international population, but consider its primary market to be the state from which it secures basic financial support. And within that state, it may target its recruitment efforts to students with designated academic performance achievements.

*Functional segmentation* requires the clustering of services according to some logic for administrative or recognition purposes. For example, the university's office of state relations will be responsible for informing the governor's office and the state legislature of both its programs and its needs, whereas its office of development would target alumni, corporate, and philanthropic givers for support. Its instructional programs would be grouped into various colleges and schools, each of which recruits from among different potential student markets.

A family service agency might use the same functional categories to target its internal publics as its external consumer publics, using such program designations as counseling, family life education, and protective services. Alternatively, it might use those categories to target consumers in certain geographic areas, but cluster its internal publics according to such categories as direct service, supportive service, or management. It might segment further according to whether those activities are performed by paid or volunteer staff. Its external input publics might be categorized according to whether they supply financial, knowledge, or personnel resources. Within these categories, some will be designated as primary markets and others as secondary.

The market may also be segmented along such *demographic* characteristics as age, sex, family status, family size, stage in the family life cycle, income, occupation, education, religion, race or ethnicity, nationality, and social class. Demographic choices may have implications for input, throughput, and output publics. Thus, an agency aiming its service at a Chicano or an Oriental population may find that this decision has implications for the composition of its staff as well as for the selection of its input publics.

*Psychographic characteristics* are somewhat more subtle and sometimes more difficult to define. They include such variables as personality, life-style, and the readiness to use a service or to contribute to it. It may also refer to the types of benefits sought by those contributing to or using a service. For example, contributing time or money to an organization may confer prestige on the provider and may increase the range of friends and personal contacts made by the contributor, thus providing the contributor with a sense of wellbeing. Recognizing this, many agencies play upon the needs for identification and of belonging among many of their potential donors. They may even target persons with those needs.

Other psychographic characteristics include the extent to which services are likely to be used, consistency of relationship, or the loyalty expressed toward the organization. If consumers do not express what staff consider to be appropriate psychographic characteristics, staff may attempt to change those characteristics, as when my boss tried to convince the lady who bought swimming to think of herself as a sharing and caring member instead of a buying customer.

Some may be lifetime users, like some welfare recipients; others onetime only users, like those who attend a single session of a family life education program. Some may be light, others medium, and still others heavy users. Thus while many members of a religious congregation may attend services only once or twice a year, others will be weekly or even daily participants. Still others will not only attend services, but also send their children to Sunday school, participate in adult education activities, and take responsibility for the institution's charitable activities.

In some organizations, supplying resources, providing services, or receiving them are associated with demands of loyalty. The extent to which persons are willing to provide financial assistance, consultation, or other volunteer time may be a direct result of the commitment made to that organization. Writing a check may require little or no sense of responsibility to the organization, but it may entail some commitment to its cause or to its activities. Recipients of a county welfare department's services may feel little loyalty to the agency. On the other hand, recipients of services in a community center may be expected not only to be loyal members, but active participants in many of the center's various activities, including committee membership and fund raising.

Decisions about any of these segments are likely to affect other decisions which have direct implications for the organization's positioning within its potential markets. Thus, geographic decisions may have an implication for demographics. For example, limiting university recruitment to a narrow geographic area may reduce the numbers of qualified students in the applicant pool or may increase the number that need financial assistance. Now look at Exercise 3–1.

---

**EXERCISE 3-1**

**Segmenting the Market and Finding Your Niche Within It**

1. Review your notes or recollections regarding the program you described in Exercise 1-1. If you prefer, use the example in the vignette with which we opened Chapter 1. You may have to make some educated guesses. What are the general markets at which it was aimed? The publics addressed? Consider input, throughput, and output publics.

2. Were those publics segmented in some way according to geographics, demographics, psychographics, or functional characteristics? Might the program have been targeted more specifically to one or more of these publics? Which of these make up primary markets? Secondary markets?

3. Was the program's niche in the market clear to its staff, to potential consumers, to suppliers of resources, and to others? Was there consensus among these publics regarding the program (its activities, services, the consumers and others served)? If not, why not?

---

## Market Positioning

Market positioning is more than a process by which an organization chooses its consumers or other publics. It is also a process by which the organization spells out the distinctive roles it chooses to play with all of its publics. An adoption agency, having surveyed the range and needs for placement that exist in a given community and the availability of families for placement, might choose to target its services only to hard-to-place or special needs children. In making that decision, agency staff and board members may have determined that there may be no need to locate healthy, Caucasian babies for potentially adoptive families.

Such services may already be adequately provided by others in the private, voluntary, or public sectors, but a survey of agency case records shows that there are few available services aimed at permanent placements of older children, children from ethnic or racial minorities, or children with disabilities. Moreover, the organization's internal publics, its staff members and its board, are committed to placing the hard-to-place. An informal assessment of the agency's potential suppliers suggests that funding and other needed support for placing children with special needs are available. Thus all the elements needed to define the agency's particular position or niche in the market seem to be in place.

Decisions about market positioning depend in part upon who else is providing a particular service and the extent to which there is competition, if any. It may also depend upon the severity of need. Moreover, it often relates to the ideological or value commitments of staff, board members, and of significant input publics who must conduct the services, allocate needed resources, and legitimate the enterprise. These decisions have implications for what might be termed *market orchestration*.

## Market Orchestration

Market orchestration refers to choosing the right mix of input, throughput, and output publics. It may require that you determine your organization's "target market range." This range may include the geographic distance that you may consider to be part of your primary market, the kinds of problems the organization is willing to address, and both the demographic and psychographic characteristics you consider of primary importance. Differences in perception on the part of suppliers and other service providers with respect to your organization's appropriate or legitimate target market range may require educational or promotional activities aimed at changing the perceptions of one or another of those publics.

The lack of consensus on your organization's legitimate domain— whom it can serve, what services it should give and in what way—creates strains just as individuals suffer role strain when their perceptions of what is appropriate come out of sync with the perceptions of others in the role-set. If an agency's claim to a particular domain or market segment is not accepted by key publics, such as consumers, it may have to reach out to new consumer publics or engage in promotional activities aimed at changing the nature of the demand from potential consumers.

Differences in perceptions between different kinds of publics (e.g., funders and clients) may not be as serious as differences within a particular type of public. For example, middle-class teenagers may be unwilling to join a church or community center if that organization also provides services to lower-income or otherwise objectionable youths whom they consider undesirable associates. "Soshes" may be intrigued by "greasers," but not enough to associate with them on a regular basis.

## Images and Markets

In relating to each of your organization's markets, it is important for you to be clear about what it is your agency can or intends to do that makes it especially attractive to that market. Its ability to do that will depend on how it is perceived by key decision makers in each of those markets. To a certain extent, we are talking about shaping the image of your organization and bringing that image into line with the image that targeted markets have of the kinds of organizations with which they would like to do business. Images, however, are not acquired at will or even by effective public-relations efforts. They are largely the functions of actual deeds and the previous history of an organization. Achieving a desired image may require drastic changes in the organization's activities and those changes may have to transpire over time. Thus, establishing exchange relationships with key elements in an organization environment may not be all that easy. It may require careful planning and long-term investments.

When I first began planning the School of Social Work's Continuing Education Program, I found myself fortunate to be employed by an institution that was seen as a major intellectual center, located in a lively and attractive community. But I also had to deal with some negative images.

The School was not perceived to be responsive to agency or local needs. It had the reputation of being very *ivory tower* in orientation, and many of its faculty were identified more with social science disciplines than with social work practice. Bringing continuing education programs to local communities, and establishing collaborative relationships with state and local agencies did much to change the image. It not only induced consumers to attend, but it induced federal, state, and local funders to provide us with the necessary financial resources to operate and expand the services.

Like most organizations, however, we found ourselves unable to respond to the growing demand for those services. Although our resources were expanding, the sources of supply were not stable, as is often the case in organizations that depend heavily on grants and contracts. We had to limit our growth. We had to decide on which populations to target the ongoing services and on which to target one-time or ad hoc services. "Should we train agency administrators and supervisors, direct service practitioners, paraprofessionals, volunteers?" we asked ourselves. "Should we aim most of our efforts at the child welfare or mental health fields? Or should we target other service sectors, such as the field of corrections, where few if any educational services were being aimed? Did we have a responsibility to enter a market that was clearly underserved, and could we develop the capacity to do so?"

Such decisions are not always made on the basis of an organization's particular interests or commitments. The decision may be made on the basis of the resources that it can command. To better comprehend this point, let's look at a situation that is at least somewhat familiar to most of us: college recruitment. And let's focus on recruiting for the football team. If they had their druthers, most college athletic departments would recruit the best athletes available, without in any way having to lower academic standards. No athlete would be recruited who could not compete in the academic arena as well as on the athletic field.

Some universities, like UCLA or Michigan, might be successful in such recruitment efforts. They have superb academic reputations, and are most successful on the football field. Their reputations, when combined with athletic scholarships, generally put them in a pretty competitive position. However, other schools may not be that fortunate. They may have to choose to recruit on the basis of either athletic or academic qualifications. In order to mount a winning team, they may have to compromise on academic qualifications—presumably assuring themselves of a team that can play. A winning team is likely to yield the approval of alumni and other supports on which the university or college may be dependent for a variety of resources. On the other hand, criticism that the university has lowered its standards, or that it is not properly educating its athletes, may generate negative public opinion. The image of the total university may suffer, even as its football team thrives.

As another example, let's refer back to the small regional liberal arts college we mentioned earlier. Although we can assume that it wishes to attract an able student body, the college's ability to attract students will depend to a large measure on its image. And that image is likely to be shaped by the quality of its faculty, the composition of its current student body, and its previous history. Some schools are known as "diploma mills"; others are known as "a great place to have good times." Some are known as centers of scholarship and learning; some as "hippie hangouts" or places where "artsy" kids tend to go. A school may be comfortable with its image and may have determined that its niche in the consumer market is the pre-college population that approximates, in its characteristics, that particular image.

If, however, the college is not comfortable with that image, or wants to change it by attracting a wider array of students, it will have to reshape its programs and activities to satisfy the needs and demands of newly sought populations.

We can apply the same kind of thinking to the college's other markets: the suppliers of research grants and endowment funds; other colleges and universities with which it might cooperate on exchange programs and which are its competitors for academically able students. Its niche in those markets will also be determined by internal publics like the faculty and others who provide services to students and engage in scholarly activities. To occupy a new niche in any of these markets, additional faculty may have to be recruited; some on the basis of academic reputations, others, perhaps, on the basis of their ability to relate to various ethnic populations.

As with the liberal arts colleges we are discussing, your agency's niche in the market may be narrow or broad. You may attract a wide variety of clients with a correspondingly wide array of problems or you may also limit your services to very specific populations. Perhaps you find yourselves attracting many different kinds of clients whereas most of the staff are convinced their services should be offered to a narrower variety of people in need.

Current clients may include persons with specific ethnic, racial, or socioeconomic characteristics. You may wish to attract others. Current clients may feel only a minimum commitment or responsibility to the agency. Perhaps you are seeking other consumers who feel committed to reciprocating for services received by taking on responsibility for other clients once they have been helped with their problems. Perhaps you seek clients who are capable of participating in decision- or policy-making groups or in finding new sources of financial support for the agency.

Determine how broad or narrow a niche in the market you wish to carve out and the position within the broader market you wish to occupy. Exercise 3-2 will provide you with an opportunity to reexamine your current position and to determine how close it may be to a desired position.

---

## EXERCISE 3-2
### Market Positioning

1. List the major consumer publics that you are trying to attract (e.g., college students with high IQs, parents willing to adopt special needs children, and so on).

2. Now go back over that list and check those populations that are already attracted to your organization.

3. With a different color, check those that are most attractive to your organization.

4. Locate each of these populations where appropriate in Figure 3-1. For example, those that are both attractive to your organization and attracted to it would go in the box in the upper left-hand corner. Those that are attractive to your organization, but are not attracted to it would go in the upper right-hand corner. Those not attractive to your organization, but tend to be attracted to it would go in the lower left-hand corner. And those that are neither attractive nor attracted would go in the lower right-hand corner.

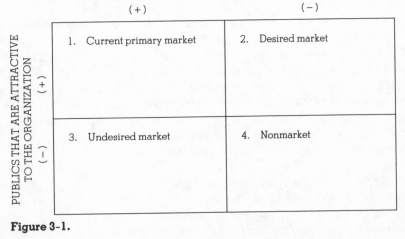

**Figure 3-1.**

You have now identified (1) your current primary consumer market, (2) the desired market, the one you wish to induce to seek services from your organization (and which in time may become its primary market), (3) the undesired market, the one you wish to treat as a nonmarket, and (4) those publics which in fact are currently the nonmarket. Should any of these publics be treated as elements or components of a secondary market to which some resources and services must be directed?

I suspect that this was not an easy exercise to complete, nor was Exercise 3–1. We too often perceive our markets as undifferentiated masses. At best we take into account some demographic, geographic, and functional, variables. If we pay attention to psychographic characteristics, it is in reference to functional problems we perceive in our consumer populations, problems that are to be corrected through our service programs. But those psychographic characteristics, as we now see, may be equally as important, or even more so, in determining toward which segments of the market to aim our services.

The same approach to segmenting the market and finding our organizational niche within it can be used in establishing strategic relationships with input and throughput publics as well. Put yourself in the position of a staff or volunteer recruiter and trainer. How would you use these exercises to segment or position the agency, or your department, vis à vis paid and volunteer staff? Put yourself in the position of a fund-raiser or grant seeker. How would you use these exercises with reference to resource suppliers?

## Review

Marketing is in part an effort to respond to or to generate demand. But demand depends, in part, on the degree to which there is consensus, disagreement or indifference to an issue being addressed, a population in difficulty, or a program in the making. Planners and others concerned with the development and delivery of human services must develop strategies that are appropriate to this "acceptance" environment. Cooperative strategies make sense when there is general agreement on goals or means, whereas promotional strategies are more appropriate to conditions of indifference, and competitive strategies are called for when there is opposition to be overcome.

To a large extent, such strategies will be affected by the image the organization projects to others in its task environment . . . those key publics upon which it is dependent for survival and/or for achievement of its program missions. That image is likely to be shaped by decisions made with reference to any one of the key publics. Thus, a decision about targeting services to a particular consumer population is likely to affect the organization's potential to recruit resources from other publics. Finding one's appropriate niche in the market is, therefore, a dynamic process in which the

activities aimed at one or another public are likely to affect the organization's relationship to other publics.

Decisions about primary, secondary, and nonmarkets are best made on
the basis of careful market segmentation. Markets can be segmented on the
basis of geographic, functional, demographic, and psychographic characteristics. Finding an organization's niche in the market requires a careful
pinpointing of those characteristics the organization considers desirable
with reference to its programs and services and essential to securing the resources necessary for its operations.

# PART II

# The Tools and Mechanisms of Exchange

# 4  EXCHANGES WITH OTHER SERVICE PROVIDERS

THE SUCCESS OF virtually any organization's programs is likely to depend on the nature and quality of the exchanges it maintains with those other organizations with which it is interdependent. For human service agencies, interorganizational exchanges with other service providers have emerged as a focal concern as agencies seek to coordinate with each other and to provide more comprehensive and continuous services to clients. Few programs can be designed that do not require at least some exchanges with other service providers. No resource-development strategy is complete without consideration of competitors for scarce resources and collaborators in their utilization. These other service providers can be defined as "markets," as publics that provide inputs and consume outputs. You may still find it curious to define other service agencies as potential "markets." An example from practice may help clarify the point.

A few years back I was involved in the training of foster care workers in a metropolitan public welfare department. The Child Welfare units had just been charged with moving children out of temporary foster care and into more permanent placements. The goal was to achieve a permanent placement for each child within a 6-month period. Any of you who have worked in child placement know that that is no easy trick to perform.

In order to be helpful, my staff and I decided to interview a number of child welfare experts in different parts of the country whose own programs had successfully moved in the direction of permanency for children. What follows is an excerpt from one of our interviews with the director of a highly successful program.

## Kids Should Be at Home

"When we decided to change most of our efforts from placing kids in foster homes and then managing them as they moved through the foster care system, to relocating them with their bio-parents . . . well, it required a whole new way of operating. In the old days, we just recruited the best foster parents we could find. But now we also do everything possible to support the bio-parents in their efforts to keep the child at home.

"This requires that we work cooperatively with the schools, the health clinic, the library, and every other resource that might be helpful to the child and his family. We developed joint projects with the Corktown Mental Health Clinic; participated in case conferences with the staff of at least eight different agencies; increased the range of our referrals; set up collaborative follow-up and case management procedures. We worked together with the juvenile and probate courts to set up a jointly sponsored volunteer program.

"An interesting consequence of working with the courts was the establishment of relationships with a number of civic associations. Many of the courts' volunteers had been members of the Kiwanis and of several of the churches in the area. Since we did most of the training of the volunteers, the organizations from which they came began seeing the Welfare Department's wards as their problems and not only ours. The Kiwanis ran an annual picnic at which kids and their bio as well as foster parents could begin to interact.

"We had an interesting problem when the question arose about whether to invite kids to the picnic once they had been placed in adoption. Some of them could not be reunited with their bio-parents so had to be placed out for adoption. Now the question was whether or not to invite the adoptive families with the bio-parents and the foster parents to the same picnic. Not knowing exactly how to deal with it, we turned the problem over to the self-help groups we had established.

"For some time we had been working with foster parents in groups, in fact fostering their own development of support groups with technical assistance by our caseworkers. We thought we would try the same thing with bio-parents who had lost one or more kids to the courts and who are now trying to regroup themselves. If they are going to regroup, we thought we would give them some group support or let them support each other.

"In fact, what we did is set up a number of self-help groups in which our caseworkers served as facilitators. It wasn't long before one of the staff got the idea of a kind of 'inter-group,' that included experienced foster care parents who were preparing kids to re-enter their bio-families and members of those bio-families who were kind of anxious about their ability to take care of their kids properly now that the kids had been away from them for so long.

"While my staff had originally resisted some of these activities, we soon found that involving clients and foster parents in their own self-help, and then in helping each other, increased our own capacities and our own effectiveness. It has taken a lot of effort, but without linking up with the organizations, with our foster care partners and with our new client partners, we never could have shifted our own services as successfully or as radically as we did. The picnic? We invited everyone. No problems."

The vignette presents an interesting example of how one public agency's success was directly related to its work with other public and voluntary service providers, with civic associations and with organized client groups. In this chapter, we will explore the range of exchanges possible between an agency and other service providers. In Chapter 5, we shall examine relationships between agencies and their consumer populations, particularly the involvement of consumers in program development and in service delivery. Exchanges with funders and other resource providers are dealt with more fully in Chapters 12 and 13 on fund raising and grant seeking.

You may already have given a great deal of thought to the issues discussed in these chapters and indeed, may have considerable experience in the programmatic activities described. You'll now have an opportunity to reexamine the issues discussed from a strategic marketing perspective. Keep in mind what you have already determined about market segmentation and your organization's niche in the various markets in which it operates.

## The Costs and Benefits of Coordination

Many people not familiar with the delivery of human services at the community level assume that agencies have a natural tendency to coordinate their activities. All too often, nothing could be further from the truth. Instead of naturally gravitating toward each other, organizations and groups are more likely to be governed by self-interest that works against some forms of coordination while encouraging others. Coordination involves certain costs.

It requires giving up full authority over a program or program components, as these become shared with others. It requires investing time in maintaining exchange relationships that some feel might better be allocated to providing services to clients. It means operating at the boundary of one's organization or outside of it, rather than in the more familiar and perhaps more comfortable surroundings of the agency itself. Thus, the costs of coordination may be substantial.

The benefits, however, may also be considerable. They include more comprehensive as well as more continuous services. Continuity refers to the sequencing of services, each of which becomes a link in a chain. The success of one link in the chain can only be evaluated on the basis of the integrity of the chain itself. For example, a mental hospital could hardly evaluate the success of its discharge program, regardless of how much preparation it provides its patients for reentry into the community, unless there were appropriate community care facilities and support services available to patients following discharge.

Comprehensiveness refers to the scope of services provided in relation to a client or a consumer population problem. For example, a job training program that focuses only on trainee skill development would hardly be considered comprehensive. But a program that includes training, job development and job placement, family life education, and health and mental health services provided to the trainee and his or her family members, would be comprehensive.

The anticipated benefits of coordination are (1) improved service to clients, (2) reduction in expectation or demand in a single agency to be all things to all people, and (3) elimination of gaps and holes in the network of services. In many cases, coordination also improves efficiency through reduction of duplicate efforts. Effective coordination is not only desirable, but it is generally feasible, although it does require careful planning.

A wide variety of "linking mechanisms" can be used to orchestrate the activities of several organizations in order to increase the availability of services, their accessibility, their effectiveness, their efficiency, and their responsiveness to various publics. These linking mechanisms are formalized exchange procedures. Like other forms of exchange, it is not necessary for all parties to the exchange to receive the same benefits, or even to benefit to the same extent. It is only important that each party perceive the benefits it receives from the exchange as outweighing the costs. It's not even important that the benefits be accrued at the moment the exchange takes place. What is important is that each party trusts that its investment will have sufficient payoff to warrant that investment.

Although many of the linking mechanisms that I shall be describing have implications for agencies, client populations, and civic associations, we'll focus in this chapter on those that are typically used in the interagency arena. Many of these linkages are voluntary; that is, they are not required by some outside source. Some, however, are mandatory, as when a state agency requires that a county welfare department contract out for the provision of community-based care to a group organization that manages homes.

Although some exchanges may be ad hoc, as when a worker from one agency calls a colleague in another agency to ask for advice on a knotty problem, others include standardized procedures, like those used in interagency referrals.

## Strengthening the Linkage Mechanisms Between Agencies: A Marketing Problem

In Figure 4–1 I have categorized the more frequently found interagency linkages under four main headings: Meeting Immediate Client Needs;

A. Meeting Immediate Client Needs

    \_\_\_\_\_ 1. Case consultation
    \_\_\_\_\_ 2. Case conferences
    \_\_\_\_\_ 3. Case management
    \_\_\_\_\_ 4. Joint intake, screening, diagnosis
    \_\_\_\_\_ 5. Referrals
    \_\_\_\_\_ 6. Treatment teams
    \_\_\_\_\_ 7. _____
    \_\_\_\_\_ 8. _____
    \_\_\_\_\_ 9. _____

B. Meeting Agency Personnel Needs

    \_\_\_\_\_ 1. Co-location of staff
    \_\_\_\_\_ 2. Loaner staff arrangements
    \_\_\_\_\_ 3. Joint training and staff development
    \_\_\_\_\_ 4. Staff outstationing
    \_\_\_\_\_ 5. _____
    \_\_\_\_\_ 6. _____
    \_\_\_\_\_ 7. _____

C. Gathering, Exchanging, and Disseminating Information

    \_\_\_\_\_ 1. Information clearinghouse
    \_\_\_\_\_ 2. Interorganizational technical assistance
    \_\_\_\_\_ 3. Joint program evaluation
    \_\_\_\_\_ 4. Joint promotions and community education
    \_\_\_\_\_ 5. Management information system
    \_\_\_\_\_ 6. Needs assessment or special studies
    \_\_\_\_\_ 7. _____
    \_\_\_\_\_ 8. _____
    \_\_\_\_\_ 9. _____

D. Integrating Programs and Administrative Procedures

    \_\_\_\_\_ 1. Joint budgeting
    \_\_\_\_\_ 2. Joint funding (allocation)
    \_\_\_\_\_ 3. Joint fund raising
    \_\_\_\_\_ 4. Joint program design
    \_\_\_\_\_ 5. Joint program operation
    \_\_\_\_\_ 6. Joint standards and/or guidelines
    \_\_\_\_\_ 7. Purchases of service
    \_\_\_\_\_ 8. Sharing facilities and/or equipment
    \_\_\_\_\_ 9. Standardized procedures
    \_\_\_\_\_10. _____
    \_\_\_\_\_11. _____
    \_\_\_\_\_12. _____

**Figure 4-1**   Inventory of Potentially Useful Linking Mechanisms

Adapted from Armand Lauffer, *Assessment Tools*, Sage Publications, Beverly Hills, Calif., 1982, pp. 39–41. Adapted by permission.

Meeting Agency Personnel Needs; Gathering, Exchanging, and Disseminating Information; and Integrating Programs and Administrative Procedures. You'll notice that I have left several lines blank under each category. You may know of other important linking mechanisms that your organization, or others with which you are familiar, utilize extensively.

The utility of these linkages for program design, and their significance for the pooling of resources to achieve complementary objectives will soon become apparent. The costs involved are sometimes not at all apparent. Unfortunately, many agencies are reluctant to engage in anything more than the most perfunctory exchanges for fear of loss of autonomy, of exposure to outside examination, or because of the expected demands on staff time. Even where administrators agree on the importance and the value of these linkages, they may not be able to agree on each organization's responsibility for aspects of the exchange process. Moreover, previous negative experience with similar exchanges may have lowered the trust level between potential collaborators.

Establishing effective and ongoing linkages between providers poses an interesting set of marketing problems. What is the product you are marketing: new and intrinsically rewarding activities and relationships, instrumental objectives like cost-saving or the establishment of more effective and responsible services, a change in the images of the cooperative organization, or greater access to needed resources?

The linking of service providers into a coordinated and comprehensive system takes time. It takes time to design a linking mechanism, to promote its adoption by providers, to negotiate or mediate agreements between providers, and to evaluate the effectiveness, efficiency, or appropriateness of the mechanisms in question. Many linking mechanisms are not quick to prove themselves. Comfortable working relationships are not easy to achieve. Even those linkages that seem to be fully operational need continued attention and support if the gains made are to be protected and further progress promoted.

The development of such exchanges and their maintenance may be affected by a number of variables. These include (1) the skill and capability of the individuals involved and their development; (2) the money and other resources at the disposal of one or more of the partners to the exchange, which may serve as inducements or which may make an exchange relationship more attractive; (3) the extent to which public opinion and environmental conditions support and foster such coordination; (4) the complementarity of the objectives and concerns of the parties to the exchange; (5) the complementarity of the policies and procedures that govern the functions of those organizations; (6) the existence of necessary logistical supports; (7) and such other variables as good will, trust, or perhaps even the extent to which participating organizations view the exchange relationship as "taking them off the hook" through the sharing of responsibility. To what extent do these conditions prevail in your agency's efforts to expand its linkages to other providers?

## Developing an Agency Resource File

Perhaps I've jumped the gun by moving directly into the arena of inter-agency exchanges without so much as describing the potential linkage mechanisms or even discussing how other service providers might be designated as part of your organization's market. You may not know enough yet about what other agencies in the community do to determine the nature of the exchanges that could or should take place between them and your organization. Discussion of referrals or the development of a management information system may be premature until we know more about the operations of each of the other agencies, or what they perceive to be their mandates and their service domains. The following vignettes may suggest some different reasons for developing a resource file that describes the work and concerns of other agencies.

### A Personalized Program Resources File

"When I started my present job I wasn't only new to the agency, but I was also new to substance abuse work and to the community. I'm kind of an assertive person. So when I found the agency had almost no orientation at all for new workers, I asked my supervisor for a reduced load for the first three months or so in order to have time to know the community's resources. I argued that if I was going to be a drug counselor in the school system, I had to know what resources I could tap on behalf of the kids and families who were my clients.

"It happens that this is a rather innovative agency. Worker loads are kept rather low so that we can do more than just counsel kids when they get into trouble. A lot of time is devoted to preventive work. We've got some room to maneuver in terms of the balance between preventive and rehabilitative work. My supervisor was supportive. She suggested that if I really wanted to know what the resources in the community were, I should start by checking with some of the kids who had been seen by a number of agencies over the years. Ours is the kind of agency that involves kids in helping each other so that this was not going to violate any confidence. She gave me three or four names both from my own caseload and from hers.

"She was right. What a gold mine! I not only found out which agency did what, but where there was a helpful caseworker, where I might find a sympathetic doctor, or how a degrading procedure at the local health clinic could be avoided. I also found out how different teachers in one of the local schools treated kids with drug problems and what I could expect from the school psychologist, the counselor, and the principal.

"But these kids couldn't give me all the information I needed. Luckily there was a community directory put out by the Welfare Council that listed all the other health and welfare agencies in the county. I found some of my co-workers really helpful in filling in the details about the procedures for referring clients and for communicating information between agencies. Just like the kids I spoke to, they were able to tell me how to cut through some of the red tape and bureaucratic tangles that I'd be likely to get into in relating one agency to another. It wasn't long before I had developed my own personalized resources file, one that I was able to update as I got to know people better and had more experience in the community."

## A Taste for Children

"Our agency has been in the child welfare business for years. You know, when you're in the same business a long time, you begin to take certain things for granted. You look at things from the same old perspective. And you tend to interact only with those other people who feel the same way as you do about things.

"I suppose things would have remained the same if it hadn't been for Harriet Kaplan, the mother of two 'bio' and three adopted kids. Harriet's a dynamo. When she was elected president of the local chapter of the Council of Jewish Women, she was looking for something new and different to do. It happens that her election coincided with a newspaper campaign of ours, a 'child of the month campaign.' Each month we place a story in the newspaper with a picture of a child who is free for adoption. We're talking about kids with developmental disabilities. Older kids, you know. Well, Harriet called me one day and asked if she could come to talk with me.

"We talked a bit about our agency and our efforts to find permanent homes for children. She wanted to know what other agencies did and how we related to them. To be honest with you, I knew a great deal about some of the agencies in town, but very little about others. By the time our conversation ended, Harriet had a campaign all worked out in her mind. She would help us develop a resource file so that we could make better use of other program resources. Together with volunteers from the Council of Jewish Women, she would knock on any agency door that was currently serving children or that should be.

"We worked together on a form to be filled out on each agency. Harriet's group went to work collecting information. Once they had it all collected, they organized it into a community directory with a twist. It looked like a recipe book. They called it a *Taste for Children*. The book was an instant success. Parents wanted it. Agencies wanted it. But Harriet's group didn't stop there. In their interviews, they had uncovered a number of practices they thought were less than beneficial for kids or their families. They also found other agencies that were doing super work but which were understaffed or underfinanced, and certainly underrecognized.

"To correct what she thought were some inequities and inadequacies, she decided to take her *Taste for Children* on the air. Every Wednesday evening, she had a half-hour interview show on our cable television station. She began by interviewing the directors or key staff people of the more successful agencies in town. Then she added a panel of consumers—parents, kids, consumer groups—who would question the person being interviewed and react to what he or she said.

"And she allowed agencies to advertise—not for money of course—that wasn't permitted in the cable television charter. But agencies could take 30 seconds to tell about their services after they had passed before one of Harriet's interviewing teams. After a while Harriet began interviewing agency representatives from those organizations that she and her group felt were not serving children adequately. Sometimes there were fireworks! The interviewing panel really took after some of the agencies that seemed to put their own interests above those of kids and families.

"Well, what started out to be a resource file for use by our agency became a public forum for child advocacy. It's taught me a great deal about what happens when you begin gathering information, and especially when you make that information public."*

The child welfare workers quoted had several reasons for developing resource files: finding out what other agencies do to increase the likelihood of collaborative relationships, developing a personal information system that the individual worker might use in making contacts to serve the needs of individual clients; and broader community use in advocacy on behalf of a client population. There are many other reasons why you might wish to develop a resource file.

The information in it might be drawn from many sources and many persons: volunteers who interview others under your direction, colleagues at the agency, workers at other agencies, and consumers. Much of the information may be available in community directories, such as those published by a community mental health center, a public welfare or public health department in your county, or the health and welfare council.

Consider making personal visits to agencies, and getting to know what they look like from the inside out. If you don't know where else to start, start with the Yellow Pages. You may have to use a variety of information sources in order to develop your own file. Once you've decided which agencies to visit, it might be helpful to categorize them in some way that you find helpful. In Figure 4–2, a worker in a family service agency identified all the organizations in her community that provided services, directly

*From Armand Lauffer, *Getting the Resources You Need*, Sage Publications, Beverly Hills, Calif., 1982, pp. 36–39. Reprinted by permission.

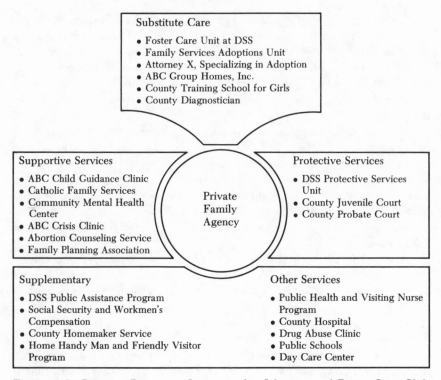

**Figure 4-2** Program Resources Inventory for Adoptive and Foster Care Children and Families

From Armand Lauffer, *Getting the Resources You Need*, Sage Publications, Beverly Hills, Calif., 1982, p. 32. Reprinted by permission.

or indirectly, of importance to children needing placements in foster or adoptive care settings. Notice that some agencies appear more than once.

Before moving on to a more detailed examination of exchange mechanisms, complete Exercise 4–1. We will then be ready to examine in some detail the linkages that are both possible and desirable between service-providing organizations. We will begin with those linkages aimed at meeting immediate client needs and then move on to those that deal with

---

**EXERCISE 4-1**

**Building Your Own Resource Inventory**

1. Decide whether the categories of the columns in Figure 4–2 are applicable to your situation. Would you divide some into more specific categories? Consolidate others? Add categories? Use the

*continued*

**EXERCISE 4-1 continued**

categories that make the most sense to you; write on a blank sheet of paper or a piece of newsprint. Do not be limited by the format in the examples. Be creative. You might find another format that is more graphic or easier for you to use.

2. Now start your inventory by listing what already exists. Using a black pen or marker, write in all the program resources of relevance to a particular consumer population found in your community.

3. Having specified what is, add what might be. Using a red pen or marker, add services that are not found in your community.

4. Go back over your inventory of "what is" (the one written in black) and underline in red those you feel need considerable modification.

agency personnel needs, the gathering and exchange of information, and finally the establishment of integrative and administrative mechanisms.

## Meeting Immediate Client Needs

No agency is capable of providing for all the needs of all its consumers. Agency personnel often interact on behalf of their clients with staff of other human service programs. This interaction may take the form of (1) case consultation; (2) case conferences; (3) case management; (4) joint intake, screening, and diagnosis; (5) referral, and (6) the use of treatment teams.

*Case consultation* is often an informal process in which staff from one agency asks for advice from staff at another regarding the needs of a particular client or class of clients. It can also become routinized as part of the formal relationships between organizations. Teachers at a local junior high school, for example, may know that under a contract between the School Board and the Mental Health Board, they can always call for advice on dealing with a substance abuse problem from specialists at the Community Mental Health Center.

*Case conferences* are well-worn techniques, used for many years by social agencies to regularize ad hoc consultation procedures and to increase the likelihood that staff with comparable interests or concerns can learn from each other. Typically, social agencies with clients in common assign direct service staff to attend regular or bimonthly meetings to discuss the progress of individual cases. The client or client family may be tracked through the system so as to identify those points where he or she was well served or where the client may have been side-tracked or dead-ended. Participants in the conference, some of whom may represent different disciplines or professions, consult with each other in the development of a treatment plan and on the assignment of responsibilities for care.

*Case management* procedures go one step further. Responsibility is assigned to one worker or one agency for making sure that clients receive all the services which are due them and which they require. This may entail making appointments for services, providing the client with transportation to get to necessary sources of help, checking periodically with other providers to make sure the client is receiving proper treatment, and determining when a case should be closed out.

*Joint intake, screening, and diagnosis* may be conducted centrally by a single organization for several participating organizations, or it may be decentralized, each participating agency conducting all or part of the process for its partners. The process may begin with *outreach* efforts aimed at informing potential clients of the services available to them. *Intake* itself is a process whereby clients are accepted for service. It may begin with "interception screening" which is, in effect, a pre-intake procedure in which clients, who inquire over the telephone or walk in, get information on where to go for help or how to apply for it. More detailed screening may subsequently take place on a "sectoral" level. Clients with health problems may be referred to a health intake worker, whereas another worker may be responsible for the intake of clients requiring educational or recreational services. *Diagnosis* generally follows intake and screening; it includes the assessment of the totality of a client's needs and frequently results in the development of a comprehensive plan for treatment. Based on diagnosis, the client may then be referred to an appropriate worker or to another agency for help.

*Referral* is a process by which a client is directed to another provider for service. At the simplest level, the intake worker will inform a client about where and how to go about getting another service, whereas in another case, he or she may contact the service provider to facilitate entry. Referrals sometimes include procedures required by the referring and accepting agency. For example, some agencies will not accept referrals unless some preliminary screening and diagnosis has been completed on forms of their own design. Effective referrals often require contractual agreements between the parties to the exchange. Without such agreements, rejection or misdirection of clients is not uncommon. The creation of centralized intake and referral systems can serve to cut down instances of rejection. If potential clients are properly screened, service agencies need not reject applicants outright when they cannot provide the required service. They need only refer the applicant back to the centralized referral agency or request information from an intake worker about where to more properly refer the applicant.

*Treatment teams* are frequently the outgrowth of other linkages. Multidisciplinary or multi-agency in nature, they involve the coordinated efforts of several service providers. For example, a treatment team might include a rehabilitation counselor, job trainer, job placement officer, methadone maintenance provider, and others. One agency may designate a staff member to be the informal team captain to assure that the services will be properly provided. Unlike case management in which different persons may work in isolation from each other on behalf of a particular client, members of treatment teams generally interact with each other on a fairly regular basis around the needs of many different clients. In effect, although they may be employed by different agencies, they operate almost as if they were employed by the same organization to work on issues related to a particular client population.

## Meeting Agency Personnel Needs

Interagency linkages can also be promoted through staff exchanges of various kinds. These include (1) staff outstationing, (2) co-location, (3) loaner arrangements, and (4) joint training and staff development. Let's start with examining the difference between outstationing and loaner agreements.

In *loaner* arrangements, a staff member employed by one agency will be placed on loan to another. The worker will operate as if, in fact, he or she were an administrative and programmatic member of the second agency's staff. For example, a specialist in substance abuse from the community mental health center may be placed on loan to the aforementioned junior high school. Operating as a member of the school's social work and counseling staff, he or she will attend all faculty and staff meetings. Although the counselor on loan will continue to be a salaried member of the community mental health center staff, collegial relationships will be shared, derived in large part from the host agency (the school). *Outstationing* is similar in that it also involves situations where one agency places its staff members at the disposal of another.

In outstationing arrangements, however, the staff member involved remains responsible only to his or her own employer. For example, an outreach worker may be located in the community, touching base with a number of agencies. This worker may be available every Tuesday afternoon at the public library, on Mondays and Wednesdays in Recreation Department facilities, on Thursday at a settlement house, and so on. An SSI (Supplemental Social Insurance) adviser from the Social Security Administration may be available every Tuesday and Thursday mornings at the downtown Senior Citizens Center.

*Co-location of staff* occurs when two or more agencies assign personnel to a common location, one which may be separate and apart from the facilities generally used by the two agencies involved. Co-location may, in operation, be identical with the *interorganizational treatment* teams we discussed earlier, although a treatment team may be able to operate effectively without necessarily being located in the same facility. Co-location does not require a fully integrated service. For example, when several agencies locate staff members in a "multiservice center," they are co-locating but not necessarily assuming that their staff members will operate as members of a combined team. Each may be doing the business of its own agency, much the way outstationed staff do.

*Joint training and staff development* are special examples of cooperating on an interorganizational level. Such activities may be centralized, as when the United Way trains staff to work with boards and committees or when an Area Agency on Aging trains the directors of its constituent agencies in the use of a new information processing system. Cooperation on issues pertaining to development and training can also occur on a bilateral or multilateral basis between organizations, and at the same level.

For example, a family service agency, planning to invite well-known family therapist Jay Haley or Virginia Satier to conduct a workshop for its staff, may arrange for other local agencies to share in the experience and/or the expenses. An agency that has developed specialized expertise in dealing with problems of the disabled may conduct workshops for the staffs of other agencies who work with disabled populations, at no cost to the other agencies. Finally, an agency that has developed a useful manual on public relations or promotions may wish to share that manual with other like agencies, reproducing it at cost.

## Gathering, Exchanging, and Disseminating Information

As services proliferate, and as consumer populations express increasing needs for a wide variety of services, the management of information about clients and services becomes of central importance. Information systems are expensive to develop. They have limited utility when they are limited to a single organization or service program. For this reason, agencies may establish cooperative arrangements for information management. Agencies are involved in (1) the use of information clearinghouse, (2) provision of technical assistance, (3) joint program evaluation, (4) joint program promotion and community education, and (5) the joint conduct of needs assessment or other special studies.

*Information clearinghouses* generally require that staff at one location undertake responsibility for collecting, classifying, and distributing information to several agencies and other community organizations on such issues as labor market conditions, job openings, and client services available. *Interorganizational technical assistance* refers to situations in which staff of one agency provide specified technical tasks for others, or instruct others how to perform those tasks. For example, when a community development corporation provides help to one of its constituent agencies on preparing proposal narratives and budgets for submission to state or federal agencies, it is providing technical assistance. The United Way may likewise provide technical assistance for its member agencies on budget preparation and submission. Such technical assistance need not relate to fiscal issues alone. It can be provided on such matters as developing a newspaper or television commercial campaign, using behavioral or token economy methods in group home management, or working with reconstituted families.

Technical assistance may be very similar to consultation, but it generally does not focus on specific cases; it is directed at a category or a type of activity. Nor need technical assistance be offered only by central organizations like the United Way or a community development corporation. It may be provided by any agency or organization that has a particular competence which is being sought by others. The child placement agency, whose director was quoted in the second vignette, has provided consultation and technical assistance to agencies throughout the country.

*Joint evaluation* may be the only feasible approach. Sometimes, centralized planning agencies conduct evaluation of their member agencies or of specific projects assigned to those agencies. Evaluations can also be conducted on the effectiveness or the costs of the interorganizational linkages we have been discussing.

Combined *needs assessments* or *special studies* are conducted for much the same reasons. Individual agencies may not have the technical or financial resources to conduct large-scale needs assessments. It is frequently much more efficient to conduct assessments that can be utilized by a number of agencies rather than to have each duplicate the efforts of the others in describing targeted populations or their needs.

The information gathered through needs assessments or program evaluations often makes up the basis for *shared management information*. Organizations using management information systems (MIS) may collaborate in gathering data on client populations, on resource capabilities, and on other areas of concern. Frequently these systems are computerized, with agencies sharing in the cost or time needed for use of computer facilities. The growth in availability of low-cost microcomputers and telephone-access systems makes it especially attractive to share in the development and management of MIS.

## Integrating Programs and Administration

Many of the linking mechanisms we've already discussed clearly have implication for collaborative administrative or programmatic activities. In this section we will discuss (1) joint budgeting, (2) joint funding, (3) joint fund raising, (4) joint program design, (5) joint program operation, (6) joint standards and/or guidelines, (7) the purchase of services, (8) sharing facilities and/or equipment, and (9) the establishment of standardized procedures.

*Joint budgeting* is an interesting process. It occurs when several organizations agree to share decisions regarding the financing of existing programs, but not necessarily on an exchange of funds between them. For example, in planning a picnic for children in foster and adoptive placement, and others who have been returned to their birth parents, several organizations may decide to budget jointly. The public welfare department's child placement division may allocate part of its budget to informing children and families of the time and location of the picnic. The Kiwanis may agree to contribute food and refreshments, while the churches involved may agree to contribute volunteers for transporting people to and from the picnic.

Other organizations may agree to provide sports equipment and to coordinate athletic activities. If the picnic is an annual event, each of these organizations may show special allocations for this picnic in their budgets. Although no money is ever exchanged, the picnic operates as if it had a single budget, the actual cost being shared, according to some agreed-upon formula, by the parties involved.

In contrast, *joint funding* refers to processes in which two or more service providers collaboratively finance a service program or project. These arrangements are common when funding regulations allow the use of "in kind" contributions as local share requirements for receiving a grant. Combining funds or in-kind contributions from different agencies makes it possible to realize shared objectives. An outreach service, for example, might be too costly for a single agency, but within reason when collaborating organizations pool their funds. Cost-sharing also occurs when two or more organizations agree to allocate funds to a third, perhaps a new organization, so that services will become available which both of the contributing partners feel are essential, but which neither feels capable of providing.

Collaborative allocations sometimes require *joint fund raising*. Agencies sharing facilities might also share in a capital fund drive. Other organizations may engage in a joint effort to raise funds for a needy population for which they both have responsibility. Many sectarian organizations engage in joint fund-raising efforts on a regular basis and may even delegate responsibilities for fund raising to a specialized agency. Thus, for example, the Jewish Federation in many communities serves as the fund-raising arm of all of its member social service and educational organizations. The United Way provides much the same service on a nonsectarian community-wide basis.

Collaboration on funding and fund raising, as well as many of the other exchanges discussed in this chapter, frequently leads to collaboration on *program design*. The foster care program described earlier could not engage in as wide a range of exchanges as described in the vignette had the collaborating institutions not been involved in at least parts of the program design process. Organizations seeking funding from a government or foundation source may be required to show that other key actors in the community have been involved in the program design, and that the projected program efforts are widely supported. Agencies frequently cooperate in the design of specialized, and perhaps time-limited, projects aimed at populations with very specific problems. For example, during the recession years of the early 1980s, many organizations pooled a variety of resources, including staff time, in joint efforts dealing with the consequences of hunger in their communities.

Their activities may have gone beyond program design to *joint program operation*, with each of the participating organizations assuming similar or perhaps complementary activities in the collection and distribution of food to needy families. Joint program operation need not be a response to crisis situations, however. In the mid-1970s, I was involved in helping facilitate the establishment of a community mental health laboratory in the Detroit area.

The laboratory was a joint creation of the 40 community mental health agencies. Its board was made up of representatives of those agencies, appointed on a rotating basis. In addition to promoting continuing education and training, the lab staff facilitated the exchange of other resources and technical expertise among member organizations. The board applied for, and received, a grant from an outside funder. Member agencies also paid fees for the services they received.

There are times when such intensive interactions are not possible. However, agencies may engage in the development of standards for practice that are intended to improve services. For example, in one community, all the substance abuse agencies set up several task forces to establish standards for practice. The resulting statement spelled out the desired ethical behavior of the practitioners as well as standards for staff development and training.

It is not unusual for professional associations to establish standards or guidelines for their members or member organizations. Thus, the American Hospital Association establishes guidelines for its member institutions. The National Association of Social Workers has a code of ethics that serves as a guide for individual practitioner behavior, and it has guidelines for salaries and other benefits that it recommends to employers.

You are probably familiar with *purchase-of-service* agreements by which one agency pays for services from another. When a foster care agency pays families to provide foster care, it purchases their services. When the same agency places children in the group home, it purchases services from the group home operators. Purchases of service are generally accompanied by requirements that the contractor must live up to. Such agreements are generally formalized with the obligations of both parties clearly spelled out.

Frequently this requires the establishment of *standardized procedures*. Such procedures facilitate the establishment of other linking mechanisms as well. For example, central intake and referral procedures may require establishment of a standardized intake form. This form derives from the procedures that all participating organizations have agreed to abide by. When the organization managing a centralized MIS system instructs participating organizations on what kind of information to gather and how it must be reported, it has standardized procedures. Standardized procedures make it possible for agencies to engage in many kinds of exchanges on a routine basis. Until procedures become standardized, many exchanges may be conducted on an ad hoc basis, each occasion creating a minor crisis as staff have to figure out how to do this or that, without creating disruptions in the regular operations of the organizations in which they are employed. At this point try Exercise 4–2.

---

**EXERCISE 4-2**

**Itemize Existing Linkages**

1. Think about an agency you are familiar with, or interview staff at an agency you want to know more about. Identify the interagency linkages discussed in this chapter that currently exist between it and other providers of services. On Figure 4–1, check those linkages that currently exist.

2. Review the discussion in Chapter 3 on segmentation of the market. On what basis were these interagency exchanges established: geographic, demographic, psychographic, or functional? Explain briefly.

3. Determine if these linkages tend to cater to the needs of particular populations, such as retarded children, people whose incomes fall below a certain level, or the aging with cardiac problems.

---

## Review

One of a service organization's key markets is made up of other service providers. These include human service agencies, civic associations, and organized consumer self-help groups. In this chapter, a range of linking mechanisms—formalized interorganizational exchanges—between human service agencies were described. They can be grouped under four categories: (1) those that are aimed at meeting immediate client needs, (2) those aimed at meeting agency personnel needs, (3) those involving the gathering and disseminating of information, and (4) those aimed at integrating programs, and program administration. These operational-level exchange mechanisms are intended to make services more continuous and comprehensive and thereby improve effectiveness and efficiency.

Some of the principal linkage mechanisms are described below.

*Case conference:* Staff from two or more organizations discuss the needs they have in common and consult in the development of treatment plans.

*Case consultation:* Staff at one organization ask advice from staff at another agency regarding the needs of particular clients.

*Case management:* Staff at one agency are given responsibility for coordinating the services provided by several organizations to meet the needs of particular clients.

*Co-location:* Two or more agencies have staff and separate facilities at the same location—coordination of activities is optional.

*Community needs assessment:* The gathering and analysis of information on community needs by one organization on the behalf of others, or by several organizations in cooperation.

*Fund raising:* Organizations cooperate in funding drives, establishment of endowment funds, or in securing grants or contracts.

*Funding (allocation):* Organizations contribute dollars or in-kind resources for the funding of a collaborative project or for setting up an independent program.

*Intake, screening, diagnosis:* Two or more organizations develop a common system of processing new clients and diagnosing their needs so as to coordinate and improve the delivery of services from all relevant agencies.

*Joint budgeting:* Two or more organizations coordinate the development of their annual budget so as to take into account how each organization's budgetary decisions affect the budgets of the other agencies.

*Loaner staff:* Staff from one organization are assigned to work (temporarily) under the direct supervision of staff of another organization to carry out activities for that agency.

*Program design:* Two or more organizations unite their efforts to plan and find resources for an effort.

*Program evaluation:* Two or more organizations unite their efforts to examine the effectiveness of an effort.

*Program operation:* Two or more organizations unite their efforts in the implementation of a program.

*Public relations, news releases, and community education:* Two or more organizations join efforts on behalf of a client population or their own resource needs, in educating the public or raising critical consciousness.

*Purchase of services:* One organization pays for specific services (such as outreach, intake, transportation, or diagnostic services) from another agency.

*Referral:* Two or more agencies regularly refer clients back and forth, keeping track of their capabilities for providing services and monitoring the effectiveness of the referral process in meeting client needs.

*Sharing facilities or equipment:* Permanent or ad hoc exchange of facilities such as meeting rooms, offices, libraries, and equipment, e.g., word processors, microcomputers, printing equipment, and audio-visual equipment.

*Staff outstationing:* Staff from one organization are assigned to do their work in the facilities of another.

*Standardizing procedures:* Two or more organizations use the same procedures to respond to particular client needs.

*Technical assistance:* Experts from one organization provide consultation or technical assistance to another in return for similar or other benefit.

*Training and staff development:* Two or more organizations cooperate on training and development by cosponsoring events, sharing successful programs, or trading their expertise.

*Treatment teams:* Staff from two or more organizations coordinate services to meet the needs of mutual clients through continuous and systematic interaction.

Any of these mechanisms might increase the marketability of your organization's programs or of its clients. Your organization's strategic marketing efforts will have to take account of the extent to which the organizations with which yours is linked make up a market to be penetrated or can become partners in the penetration of still other markets.

# 5 EXCHANGES WITH CONSUMERS AND NATURAL HELPERS

TRADITIONALLY, THE BUSINESS marketing literature has focused on consumer interests and on the response to those interests, or activation of consumer demand. These are not unimportant concerns to marketers of human services, but the activation of demand for such services tends to be less central to program planning than does the response to consumer interests. More of these services now accept consumer definitions of their own interests and consumer demands in developing and delivering services. Unfortunately, as the following vignette demonstrates, agency program planners are not always as skillful as necessary in the establishment of effective exchanges with organized groups of consumers or with others involved in self-help and mutual aid.

### Starting Up a Widows' Group

"The first meeting was a disaster. I had heard of Phyllis Silverman's work in organizing widow-to-widow groups in the Boston area and thought it would be a good idea to organize a similar group here. Having been widowed only 2 years ago, I had empathy for many of our clients who were in a similar situation. I asked each of the other caseworkers at the agency to refer clients to a new group I was forming. At the first meeting, 11 women came. They ranged in age from 45 to 63.

"Since I knew their life circumstances were all a bit different, I thought I'd initiate the process by talking about my own widowhood. I talked and everyone listened politely, but when I tried to get other people to volunteer their feelings or their experiences, it was a disaster. Nobody said anything. Finally, Monica Merle, an attractive woman in her mid-fifties, spoke up. But she wasn't sure what to say either. I had a feeling she was just talking to fill the silence, and in fact try-ing to help me out of my difficulty. Some situation. Here I'd convened the group to help them, and one of the members was trying to help me.

"Following Monica's comments, a few women raised their hands and asked what the purposes of the group were. I said a few trite things about all of us having experienced similar losses, and how we go through different stages of grief until we're able to cope with the world around us again, and how I thought it would be helpful if we shared our coping experiences. I don't think anyone was really con-vinced. I was beginning to doubt the value of the group myself. But at least every-one agreed to come back the following week to try again. As she was putting her coat on, Monica asked if it was okay if she were to call me later in the week. She had one or two ideas about how to get the group moving. I was delighted.

"'I have been active in many organizations and have served on a lot of com-mittees and I always find that they have a difficult time focusing on what they should be dealing with. Some people take the lead and everybody else gets squeezed out. I've had a lot of success with a technique that gets everybody in-volved. Here's how it works.' I listened.

"Monica's idea was great. It was to use the nominal group technique to gener-ate expression of needs and concerns so that we could get things out on the table. And it did work! At the end of the second meeting, one of the women remarked that she couldn't have believed that anyone else had gone through what she was experiencing. It was good to be among others who understood.

"By the fourth meeting, I found myself in a quandary. Monica had begun to take on official leadership of the group. I was feeling unneeded. That was OK; this was to have been a mutual aid group, anyway, not one of our more usual treatment groups in which staff play the convenor and facilitating role. The prob-lem was that my boss was having difficulty with the idea of a group operating un-der the agency's auspice in which a staff person wasn't in charge. 'Who would be held accountable if someone were hurt in the helping process, and how would we be sure that the help given would be up to our standards?' is the way he phrased his objections.

"My relationship to Monica and to the group was another problem. I had learned a lot from Monica. I welcomed her openness and her willingness to take a leadership role. So did many of the other women. The problem was that Monica was a dynamo and hardly anyone could keep up with her, or for that matter get their ideas on how the group should be run discussed, if Monica had other ideas.

"Still, Monica was a member; and that's how other members viewed her, even if they sometimes were put off by her. I was staff, and as much as people in the group seemed to trust me, I was beginning to feel unwelcomed in the group un-less it was to give specific information when asked, like what the procedures were for getting social security benefits, or where to go for low cost legal advice."

The worker quoted identified three problems: her boss's expectations; her relationship to Monica, a member of the group; and the changing expectations of her role expressed by other members. What other problems did you spot? What accounts for these problems? Might they stem from the way in which the agency had previously treated its consumers? Do they result from lack of clarity about the purposes of the group and the expectations of staff and group members of each other? Were participants in the group viewed by the agency as clients? How did they view themselves: as clients, members, customers? If as clients, were they perceived as patients, victims, deviants? Was the group described to be a variant of the agency's other treatment groups, but with somewhat greater responsibilities allocated to its members? What, in fact, were the expectations of group members? By whom? Were these made clear? To whom did the group really belong: the agency, the worker, its members?

## Defining the Consumer as a Client

The way in which consumers are viewed has a significant impact on the way in which they are treated. In general, the term *client* implies a dependency relationship. Clients who are called *patients* are generally perceived to be in need of help because they do not have the expertise to treat themselves. The health provider is presumed to be expert in diagnosis and treatment, for which he or she takes responsibility, perhaps delegating some responsibility for nontechnical activities to the patient or to the patient's family or friends. The patient is expected to be relatively passive, to do as instructed, if he or she wants to get better. Patients may or may not be the cause of their own problems.

In contrast, clients who are called *victims* are perceived as not being responsible for the trouble in which they find themselves. Their problems may be the consequence of an accident, of discriminatory or purposefully vicious or harmful treatment, or of economic and social forces outside their control. Such clients can be helped to deal with the consequences of these circumstances but not necessarily with the circumstances themselves or with their causes. Some agencies provide help and succor to victims. Some engage in actions aimed at ameliorating the conditions that lead to the problem, or in action programs aimed at changing those conditions.

*Deviants*, however, are often blamed for their own problems. They are perceived as having chosen to act in ways that are considered irresponsible or immoral by society. Drug addicts, criminals, alcoholics, and others are frequently defined as deviants. So are juvenile delinquents, children who act out in the classroom, and other persons whose behavior somehow is outside the norms of the society or the group of which they are a part. Treatment efforts are frequently aimed at changing the deviant client, modifying his or her behavior in such a way that it becomes more acceptable and less problematic to others.

What might be the consequences in terms of services or intervention efforts if an unemployed and depressed auto worker were to be perceived as a deviant, a victim, or a patient? What about a child needing a foster home; the child's parents who may have abused the child? An alcoholic mother?

## Agency-Client Relationships

The involvement of agency staff with consumers as *members* of self-help groups is, for many, a relatively new phenomenon, and for this reason we will be devoting considerable attention to it in this chapter. The more regular practice has been to treat consumers as clients. In so doing, the agency or the professional practitioner sets the conditions for exchange. A university determines its entry criteria, when service will begin and end, the nature of the service, and the obligations to be fulfilled by students if they are to remain in good standing. The more desirable the university and what it has to offer, and the fewer the alternative sources of supply for the consumer, the more likely it is to influence the behavior of students. This capability to influence is based on a number of sources of power held by the university and its staff: professors, counselors, dormitory supervisors, and others.

First, there is the *power to reward* either extrinsically through recognition, scholarships, grades, athletic letters, certificates of accomplishments and diplomas or intrinsically through providing opportunities for meaningful social and intellectual experiences. Second, there is the *power to penalize* or to *coerce* through the threat of exclusion: poor grades, nonadmittance to a desired class, suspension, or expulsion. Certain universities and certain classes are attractive and thereby potentially influential because of the *expertise* of their faculties and the facilities used for instruction. Others hold a recognized position of esteem that increases the rewards of being associated with them. Faculty and other functionaries also hold power through the positions they maintain within the structure of an enterprise: Department heads, full professors, graduate assistants, and other instructional personnel are influential because of their positions. So are financial aid officers, newspaper editors, football coaches, and residence hall directors. Finally, there is *referent power*, the potential to influence because of the many mutual obligations that emerge over time as students interact with each other and with university functionaries and staff.

Students, however, are not without some power of their own. First of all, they can choose not to attend a particular university or for that matter, any university. This is happening more as young people seek other alternatives or as they find themselves unable to afford the high costs of tuition and maintenance. They can also choose to attend schools nearer home or to attend part-time, thus inducing universities to change their programs to accommodate to consumer needs. Second, they can show their preferences for certain courses or programs by enrolling in some and not in others, thus shaping the behavior of the instructional establishment. They can also delegitimize the authority or position of certain departments or instructors through individual and collective behavior. A change in societal norms and activism on the part of students in the 1960s did away with the universities' claim to *in loco parentis*, whereby universities and colleges determined who could have access to whose dormitory rooms and at what hours. It also involved students in the processes of curriculum development and course design and increased the range of opportunities for independent learning and for personalized instructional programs.

To a large extent, student activism preceded a broader consumer activism which emerged in the 1970s. How has this activism affected social agencies and other human services? How has it affected an agency with which you may be affiliated or about which you are otherwise informed? If students have been largely successful in redefining their position of relative powerlessness as clients, essentially output constituents, into a position of greater power as input constituents, partners in or *members* of the academic enterprise, or perhaps as more knowledgeable customers, are there parallels in other organizations?

## Members and Customers

In contrast to clients, both customers and members are perceived to be more autonomous, responsible, and self-directing in their relationships to an agency. *Customers* are expected to either pick and choose what they wish to purchase from an agency, or not to buy at all. Whatever the decision, the customer is generally, if not always, right. Staff may suggest one or another service or product, but the customer is always the one who determines what is in his or her best interest. A library user is a good example, so is a participant in a professional conference or university-based C.E. program who selects the sessions or workshops he or she will attend.

*Members* have more than autonomy. They also have authority, and with authority comes responsibility. Members are theoretically equal or nearly equal partners with staff in the development and the delivery of service. Although there are nearly always limits on the kinds of services provided, the member is involved in shaping the programs or policies of the organization to which he or she belongs and in determining what kinds of services members should be entitled to and under what circumstances.

There are considerable differences in the expectations of customers and members. The way in which the woman who "bought swimming" at the community center viewed her responsibility and her privileges was quite different from the staff's perceptions. That example, drawn from the vignette in the Introduction, is typical of the tensions often expressed in churches, civic associations, settlement houses, and other membership associations—including self-help groups.

Customers and members generally pay fees for services received or for membership in an organization. As is true for clients, those fees, particularly if they are substantial, may put them in a relatively powerful position. An agency may be dependent on those fees and may thereby seek to satisfy its customers through the provision of services which are considered appropriate compensation for the cost incurred. Members may be recruited who possess certain geographic, demographic, or psychographic characteristics that will be considered attractive not only to the organization, but to other potential members. To some extent this may also be true of customers, particularly if an agency promotes its programs on the basis of the kinds of people it serves as well as the kinds of services it provides.

Consumers who have *complete control over the initiation of the interaction* operate as customers in the free market (much as you may have when you purchased this book). An offender who has been referred to counseling, as a substitute for a prison sentence, by the court (i.e., someone who has been defined by society as a deviant) has little if any control over the initiation because of the coercive measures that might be imposed should he or she refuse treatment. Moreover, the greater the individual consumer's resources (alternative sources of supply) and the more the organization needs those resources (e.g., a small liberal arts college under threat of closure because of lack of funds), the greater the consumer's control over the initiation of the interaction. This is particularly true if the consumer knows about the organization and the benefits he or she can gain through an exchange relationship. For persons concerned with marketing, this may suggest: (1) a promotional effort on behalf of the organization and its programs; (2) the need to better understand the potential consumer's needs, interests, and resources; or (3) the establishment of an effective referral, recruitment, or outreach system through which consumers may be induced to initiate a transaction.

Consumers and service agencies are dependent on each other to the extent to which (1) each needs the resources that the other controls, and (2) other sources of supply may be available at a reasonable and acceptable cost. Consumers may possess resources important to the agency: legitimacy, money, social contacts, energy, or information. Agencies may possess equal or greater importance: technology, access to other organizations and services, and so on. The closer the fit between the attributes and skills of the individual in need of service and the technical requirements and capacities of the service organization, the greater the interdependence of the two. Why else are some vocational rehabilitation agencies accused of "creaming" when they select clients who are most likely to succeed, or why else do colleges attempt to recruit students who most closely match faculty capacities and interests? A similar claim might be made that the greater the reliance of agency staff on the clients' beliefs (such that they affirm service ideologies), the greater their interdependence. *Power* shifts in one direction or the other to the extent that one or the other system functions independently or dependently.

The closer the organization and its consumers are in their *beliefs and norms of behavior*, the more likely they are to *trust* each other. I am referring here to a belief about the likely outcome of the relationship and the manner in which each of the parties participates in it. If staff is to infuse the relationship with trust, they must believe that consumers will not misuse or abuse the relationship and that they are motivated to benefit from it. By the same token, consumers must trust the motivations of staff, their technical competence, and their modes of behavior. Trust is enhanced to the degree that there is congruence between consumer goals and organizational output goals as well as to the extent that the organization treats the consumer as a subject instead of an object (i.e., as a partner or member, rather than a deviant, a dependent patient, or an unresponsible—read *irresponsible*—victim.)

Perhaps we are now better able to understand some of the difficulties experienced by the worker who attempted to start up a widows' group. Before moving on, complete Exercise 5–1.

---

### EXERCISE 5-1
### Agency-Client Relationships

1. Reread the vignette with which we opened the chapter. Based on other experiences you may have had with human service agencies, consider to what extent both staff of the agency in question and participants in the widows' group may have considered those persons to be clients (patients, victims, and deviants), members of the agency, or customers. If the agency's staff or its consumers defined the consumers differently, what effect might that have had on their expectations for the group's first meetings?

2. To what extent did the agency or its consumers have control over the initiation of the relationship? What other sources of supply did each have and how badly were these needed by each? If the vignette does not provide enough information, where would you obtain it? What might you be looking for; i.e., what would you need to find out?

3. To what extent does each party depend on one another? To what extent does the establishment of the group increase or decrease the dependence of the consumer on the organization? What effect might this have on the organization: in particular, on some of the staff who do not have any relationship to the group and who may never have worked with self-help groups?

4. To what extent does the establishment of the group change the norms that govern the relationships between the agency and its consumers and how do such changes affect trust between the parties?

Perhaps it was a bit unfair of me to ask you to complete the exercise before reading on. We are now about to examine the phenomenon of membership in associations and self-help groups and other forms of non-professional helping systems, and their relationships to organizational and institutional service providers. Nevertheless, the preceding discussion and the exercise activity will provide you with a firmer set of concepts upon which to anchor your understanding. Let's now turn to an examination of the exchanges involved in three kinds of partnerships, each of which assumes full or partial membership in the agency. These partners include lay service providers and members of self-help groups. Both belong to the natural helping system with which many agencies have become increasingly interdependent.

## Lay Service Providers: The First Line of Help

People often seek help from others like themselves. They may fear the cost in time, money, and psychological dependence that frequently accompanies service from an agency. They may be unwilling or reluctant to approach professional care givers for fear of either being defined as deviants and victims or being required to assume the responsibilities of membership. They may prefer the more personal and immediate help from lay service providers in the natural helping system.

Grandparents, friends, and neighbors often take care of younger children when parents are at work or temporarily incapacitated. It is not unusual for neighbors to talk to each other about child-rearing problems they share in common: "Marvin was teased at school yesterday because his hair is curly. You have adopted kids with interracial backgrounds, too. Have you had to handle discrimination in the schools with your kids?" A parent with a multiracial adopted child asked another adoptive parent, "How did you do it?"

Sometimes friends, relatives, or neighbors are not able to help either in providing service or in referring the help seeker to a professional or institutional provider. Nevertheless, there may be others in the neighborhood or community who are exceptionally knowledgeable and may serve as lay advisors or lay care givers. Margaret Richardson is such a woman. Being herself an adoptive parent with an interracial family, she was in a good position to counsel Marvin's mother. But Margaret was involved in more than giving advice and empathic listening.

An advocate of promoting adoption for children with special needs, Margaret was instrumental in the development of a new adoption service aimed specifically at such children. Through her own experience, and through the reported experiences of others, she became a major source of information in her state. It was not unusual for her to be at her kitchen telephone 5 or 6 hours a day dispensing support, advice, and counsel.

### Tell Him I Suggested You Call

"If a parent called from a rural area in the western part of the state about discrimination, she might say, 'I'm glad you called. Betty Jenkins in Halterville and Bob and Betty Schwartz in your own town are concerned too. Did you know that State Senator Marzen is drafting a bill to deal with a similar issue? But he doesn't have quite your perspective. Why don't you contact the Jenkinses and Schwartzes and then get hold of the Senator. Tell him how you feel. You might be able to get that bill written just the way it should be.'

"Sometimes Margaret would do little more than listen sympathetically, accepting a heartfelt outpouring of anguish by parents seeking to adopt but having been rejected by a number of agencies, or by an adoptive parent who no longer felt he or she could cope with the severity of the problems presented by the handicapped child. Sometimes attentive listening might be supplemented by a bit of advice on how to handle one's feeling or on how to help a child help himself. Frequently it was supplemented by a suggestion to contact another parent in the neighborhood who had faced a similar problem a year or two ago.

"Margaret was not averse to advising people to seek professional help when it was needed, or to suggesting where it might be found. 'It seems to me you've gone beyond what a parent can endure without some outside help. The people at the Child Guidance Clinic are really helpful in dealing with the issues you present. Why not call Dr. Sullivan? He might not be able to see you, but he'll arrange for you to talk with the right person at the clinic. Tell him I suggested you call.'"*

Is there a Margaret in your community or in the neighborhood your agency serves? Could she help potential clients get to your agency's services or make better use of them? Do people know about Margaret? Take a few minutes to think about some of the ways in which you might be able to identify individuals in your own community, like Margaret, who play important roles in the helping process. Jot their names down on a piece of paper.

Margaret represents an impressive example of someone involved in counseling, referral, and social action. In effect, she performs three linkage functions. Beyond that she also heightens people's awareness of their situation, raising their critical consciousness about the issues that affect them and that indirectly affect larger numbers. People turn to her because she facilitates their exchange with others, and as Margaret does this, she gains greater expertise, credibility, and the sense of having done something worthwhile. Some of her needs are being met as she services others.

Margaret is not alone in this respect. The givers and the receivers of help each benefit from the relationship; otherwise they would be unwill-

*From Armand Lauffer, *Getting the Resources You Need*, Sage Publications, Beverly Hills, Calif., 1982, pp. 113–114. Reprinted by permission.

ing to maintain their voluntary exchange. The help exchanged may require only time. "I know you're feeling poorly. Let me pick up some things for you when I go to the supermarket later." Sometimes help is sought from others who have experienced similar difficulties. "It is just my lumbago acting up, and a little liniment will fix me up in no time." "What you need is to get off your feet for a couple of days; let me fix your meals." "Try lying out in the sun during the day and using an electric heater at night. Make sure you lie on your back and not on your stomach. That will fix you up."

Friends and relatives may also suggest a need for professional help. "If the treatments don't work, I know a good chiropractor." Often, people may pass through such an informal network of lay helpers on their way to professionalized services. "That's about all the food I can spare. We are in trouble, too. Wish I could do more. The Salvation Army people will help you out; they understand and they got a food store open on Thursdays." "When I had my foot problem, nobody could help me as much as the chiropodist on the corner of Main and South. Why don't you try him?"

Those referred by natural helpers to professional providers may return to those same friends or neighbors to evaluate the services received. For example, an older person referred to a physician by a friend may check with that friend later to discuss the care received or promised in hopes of making some decision about whether or not to continue going for professional care. An effective professional care-giving system often requires an equally effective lay service network. A physician prescribing home treatment may know that his or her recommendations are impractical without the help of friends and relatives and may attempt to reach out and activate members in the lay service system through the patient. "You know that it won't be possible for me to check on what you're eating. Here is a list of tips you should share with your wife. Make sure she prepares everything the way it is spelled out here. If she runs into any problems, have her call my nurse. She will tell her where she can get the best bargains on some of these foods."

Similar examples exist with regard to other needs in such areas as housing, transportation, and job placement. In effect, the lay service provider is an extension of the professional care-giving system, a junior partner of the professional or agency-based care giver.

In some ways, the lay helping network is a much more flexible and responsive system.* There is never a long waiting list or red tape to be unsnarled. Help can be scheduled at one's own convenience. It deals with issues and provides assistance that would be too costly for agencies or other more professionalized service providers: helping people shop, preparing

*Parts of this discussion are drawn from Armand Lauffer, *Social Planning at the Community Level*, © 1978, pp. 178–179, 181. Reprinted by permission of Prentice-Hall, Inc., Englewood Cliffs, N.J. I am also indebted to my colleague Tom Powell for much of my understanding of self-help groups.

meals, and doing the many other things required to maintain full or partial independence. Because lay helpers are often similar in background to the persons in need of help, there tend to be fewer conflicts in values or cultural misunderstandings between help givers and help seekers. Moreover, reliance on the natural helping system reduced the stigma attached to becoming defined as a client—a patient, a deviant, or a victim—statuses that imply a loss of independence or competence.

There are, of course, many disadvantages to total reliance on the lay helping network. The growth of social agencies and other professionally provided services is a response to the inadequacies of the natural helping system. These inadequacies include (1) misdiagnosis or inadequate treatment, (2) quackery that is not corrected by a system of professional accountability, and (3) the unavailability of help when it is needed. Even when help from friends and family is available, such help may so drain the energy and emotions of those providing it that relationships become characterized by guilt, resentment, and even retaliation. For these reasons, partnerships between agencies and lay helping systems are really essential.

"When I couldn't manage anymore, I just had to move in with my daughter," reports a widow of 15 years. "We wanted Mother with us, even if we didn't have much room," her daughter explains. "It was when she became too ill to care for herself and medical expenses mounted that we went to the welfare department. Next week she is going to a nursing home. It breaks my heart, but the tensions on everyone in the family are just too great. We can't cope with her needs anymore. And she can't cope with them herself."

Because neither families nor agencies are the answer for all persons in need, and because the ad hoc nature of much of the lay service network is variable in effectiveness and availability, people have increasingly banded together to form mutual helping groups. To a large extent, these groups are parallel to other developments in the consumer movement: efforts by people to take charge of the conditions that affect them. In self-help groups, the distinctions between being a consumer and being a provider are blurred.

## Self-Help Groups

Until only a few years ago, one would have been hard put to find a reference in the professional literature to mutual-aid or self-help groups. Today, they can hardly be ignored. There are more than 8,000 national associations of self-help groups today. Although some may include two or three chapters, others, such as Alcoholics Anonymous and Weight Watchers, have enormous memberships and even larger nonmember customer groups. Weight Watchers, for example, not only involves participants in group activities, but has many hundreds of thousands of other consumers whose connection to the organization may be through the purchase of a container of low-calorie cottage cheese or a booklet on the dieting process.

Self-help groups are formalized expressions of the lay service network. In many respects they are a substitute for the extended family and for earlier more integrated communities. They have become a necessity in a society where geographic and social mobility are ubiquitous and where rapid, almost wrenching changes in personal status might otherwise be destructive to both individuals and to society.

When people organize themselves into self-help groups or join existing ones, they are redefining themselves from victims, deviants, patients, or even customers into full-fledged partners in the help-giving process. If self-help groups are organized for expressive as well as instrumental purposes, they provide their members with an opportunity to satisfy their need to associate, to socialize, to maintain mutual support. They provide people with identities, with reference groups, with the sense of being "a part of" instead of "apart from." Their instrumental purposes depend on the type of organization the self-help group is.

Thomas Powell, one of my colleagues at Michigan, has studied hundreds of self-help groups around the country. Powell divides these groups into those that aspire to contribute to the welfare of their members and those that also aim to affect the larger society.

Among the former are Widows-to-Widows and Overeaters Anonymous. Among the latter are the National Alliance for the Mentally Ill and the Gay Liberation Front. Two parent groups demonstrate these differences in orientation: Parents Anonymous is concerned with helping parents cope with abusive or neglectful behavior toward their children, whereas Parents Without Partners provides support for variant life-styles based on circumstances outside the control of the membership. Some groups have built on both objectives, changing their own members and changing society, into their purposes. Some, like MADD, Mothers Against Drunk Drivers, have taken on a social action and a public education mission in addition to supporting those who have been victimized.

Some groups require cultlike adherence to a set of norms or to an ideological position. They may, like Synanon, even require that members live together or in close proximity. Critics of self-help therapeutic communities have charged that residents become so dependent on these communities that they cannot survive outside. Moreover, some self-help groups have only limited tolerance for what they consider to be deviant behavior.

While behavior that was once defined as deviant outside the group has now been redefined as the result of victimization, the new norms imposed by the group may turn out to be equally intolerant. Members who do not subscribe to the group norms or fulfill their membership obligations may be expelled. Those who choose to leave of their own accord may be defined as renegades. Because such groups are inclusive, they make it difficult both to join and to leave without creating enormous disruptions in the participants' lives.

Others are much less inclusive, demanding only limited participation and involvement. Sometimes support groups are organized for the relatives of troubled individuals, rather than for those individuals themselves. Some, like Parents of Retarded Children, not only provide mutual support, but may also refer members to various social agencies.

Despite their many advantages, there are also problems with overreliance on self-help groups. Members may be no more technically competent to provide needed services than are other lay service providers. Some substitute quasi-ideological or mystical beliefs for scientific or more rigorously tested professional practices. Some, as I've noted, may require even greater loss of autonomy than does professionally provided help.

These cautions notwithstanding, social agencies have become increasingly involved with self-help groups. Their involvements include referrals to self-help groups that provide specialized services, acceptance of referrals from such groups, the formation of self-help groups where such groups are seen as beneficial to agency clients, consultation to or from the groups, training activities that include representatives of both, joint social action, and promotional or fund-raising activities.

There are many reasons for this involvement. Members of self-help groups are frequently energetic and highly talented people, and their activities not only are helpful to those who affiliate with them, but add significantly to the repertoire of the professional provider as well. Involvement of agency clients or potential clients in self-help groups can reduce the cost to the agency of providing needed services. It also increases the likelihood that services will be provided in a continuous and comprehensive manner. Sometimes it's the only game in town. Without self-help groups for burn victims, for adults who were adopted when children, for the recently widowed, there just might not be any services available for some persons in need.

## Types of Partnership Relationships Between Agencies and the Natural Helping System

In Fig. 5–1, you will find an inventory of possible partnership relationships between human service agencies and lay service providers and/or self-help groups. Some of them were discussed in this chapter. Others, such as case management and staff outstationing, were discussed in Chapter 4, but are equally relevant here. For example, an agency-based case manager might be responsible for seeing to it not only that services by other agency providers are delivered properly, but also that the client was properly received in a self-help group with which the agency has a referral

| Linkage Mechanism | Natural Helper |
|---|---|
| _____ 1. Case management | _____ |
| _____ 2. Co-location of staff | _____ |
| _____ 3. Fund raising | _____ |
| _____ 4. Information dissemination or community education | _____ |
| _____ 5. Joint promotional efforts | _____ |
| _____ 6. Junior (directed activity) partnerships | _____ |
| _____ 7. Loaner staff arrangements | _____ |
| _____ 8. Program development | _____ |
| _____ 9. Referrals | _____ |
| _____ 10. Social or political action | _____ |
| _____ 11. Staff outstationing | _____ |
| _____ 12. Training | _____ |
| _____ 13. | _____ |
| _____ 14. | _____ |
| _____ 15. | _____ |
| _____ 16. | _____ |
| _____ 17. | _____ |
| _____ 18. | _____ |

**Figure 5-1**  Inventory of Possible Linking Mechanisms Between Human Service Agencies and the Natural Helping System

agreement. The process might also go in the other direction, where a senior or more experienced member of a self-help group (like Widows-to-Widows, Recovery Incorporated, or Women for Sobriety) sees that a new member goes to the appropriate human service agency for help (the social security office, community mental health center, and so on).

Any of the linkage mechanisms listed can go in either direction or be initiated by either partner in the exchange relationship. Agencies might train members of self-help groups or members of the lay service network. Natural helpers might conduct staff development activities of agency staff or join with them in the design of a community-wide education program. A community mental health center's substance abuse counselor might team up with a member of a group of former abusers to provide services in a community center at a junior high school (co-location or outstationing). Junior partnerships are generally initiated by the agency or some other provider of professional services (like the example of a physician enlisting family members in the care of a postoperative patient). There are circumstances, however, in which members of self-help groups or other lay providers initiate the treatment program and utilize members of the professional or agency staff as junior partners.

When Margaret Richardson referred someone to the child guidance clinic, she not only gave Dr. Sullivan's name, but was likely to follow up with a call to the staff members assigned, providing consultation and instruction on difficulties faced by adoptive parents and their children. When she counseled someone about the procedures used by the welfare bureau's adoption's department, she told them not only about the procedures involved, but how to instruct the welfare staff on some of the procedures or policies with which they might not be thoroughly familiar. Exercise 5–2 will reinforce your understanding of this exchange.

---

**EXERCISE 5-2**

**Linking Agencies and Natural Helpers**

1. Go over the inventories of partnership linking mechanisms in this chapter and in Chapter 4. Think about the exchanges you are familiar with between agency and other professionalized service providers and natural helpers (members of the lay helping network or members of self-help groups).

   Check those linkage mechanisms your organization currently employs with one or more natural helpers (on the line to the left of the number, i.e., "✓ Staff Outstationing").

   What other linkage mechanisms are in operation or should be? Add them in the spaces given (13–18). How would you describe or define these?

2. Now identify one or more persons or self-help groups involved in the exchange and list them on the line to the right of the linkage in question.

3. If there are no individuals or groups involved with your organization in a particular category, should there be? If so, in a different color of ink or pencil, specify who. If additional persons or groups should be involved, add them as well (in the same second color). You may need more space. Use additional paper if necessary.

---

## Difficulties in Establishing and Maintaining Partnerships

If you had some difficulty in completing Exercise 5–2, you are in good company. Partnerships between agencies and their consumers or clients are hardly yet the modal pattern. Agencies are much more likely to treat their consumers in the more traditional roles of client-patient, deviant, or victim. The reasons are not difficult to comprehend. Despite many common concerns, professional and lay care givers have distinct and separate characteristics.

In each system, care givers are guided by different kinds of knowledge and experience. Lay knowledge arises out of individual or shared experiences, whereas professional knowledge tends to be more technical in nature, representing the collective wisdom of experience combined with the ordered knowledge of science and research. Practitioners in each system are governed by different norms. Whereas lay care givers are affected by those norms inherent in their own subcultures or local communities, professionals are influenced by the values and ethics inherent in their occupational and professional communities, values that are modified by the bureaucratic norms of the organizations in which they work.

This might be a good time to go over your earlier responses to the instructions in Exercise 5-1. How might your current understanding have modified your answers regarding the initiation of contact, the relative power of each partner to the relationships, the norms and trust essential to successful transactions?

The vignette that follows provides an example of a more comprehensive approach to agency-consumer exchanges. In the widows' group example, a worker made an independent decision to start a group without much understanding of the mutual-help process, of its implications for the agency, and of the demands it was likely to place on those to be recruited for membership. In the example that follows, a school makes a decision to extend its services into the community, and to bring the community into the building, without quite anticipating all the serious problems that might arise. Both vignettes illustrate the possibilities of effective exchanges between agencies and natural helpers, but both also demonstrate the difficulties involved.

The neighborhood school apparently planned most carefully for its development of exchange relationships with the neighborhood. It had to overcome a number of problems, however, that were caused by a seeming incompatibility between the formal system that the school represented and the informal patterns of relationships that existed in the community.

### A School Opens Its Doors

"I took this assignment knowing it would be tough, but knowing the possible payoffs were great. I had been vice-principal of another school, and frankly it was a 'cush' job. So when I was offered the principal's job at Everett Elementary, I was a bit ambivalent. It's in a low-middle-income neighborhood, one that is in transition. At the time I was offered the job, there were a number of neighborhood groups active in trying to stabilize the community and to build in a sense of pride. I think that, as much as anything else, is the reason I took the job.

"If there was evidence of motivation aimed at self-improvement in the community, I reasoned, there was the potential for motivation to learn among the school kids as well. And where motivation is high, an educator can achieve a lot. Let me explain.

"Schools can't educate people who aren't ready to be educated. And a kid's readiness to learn has very little to do with what goes on in the school. It's what goes on in the community, at home, on the streets, that counts. Too many educators focus on the content of education, on the curriculum, instead of on the children. And even when they do pay attention to the child, they see themselves as competitors with the child's family, maybe even the child's ethnic and cultural heritage. That's a no-win game. Even if the educator thinks he is winning, the child or the family end up losing. Education isn't a contest in which the educator scores points if someone else loses.

"In a real people-centered educational program, the child, not the curriculum, is the focus of concern. And since the child is part of the community, it stands to reason that the educational program of the school should not be closed off from the community. Unfortunately, that's not how things work. Most schools operate like prisons. I don't mean that they are all punitive. But they operate on a 'closed door philosophy.' Education takes place in the school, and community influences are kept out.

"Although there is always some community participation, community people are generally relegated to certain roles . . . like lunchroom monitors, teachers' aides, or PTA members who raise money for special projects. The presence of too many parents in the school is often viewed as an impediment to good education.

"I've had teachers tell me that parents are too emotional about their kids and that is why they just don't make good judgments. I've had others complain that the family child-rearing patterns and the ethnic or cultural values in the community are antithetical to the values of the school. Now that may be true. But the fault isn't in the community. It's in the school and its staff. You can close the community out of the school building, but you can't close it out of the child.

"Now I'm not suggesting we go to the other extreme of opening up the school or even trying to run a school without walls. I believe in a more balanced approach. There are times when the school should close its doors, and there are times when those doors should be wide open. If we turn all the responsibility over to community people, we face the danger of seriously weakening professional standards and diluting professional expertise. But if we keep our distance, we face the danger of setting up a situation in which the children will have to resolve the contradictory influences of school and community. And in that kind of game, we'll all end up losers.

"There are times when the teachers know best and there are other times when the knowledge of the ordinary citizen (like about taking the bus or fixing a pipe in the basement) is just as great or even greater than that of the teacher. There are times when what the teacher does in the classroom can be undone by parents and siblings and neighborhood friends at home. And there are important areas of concern at home that might be put down, unwittingly, by a teacher who is not sensitive to a child's emotional or psychosocial needs.

"Every school has to adapt to its neighborhood. Parents and children and others in the community have to adapt to the school as well. There are ways in which both sides can be helped to adapt to each other without giving up too much, and perhaps by gaining a great deal. Here's what we did to adapt after I took over as principal.

"First, we used CETA funds to hire community people for the jobs of co-leaders of parents' clubs. There was a family club for each grade level. The teachers and community people were the co-leaders for each group. Parents could join on a voluntary basis. Each club had three purposes: (1) to discuss ways in which they (parents) could work together to help kids with school-related problems at home (like motivating them, helping them with homework); (2) to help in the classroom with subject matter that they know something about (like baking a cake or planting flowers); and (3) to raise money or to get supplies and equipment needed for classroom or schoolwide projects.

"The groups that worked best were those that the teachers took the least active role with. Once parents got the hang of it, and this required well-trained community co-leaders, these groups became a significant influence in the kid's education.

"We also gave our teachers time off to do some public speaking about the schools and what our objectives were. Sometimes alone, and sometimes with their club co-leaders or with parents, they made presentations to local church and civic groups. One result was that children's artwork began to appear in neighborhood stores and in the shopping center. Another was that the school's band and many of the classes began performing in parks and in shopping areas on warm days. Because we encouraged others to walk in, several local musicians volunteered to work on a jazz combo with kids after school.

"The neighborhood weekly newspaper was our biggest booster. And this was not by accident. Parents and teachers, sometimes as co-authors, wrote folksy stories about what was happening at Everett. Some of our volunteers wrote about their work too. We even began publishing a weekly Everett School Family Recipe column. Merchants donated supplies for some of our special projects when we announced them in the paper or when members of the parents' clubs approached them. Every other week I wrote a column for the paper, explaining something about our educational philosophy or in some other way informing them about what we were doing and why it was important to all of us—parents, teachers, and neighborhood residents, not to mention the kids themselves.

"At first, I encouraged community groups to use the building after school and in the evenings. Later, as we got community people involved, we had to limit the building's use by outside groups. There was just too much going on for the children and their families: sports clubs, scouts, a 'chitlin's and rice' cooking club, even a bike-repair club. It was like a settlement house, a real neighborhood center; run almost entirely by volunteers, but with some help from staff of the City Recreation Department and Community Development Corporation. Of course, some teachers objected to having their classrooms messed up on occasion. But they sure appreciated the kind of motivation that kids had in coming to school!"

Clearly, the principal, through carefully planned and executed efforts, had succeeded in reducing the distance between the school and the community. A year after this interview was conducted, she had also arranged for the child guidance clinic to locate a detached worker at the school on Tuesday and Thursday afternoons and was negotiating other linkages with the city's historical museum, the AARP (American Association of Retired Persons), and several other social agencies. Exercise 5–3 will formally analyze this effort.

---

## EXERCISE 5-3

### Determining the Reasons for Success or Failure of Agency-Natural Helper Relations

1. Starting with the vignettes in this chapter or your own experience, identify the variables that led to the success of or to the difficulties encountered in an effort to develop exchanges between an agency and natural helpers in the community. Consider the following variables in your analysis:

   How consumers were defined by the agency
   How natural helpers (members of the ad hoc lay system or of self-help groups) viewed the agency
   The issues or problems addressed
   The kinds of linkages employed and the resources needed to put them into effect
   The philosophical or cultural orientations of the key actors (i.e., technologies, norms, trust)
   Vested interests of the key actors

   And add other variables you consider of equal importance.

2. Assume that you have been asked to design a complex of exchanges between your organization and members of the natural helping system of which your consumers are at least potentially a part. And assume, further, that you were asked to design those exchanges so that they might maximize the extent to which natural helpers will become partners in the agency's enterprise.

   *continued*

---

**EXERCISE 5-3 continued**

Develop a plan for implementing those exchanges. Your plan should include the following components:

The objectives to be achieved
The types of linkage mechanisms to be employed
The resources you will need to implement the plan
The kind of planning process that will be employed and who will be involved

In completing the exercise, you may wish to refer to Chapter 8, "Designing the Program." What kinds of problems do you anticipate in design or implementation?

---

## Implications for Strategic Marketing

Implications for the strategic marketing approach are perhaps too obvious to warrant extensive discussion here. Agencies concerned with reaching and relating to various consumer populations will have to consider how and where they are to be reached, the nature of their interdependence, and the extent to which the goals of each will be reflected in relationships of mutual trust. From a program-development perspective, consumers are clearly seen as a key resource.

## Review

The traditional definition of agency consumers as "clients" may limit the range of exchanges between an agency and key publics in its environment. Clients are people to be served, and they are generally perceived as dependent on a professional care giver for service. The perception that clients may be victims, deviants, or patients further circumscribes the ways in which they will be treated by professional providers. In contrast, the definition of consumers as "customers" is likely to shift the responsibility of choice of services from the professional to the purchaser. The definition of the consumer as a member may increase the likelihood that consumers will become involved in the help giving or planning.

Most persons receive assistance from natural helpers before, during, and after getting help from formal service agencies like health clinics, child welfare organizations, and schools. The lay helping process is generally ad hoc in nature. Increasingly, however, people in need of help are banding together in mutual-aid groups organized for both expressive and instrumental purposes. Ad hoc networks and mutual-aid or self-help groups have the advantage of being more personal, quicker to respond, and sometimes more individualized in their services than more formal and bureaucratic agency-based services can be. Members of the natural helping system, however, may not have the necessary expertise to provide certain kinds of help, and in some cases demand more of those in need than they may be able to give in return.

Although, for the most part, the formal and the natural helping systems exist side by side, more agencies and self-help groups are trying to develop exchanges between them. Such exchanges are made possible through a number of linking mechanisms. Among them are case management, colocation of staff, fund raising, information dissemination or community education, joint promotional efforts, junior partnerships, loaner staff arrangements, program development, referrals, social or political action, staff outstationing, and training.

Effective partnerships between agencies and natural helpers can be initiated by either side. Like other exchanges, their purposes must be clearly understood and the responsibilities of each side must be agreed upon. Linking mechanisms, if they are to be maintained, must be perceived as beneficial to each of the partners in the exchange. The nature of the interdependence of consumers and provider organizations is likely to be affected by (1) who controls the initiation of the relationship and what other options each side may have, (2) the power/dependency relationship that unfolds throughout the exchange process between both parties, and (3) the norms that govern those interactions and the trust that emerges from them.

# 6 NEGOTIATING YOUR WAY TO NEW PARTNERSHIPS

PARTNERSHIP ARRANGEMENTS BETWEEN an agency and its many publics don't just happen; they are built by the parties to the exchange. The process by which the parties come to terms, arrive at an agreement, or transfer assets between them is called *negotiation*. Success in the strategic marketing process is very dependent on the outcome of negotiations. It requires the ability to negotiate effectively on one's own behalf or on the behalf of one's organization or constituency. As a program specialist, an agency administrator, or someone responsible for implementing a marketing strategy, you will have opportunities to negotiate with many publics. Interagency linkages like purchase-of-service agreements and client referrals require negotiated agreements. Collaborations between service agencies and self-help groups may require negotiated agreements on the responsibilities of both parties to the exchange.

Some negotiations are the results of actual or presumed conflicts of interest; labor-management issues are frequently presented this way. However, even when interests seem to diverge, they can be made to complement each other. As the representative of a staff committee, you may find yourself negotiating for improved working conditions, arguing that these will result in improved client services, playing down the conflict, and playing up areas of joint concern.

Agreement to negotiate requires that both sides feel they can get something of value out of the process. The possible consequences of non-negotiation must be perceived as being worse than the possible outcomes of striking a bargain. Both sides must recognize that they may not each get everything they want, that accommodation may require compromise and the postponement or elimination of some objectives. Although each side will try to achieve most of its objectives at a minimal cost, each must believe that a settlement is not only possible, but sincerely desired by the other side as well.

## Formal and Informal Negotiations

Negotiations can be conducted in an informal way or may be highly formalized. Labor-management negotiations, for example, are rule-governed, with many of the procedures spelled out in legislation and in the regulations that accompany legislation. Generally, the procedures for negotiating contracts or grants between state and local agencies are also clearly spelled out. Sometimes, the process is almost totally informal, as when colleagues from two agencies agree on who will assume case-management responsibility for a particular client or when staff in two units within the same organization agree to a temporary staff exchange that is never ratified by anyone from the central office. The more ad hoc the exchange, the more informal the negotiations are likely to be. Nevertheless, even many formal processes are complemented by informal negotiations, as the following vignette illustrates.

### Get Me a Grant

From an announcement in the *Congressional Record*, I became aware that the Children's Bureau was interested in promoting the training of child welfare workers in each of the states. I called the grants officer in the regional office to get further information. Just over $800,000 was available for training in our region, a six-state area. I found out more about funding priorities and asked if I could call back after we had done some thinking about how we might respond. "I would welcome your suggestions," I said. "Please call" was the response. Two weeks later I called back to spell out what we intended to do.

In addition to training a designated number of staff throughout the state, I explained, we would design training materials to be packaged as modules for use by supervisors at the work unit level. Moreover, these materials could be made available at cost to other states within the region. So we'd not only conduct required training this year, but establish the capacity and the resources to continue training throughout the region. The feds, I was suggesting, were going to get a big bang for their buck.

So far I hadn't said anything that was not to be spelled out in greater detail in the formal proposal. But by sharing these ideas, I was able to elicit suggestions about what would be acceptable and what would not. The hitch was in the amount of money we intended to ask for: $360,000.

"We'll never get this through, Armand," the grants officer told me. "You're asking for more than 40 percent of the total amount available to the region. We've got to be fair to other states, too." "Fairness is just what we're talking about," I replied. "You know that there's only one other university in the region capable of producing anything as effective and long-lasting as this project, and it's located in the state that has received considerable training sums from HEW during the last 4 or 5 years. In all that time, Michigan hasn't received a single grant. And let me tell you, our Department of Social Service people at the state level aren't happy about this. Nor is our congressman. They feel we've been short shrifted. Perhaps Michigan's applicants haven't submitted adequate proposals in the past, but you know that this one is right on target."

"You probably know that 40 percent of the children in Region V who are on ADC [Aid to Dependent Children] live in Michigan," I continued. "So asking for 40 percent of the training funds isn't out of line. Neither you, nor I, nor anyone else wants any political flak around this issue. But I know how our political people are feeling. If the proposal is no good, your review committee should drop it from consideration. But if it is sound and we don't get adequate funding to do it right, someone's going to get upset."

The issue was no longer whether we were going to get the grant or not, the issue was how much. Ultimately we settled for $320,000. I knew what I wanted for the project, and how much support I had. More important, I knew what the funder wanted, and I provided the funder with the information that was necessary for dealing with pressures from other applicants. As in other successful exchanges, the funders were as happy to find us as we were to find them. It resulted in a successful partnership, one that was to include a half-dozen or so more grants in as many years.

Both the federal official and I were fully aware that we were engaged in a negotiating process and that I was using tactics as part of a game plan. Serious problems can arise when both sides do not agree on the legitimacy of the tactics used or if they play the game by different sets of rules. I use the term "game" advisedly. Games have rules that govern player moves: what they can do and how. Games also have rules that determine the end of play: who wins and who loses, the final score, or when to stop playing. A win for one side need not require a loss for the other. Both can end up improving their positions. Serious errors are made if negotiating issues are defined as distributive, when they might better be defined as integrative, leading the parties to seek ways in which they can share benefits rather than struggling over them. Problems also arise when one or the other side finds itself negotiating with a "phantom."

## Knowing with Whom You Are Negotiating

When teachers negotiate a salary increase with the local board of education, only to find that the board is unable to deliver on its promises because of a decrease in the property tax or because the citizenry has not voted for a millage increase, the teacher's union has negotiated with a phantom. It may later accuse the board of negotiating in bad faith. An interesting example occurred in a metropolitan midwestern city some years back. Social workers in all of the community's voluntary agencies struck for higher wages and more extensive fringe benefits. Agency administrators agreed to their demands, most of which they felt were legitimate. However, the United Way (U.W.), which sets salary standards, refused to change those standards or to permit agencies to pay staff according to their newly negotiated salary ranges.

The executive of the U.W. explained, "We haven't raised enough funds in our campaign to be able to pay those salaries without reducing the number of staff in each of our member agencies. That would necessitate cutting service. We are not about to do that." Administrators went back to their workers explaining that they could not increase wages or benefits beyond the U.W. standards without risking cuts in appropriations.

The union representing the workers then approached the U.W. with its demands, but the U.W. executive refused to negotiate. "They're not our employees," he explained. "None of them work for us. They work directly for their own employers." It seemed that no matter where it turned, the union was negotiating with a phantom. There was no way out but to have the agency administrators organize themselves into a negotiating committee, working on behalf of the union in putting pressure on the United Way: an interesting twist indeed.

You've probably experienced a negotiating process in which you thought you had arrived at some accommodation with a teacher, staff members of another agency, or representatives of a consumer group, only to find that someone in authority refused to accept the outcome of those negotiations.

"We agreed to provide our printing facilities to the Parents Alliance for a joint fund-raising effort. They were to design the copy and send out the flyers," complained an agency program coordinator with whom I was consulting. "But the copy wasn't what we had agreed on, and they were so late getting the materials out that the fund-raising effort fizzled. I think the people we were negotiating with never got the OK from their leadership, so they just couldn't put the time in to do it right." When negotiations or their outcomes fizzle out, the parties involved not only are disappointed but often harbor such misgivings about each other that future efforts to achieve mutually beneficial objectives are ruled out.

## Why People Negotiate: Distributive and/or Integrative Gains

Negotiations may arise from the attempts of two or more parties to either reach some accommodation regarding disputed issues or collaborate on the achievement of mutually beneficial objectives. Examples of the former are found in labor-management or client-agency confrontations. Examples of the latter include the establishment of linking mechanisms between human-service agencies or between agencies and consumer groups. The first requires a *distributive* bargaining approach, the second, an *integrative* approach.

Distributive bargaining derives from actual or perceived conflicts of interest. To achieve its objectives, each side tries to induce the other to give something up, to make a concession. In integrative bargaining, on the other hand, each side has goals or objectives that can be achieved only through collaboration. These goals need not be the same; they only need to complement each other. For example, one agency may be interested in referring its clients to the other, whereas the other is interested in expanding its client population. In integrative negotiations, bargains are struck when both sides share in their perceptions of the benefits to each organization or to the total community through arriving at accommodation. It is not necessary that each party benefit equally, it is only necessary that each perceive accommodation to be in its own interest. In distributive negotiations, conflicts are resolved when both parties agree that accommodation is less costly than some other situation, and when both share the same perception of each group's capacities to do harm to the other if accommodation is not reached.

## Types of Issues Around Which Negotiation Takes Place

Whether the negotiations are distributive or integrative, the types of issues addressed will be (1) substantive, (2) procedural, and/or (3) symbolic. Substantive issues specify who does what with whom, when, where, and how. They spell out obligations and define the kinds of relationships, if any, that are to be established between the parties. Substantive issues can be discussed rationally, calculated economically; they are therefore the easiest to deal with and tend not to be emotionally charged. People can agree on what to agree about and on what to disagree about. Issues can be stated so that each side develops empathy for the other's position. The same is not necessarily true of procedural or symbolic issues.

The procedures to be used in the negotiation process are frequently perceived as being powerful influences on its outcome. Typical procedural issues to be resolved include the timing and the location of the negotiations, who represents whom, how the agenda items are to be brought up, which substantive issues are to be dealt with first, when outcomes or stalemates are to be presented to the larger public, and the kinds of grievance mechanisms that are used. Even the size of the table and its shape may generate hurdles that are difficult to cross.

Procedural issues can be very troubling. Let's take the issue of location. It may be difficult for both sides to agree on *where* to negotiate. Negotiating in one agency's offices may seem to put it at an advantage. Its negotiating team will be familiar with the surroundings, can set the room up in the way they find it most agreeable, may have access to needed information and to decision makers. On the other hand, there are some advantages to meeting on the other party's territory. Visitors may be able to defer decisions by claiming they have to "check back at the home office."

Symbolic issues, because they are more abstract, are even more difficult to accommodate. Frequently they relate to people's perceptions of themselves, their dignity, or their identify as a part of a larger entity. In the mid-1960s, the term "black" as a replacement for the words "colored" or "Negro" took on great symbolic meaning, frequently beyond the substantive issues that were being negotiated. Exercise 6–1 will help to clarify some of your confusion.

---

**EXERCISE 6-1**
**Identifying the Variables**

1. In your personal or occupational experience, you have undoubtedly been involved in a variety of negotiations. In the space below, identify three situations with issues which were originally defined as distributive, but which you think should have been defined as integrative. Select any one of these to work on.

   _____

   _____

   _____

2. Describe the procedural, symbolic, and substantive issues that were subject to dispute. Which of these seemed most important to each of the parties at the start of the process? At the end?

3. Describe how the negotiating process was initiated.

   Who initiated the negotiations?
   Who was delegated or assigned to negotiate?
   If there was a negotiations team, how was it organized?

4. What were the outcomes of the negotiations? Did they fizzle out? Result in a stalemate? Generate an accommodation acceptable to both sides? Was the resolution firm or did it begin to unravel soon after it was agreed to?

*continued*

---

**EXERCISE 6-1** *continued*

5. Did either of the parties attempt to redefine the issue from distributive to integrative? How? What led to the success or failure of these efforts?

6. Were the negotiations held informally, formally, or both? Would the outcomes have differed had there been a different balance of formal and informal interactions?

---

## Recognizing and Dealing with Needs

In any negotiating situation, it is important to be as clear as possible about your own personal needs and of those upon whose behalf you are negotiating. It is as important to be aware of the personal and constituency needs of those with whom you are negotiating. All people, and to a certain extent organizations, have a need to belong and a need to be respected. Individual negotiators frequently act so as to increase their prestige among other members of their negotiating team or that team's constituency. Sometimes the negotiator is equally motivated by a desire to be accepted or respected by members of the other team. Gaining the other side's esteem can be a powerful asset in the negotiations process. Being excessively committed to achieving it can be a powerful liability.

Agencies express similar motivations when they negotiate with each other, with consumer groups, or with suppliers. An organization's interest in establishing an exchange relationship with another organization may be motivated as much by the need to be related to that agency as by any other more measurable benefits.

What confounds many negotiating processes is the likelihood that one party may confuse demands with needs. For example, a union demand for extended maternity benefits may really reflect a need that could be better met through the establishment of a day-care center on the employer's premises or a job-sharing arrangement. Demands for higher wages, as we learned in the early 1980s, may have worked against unions, particularly when they resulted in plant shutdowns and massive layoffs. Thus, it is possible that any negotiator may, out of ignorance, work against his or her own needs.

It is not always easy to recognize needs, especially when they are hidden. Needs may be purposely hidden so as not to reveal too much too early in the negotiation process. For this reason, negotiations frequently go through a period of testing in which each side seeks to understand the other side's needs. Representatives of each side may ask each other fact-finding, opinion-seeking, direct, or open-ended questions. Fact-finding questions include: "who, what, where, how, and when." Opinion-seeking questions may be phrased as "Do you think that if we . . . ?" A direct question might be: "If we agree to this point, will you agree to drop the second demand on your list?" A more general or open-ended question might begin with the words: "Tell us what you are interested in."

To be effective in negotiating, one may have to work not only for one's own needs or those of one's constituents, but also for the needs of the other side. If the other side's needs are not at least partially met, no accommodation may be possible. This is as true of integrative as it is of distributive bargaining. At other times, it is clearly in one's interest to work against the other side's position. There may even be times when it is strategic to work against one's own needs in order to establish trust, which may lead to success on some other issue or at some future time. This tactic is called a gambit; it is much like a chess opening in which the first player sacrifices a pawn or some other piece for an advantageous position.

Uncovering the other side's needs requires good listening skills. Knowing what the other side is really saying may help you to rephrase a demand. "Do you mean, when you ask for maternity benefits, that you are concerned about providing income for women who have just borne children?" Gerard Nierenberg, a master negotiator, suggests that listening for "tip-off" words will also help you avoid a trap. If someone says, "To be frank," you can be pretty sure that person is hiding something. If at the end of a session, someone says, "By the way," you can bet that person has been thinking hard about the coming revelation for quite some time. And if someone says, "Before I forget," that probably means he or she wants you to remember. Listen not only to *what* the other person says, listen also to *how* it is said. Is it said with conviction? With sincerity? Do the gestures that accompany a statement demonstrate empathy and concern, honesty, dishonesty? Be careful not to read the wrong thing into what is being said. People with different ethnic or social backgrounds may express themselves in ways that have important meanings for their constituents, but which may be interpreted incorrectly by yours. See what Exercise 6–2 can show you.

## EXERCISE 6-2
### Recognizing Needs

Take either the situation you described in Exercise 6–1 or one of the two cases described in this chapter: my informal negotiations over the size of a grant with a federal official or the negotiations between a university president and the minority students who had taken over a communications building.

*continued*

**EXERCISE 6-2 continued**

Based on the limited information you have available, but also on the basis of your experience in other situations, answer the following questions:

1. What were the needs (expressed and implied) of both parties? Were the needs of the negotiators and their constituents identical? If not, how did they differ?
2. Did one side or both misperceive its own needs or those of the other side? Of their constituents? If so, what were the consequences of such misperception?
3. Did either side or both actually work toward meeting its own needs, or were their actions counterproductive?

*Note:* Your responses to these questions will depend on how you define needs. Consider your own definition, or build on the definitions you may find in the literature. Maslow's needs hypothesis, for example, orders human needs on a hierarchy from the lowest or most basic, security, to the highest order, self-realization. In between are the needs for belonging and esteem.

## The Importance of External and Internal Environmental Factors

Negotiators and their constituents are subject to influence by the key publics in their environments. The outcome of a negotiation process is sometimes as much the result of what these publics expect as of the skill of the negotiators. A teacher strike, for example, is likely to succeed as long as parents continue to believe that the teachers are in the right and they (the parents) are not too badly inconvenienced by it. The longer schools remain closed, the less sympathy is likely to be expressed for the strikers.

The extent to which new resources are available may strengthen the position of the side seeking them. Conversely, a shortage in resources or alternative sources of supply may weaken the position of those in need. For example, if the department of mental health needs ten new foster homes, and there are only one or two operators willing to establish new homes in a certain community, the department may be willing to make special concessions to those operators. Sometimes accommodations are arrived at when institutions of social control choose to impose their domination over the process. Thus, the civil service commission may step in to resolve a labor dispute. The police may step in to dissipate a confrontation between residents and managers of a public housing project. An area agency on aging may step in to dictate the terms of an agreement between agencies working toward the establishment of a network of comprehensive services.

The internal factors are equally complex: (1) the composition and internal division of labor within each side's bargaining team, (2) the relationship between team members and members of the opposing team, (3) the relationship between each team and its constituents, and (4) the skill of team members. We will discuss each of these separately.

## Composition of the Negotiating Team and Relationships to Members of the Other Team

Negotiations need not always take place between multimember teams. One of the first things that you will have to consider is whether negotiations should take place between individuals, between teams, or between an individual and a team. The decision is as important when you engage in a formal negotiation process as when the negotiations are conducted informally. The advantage of having individuals negotiate on the behalf of their constituents is that some decisions can be made on the spot, particularly if those individuals are the top executives or leaders of the organizations involved. Moreover, it eliminates the possibility that the other side will "divide and conquer" or zero in on the weakest member of a team. Using a negotiating team with several members, however, has its own advantages.

First, it allows you to involve people with different kinds of expertise. It permits the pooling of judgments before decisions are made. A large team can sometimes overwhelm the opposition. It also increases the probability that each of the team's constituent populations will be represented. For example, some years back, minority students at a university that I had been affiliated with took over the school's communications center, making it impossible to place or receive a telephone call. The students had a number of grievances that they wanted resolved.

By delegating a large team to negotiate with the university authorities, the students assured themselves that all divergent points of view would be represented. The university administration decided on a different tactic. Only the president was to negotiate with the student representatives. The president reasoned that by not overwhelming the students with equal numbers, he could increase their sense of confidence in themselves, and in so doing move more rapidly toward an accommodation. Moreover, since he was in a position to make decisions on some of the students' demands, there would be no need to delay the resolution process by involving others.

Interestingly, he also reasoned that by meeting with the students alone, he could avoid making some decisions when more time was needed to think or to negotiate with other publics at the university. For example, in response to a demand related to curriculum, he was able to point out that academic issues were not his prerogative, and that he would have to discuss this with the faculty senate. On an issue that had to do with admissions, he indicated that he would have to defer to the university's director of admissions and the board of trustees. Perhaps most important was his conviction that in meeting with the students by himself, he could establish an informal atmosphere that would be more conducive to arriving at an accommodation.

"We all wanted the same thing," he later explained, "an open university, and one that not only provides equal opportunity to all segments of our society, but gives the kinds of support that would make minorities comfortable and at ease in this environment. Had I brought in a team of experts, it would have created an 'us against them' atmosphere. I wanted to defuse the confrontation, not inflame it."

The decision to delegate one person to negotiate with a team or with a total organization frequently reflects that side's power in the negotiating process. For example, a federal agency with access to dollars that are needed by local service providers may delegate an individual project officer to conduct site visits and to meet with representatives of the agency's staff, its collaborating organizations, and consumer populations. On the other hand, if the federal agency is in dire need of certain services by a potential contractor, several key officials may be assigned the responsibility of negotiating with the representative of the contracting firm or agency.

There are, of course, many situations in which negotiations between teams are called for. This is almost invariably the situation in international relations, in labor-management relations, and frequently in interagency relations. All members of the team need not be in the same room at the same time, nor need they perform their functions simultaneously. For example, two agencies exploring the possibilities of joint programming may delegate different staff members to meet with their counterparts. A bookkeeper may meet with a bookkeeper, a casework supervisor with a casework supervisor, and so on. Agreements may be arrived at piecemeal, as the subnegotiators make recommendations to their respective administrators.

Should the negotiations require the development of a formal negotiating team, you will have to think through each role on that team. Team members are not expected to operate like members of a track team, each running as fast as possible. A better image might be the basketball team in which each member assists the other in defensive or scoring plays, but even here it will have to be determined whether each player is to perform a given role or each is assigned "one on one" against the opposition.

Generally, each team will have a spokesperson and/or a team captain, who should be someone with considerable expertise in bargaining. Although he or she need not be the highest ranking member of the organization on the team, the captain should have clout with his or her constituency or have access to those upon whom decisions depend. It should also be someone who can (1) speak the language of the other side, (2) get information across, and (3) listen well. The spokesperson should be able to communicate as an equal without being condescending or subservient. The captain or spokesperson should also be patient, able to take the heat, and able to inspire confidence. The team spokesperson must be able to say no, yes, or maybe.

Clearly both sides are not necessarily on the same footing when they enter the negotiations process. One may have considerable legitimacy in the community; the other may be new or unknown. One may be a bureaucratic organization; the other may represent a loose confederation of individuals.

One side may feel itself aggrieved; the other, let down. One may be making demands; the other, responding to them. One side may view the negotiation process as a form of conflict resolution, whereas the other may not have perceived any conflict.

## Constituent Organizations

Negotiators and negotiating teams are responsible to constituencies. When two bureaucratic organizations negotiate with each other, they may represent different constituencies which are, however, generally organized in much the same way: as staff, boards of directors, consumer populations, and so on. Each side is likely to understand the other as well as the limitations imposed by organizational factors. This understanding does not necessarily exist when an agency negotiates with its consumers, for example, a neighborhood association that operates more like a primary group than a bureaucracy. Understanding the relevant structures and decision-making processes of the other side—how authority is delegated and how firm that delegation is—is of central importance to successful negotiations.

This point will become clear if we return to the negotiations between the minority students and the university president. The president, a skillful negotiator, was able to help the student delegation understand precisely what was possible and what was not under the circumstances. He helped them identify with him and his concerns just as he identified with theirs. He also pointed out what was possible now and what would occur a year or two later if they worked together. He skillfully turned a confrontation into a commitment to collaboration in which both sides had empathy for the other.

When the student delegation returned to their colleagues, still in the communications center, they were promptly denounced as having been duped, taken in by a smooth-talking bureaucrat. They were "fired," and another group of students was delegated to take up the original demands, instructed to be even more militant in their approach.

Again they met for several hours with the president. They, too, left feeling that he was on their side and that accommodation was not only desirable but essential if they were to maintain the considerable sympathy for their cause expressed by other students and faculty on campus. On its return to the communications center, this group was also accused of having capitulated to the enemy. A third delegation was sent to negotiate with the president, this time with a set of escalated demands that were "non-negotiable."

> The university president recollected: I knew what was coming, and I was determined not to be worn down by it. When you deal with people who are new to the negotiation process and who don't really understand how much power they have, or for that matter, how little, you have to do a lot of educating. These kids were not used to working together and it was the first time they had tried to take on a bureaucracy. They just weren't able to delegate responsibility to their negotiating team. If they didn't get what their constituents thought they should have gotten, the group simply sent in a new team. While under other circumstances they might have done that to wear me down, in this case, they weren't thinking all that strategically. The plain truth is that they didn't know any better.
>
> By the time they were finally ready to settle, the university had found it could operate pretty well without the telephone system. Ma Bell was ready to put in new lines, and support on campus for the students was beginning to waver. There was clearly a possibility of a backlash when rumors began spreading that outside organizers were coming in to advise the dissidents. I didn't want that to happen, so I decided to go to the communications center myself. In effect, I found myself negotiating with everybody instead of with the team.
>
> By this time, at least half the group had already spoken with me, and we had established at least some modicum of trust between us. All of us cared about the university, and none of us wanted to see it harmed. We came to a settlement that we could live with; in fact, it strengthened the entire university community. It resulted, among other things, in new access to minority populations we hoped to recruit to the university.

When constituencies are in ferment, it is difficult for them to delegate responsibility, and it can become impossible for the negotiating team to maintain its position of authority and legitimacy. This is especially true in negotiating community-based disputes, where the community group is open to all kinds of outside influences and their perceptions of strength or of the justice of their cause is easily manipulated.

Nevertheless, the fluidity of such situations frequently leads to new ideas that can be translated into programs and services, if only the two sides will listen to each other. Unfortunately, in the heat of a dispute, many good ideas are misunderstood or forgotten. Program designers would do well to keep good notes, recording ideas for reexamination in a calmer time.

## Negotiating Skills

The skills required for affecting negotiations can be grouped as analytic and interactional. *Analytic* skills include assessment, planning, and strategy development. Interactional skills are both direct and indirect, expressed in person or in writing. The ability to respond verbally with empathy instead of anger to a presentation of grievances is a skill in *direct* interaction. The ability to phrase a written response so as to increase the likelihood that the other side will empathize with your position is also direct. But the ability to write a news release that will generate consensus with your position and opposition to your opponents' is an example of *indirect* communication. You are telling your opponents that they may be getting themselves into difficulty and that you can effect that difficulty.

The *assessment process* sometimes requires a great deal of homework. It might entail finding out informally where the other party stands on the issues, launching some trial balloons so as to ascertain how the other side will respond to your bargaining position, polling the opinions of key publics around the issues to be negotiated. One side may be able to compromise, whereas the other side's constituents may make it impossible to work for anything but non-negotiable demands. If in fact they are non-negotiable, there may be no reason to negotiate at all. Clearly, my request for $360,000 was not non-negotiable. Nor were other components of the proposal, although beyond a certain point, we would not negotiate further.

Stated demands do not always reflect the real objectives of each side. A demand may be the opening position. Demands for specific concessions or agreements may reflect one side's limited awareness of the possibilities. What are the capacities of each side to change their demands over the period in which the negotiations take place?

It is also important to understand the relevant decision-making processes used by each side, how authority for negotiations is delegated, how firm that authority is, and what procedures must be used by each side to ratify any tentative decisions made at the bargaining table. Experienced negotiators know that dragging out the negotiating process can destroy the leadership position of those representing the other side. It can also threaten one's own leadership position. How long can the other side hold out? Do they have the resources (like a strike fund) to maintain their position, and for how long will relevant publics support that position?

A proper reading of the outside pressures that may force the settlement provides negotiators with some clues about whether to focus only on those with whom direct negotiations take place. There may be other publics to please. Effective use of the news media and other public relations techniques may sometimes be the fastest way to arrive at an accommodation. Unlike geometry, in negotiation, the shortest distance between two points may not be straight a line.

The *planning process* requires a variety of decisions. Who should negotiate on your behalf, an individual or a team? If a team, of whom should it be composed? Who is to play what role? Planning requires clarifying your side's objectives, not necessarily the resolutions it is willing to settle for. For example, a hospital's objective may be to locate a certain number of patients in community placements. This objective should not be confused with efforts to induce a targeted community agency to accept a given number of referrals. Based on your assessment of the other side, is it possible to lay out the specific provisions of an agreement that you are willing to settle for? Keep a number of alternative backup positions in your pocket.

There are a number of ways of developing a *negotiation strategy*. Some negotiators prefer to put all of their cards on the table, some prefer to reveal them slowly. It may be best to get the other side to reveal its positions first, and then to respond to those positions one at a time. The university president quoted earlier sums up his strategy by saying that he always gives "as little as possible, unless giving a lot results in gaining a lot, and give in only on items for which you think an accommodation is possible. Use precedents from settlements that have been made elsewhere around issues similar to yours. Consider the appropriate language or interaction style that is likely to yield results. I would not negotiate with a clerical union the way I negotiated with the students," explained the president. "If I did, they would consider me a fool, and the university an easy mark." Successful negotiators interact with various publics in different ways.

Perhaps the most important *interactional skill* in negotiation is the ability to empathize with the other side. Empathy is the ability to understand where others are coming from. It requires putting oneself in the shoes of another. It is equally important to help representatives of the other side to put themselves in your shoes or in the position of those who must ratify any agreement made. You may have to help those with whom you are negotiating to interpret what *they* have learned to their constituents.

Concomitant with empathy is the ability to generate trust. This requires open and honest communication. Successful negotiating also requires a commitment to arriving at a settlement and the ability to project confidence that the negotiating process will yield a settlement acceptable to both sides. If an agreement is acceptable to only one side but is rammed down the throat of the other, it is not likely to hold for long.

Once engaged in the negotiating process, make sure you or someone else on your team keeps a bargaining book, an inventory of what you had started out to get and the shifts in your position and those of the other sides. Be sure to record the wording of the agreements, even if they are only tentative. Consult your constituents regularly to make sure that both agreements and the language being used are understood and accepted. It may be necessary to educate those constituents throughout the process. If the language provides a problem for either side, consider alternative ways of phrasing an agreement without changing its substance. Remember that it is frequently important to appeal to a broader audience because your constituents and those of the other side can be influenced by public opinion in the forms of both support or disapproval.

## Pacing and Shifting Positions

The pacing and timing of negotiations are also critical to arriving at a satisfactory accommodation. In general, the easiest and least controversial items should be dealt with first. When a tentative accommodation on some issues is arrived at, confidence is generated on both sides that the more difficult issues can also be resolved. Some negotiations work best when they go around the clock. Others are best managed in short sessions, conducted over long periods of time.

Breaks between formal sessions can be used to re-establish working relationships with your own team and those of the other side. When things get heated or seem to reach an impasse, it is useful to take a break, even an indefinite one, so long as that break is accompanied by a commitment from both sides to reconvene when they are ready. Breaks permit the testing out of alternative definitions of problems and their solutions before they are presented formally at the bargaining table.

Closely related to timing is the shifting of positions. I've sometimes been accused of using Mau Mau tactics in negotiating, even with organizations with which there is no basic conflict. The tactic works something like this: I'll present a hard line, almost an unyielding one, only to have a colleague of mine point out to the other side that if approached properly, I can be reasoned with. It hasn't always increased my popularity, but it certainly has increased my ability to get things done quickly, and frequently to my organization's advantage.

Shifting positions is another useful tactic. I have sometimes withdrawn an agreement tentatively made when I found the other side unreasonable on some other issue. This can be tricky, particularly if it generates distrust. One way of overcoming accusations of bad faith is to point out that your constituents will not be willing to support you on the tentative decision unless they also feel the resolution of other issues is possible. It is useful to claim that you are not in full control and you must get approval for an accommodation from others.

## Turning Predicaments to Opportunities: From Win-Lose to Win-Win

All too often, negotiations are conducted on a win-lose basis, like a zero-sum game in which one party wins to the extent that the other side loses. It is my experience that this may make sense for chess or Ping-Pong, but that this perspective is altogether inappropriate for anyone engaged in marketing. Even when the presented issues seem to be distributive in nature, like the university-student negotiations described, they can be redefined in integrative terms: "We both believe in this institution, and together we can make it work better."

When either side feels that it has lost, it is not likely to invest much in maintaining an agreement. Everyone likes to win, but it is not necessary for anyone to wind up the loser or for others to come up the only winners. *It may be true that any problem can be rendered unsolvable. It is also true that any predicament can be turned into an opportunity.* If negotiations are to succeed, it is not necessary for one side to embrace the other side's position or to give up its own. It is necessary, however, for each side to recognize that it can achieve some of its goals only to the extent that the other side also achieves some of its goals. It is also necessary for both sides to feel that accommodation is not only possible, but desirable.

## Third-Party Interventions

There are times when the principals will not be able to arrive at an accommodation and so may break off negotiations indefinitely. If the consequences of such an action are likely to lead to even more serious difficulties, this may be a good time to seek help from a third party. For example, someone from the United Way might help two agencies negotiate a purchase-of-service agreement. A representative of the community development corporation might help a neighborhood group present its case before the City Council. The city attorney may help resolve a dispute between the recreation department and the transportation authority.

The third party might be expert in the substantive issues being negotiated, or in the negotiating process itself. Arbitration and mediation are the principal forms of third-party intervention. *Arbitration* refers to a process whereby a dispute is referred to a third party who is given power to enforce a settlement on both parties. There are two kinds of arbitration: voluntary, and compulsory or involuntary. In the first, both parties decide whether to accept arbitration. If they accept it, they can decide if it is to be fact-finding or binding. In fact finding, the arbitrator not only digs into the facts behind the issues, but spells out the possible consequences of one agreement in contrast with another. Information may be presented only to those involved in the negotiating process, or it may be made public. Information may be generated through any number of assessment approaches, including private interviews and public hearings. The arbitrator's report and any of the suggestions that may be included within it do not obligate any of the parties. In contrast, binding arbitration delegates authority to the arbitrator for making judgments that both parties have agreed to abide by in advance. Although binding arbitration reduces some of the autonomy of both sides, it also takes the heat off. The arbitrator can always be blamed by negotiators for making an unpopular decision. Compulsory arbitration, in which both parties are required to accept the services of the arbitrator, is nearly always binding.

*Mediation* is almost always voluntary. It may include many of the same activities as arbitration, but the mediator is likely to focus at least as much on the negotiating process as on the substance of the negotiation. For example, mediators help persons on each side develop empathy for the other and promote the confidence of both sides in themselves and in their negotiating partners. They interpret each side's relative power position, and in so doing help them become more realistic about the possible outcome of the process. They give encouragement when the going gets rough, facilitate trade-offs, and suggest alternative ways of defining the issues or of looking for solutions.

Sometimes they work with the constituencies of one or both sides, particularly when those constituencies find it difficult to accept the realities of a given situation. In this way, they too take the heat off the negotiator. The mediator may be required to put pressure on one or both sides and to accept the responsibility for such pressure as well as for a proposed solution, by accepting the role of scapegoat so as to protect the respective leaders of each side.

The mediator also arranges the timing and pacing of the negotiations, holding some issues in check while pushing others higher up on the agenda. By ordering and sequencing the events that take place—exploration, trade-offs, making commitments, and so on—the mediator can help keep the process going. For these reasons selecting the right mediator may make all the difference in settling a dispute.

Generally, both mediators and arbitrators are selected because they are both assumed to be neutral on the issues and they are skilled in the third-party intervention process. In all forms of mediation and in involuntary arbitration, the third party must be acceptable to both sides. In labor-management or community-dispute issues, both sides generally submit a list of names in order of acceptability. If the same names appear on both lists, the person with the highest ranking on each is selected. Interestingly enough, sometimes one side will put a name high up on its list because that person may be presumed to be more acceptable to the other side than to its own constituencies. For example, some years back, Third World students struck and closed down San Francisco State College. Representative John Conyers of Detroit was brought in as the mediator.

Conyers was acceptable to the school administration because he was clearly a man with the right skills and someone who represented acceptable values. But the administration understood that he would be just as acceptable to Third World students, because Conyers is a black and has a liberal voting record in Congress. The administration presumed that the students could identify with Conyers and would perceive him to be "their man."

Now see how well you do on Exercise 6–3.

## EXERCISE 6-3
### Identifying and Applying Practice Principles

This chapter is loaded with practice principles and guidelines that you may find useful in preparing yourself for a negotiating process. A practice principle is a guide to action. It is generally based on experience or on values. Examples include:

> "Negotiators must produce something of value for their constituents."
>
> "Accommodations that are defined in integrative terms (win-win) are likely to be more acceptable to both sides than those defined as distributive (win-lose)."

The first of these is written as an imperative; the second as an aphorism. Either form is acceptable. Both include action verbs ("defined," "produce,") and both are suggestive of appropriate or successful behavior.

1. Go back over the chapter or your reading notes. Identify all the practice principles you can find. Sometimes they will be stated directly; at other times they will have to be inferred from what I (the author) wrote or from the case examples I included.
2. Now find some way of grouping those principles. You might find the chapter headings useful (e.g., "Why People Negotiate" or "Negotiating Skills"), but feel free to develop your own categorization scheme. Relocate the principles you identified within your categories. Leave yourself some room, about 1/3 of the width of the page, to the right of your list, for step 3.
3. Now make two columns to the right. Label one "Acceptability" and the other one "Skill." Score each item on these two variables. Give yourself a 5 for those principles you find *totally acceptable*, with which you have neither a value nor a strategic disagreement, and a 5 for those you feel *skilled* in applying. A score of 4 means that in most cases you find the principle acceptable or that you have some basic skill in application. A score of 3 indicates you have no opinion on acceptability or are unsure about your level of skill. A score of 2 indicates you find the principle as enunciated in the chapter mildly unacceptable or unacceptable in certain situations, or that you feel unskilled in this area. And a score of 1 indicates total disagree-

*continued*

ment with the principle, or a total lack of competence to perform accordingly. Score yourself similarly on skill.

For all those items that you scored 4 or 5 on both acceptability and skill, little needs doing. But where you scored yourself high on acceptability and low on skill, some work needs to be done. And on all those where you scored yourself low on acceptability but high on skill, some reflection may be necessary. For all those on which you scored yourself low on both, some consultation with others may be in order.

## Review

Negotiation is the process whereby parties come to agreements regarding their relationships with and toward each other. It is therefore central to strategic marketing because it is used to establish relationships with key publics like funders, consumers, staff, representatives of other service providers, and so on. Negotiations can be conducted formally, informally or both. In successful negotiations, each side must trust that the other side is bargaining in good faith, and that it is capable of making commitments necessary to arrive at a settlement. Some negotiations are distributive in nature; that is, they presume a conflict of interest on both sides, and that the gains for one may result in losses for the other. More frequently negotiations are defined as integrative, when both sides expect to gain from collaboration and accommodation. While all parties to the negotiating process do not have to gain equally, the benefits of accommodation must be perceived as greater than the possible consequences of non-negotiation or nonaccommodation.

Negotiations generally deal with three types of issues: symbolic, procedural, and substantive. Symbolic issues often get in the way of achieving settlements on issues that can be discussed rationally and in situations where the costs and benefits of various alternatives can be weighed. Symbolic issues tend to be presented in non-negotiable terms, and so by definition they are difficult to deal with. Nevertheless, because they are integrally intertwined with the images and identities of the parties, they are often significant. Procedural issues may also be difficult to deal with, because they are often seen as having significant impact on the position or power of each side during the process of negotiating on substantive issues.

Negotiation is more likely to have a successful outcome when the needs of all parties to the process are recognized. Needs are not identical to demands, although they may be perceived as such. If either or both sides can accommodate to the needs of the other, the outcome of negotiation is likely to be perceived as beneficial. Experienced negotiators recognize that it may be necessary to help the other side come to grips with its real interests, in contrast with its stated position. The same may be true of the negotiator's own constituents. Environmental factors can have a significant impact on the outcome of negotiations. If key publics are supportive of one side or the other, or if they are nonsupportive of the entire negotiating process, they can sometimes make or break the negotiations. Sometimes the process is affected by agencies of social control, such as the police or some external standard-setting body; internal factors are equally important.

Of great important is *who* does the negotiating, *when*, and *where*. Negotiations can be conducted between individuals, teams, entire constituencies, or combinations of the above. When teams are used, the role of each member must be clearly understood within the team and by those with whom the team is negotiating. Probably the most important role is that of spokesperson, often taken by the same individual who serves as team captain. While negotiators must be skillful at communicating with each other, they must also be able to communicate effectively with their constituents so as to assure constituent support for any possible agreement.

Negotiating skills can be defined as analytic and interactional. Analytic skills include assessment, planning, and strategy development. Interactional skills include interpersonal as well as written communication. The capacity to empathize with the positions or situations of others is perhaps the most essential interpersonal skill.

Even those negotiations that are initially perceived of in win-lose, or zero-sum terms, can be redefined as win-win situations. This requires readiness to accept alternative solutions to newly defined problems. Sometimes, this redefinition requires third-party intervention.

The third party, a mediator or an arbitrator, must be acceptable to both sides and perceived by each as reasonably neutral. He or she must also be at least as committed to a successful outcome as either or both of the parties. Arbitration can be voluntary or imposed; of the fact-finding or binding kind. In binding arbitration, both sides agree in advance to abide by the arbitrator's recommendations. Mediators tend to spend more time on the negotiating process than arbitrators, who focus primarily on substantive issues. Thus, mediators may invest a great deal of effort on coaching each side and on helping each come to understand the position and the power of the other.

# PART III

# Program Development

# 7 INTERACTIVE ASSESSMENT TECHNIQUES

NONE OF US would consider developing a treatment plan without careful assessment of a client's problem, potential, or aspirations and of the resources in the client's immediate environment that might be activated on his or her behalf. Yet we often engage in program design and development while paying only cursory attention to the assessment process, relying all too heavily on our intuitions and assuming the correctness of our decisions on the basis of personal or professional commitments. There is another danger as well: the danger that we will design "research" projects without the necessary competence, misinterpret information, and perhaps even mistreat the public from which we gather the information. Any experienced assessor, researcher, or market analyst would shudder at the incompetence and insensitivity verbalized in the following vignette. Yet it is all too typical of agency-based practitioners who may not have thought through what information they need, what it will be used for, and the best (most useful and efficient) ways to get it.

## We'll Use the Info We Have

"I'm not big on research, but I do appreciate the use of information, so when we decided to try using marketing techniques to keep this agency afloat, I knew that I would have to learn something about market research. I got a couple of books from the library and started reading. To be honest, much of the stuff was over my head—terms like 'market segmentation' and 'penetration.' Much of it was just too technical for me.

"I figured we knew what we were after, so we would just do a survey, and that's that. So we designed a questionnaire and distributed it to every fifth household in the neighborhood, asking people to get it back to us in stamped self-addressed envelopes. We asked for lots of information. You know, on family composition, schooling and economic situations. And we asked all kinds of questions about what people might want from the agency, their feelings about the neighborhood.

"It was maybe more information than we needed. But we figured we could always store it and use it later. We did alright, I guess. About a quarter of the questionnaires were sent back, not all of them filled out just right or completed, but we used the information anyway."

Even when we do an adequate job of studying the needs or interests of a potential consumer population, we may be less than thorough in assessing such other publics as funders, the local human service agencies with which collaborative exchanges may be needed, or the aspirations and capacities of our aging employees. If interacting with various publics is essential to shaping a product or product line that is well targeted and supported, it stands to reason that the assessment process itself should be interactive and that the tools used should permit the active involvement of our various input, throughput, and output publics.

Because the methods used in assessment are often the same as those of evaluation, and because both activities may take place concurrently, the two terms are often used interchangeably. They are, however, conceptually distinct. Assessment activities are focused on the examination of *what is*, on *what is likely to be*, or on *what ought to be*. Evaluation focuses on *what happened, how it happened,* and *whether it should have happened.*

This chapter will deal only with assessment, and, therefore, logically precedes other chapters dealing with program and resource development. We need to know about our circumstances and those of other publics, of their interests and needs, before we can determine what is feasible. And we need to know what is likely to happen or is desirable, in order to set proper goals. We begin by examining the differences between asking here-and-now (what is), anticipatory (what is likely to be), and normative (what ought to be) types of questions. We will then examine the implications of each of these approaches for assessing the environments within which agencies operate and programs are developed.

In this chapter, I will share with you a variety of assessment tools I have found useful in strategic marketing. Most are relatively nontechnical. I will resist the temptation to be comprehensive in order to focus more directly on those tools that I think you will also find useful.*

*For more extensive instruction in the tools discussed, see Armand Lauffer, *Assessment Tools for Practitioners, Managers and Trainers*, Sage Publications, Beverly Hills, Calif., 1982. Some of the text and a number of the vignettes come from that book by permission of the publisher.

## Assessing What Is, What Might Be, and What Ought to Be

When we assess what is, we are directing our attention to the here and now. We might choose to examine the populations in need of service, the organizations that currently or potentially provide those services, or the relationships between providers and between providers and consumers. Assessment activities may also be aimed at examining the capacities of our own organization to respond to need or opportunity and the extent to which opportunities or support for new programs exist.

When the program planner focuses on an actual or potential consumer population, the following questions might be asked:

1.  To what extent do *debilitating* or inappropriate *attitudes*, values, and perspectives limit people's abilities to make use of available resources or to act on their own behalf?
2.  To what extent are they *unaware of available services*, programs, and facilities or the benefits and costs of making use of them?
3.  To what extent do they have the *capacity or skill* to make use of these programs or services?

Answers to these questions may be sought directly from those populations targeted for service. Alternatively, they may be inferred from observations of the behaviors of potential consumers. Another approach is to seek answers from those who already serve the populations in question and may be familiar with their needs and circumstances. Answers to these questions may lead some program designers toward an advocacy strategy aimed at empowerment or *animation*.* The ideological position of the assessor may have much to do with whether the population being assessed is viewed as victim, deviant, or client. Thus, the same questions asked by different persons are likely to yield a variety of answers.

Other program planners may focus on the programs or services provided to a given population rather than on the population itself. Here, five questions might be asked:

1.  To what extent are services of various kinds *available* and to whom?
2.  To what extent are available services *accessible* (by dint of location, hours offered, removal of architectural and psychological or social barriers)?
3.  Even if available and accessible, are services *responsive* to actual and potential consumers and what kinds of *accountability* mechanisms are built into those services?

---

*By the term *empowerment*, I mean increasing the capacities of individuals and groups to take charge of their own circumstances and to influence the conditions that govern those circumstances. *Animation* is a term current in the French literature on community development, referring to activating people to take responsibility for their own affairs.

4. How *effective* are the services (i.e., do they make a difference and for whom)?

5. Are they *efficient*; could one serve larger numbers or provide more comprehensive services for the same amount of money, or would a change in the scope of the program result in considerable cost savings?

When one examines the relationships between service providers or between providers and consumers, at least four sets of questions are raised:

1. To what extent are services provided *comprehensively*, in such a way that one service complements another instead of competing for the client's allegiance or leaving large service areas uncovered?

2. Are services provided *continuously*, so that when one agency completes its service (for example, job training in an institutional setting) other agencies are ready to provide subsequent service (job placement for a disabled person in the local community) and other supports leading to independent living arrangements?

3. To what extent are the cultures of each *compatible* with each other (terminology used, expectations about behavior, perceptions of need and priorities)?

4. What *relationships* exist between the institutionalized forms of services offered under public, voluntary, and private auspices, and the more informal services provided by natural helpers like family, friends, neighbors, and members of self-help groups?

These are here-and-now types of questions. They focus on *what is*. In anticipatory assessment one asks the same kinds of questions, but the focus is on the extent to which needs or problems are likely to be felt in the future. What might be the likely drain on existing services should unemployment double or be reduced by 50 percent in the next five years? Would one wish then to focus on the debilitating attitudes or on lack of marketable skills? Anticipating the possible consequences of cataclysmic events (like worsening economic conditions), would rehabilitation services face major reductions in funding? Or assuming current trends toward community placement, to what extent might one anticipate continued problems of availability, accessibility, accountability, effectiveness, or efficiency?

The advantages of anticipatory assessment are that it permits program planners to think ahead rather than to catch up with problems after the fact. Anticipatory assessment makes it possible for us to make decisions now that are likely to head off problems and their consequences for the populations that concern us and for which we are mandated to provide services.

There is yet a third approach. *Normative* assessment begins with an image of a desired state of affairs. We might ask ourselves what kinds of resource mix we would want available to the agency, what services we would like to see in place four or five years from now, or what kinds of consumer self-help capacities we would like to build. We also might begin by deciding what a minimally acceptable child placement, library, health, or rehabilitation service might look like (perhaps in terms of such issues as availability, accessibility, accountability, effectiveness, and efficiency). In effect, what we would be doing is developing a "competency" model that describes that which is desirable.

When a professional association like the United Way of America or the National Association of Settlements, or a government agency like the Rehabilitation Services Administration sets minimum standards for local service agencies, it establishes a competency model. Program planners in an agency can also design their own competency models; for example, spelling out what they consider to be good or effective casework services. For assessment purposes, designing the model is only a first step. It is then necessary to examine where the population or the service system is, in relation to the norms that we have specified. It is the gap between current reality and a desired state of affairs that gives direction to our program development efforts. Once we have uncovered present levels of competency and compared them with the desired norms, we can then specify our objectives and set priorities on the bases of salience and feasibility.

I have sometimes been asked which approach (here-and-now, anticipatory, or normative) works best. Obviously, there is no single answer. We often do the here-and-now kinds of assessments because we confront problems in the present that demand our attention. Yet agencies involved in ongoing planning and program development activities would hardly do themselves or their consumers justice without also engaging in both normative and anticipatory assessment activities.

Remember, each of your publics is likely to have different perceptions about the problems to be addressed or programs to be developed and different preferences regarding each. The term *perceptions* refers to how a given problem or situation is viewed. We are speaking about its image. Images are to a large extent subjective. They are drawn both from personal values and from experiences shared with others. Your organization, for example, might project a positive image of being trustworthy, progressive, forward-looking and responsive. It might project a negative image, such as being unprofessional, nonresponsive, ineffective, and so on. The image is determined in part by the organization's past history, by the type of staff it employs and by the ways in which the staff present themselves, by the organization's sponsors, by its clients, and more. This same is true of the agency's other programs whether these are of long standing or only in the thinking stages. It is quite likely that your current or potential consumer populations have different images of the organization than do its staff members. Current and potential funders may have still different images.

If you were to confer with some of your colleagues, you could probably agree on some ideal image of your organization, its programs and services. This is the image you'd like to approximate; in effect, a normative image. Without too much probing, the staff might also be able to describe its public image, how others view the organization. Finally, the staff might be able to come up with an image of the organization's real self, how its members believe it really is. When these three images are out of line with each other, or when the perceptions of the agency's various publics are not co-terminous, the organization may find itself in some difficulty.

The term *preferences* indicates the relative value of comparable items. Some clients might prefer individualized counseling or treatment, whereas others would prefer participation in self-help groups. Consumers' preferences are not always what your agency may be prepared to provide or what funders may consider to be appropriate. When these preferences are out of sync, it may be necessary to influence one or another of the relevant publics and attempt to induce them to change their preferences or to become aware of the relative merit of another approach.

## Deciding Which Assessment Tool to Use and with Which Public

"Alright, already," you may be thinking, "When do I start my survey, and how do I go about designing it?" Soon enough; but first I want to discuss four other tools with you: the nominal group technique (NGT), Delphi, force-field analysis, and task analysis. These are somewhat more flexible and easier to use with small groups or highly targeted populations than surveys. When used properly and with the right publics, they are likely to yield considerable information.

We discussed another assessment tool, eco-mapping, in Chapter 2, and at the end of this volume you will find the instructions for playing COM-PACTS II, a *Co*llaborative *Ma*rketing, *P*lanning and *Act*ion Simulation. Playing COMPACTS II will give you an opportunity to test out your ability to use all the concepts you have learned from this book on strategic marketing. You will also find that COMPACTS can be used effectively as an assessment tool; identifying preferences, expressed demand, capacities, and the potential for collaboration or conflict between various publics. But for the moment, let's get down to the business at hand: learning how and when to use the five interactive assessment tools.

### The Nominal Group Technique

The nominal group technique was developed to involve people with diverse backgrounds and opinions in assessment and priority-setting activities. Although there are many variations of NGT, they each differ from interactive groups by limiting the "group think" process and by assuring that all participants will have equal access to the assessment and priority-setting processes. These participants might include representatives of various agencies at a community meeting, consumers of agency services brought together to discuss their responses to current services, and government officials and others responsible for setting funding priorities. NGT was used by Monica, the activist member of the widows' group described in Chapter 5.

Here is how the process works. Those involved might be asked to list three needs to be addressed on small pieces of paper. The term "needs" may be replaced by other concerns such as problems to be addressed, population groups to be served, desired interorganizational linkages, or resources in short supply. The group's convenor or facilitator then collects and sorts the papers according to some logical scheme reflecting the responses. If the original inquiry focused on management problems within an agency, the responses might be logically grouped under such headings as communication, staff morale, or appropriate allocation of work-load responsibilities. Each heading is then written across the top of a chalkboard or on each of several large sheets of paper. The problem statements written by the individual participants are then placed in the appropriate categories and participants are asked if some statements might be eliminated or integrated with others because of overlap and duplication. We might now find ourselves with seven or eight items in one category, three in the next, five in the third, eleven in the fourth, and so on.

At this point, the facilitator asks each person, in the order of the seating arrangement, to argue persuasively that one or another of the items listed should be acted upon or should take priority. At this point no group discussion is permitted. Each speaker might be limited to 30 or 60 seconds, depending on how many people are involved or how much time is available. When everyone has had a turn, it is now time for everyone to vote. If there are six or seven items in one category, participants might be asked to vote for the two that ought to be given priority. If there are only three or four items, they would vote for one item only. When the voting is over, the priorities under each heading are clear. It is now time to vote on whether to work on all the items in one category before tackling another (say staff morale, before allocation of work responsibilities) or to select the highest-priority items in each category for action.

In setting priorities, consider asking questions: Which of these items should we work on first? Which problems are the most destructive to the organization? Which might be the easiest to deal with? In effect, you would be assessing the opinions of key actors in a program-development process and assessing their readiness to engage in a change process. In my experience, this process works best with groups comprising 6 to 20 participants. If more people are to be involved, it might pay to break larger groups into several smaller groups, each with its own facilitator.

The following descriptions by a community organizer of her use of NGT may help bring the process to life for you.

### Thirty Seconds to Make the Point

"We just seemed to be getting nowhere. Every meeting ended in a jumble of confusion and hostility. Mrs. Carmichael, who was a mighty powerful woman, seemed to be doing most of the talking. People were afraid to raise their voices against her. All but Lettie Benedict, who had once worked as a secretary in the mayor's office. Because of her reputed connections, the fireworks between them were something to watch. But it kept almost everyone else out of the dialogue, if you could call it that.

"I shared my problem with Mark Habib, an experienced community organizer, also on our staff. 'Look,' he said to me, 'why not use the nominal group technique? You know what the problems are in your neighborhood, at least the general categories. Before the next meeting get yourself a big pad of newsprint.

" 'On the top of each sheet, put the title of one problem category, like street repair or muggings or retail gouging. Then hang up the sheets around the walls of the clubhouse where you meet.*

" 'When you have your next meeting, give everybody a magic marker and have them go up to the wall and write their action suggestions under each category.'

"It worked like a charm. Everybody seemed to have a good time writing. Some people even started correcting other people's grammar and spelling. People talked informally about the suggestions they thought were good ones and those they thought were way out. After a while I asked everyone to sit down. I asked Mrs. Carmichael to read each of the suggestions made under each category. If there were overlaps, I asked Lettie to fix them up by consolidating them into shorter statements while Mrs. Carmichael went over to read the next set of categories.

"When we were all through, I told them now it was time to express their opinions for real. Everybody would be given thirty seconds to convince us about the action steps we should take first as a neighborhood group. They could try to convince us on the basis of how important a problem was or on the basis of how easy it was to solve. No sense in working on things that weren't going to yield up any solutions. Now you might think that thirty seconds isn't very much time. But you'd be amazed at how much you can say in thirty seconds if you really think about it. One of the problems with these people was they would talk without thinking. Talk about being amazed! Were they ever amazed at how much they got done in less than a half hour!

"We then voted on the action steps we wanted to pursue as an organization during the next month or two. Again, talk about being amazed! There was an in-

*Note the variation from the procedure described earlier. Many other variations are possible.

credible amount of consensus. We decided on three concrete action steps. True, some people were disappointed that their priorities were low on the totem pole. But at least everybody'd had a fair chance to make a contribution and everybody'd had the same chance to vote. 'This won't mean that we can't work on any other issues,' I explained at the end of the meeting. 'We've decided what we're going to do first. We'll have a chance to set priorities again next month, after we've had an opportunity to take stock on how we're doing on what we decided tonight.' "

### How the Nominal Group Technique Works

**Step 1.**   Begin with a solitary generation of ideas in writing.

**Step 2.**   Record each idea in a terse phrase on a flip chart.

**Step 3.**   Conduct a round robin feedback session from group members in which each recorded idea is clarified and lobbied for.

**Step 4.**   Allow individual voting on priorities; the group decision will be derived through rank-ordering or rating of preferences.

The advantage of this technique over more interactive group processes is that it guarantees everyone's input. It reduces the likelihood of "group think," the excessive influence of group members with a great deal of charisma, with clear personal priorities, or with higher social status. The Delphi conference provides similar advantages.

## The Delphi Method

Although the Delphi and nominal group techniques are likely to be used for similar purposes, they do not have common origins. NGT is an outgrowth of the field of group dynamics. The Delphi method emerged from the field of technological forecasting. Originally designed as a projective technique, utilizing expert panelists to predict future events or trends, the Delphi method has increasingly been used for program assessment and development. Unlike the nominal group technique, the Delphi conference does not require face-to-face interaction. Participants are rarely present in the same room, and they need not participate at the same time. The method usually uses a structured questionnaire and goes through a number of waves called iterations. Respondents are called panelists; they are selected for their presumed expertise, which may be based on the representation of particular points of view or of specified populations. An effort is made to balance the panel with people who represent diverse views.

There are two kinds of Delphi questionnaires: predictive and policy. The policy Delphi is generally normative in its orientation. Several possible policies or programs are listed on a questionnaire, sometimes with pro and con arguments immediately following the policy statement or program idea.

An example of a policy statement is "No one shall be released from the rehabilitation center until agencies from the client's local community have established a re-entry plan and designated a responsible case manager." An example of a program or service description might be: "Intake services will be located at arranged times outside the agency's headquarters at such locations as schools and community centers." Either statement might then be rated according to a number of different criteria: e.g., feasibility, desirability, or cost. Respondents would be asked to rate each policy statement on a five-point scale according to the criteria selected.

Let's assume desirability and feasibility are the two criteria to be used. If the majority of respondents agree that a policy or program idea is both desirable and feasible, no further probing is necessary. But what if half of the respondents feel that a policy is desirable while the other half feel that it is not in any way desirable? Or what if the respondents agree as to a policy's desirability but conclude that it is not feasible? This is where a second iteration (questionnaire) is required.

Those persons conducting the Delphi conference would probe for the reasons why there are differences among the respondents. A well-designed Delphi questionnaire often includes the opportunity for panelists to write in the reasons for their ratings. It also leaves space for them to add additional program or policy statements they would like other respondents to react to. The Delphi process often goes through four, five, or six iterations. The process need not lead to consensus, but it often leads to clarity.

Let's take a look at how the training director of a state department of mental health used the Delphi method.

### Delphis and Task Forces

"It didn't seem to make much sense to me to plan statewide training programs in substance abuse without getting some informed opinion on who needed the training most and who should be trained, on the context and format of such training, its location, length, and so on. There were some pretty basic questions—for example, should we focus on psychiatrists and other professionally trained mental health personnel? On lay care givers? Ex-abusers? Teachers? G.P.s? Policy and other gatekeepers?

"In the past we would convene task forces to help us make policy decisions like these. But I wasn't happy with the work of these task forces. Sometimes the people whose opinion you really want are just not available for the task force. At other times task force members get bogged down in particulars or wind up agreeing on something just to agree. I wasn't ready to give up my use of task forces, but I needed some way to counteract 'group think' and to focus task force deliberations. That's where Delphi was so ideal.

"Before convening regional task forces, I designed an exploratory Delphi questionnaire with eighteen issue statements and sent them to all those people who had agreed to serve, plus a number of others whose opinion I wanted to include. Each issue was stated in policy terms: 'Training should be conducted in the home community or on the job rather than at state or regional centers.' Or 'Users and ex-abusers should be trained to give help to their peers in trouble.'

"I asked the respondents to rate each item on a five-point scale according to a number of dimensions. For example, I asked them to indicate whether a proposed policy was highly desirable, desirable, neutral, undesirable, or highly undesirable. I then asked them to rate each statement again in accordance with such criteria as estimate of cost, probability of attendance, and feasibility in terms of resources. I left space at the bottom for respondents to add as many as five additional statements, if they wanted to, or to comment on my eighteen.

"After summarizing the responses, my staff and I shared the results with each task force. We accounted for regional differences. That way each task force could see how their thinking related to that of other regional planning groups. These preliminary inputs helped to cut down on some of the confusion that usually prevails at first meetings. Based on the first Delphi responses and the discussions reported by my staff at each of the regional meetings, I designed the second Delphi questionnaire.

"On those items for which there was a great deal of consensus, on desirability and feasibility, no further work was needed. We could just proceed with our planning. But on those items where there were big splits in opinion, or where people thought the idea was good but the feasibility poor, we needed to do a lot of probing. In some cases the clues came from the comments at the bottom of the first questionnaire. We then took what people said during the first task force meeting and put it into our second level of questionnaires. Following several more waves of questionnaires and task force meetings, we were able to arrive at some agreement on a statewide program with considerable variation at the local levels.

"There are times when I'm tempted to use Delphi instead of task forces altogether. I have, in fact, in conference planning. Delphi is neater; it sharpens opinions and does not degenerate into 'group think' where the least controversial policy is the one arrived at, or where some persons sway the rest by the sheer force of their personalities, status, or just plain stubbornness. With Delphi, the respondents can stay anonymous and are more apt to take risks and to be more honest about their thoughts and feelings."

### How the Delphi Method Works

All Delphi conferences go through four phases:

1.  The subject is explored and each individual contributes additional information.
2.  The degree of agreement or disagreement in the group is assessed on each point.

3. Underlying reasons for differences are brought out and probed for clarity.
4. Previous information is analyzed and fed back for consideration.

Like the nominal group technique, the Delphi conference guarantees equal input by all parties. Unlike NGT, Delphi even protects the anonymity of the respondents, whose identities need not be revealed on returned questionnaires. Studies of both NGT and Delphi conferences reveal that participants generally feel that they lead to quicker and more effective decisions. Time is not lost in meaningless and often aimless discussions.

*Future* or *projective* (*predictive*) Delphis, in contrast with *policy* Delphis, are designed to anticipate the likelihood of future events or conditions such as available resources, client demand, or public concern. The assumption behind them is that by selecting respondents for their individual or collective expertise, we are likely to make good predictions. The same steps or phases are used, but the items to be rated are written in predictive language and the rating variables are predictive rather than evaluative in nature. For example, a statement like: "The demand for family counseling will double over the next 5 years" might be rated on a five-point scale from "highly likely" to "highly unlikely" and from "highly significant for this agency" to "highly insignificant."

## Force-Field Analysis

Force-field analysis (FFA) originated in Kurt Lewin's attempts to infuse the social sciences with rigor of the physical sciences. It has, over the years, become a frequently used assessment tool applicable to any stage of program design, resource development, and marketing. FFA employs a sophisticated mapping technique. One might begin the process by defining a desired change or change goal. The next step would be to identify all *driving* and *restraining* forces that influence that goal. Driving forces are those that may currently or potentially be activated in the direction of change. Here we might be talking about the weight of public opinion or the support of key individuals and organizations in the community, those we might identify as elements of the consensus environment.

Restraining forces include all those against change. Such forces include inertia, poor experiences with similar efforts in the past, the state of the national economy, and resistance on the part of client populations or others who might feel their vested interests to be threatened by the proposed change. In sketching a force field, you might wish to use one color to record the *actual* and another for the *potential* driving and restraining forces. The next step is to identify those forces over which you (or your agency) have control, those over which someone else has control, or those over which no one seems to have any control (like the state of the economy).

Once you have defined the problem situation or assessed a need and made a preliminary decision about a change goal, you are ready to use your force-field analysis. Unlike some of the other tools discussed in this book, FFA is used to assess the forces in the ecological environment that contribute to a problem or that can be activated to achieve desired objectives. Some of these may be dismissed out of hand as impractical or out of sync with the agency's perception of its mandate. Usually, however, there is a range of actions that have a varying potential for solving a particular problem; any of these actions may be acceptable to the critical actors in the organization. At any point in the process of program planning and resource development, FFA can be used to explore the feasibility or acceptability of an action or to choose from among alternative possible actions.

## We Threw a Party and Nobody Came

"We're not new to the neighborhood. The center has been here since 1935, and over the years we've changed much in response to new needs, changes in government programs, and most of all to changes in the composition of the neighborhood. Back in the thirties, the community was made up mostly of Italian and Jewish immigrant families, with a few second-generation Americans. Our purpose then was to Americanize our members. We had literacy classes, job training programs, citizenship workshops, clubs for kids. By the forties, we found ourselves shifting emphasis to deal with the consequences of World War II. We increased the number of children's programs after school to accommodate to the many women who worked in the plants or who ran the family businesses while their husbands served in the army.

"We started preschool programs and found ourselves with a growing proportion of senior citizens—'Golden Agers,' we used to call them. We also reached out to new populations that were moving into the neighborhood, Negroes from the South and rural families from Appalachia that had come to work in the defense plants. Some of these families were even more in need of help in dealing with an urban environment than the earlier immigrant populations from Europe, who at least had had some city experience.

"Later, in the fifties, we got into street-corner work with teen and young adult gangs, and by the sixties, with the growth of federal government programs, our service expanded dramatically to include tenants organizing in both public housing and in the most dilapidated areas of the neighborhood, where 'slumlords' had permitted their buildings to deteriorate. A few years later, we got into the community mental health business, into civil rights organizing, legal aid, and community development projects in cooperation with municipal authorities. So you see, we are not bound by preconceptions. It is a pretty dynamic agency, with a very highly qualified staff, some of whom have been around for a while. And we know the neighborhood, or so we thought, as do many of our board members, who continue to include some of the Jews and Italians who grew up in the area and moved away, but continue to feel a commitment to the center.

"When a number of Vietnamese families moved into the neighborhood, and then Lebanese families, we reached out to both groups as we had to others in the past. We even threw an open house. No one came. Nor were we successful in providing either group with services through our mental health center or our job training program. The legal aid service had suffered heavy cutbacks in federal funding, and we were down to a single paid attorney and volunteers from the law school, so we could not extend a service for which these new Americans were probably much in need.

"To try and figure out why people weren't coming, I called together a meeting of key staff—department heads and outreach workers. We used a technique we had learned from a consultant to our mental health staff some years back: *force-field analysis*. First, we identified all the *constraining* forces—those we figured were the probable reason that we had not been successful in reaching these new populations. Here is the list we came up with:

Both new immigrant populations are family oriented, tending to depend on themselves and extended kinship networks rather than public institutions.

Neither group has had experience with the center and its programs, or understands how it can help them; it is foreign to their traditional patterns.

Staff have not attempted to redesign existing programs to accommodate to these patterns.

There are no Vietnamese or Arab staff members on the staffs of any of the center's programs, nor are any of the staff members conversant with the languages or cultural patterns of these two groups.

No representatives of these groups have been involved in program planning, development, and outreach; in fact, since few have received any service at all, there are no natural 'lay referral' agents out there.

"We then went over the list, identifying those items over which we had immediate and direct control, that is, those that we could do something about. We also identified those that would require some changes in the potential consumer population. Finally, we identified those resources we would need—like grants, new staff, consultants—in order to make the necessary changes.

"We then went through an identical process aimed at identifying the *driving* forces—those that could be used to support our efforts to expand or extend services to both groups. Our list included:

Staff and board commitment.

Real needs on the part of the potential client groups that were not being met anywhere else.

A presumed interest (based on our experience with other immigrant groups) on the part of both the Lebanese and Vietnamese to become integrated into the society, or at least to see their children integrated.

The potential availability of needed resources from government and United Way funders, from the nearby university, and from immigrant aid societies in other communities who have had some success in integrating and in serving both these national groups.

"Finally, we went through the process of identifying those forces we had control over and those we could influence. The next steps—designing outreach efforts, securing the needed resources, and program development—flowed naturally."

It is my impression that the agency administrator quoted made only partially adequate use of force-field analysis. He missed the boat on several counts. First, the process itself can be applied in a more sophisticated manner, accommodating much more information and assessing the potency and consistency of the forces identified, in addition to their amenability to manipulation. Second, he could have involved others, including representatives of the populations to be reached, in a parallel process. Third, by not being more specific about the problem(s) to be addressed and the specific objectives to be reached, the force-field analysis as described tended to be somewhat diffuse. I doubt that it really led "naturally" to the next steps he indicates. I suspect he and the staff had to do a good deal more to make the necessary transitions. Let's look at how FFA works.

### How Force-Field Analysis Works

**Step 1.**  Describe the problem or need in succinct terms.
**Step 2.**  Specify the goal or objective to be reached.
**Step 3.**  Identify all the restraining forces.
**Step 4.**  List the driving forces.
**Step 5.**  Estimate the potency, consistency, and amenability to change of each of the forces listed.
**Step 6.**  Now identify the actors you feel are best able to influence the forces that are amenable to change. Jot down their names.
**Step 7.**  Identify those forces you consider to be *working* forces, because they are high in potency, consistency, and amenability to change.
**Step 8.**  Now identify those you consider to be unpredictable forces, because they are uncertain as to amenability, potency, and consistency or because they are low in consistency.

You will find the force-field balance sheet (Figure 7–1) useful in recording your assessments.

Some of the terms I have used may seem like technical jargon. They are, but these terms are not difficult to learn. In force-field analysis, the term "critical actors" refers to those individuals or groups that must support a change effort or the maintenance of the status quo so that change becomes a reality or status quo remains one. This group may include funders, administrators, parents, informal leaders in the peer group, or any of a number of resource gatekeepers. "Facilitating actors" are of two types: those whose approval must be obtained before matters can be brought to the attention of critical actors and those whose approval, disapproval, or

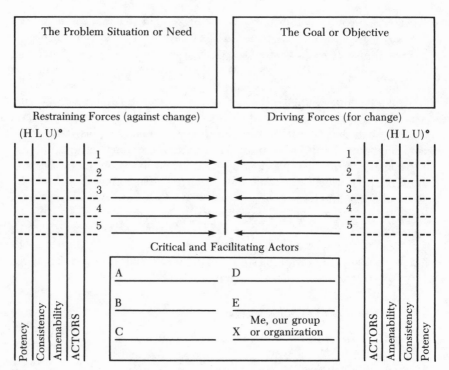

Critical and Facilitating Actors

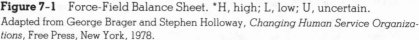

**Figure 7-1**    Force-Field Balance Sheet. *H, high; L, low; U, uncertain.
Adapted from George Brager and Stephen Holloway, *Changing Human Service Organizations*, Free Press, New York, 1978.

neutrality may have a decisive impact on critical actors. Distinguishing between these two categories may be helpful to you in the design of a marketing strategy.

"Forces" are to all those factors in both the internal and external environment that tend to prod an organism to shift directions or to maintain the status quo. These forces exist in "fields," essentially the environments we have been talking about, which can be mapped out using the force-field map. "Driving forces" are those that, when increased, alter the behavior of those affected in some desired or planned manner, whereas "restraining forces" are those that, when increased, reinforce the status quo or lead to continuation of a condition that is the antithesis of the change goal.

There may also be some "redundant forces" that either are not amenable to change or are not under the control of any of the critical actors. "Unpredictable forces" either are designated as uncertain in amenability to change, potency, or consistency, or are rated low in consistency. On the other hand, "working forces" are those judged to be moderately high in amenability, potency, and consistency. These are the principal forces to be modified or acted upon in a planned change effort. The greater the number of working forces on both sides of the force-field balance sheet, the greater the likelihood of successful intervention.

By "amenability to change or influence," I refer to a force's potential for modification, that is, for being *decreased* if it is a restraining force, or for being *increased* if it is a driving force. When a force is judged to be amenable to change, it is important to identify those facilitating and critical actors that can make a difference in the desired direction. "Consistency" indicates the extent to which a force is expected to remain stable over time, should there be no efforts at intervention. Finally, the term "potency" refers to the actual or potential impact of a force on maintaining the status quo, resisting change, or achieving the change goal. Here we are concerned with the force's potential strength, the extent of its influence, its power.

## Task Analysis

Task analysis, which I will be describing next, has a somewhat different origin and a very different use. As you will see, it can be used to define both staff and organizational tasks associated with marketing and program design. It emerged from an attempt made during World War II to categorize all the tasks performed in the newly created U.S. Air Force. The intent was to create job descriptions and to articulate them functionally so that the Air Force could perform its missions. Since then, task analysis has gone through a number of refinements. Some years ago, Sydney Fine, who had worked on the Air Force project, fashioned a national "task bank" in which some 600 tasks performed by staff members in public welfare agencies were categorized. Each task was defined in operational terms. The performance standards for that task were also indicated either in qualitative or numerical terms and the educational and experiential requirements for performing that task were identified.

A job, when properly designed, is composed of a number of tasks that are functionally interrelated. A work unit of several people in an organization would be considered functional if the tasks performed by group members are assigned so as to complement each other. By analogy, a work unit within an agency might perform its tasks best if it were functionally interrelated with other work units. And to take it a step further, service agencies or service programs would be functional if they performed their tasks appropriately in light of the tasks being performed by other programs and services in the community and nation. Those familiar with systems theory and operational analysis will recognize the schema.

Let's take a step back and reexamine what we mean by the term "task." Technically, a task is the smallest unit of work that can be described. The best way to identify a task is to think of the action verb that might be used to label it. Examples of action verbs include: writes, organizes, categorizes, types, counsels, and refers. The complete task statement requires more than an action verb, however. It requires that one specify:

1. Who
2. Does what
3. To whom and to what
4. With what (tool, instrument, technique, or method)
5. For what purpose
6. Under whose directions

If you forget that sequence, try remembering this: (1) the butler; (2) laces; (3) Mrs. Scarlet's tea; (4) with arsenic; (5) in order to do her in; (6) on behest of the upstairs maid.

An example of a marketing task might include the following: "The (1) market analyst (2) designs (3) an assessment strategy (4) using force-field analysis (5) for purposes of determining the constraints on and supports for an outreach effort (6) on instructions of the agency's executive committee." We might label this task according to its action verb, *designs*, but this might be too general. It might make more sense to label it *designing assessment strategy*. If we were using a task statement of this sort to assess current agency practice (the here and now), we might then identify current levels of performance as well as entry requirements for persons performing marketing tasks.

We might also use task analysis for purposes of normative assessment. If we were to define a set of desired performance criteria for marketing behaviors, we might then contrast *what is* against our perceptions of *what ought to be*. The same assessment tool can be applied to examining the functional relationships between departments within an organization, or agencies, programs, and services at the community level.

Like the task analysis approach within an agency that involves all staff members in the assessment process, analysis within a larger arena is best done when it includes representatives of those institutions and organizations that are likely to be affected by programmatic changes.

Remember, however, that this process works well only when there is consensus on the issues that are to be addressed and/or the approaches used to address those issues. When there is disagreement, it is often important to understand the forces that lead to conflicts of interest and how one might overcome those forces.

Let's eavesdrop on another example from practice.

### A Staff Group Becomes a Team

"We'd had time-and-motion problems around here for years. Everybody complained about the paperwork, and we didn't have enough time to see clients. It was about a year after we'd shifted to a more goal-oriented, somewhat behavioral orientation to treatment that Sally Margolis came up with the idea of using the same orientation to help organize staff members' activities so as to have greater payoff for the clients and the agency. That meant having a clear idea of what in the things we did was 'functional' and what was not.

"Sally had just come back from a national conference in which she sat in on a workshop conducted by Sydney Fine, who I guess invented functional job analysis. Sally's our staff development specialist. Her enthusiasm and her expertise are what helped us carry through the process of analyzing everybody's job and figuring out where and when the task might be best performed, and by whom. It wasn't an easy process. But it did have great payoff.

"The way it worked for us was that Sally and a small team (I was on it) interviewed everybody at the agency. We used a standard form and got everybody to spell out, in as precise terms as they could, the tasks that they performed. We learned from Fine's work that a task is the smallest unit of work that can be described. And to describe a task, you have to build it around an action verb, like 'counsels,' 'records,' 'reports,' or 'refers.' And then you have to build a sentence around that verb. Here's an example of a task statement from our agency's 'bank' of tasks.

> The adoption worker writes letters to adoptive parents confirming agency decisions to place a child in their home and informing them of the necessary procedures in order to provide them with the information needed to begin the adoption process, under direction of the adoption supervisor.

"Once you've written your task statement, the next challenge is to identify the educational or work or skill-level prerequisites for entry level into a job in which that task must be performed. Then you design performance criteria so as to evaluate the level at which the task is being performed. Those two steps are useful for a couple of reasons. First, they allow us both to screen applicants and to evaluate their performance while on the job. It helps the supervisor and the worker jointly to evaluate the worker's achievement and his or her skill and knowledge deficits. Second, it creates a framework for staff development and training. After we were through with the process of identifying all the tasks that were being performed in the agency, it was possible for Sally to involve a committee of staff in specifying where they felt we all had deficits, or to spell out the levels of performance they thought we all ought to be striving for.

"Actually, now that I think about it, task analysis did something else for us. It helped us to shift around tasks in relationship to competence and interest. As long as the tasks assigned to a work unit were performed, it didn't really matter who performed them. It became possible, therefore, for us to modify individual job descriptions. One of our foster care workers, for example, was really good at working the court system. She took on all the tasks related to the courts on behalf of all the workers in her unit. It saved everybody some time, gave her a lot of gratification and a lot of reward from the colleagues, and it made it possible for other workers to spend more time with foster parents and kids. Being goal-oriented, we discovered, wasn't only an individual process but was a group process as well."

As this vignette illustrates, task analysis is used primarily for assessing what staff do on the job and within the agency. But task statements can also be written to describe what should be done, how it should be done, and at what level of performance. Moreover, task statements can be grouped and regrouped into alternative arrangements, resulting in different kinds of job descriptions from those that the agency may currently be following. It is an extremely important tool for anyone intending to modify a service or to develop a new service or product line. It helps you determine what needs to be done and who should do it. It helps program managers to finish what they set out to do. And it is likely to be impressive to potential funders, particularly if the tasks described clearly articulate with the services promised in a project proposal or program outline.

But task analysis need not be used only with your internal publics or as a selling point with your external input publics. It can also be used as a way of spelling out the responsibilities of various partners or collaborators in the provision of services at the community level. The following vignette describes a system-wide use of task analysis.

### A Case-Management System of Linkages

"When I got the assignment of designing a case-management system for the agency, I thought that task had come at me from left field. Yet when I thought about it, I realized what a great opportunity it was to take a tool designed essentially for administrative purposes and to redesign it for community organization purposes. Here's what I did.

"I used the same kind of mapping sentence you use to spell out the tasks that are to be performed by individual workers. In this case, however, I spelled out the tasks to be performed by staff in different organizations and then grouped those tasks in a way in which each agency knew what its functional responsibilities were to be. In order to make sure I wasn't imposing anything on anybody, I tested my model out with representatives of each of the agencies to be involved with us. They made some suggestions for changes and improvements.

"The sticky point came when we had to identify performance criteria. That meant that each agency was going to have to agree to the criteria by which their involvement in the case-management process would be evaluated. It took a little give and take and some horse trading. But I think we came up with a workable system.

"I found the task analysis approach so helpful that I'm planning to use it next month to work out the joint responsibilities to be shared between six agencies for a multicounty media campaign to highlight the needs of the elderly and disabled."

It is also possible to use a simplified version of task analysis in family or group therapy, particularly where responsibilities for certain behaviors (such as cleaning house, shopping, initiating recreation activities) are either heavily lodged in a single person or unclear in terms of who has responsibility or jurisdiction. Members of a political or action coalition might also find task analysis useful as a way of specifying responsibility for parts of an action process.

## How Task Analysis Works

**Step 1.** Identify a task, the simplest unit of work you can describe. The easiest way to start is by thinking of an action verb and then asking who performs that action. Write the description of that task on the task statement form (Fig. 7–2, p. 140).

**Step 2.** Now specify the entry-level requirements for that job. For instance, "MSW with two years' experience, three years of work as a clerk typist, cheerful, empathic personality," and so on. Different tasks will require workers to have varying kinds of experiences or personal characteristics.

**Step 3.** Now specify the performance criteria. If a worker's task is to "receive, route, and transfer in telephone calls," the performance standards might be written in qualitative terms like "He's tactful and pleasant with callers"; "routes call correctly and promptly"; "does not leave the caller hanging or disconnect the caller prior to indicating that the call cannot be completed at this point." Each of these might further be quantified by ranking on a five-point scale from *highly acceptable* to *highly unacceptable* performance.

**Step 4.** Rate the task on the basis of any criteria you find helpful. We suggest *importance* (to the functioning of a unit or department), *frequency* (reflecting how often the task is expected to be performed), and *difficulty*.

**Step 5.** Complete similar statements for other tasks. Once all the tasks associated with a given person's work, or perhaps with all the staff in a given department or work unit, have been described, these tasks can be reclustered according to function. Such functions generally require the performance of a variety of tasks. Which task might be associated with outreach, fund raising, program evaluation, negotiations, or marketing services?

Let's explore the use of task analysis in the development of your organization's marketing strategy. What are the tasks associated with locating and relating the input publics who are most likely to supply the organization with needed resources? What tasks are associated with establishing collaborative relationship with potential competitors and collaborating agencies? What tasks are associated with building up public opinion in favor of a program, generating public support, or simply generating awareness about the existence of a problem or a population in need? What tasks

The Task

1. Who                               2. Performs what action

3. To whom or to what

4. Using what tools or methods

5. To what end or purpose

6. Under what directions or whose supervision

---

Entry-Level Qualifications or Requirements

_____    _____

_____    _____

_____    _____

---

Performance Criteria

_____    _____

_____    _____

_____    _____

How performance criteria will be rated _____

---

Task Rating (H = high, M = medium, L = low)
_____Importance    _____Frequency
_____Difficulty    _____Other criterion

**Figure 7-2**    Form for Describing a Task Statement

are associated with other promotional activities, such as advertising, preparing stories for the press, putting out a newsletter? And what tasks are associated with the design of a project proposal, its budget, and its evaluation procedures?

## Surveys

Now that we have had a chance to explore a number of alternatives, it is time to examine how and when survey instruments might best be used for assessment purposes. Before deciding to work on a survey, ask yourself the following questions: (1) Are the facts you need already available from other sources? (2) Could one of the other methods we have discussed yield the necessary information from targeted groups more effectively or efficiently? (3) Is the use of a survey likely to serve as a temporizing instrument to postpone or avoid action? (4) Can the survey be used to motivate or activate people as well as to yield information on which such action might be based?

Once you have answered those questions, you will have to decide for what purposes the survey might be used and who the respondents are to be. Those respondents are likely to participate if they believe that they are knowledgeable about the issues you are concerned with, and if they feel confident the information gathered will be put to good use with no danger of its harming them. Sometimes extrinsic inducements (like a payment in cash, grocery store coupons, or some other reward for completing a questionnaire) may be necessary to assure involvement. Promising to inform respondents of the results of a survey may be sufficient reward if they are already interested in the outcome and its uses.

Surveys are generally conducted through the use of questionnaires, and these may require that the respondent complete the questionnaire by checking appropriate boxes or writing in more open-ended responses. Even when the survey is conducted by telephone or in person, the surveyer gathering the information uses a questionnaire or schedule to guide the discussion. Once you have determined the reasons for using a survey procedure, the kind of information you are seeking to gather, and the population to whom the questionnaire is to be addressed, you will have to consider the extent to which those surveyed can understand the questions asked and have sufficient knowledge to answer them.

Respondents will also want to know why you are gathering the information and the use to which the information is to be put. If you are using the survey for purposes of market analysis and program planning, clients or potential clients may wish to be assured that their knowledge or their perspectives about their own needs and problems will be considered in the development of a new service or the expansion and modification of an existing one. Staff being surveyed may wish to be certain that their judgments, about the extent to which the work place provides a satisfying and motivating environment, will really be used in making changes.

Sometimes, surveys are used to determine how clients are being helped, how staff are allocating their efforts, or how programs and services are perceived by their various publics. Such information can be used for monitoring or adjusting rather than planning and development of programs. As with the other assessment techniques we have discussed, the questionnaire can also be used to evaluate programs by generating information on subject satisfaction or program outputs. In this chapter, however, we will concern ourselves primarily with the use of survey instruments for assessment purposes.

Questionnaires are extraordinarily versatile, both in their form and the way in which they are administered. As I noted earlier, surveys can be conducted through questionnaires, by telephone, and through interpersonal contact. They can be conducted with individuals or with groups. Mailed questionnaires are self-administered. Others are administered interpersonally. Respondents may be asked to complete (1) open-ended questions, after which a blank space is left so that the respondent or surveyor may write in the respondent's answer; (2) forced choice, in which respondents are required to check appropriate response categories; (3) or a mix of closed and open-ended questions.

The choice of format will depend on whether the questionnaire is to be self-administered, the kinds of information you are seeking, and the ease or difficulty in collating, summarizing, and grouping the information generated. Open-ended questions require less advance knowledge on your part about the kinds of responses that those questions are likely to elicit. You will find them most useful in generating information about subjects on which little is known or for which response categories may be difficult to anticipate. But they will cost you a great deal in terms of the time needed to analyze and summarize them. On the other hand, closed questions will yield data that are easily processed, lending themselves to categorizing and counting; but, because they force responses into narrow categories, they do not permit introduction of new information the assessor may not have thought to seek. Further, by suggesting responses they may lead the respondent away from his or her own answer. Examples of open-ended and closed questions are given in Figures 7–3 and 7–4.

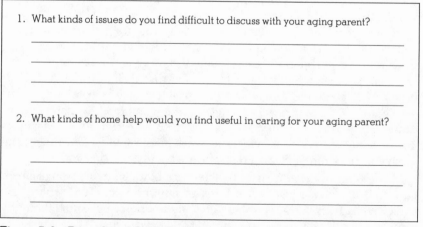

1. What kinds of issues do you find difficult to discuss with your aging parent?

2. What kinds of home help would you find useful in caring for your aging parent?

**Figure 7-3**   Examples of Open-Ended Questions

1.  Which kinds of home help would you find most useful?

    List in order of importance (1, 2, 3, 4).

    _____Home visiting, particularly when I have to be out of the house

    _____Meal preparation

    _____Taking my parent out shopping or on other trips into the community

    _____Para-nursing care

2.  How often do you need this help?

    a. Every day

       _____2 hours, _____4 hours, _____8 hours

    b. One day per week

       _____2 hours, _____4 hours, _____8 hours

    c. Two days per week

       _____2 hours per day, _____4 hours per day, _____8 hours per day

3.  Indicate the extent to which you agree or disagree with the following statements:

    a. The home visitor should be an elderly person.

       Strongly Agree_____, Agree_____, Disagree_____,

       Strongly Disagree_____

    b. The home visitor should always be the same person, rather than having the visits shared by different people with different expertise or time availability.

       Strongly Agree_____, Agree_____, Disagree_____,

       Strongly Disagree_____

**Figure 7-4**  Examples of Closed Questions

I have known a lot of people one might consider to be experts at marketing, who use surveys less for purposes of gathering information than for stimulating interest and generating commitments. In effect, they use surveys to inform people about the potential of a given service, or to generate demand for it. The three following vignettes are illustrative.

### A Continuing Education Survey

"To tell you the truth, I had a pretty good idea about what people were willing to buy and not buy. The problem was that people were not accustomed to coming to this university for continuing education. I was concerned about several things. First, I wanted them to know we were about to start a new service. Secondly, I wanted them to feel that we really cared about their inputs into that service so that their image of who we were and how we dealt with them might be changed. Third, I wanted them to begin to think, or to imagine themselves involved in one of our continuing education activities, in effect softening them up for the brochure we would be mailing out at a future date. Finally, I wanted to identify people who might be willing to take some responsibility for recruiting later on down the line, and perhaps for organizing advisory groups that might further be involved in program development some time in the future.

"So when I designed the questionnaire, I made sure that it not only stimulated their interest about the subject matter of C.E. but got them involved in telling us about the kinds of people they felt we should be using as instructors and specialists. Moreover, I queried them on the kinds of facilities and other externals that I thought might be attractive. Finally, I included a bunch of questions related to what I thought might be the most important motivator: what they would be able to do with their continuing education. These questions had to do with their career interests: like moving up the administrative line, being able to perform treatment more effectively, shifting from child welfare to work with the aging, getting a grant or other sources of funding, and so on."

### Spouse Abuse

"We knew that most of the women coming to our shelter were married to men who worked at the Ford plant or whose husbands were laid off from that plant. And we knew that there was a lot of hostility about our agency in that plant. We were seen by many of the men at the plant as people who were kidnapping their wives and kids, and that perception was pretty widespread, even among those men whose family relationships were no problem at all. And we also knew that there was a move on to find the address of the shelter and spread the word about where we were. This would leave many of our clients in danger, in fact putting our whole operation in jeopardy. We had to do something. Shelters that are easy for abusive spouses to locate are hardly safe.

"And we decided to do it by moving right in where we were likely to meet the greatest amount of hostility. Instead of calling meetings of workers and explaining our position, something that would be likely to generate hostility that we might not be able to handle properly, we decided to give them an opportunity to vent their hostility, ask their questions, and to participate with us in trying to find some solutions to the problems that some of the men and their co-workers faced. That is why we decided to do the telephone survey.

"We started off by asking what they knew about the shelter, giving them a chance to ventilate, giving us an opportunity to determine where their perceptions were on target or off base. We then asked a bunch of close-ended questions, in which they could spell out their preferences about how abused wives or abusing husbands might be helped, what concerns should be considered in dealing with the children involved, and how husbands and wives might be helped to solve their own problems with a minimum of external interference.

"You would be amazed about how rapidly the atmosphere around the plant in relation to our services changed. And you would be amazed at how much we learned, incidentally, about how we were viewed in the community, and how the whole issue of spouse abuse is viewed. We even uncovered a number of incidents of spouse abuse aimed at husbands, issues we had not been aware of before, and around which we began to offer a new service."

## Arousing the Neighborhood

"It has been my experience that people in low-income neighborhoods have sometimes been surveyed to death. They not only are tired of being studied by university students, but they are pretty skeptical and suspicious about outsiders coming in and asking them questions. What's even more problematic is that many of them find it difficult to articulate in words what their true feelings are. This is especially so when there are language barriers, because of ethnic or cultural differences, between those conducting the survey and those who are asked to respond. Some people think better in terms of pictures and images than they do in words. That is why we decided to use photographs when we go into a new neighborhood.

"Here is how it works. Two of our staff, generally guided by one or two neighborhood residents with whom we have established relationships, walk around the community taking photographs. We zero in on issues that we know are going to be viewed as problems: areas where there are lots of garbage, broken lights, ripped-out telephone booths, uncomfortable or unsheltered bus stops, broken steps on the houses, and so on. We also focus on places where buildings are particularly close together or where homes are adjacent to public buildings like schools and businesses. And then we turn our camera on some of the characteristics of the neighborhood that we figure are likely to be positively evaluated: a pocket park, a popular meeting spot like a beauty parlor or bar, and so on. Finally, we take photographs in other neighborhoods, sometimes adjacent ones, of images that we think are likely to produce positive responses.

"We then print the photographs, and select the ones that we think represent images of what people might think of as a good community and those that they might think of as problems to be overcome. We paste these up on our questionnaire form and develop a bunch of questions for each image. Once the questionnaire is constructed, we photocopy it so that the photo image and the questions appear adjacent to each other. Then when we go out into the neighborhood, we can show our respondents the pictures, ask them the questions we have, and show them how we are writing in their responses right next to the image. Eventually, we generate a new picture: a picture of what people in the neighborhood perceived to be the image they would like to aim toward, and an image of the kind of issues or problems they would like to address or overcome.

"What I found is that this approach generates greater information than we might have gotten if we used only words and no pictures. It also gets people thinking and ready to act. When we call our community meetings and organize our block clubs, we have already got beginning agendas on which to move. Now I know that some of my more scientific friends might be a little bit skeptical about my methods. Sure, there is a danger of skewing the results by the pictures you have selected for people to respond to. That is hardly the issue. For me the issue has to do with perception, perception has to do with motivation, and motivation has to do with action. I see it all interrelated."

These are examples of interactive survey assessments, in which participants may not only interact in responding to the questionnaire but are expected to interact with each other and with the assessors around other issues: program planning and design, participation in these programs, focus and demand. The following list gives the steps you should follow in constructing and conducting the survey.

*How Surveys Work*

Step 1.    Decide what you want to find out, from whom you want to find it out, and what kind of survey you want to use.
Step 2.    Decide for what other purposes (besides generating needed information) the survey is to be used.
Step 3.    Design and pretest your survey instrument, sometimes involving potential respondents in the process of design and/or in the pretest. Modify your survey instrument as required.
Step 4.    Conduct the survey.
Step 5.    Edit, collate, and code the responses.
Step 6.    Summarize those responses in a report and distribute it to the appropriate publics.

Now it is your turn. Complete Exercises 7–1 and 7–2.

---

**EXERCISE 7-1**
## Designing an Assessment Strategy

1. Select a marketing issue or problem that requires assessment before action can be taken. Pick a real issue, one that is of concern to an agency or other organization with which you are affiliated.
    Think about each of the tools you met in this chapter. Consider also the eco-mapping technique you were introduced to in Chapter 4 and any other assessment tools you are familiar with. Which of these might yield significant information? With which publics should they be used; i.e., from whom should you gather the information and who should be involved in the process of information retrieval?

2. Design an assessment strategy. Be sure to include use of all tools that are relevant and to specify in what order or for what purpose
*continued*

## EXERCISE 7-1 continued

they are to be used. What publics are to be addressed? What do you want to find out? What will you do with the information?

Should the assessment process focus on here-and-now, anticipatory, or normative issues? All three? Who will conduct the assessment process? How long will it take?

In addition to generating information, what other purposes do you have in mind for the particular tool or tools you selected? What are the possible unanticipated consequences of using these tools? If some of the consequences are potentially negative, how can you minimize the dangers?

## EXERCISE 7-2
### Conducting an Assessment Process

1. Select one of the tools you have determined to include in the assessment strategy. Prepare the tool for use, following the instructions in the chapter or guidance you have received from other sources like colleagues or the literature.

2. Conduct a test run of the assessment process with this tool. To do this, conduct it with a small number of respondents for two purposes: to get the bugs out of the instrument so that it may subsequently be used with a larger respondent population; and to gain experience and beginning mastery over the tool.

3. On the basis of this experience, how might you modify the instrument you designed? Would you use it with the population for which you had originally planned it? Do you need more experience before using it "for real"? Does your experience with the tool suggest some needed modification in the strategy you designed for Exercise 7-1? If so, make the changes.

## Review

The assessment process in strategic marketing can be aimed at output, input, and through-put publics. It can focus on here-and-now, anticipatory, or normative concerns. Five assessment tools were presented in some detail: the nominal group technique, the Delphi conference, force-field analysis, task analysis, and the survey method. NGT is particularly useful when small numbers of key informants are brought together. It uses a structured approach to elicit priorities, guarantees each participant equal access to the process, and minimizes the effect of group think. Delphi can be used for similar purposes. By means of an interactive questionnaire, it acquires the advantage of involving persons who cannot or should not be brought together, at least for part of the assessment and decision-making process.

Force-field analysis involves participants in identifying the restraining forces that militate against change and those driving forces that can be activated for purposes of change. These forces are mapped out in such a way as to provide the assessors with insights into the potency, consistency, and amenability to change of each of the forces identified. Task analysis zeroes in on the smallest unit of work that can be easily described. It can be used in assessing what internal and external publics do or ought to be doing and what standards should govern their behavior. Survey techniques, like the other tools described, can be used both to generate needed information and to activate or prepare respondents for subsequent action. Examples are given of open-ended and closed questionnaires and of their uses with a variety of publics in person or through the mails and by telephone.

Any of these tools can be used alone or in tandem with one another. NGT might yield a number of problems that key publics would judge to require action. A survey might then be conducted to determine the scope of the problem(s). A Delphi questionnaire might then be mounted with outside consultants for purposes of identifying desirable programs through which the problems might be addressed. FFA might be used to analyze the forces that restrain action or that might be activated to implement the desired program. Task analysis might then be used to specify the responsibilities of key actors for the required intervention process.

# 8 DESIGNING THE PROGRAM

PROGRAM DESIGN in the human services is often depicted by academics as both a rational and a normative process. It is both, but, as the former student quoted below suggests, something is missing: the connection between a conceptual framework and a guide to action. This chapter offers no adequate solution to this problem, but it may help you to use some of the rational and normative tools available to you more fully in all aspects of the planning and marketing processes: assessment, promotions, fund raising, and so on. Let's start by examining the perspective found in much of the literature and in many graduate curricula.

## It's Different When You Get Out in the Real World

"I learned a lot about program design while working on my masters degree— or so I thought. I learned about chart making, about careful problem analysis and definition, about goal setting. It's what you call the rational model. It's not a bad model. It gives you something to strive for.

"But once on the job, it was like I never learned it at all. The model stayed in my notes. I found myself ad hocing like mad. It was six months before I remembered that there were a couple of tools I learned in school that might be useful. I don't know how typical my experience is, but I must say, something was missing somewhere. It's different when you get out in the real world."

According to the normative model found in much of the planning literature, the process should begin with someone's awareness of a problem situation or of a more desirable state of affairs. The problem is studied and defined by those who take on the responsibility for planning. Goals are selected and translated into subgoals or operational objectives. All relevant alternative means of achieving those objectives are then examined and weighed against each other. Choices are made between alternative program components on the basis of feasibility, likelihood of yielding results at an acceptable cost, and so on. A monitoring and feedback system is generally included, so that corrections can be made if the process gets off course or if the targeted goals prove to be illusive or unattainable.

The implementation of the program is also monitored, and its procedures and outputs are evaluated at some point predetermined by the planners or their sponsors. You will find this model expressed in various ways in the writings of Kahn, Gilbert and Specht, Perlman and Gurin, Lauffer, and others. There is nothing wrong with this model, if we perceive it as a model instead of a description of reality. Critics of the rational model point out that it reduces the complexity of the planning process to a series of steps that do not conform with political realities, that choices between all conceivable alternatives are not possible because these can never be known. The planning process itself "alters alternatives" as means and ends become intertwined. Proponents of an "incrementalist" approach to planning, like Lindblom and his followers, suggest that we can at best tinker at the edges, making modest changes in response to opportunities that present themselves or that we can promote through our actions.

This incrementalist approach is supported by those who argue for a transactive or developmental approach to planning and design. Here, face-to-face interactions, interpersonal exchanges, become the key to arriving at mutual understanding in the adjustment of interests. These, in turn, lead to the emergence of consensus and of activities that lead through a process of mutual adjustment toward the achievement of agreed-upon objectives. This perspective is found in the writings of planners like John Friedmann and organizational development specialists like Havelock, Lippitt, Mann, Niehoff, and Likert.

Charles Perrow challenges the rational model further by pointing out that there tends to be a difference between an organization's stated goals, or program objectives, and the actual functions the organization performs for its key publics. Those functions may be to regulate certain publics, to absorb part of the work force, or to provide resources to organizations, frequently at the public expense. Yet its stated goals are to "rehabilitate," "train," or "improve social conditions." Stated goals and objectives, he argues, may be more important for securing funding and elite support than for achieving objectives on the behalf of populations in need and for legitimizing an organization's efforts, even when those efforts may have little to do with goal achievement.

The *strategic marketing* approach can accommodate all these perspectives; it recognizes the interdependence of agencies with their key internal and external publics. Although information is likely to be limited, and decision makers are fallible, the market nevertheless aims at rationality by accommodating the often divergent interests of these various publics.

The planning process can begin at any point in the chain of events and activities. Thus, while engaging in promotions (a step the rational planners might identify with implementation), the strategic marketer may actually be assessing needs and setting the stage for increased public awareness. This, in turn, may lead to support for action plans or programs. The exploration of such issues as *place* and *price* may lead to the design of services for which demand may be promoted. The nature of the program to be established will be shaped by the various publics that become partners in its development or conduct. It can also be shaped by suppliers on whom the agency is dependent for clients, funds, or other essential resources.

In this chapter, we will be testing out a fairly straightforward and rational approach to problem solving. It suffers from all the faults suggested above, but it has one advantage: it can be learned and shared with others. In no way a total planning process, it is perhaps no more than a structured idea inventory. Consider this approach one way of getting started and perhaps of increasing the likelihood that you will bear in mind much of what both the proponents and critics of rational planning suggest. The process begins with problem definition and concludes with an examination of intervention alternatives. Issues pertaining to implementation, monitoring, and evaluation will be dealt with in other chapters.

## Defining the Problem

Sometimes, "defining the problem" is the problem. In Chapter 7, we explored the use of a number of assessment tools including surveys, eco-mapping, and the use of force-field analysis for specifying problems to be acted on. We also explored the difference between here-and-now, anticipatory, and normative assessment. What we didn't discuss were the twin possibilities that the problem may be improperly defined or misunderstood. The problem of problem definition may have serious consequences for any kind of marketing program. I'll share three examples with you.

As a graduate student, my brother-in-law was involved in a study of freeway traffic between Detroit and its suburbs. Serious bottlenecks were a daily occurrence during rush hours, between 7:30 and 9:00 A.M. or between 4:00 and 5:00 P.M. Accidents were on the rise, commuters were complaining, and some were threatening to move their businesses out of the inner city.

With a grant from the highway authority, my brother-in-law's university began a study on how to get cars in and out of Detroit without massive new highway expenditures. The goal was to reduce the number of traffic jams, accidents, and frazzled nerves. "That's where we failed," my brother-in-law explained to me. "We had defined the problem incorrectly. The issue wasn't how many cars we could get in and out of Detroit efficiently. The issue was how many people can be moved in and out at a relatively low cost and with a reduction in accidents and frazzled nerves." Had the problem been defined that way, new options "including commuter trains and commuter buses" could have been examined. "But then," he added, "I guess we wouldn't have been doing the study in Detroit."

General Electric (G.E.) faced a similar kind of problem several years ago in one of its major corporate divisions. The influx of low-cost radios from Japan and Hong Kong were undercutting G.E.'s ability to market its own radios. Several other radio manufacturing firms had already gone under. At first, G.E. determined to find a way of reducing either competition from abroad or the cost of its own manufacturing efforts. Both problem definitions limited the options for action, and many alternative solutions were being precluded.

When G.E. instituted a new approach called "strategic planning," it was able to specify what it was really concerned about. This required divorcing itself from its preconceived notions and commitments to current operations—such as manufacturing radios. The problem, redefined, was *how to distribute radios* to the American public at a profit. Once so defined, the operational options become relatively broad. G.E. eventually opted for discontinuing its manufacturing operations in the United States. It currently manufactures abroad, purchases products from its former competitors, and distributes at a substantial profit in the United States.

Let's look at a comparable situation in a social service agency. "The problem," a colleague recently confided, "is how to keep the address of the safe house unknown, so that abusive husbands won't come there and threaten their wives and children, yet sufficiently known that battered wives can go there for safety." "Wrong," I responded. "The problem is to assure the safety of abused wives and children. Now let's see what we need to do in order to assure achievement of our safety goals." Suddenly, a wide variety of new options were available to us: community education, telephone alert systems, friendly visiting by former abusers to current abusers.

In each of the examples given, either the original problem was unimaginatively phrased or the planners and program designers had moved too rapidly toward the specification of the problem. Rather than examine the general problem and then go to specific problems that might be attacked operationally, they moved directly to a specific problem without the benefit of having explored alternative problem definitions.

Once the problem has been defined, it must be broken down into its components parts as well as described in sufficient detail to be acted upon. If your concern is with preventing delinquent behavior, you would not want to gather data on everything known about delinquency. The agency's previous history and its missions may limit the range of interventions possible. Other limitation are imposed by the expectations of relevant publics, the resources available, the consensus environment around a particular issue, or the target population to be served.

The more that is known about the *local* manifestation of a problem, the more likely your intervention will be properly targeted. You need not limit yourself to localized information or to your own information-gathering activities. A great deal of information may already be available in agency reports, government statistics, and newspaper articles. On any given problem, there is likely to have been considerable research conducted elsewhere; don't hesitate to hit the library and to review journal articles. Going into the literature may also be helpful in clarifying your understanding of the problem.

## Selecting Goals and Objectives: The Development of Strategy

A goal, according to *Webster's New Collegiate Dictionary*, is the "end of a journey," the termination point that is aimed at. As the Detroit-area freeway experience suggests, goals are directly related to problem statements. The problem statement tells us where we are; the goal statement tells us where we want to go. The more specific the problem statement, the more explicit the goal statement. In order to plan our trip, it may be necessary to schedule a number of stops along the way. These stops are the objectives, essentially subgoals defined in operational terms. One of the objectives in the freeway plan might be:

> to double the number of people who can be conveyed into the inner city during the hours of 8:00 to 8:45 A.M., without an increase in accidents or reports of frazzled nerves, within the next 18 months.

To state an objective in operational terms, you will have to consider who or what is to be changed, in which way, at what level, and in which time period. In effect, the objective is a specification of outcomes in measurable terms. The goal of Goodwill Industries, for example, is to increase the independence of disabled people. The objectives of one of its projects may be to: (1) place 40 disabled adults in jobs within a 12-month period and (2) double the number of disabled people who can live independently in their own homes in this same period. It may be necessary to achieve some objectives before others can be reached, whereas in other situations, objectives must be achieved in tandem. The selection of objectives and their sequencing or their clustering are, therefore, strategic decisions.

## From Objectives to Intervention Alternatives

The objectives we have just defined may be gained in many ways. If the presenting problem was defined as a lack of service to a given population, the goals and objectives may lead to the consideration of a number of service alternatives. If the problem was couched in terms of lack of public support, the intervention alternatives may include a variety of political tactics: lobbying, community education, and other promotional campaigns. There are always more intervention possibilities available than we can take advantage of. Unfortunately, we are all too often unaware of them. Like some G.E. executives, we may tend to be limited by tunnel vision and focus only on doing better what we are used to doing, whether it is producing radios or counseling pregnant teenagers. We will shortly examine the use of a branching-tree exercise intended to generate a wide range of alternatives, but no planning tool is a substitute for experience.

The experiences need not be yours or your colleagues'. These should not be discounted, but can be complemented and supplemented by the experiences of others. Although we can learn much from others, their experiences, unfortunately, are not so easily retrievable. Some may be recorded in what is referred to as "fugitive" literature: newspaper descriptions, papers presented at professional conferences, and unpublished project reports.

You almost need to "know someone who knows someone" in order to locate the information you are seeking from such a source. However, there are a number of search services and information-disseminating organizations through which you may be able to locate some of this literature. A reference librarian may be the first person you should talk to. Check with your public library, a local community college, or perhaps the librarian of a school of social work or a school of business at a nearby university. It may be possible for the library to conduct a computerized search for you at a relatively low cost. The librarian can teach you how to make your information request so that you don't shoot in the dark.

You may already have access to a number of search services. For example, if you work in the field of aging, you may have had experience getting information from Project SCAN at the National Clearing House on Aging. If not, write to Project SCAN, P.O. Box 231, Silver Spring, MD 20907 for information on programs as varied as transportation for the elderly or home-based nutrition services. Alternatively, you can call them at their toll-free number (800 638-2051) and speak to an information officer who will do a computer search on the projects dealing with the problem you are concerned with. These projects will generally have been identified as successful models by referent panels in their own states.

Project SHARE at P.O. Box 2309, Rockville, MD 20952, regularly publishes annotated bibliographies of reports and other documents that rarely become available commercially. It also commissions and publishes periodic monographs on issues of direct interest to those managing and planning human services.

If you have asked a federal agency for an information packet relating to its grants programs, chances are that you will receive not only the application forms and guidelines but also brief descriptions of projects that have been funded in recent years. Sometimes these are in the form of single-page descriptions; at other times they are bound in books of funded projects over a two- or three-year period. Search through them; identify those projects that are most likely to be similar to that which you are planning and from which you might learn something; then contact the project director by telephone or through the mails.

What other search services are available to you or your organization? Are there staff at the national association with which your agency is affiliated who can get you started? Are there consultants in your own locale who can be helpful?

Whether you get outright help or not, the work of exploring alternatives and deciding between or among them will still have to be done by you, your colleagues, and perhaps others such as task force and board members. Exercise 8–2, further on, should be helpful.

### Identifying the Possible: Using the Branching Tree Exercise

In the two exercises that follow, you will have an opportunity to test out an approach to identifying all the possible components of a program. These exercises are far from a complete planning system. They can, however, help you structure the brainstorming process that often takes place prior to the development of a program proposal or plan. Do Exercise 8–1 first.

---

**EXERCISE 8-1**

### General Problem Identification

1. Begin by determining the kind of problem you are going to be dealing with. In the checklist below, three categories of problems are identified: *Type A, those lodged in a particular population*, e.g., an agency staff (throughput public), a client population (output public), or those who provide the agency with needed resources (an input public), such as the citizens in a given area whose support is necessary to achieve an objective; *Type B, those clearly related to service delivery* or some part of the service system that is unavailable, inaccessible, ineffective, inefficient, or unresponsive; and *Type C*, those that are *lodged in relationships* between providers, between suppliers and providers, or between providers and consumers—relationships that are characterized by inadequate resources, lack of continuity, or lack of comprehensiveness.

Check the types and subtypes of problems that you are interested in addressing. Focus on a specific situation of concern to you

*continued*

## EXERCISE 8-1 continued

(e.g., services to the aged, community involvement in fund-raising, or safety for women).

| Type A | Type B | Type C |
|---|---|---|
| *Problems in a Population* | *Problems in Service Delivery* | *Problems in Relationships* |
| Lack of knowledge | Unavailable | Inadequate flow of resources |
| Lack of skill | Inaccessible | |
| Debilitating attitude | Ineffective | Lack of continuity |
| | Inefficient | Lack of comprehensiveness |
| | Unresponsive | |

2. Now, in narrative form, describe the problem or problems you wish to address. Be as specific as you can, using the descriptive terms from the checklist above. List all those problems that you think your organization is or should be concerned with.

Now read through the instructions and follow the example in Exercise 8–2 (the branching tree). A second suggestion for conducting this exercise is found after the Review section at the end of this chapter. It deals with the problem of interagency linkage and exchange.

## EXERCISE 8-2
### The Branching Tree Program Design Exercise

*Step 1. Problem Identification*

Now take the general statement you jotted down in step 2 of the previous exercise and identify each of the individual problems that made up the statement. Some of them might be Type A, some Type B or C. In the example below, I've listed each of the problems that a planner for Council on Aging included in his statement. Note that the problem type is identified at the right. I took these from his checklist in step 1 of the previous exercise.

Use a blank piece of paper, and follow the format shown below. You may have to do some investigating to check out the dimensions of the problem: Who is affected? To what extent? Who is aware of the problem and who is concerned?

| Problem 1 | $P_1$ | People in the community are generally unaware of how many of the community's elderly are isolated socially and from needed services. | *Probable Problem Type* <br> *A*, knowledge |
|---|---|---|---|

*continued*

## EXERCISE 8-2 *continued*

| | | | |
|---|---|---|---|
| Problem 2 | $P_2$ | Many of the elderly are having difficulty with personal management, especially those who are single. | $A$, possibly all 3? |
| Problem 3 | $P_3$ | Services to the isolated elderly are generally inaccessible or unavailable. | $B$, availability, accessibility $C$, resources? |
| Problem 4 | $P_4$ | The attendance at a congregate meal site is not up to capacity. | $A$, possibly all 3? $B$, accessibility? responsiveness? $C$, flow of client referrals? |

### Step 2.    Problem Specification

Having investigated the problem, break it down into its component parts, identifying those that are appropriate to your organization and those that might fit into another organization's mandate or sphere of activity. On a preliminary basis, it may be possible to do this by exploring the problem's dimensions with other staff at the agency, with an interagency group, or with a task force comprised of people representing resource suppliers, legitimators, consumers, and providers.* For exercise purposes, you might try spelling out the components of the problem by relying on information you already have at your disposal.

If you were taking Problem 2, for example, you might break it down as follows into Problem 2, components 1, 2, 3, etc. They would be labeled $P_{2.1}$, $P_{2.2}$, $P_{2.3}$, and so on. Which of these might be Type A-related? Types B or C?

| | | | |
|---|---|---|---|
| $P_2$ | Many of the elderly are having difficulty with personal management, especially those who are single. | $P_{2.1}$ | Nutritional deficiencies are particularly severe in rural areas. |
| | | $P_{2.2}$ | Poor management of personal budgets |
| | | $P_{2.3}$ | Poor housekeeping; inability to handle repairs |
| | | $P_{2.4}$ | Inability to get around both inside the home and in the community |

*See Chapter 1 for assessment tools you might find helpful in exploring dimensions of the problem.

*continued*

## EXERCISE 8-2 continued

### Step 3.   Goal Determination

Take each of the more specific problems and determine the goals to be reached.

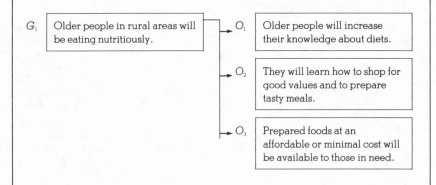

$P_{2.1}$ | Nutritional deficiencies are particularly severe in rural areas. → $G_1$ | Older people in rural areas will be fed nutritious meals.

### Step 4.   Rephrasing Goals in Terms of Operational Objectives

Take each of the goal statements and examine the possible objectives that flow from each. These can be written in measurable terms later.

$G_1$ | Older people in rural areas will be eating nutritiously.

$O_1$ | Older people will increase their knowledge about diets.

$O_2$ | They will learn how to shop for good values and to prepare tasty meals.

$O_3$ | Prepared foods at an affordable or minimal cost will be available to those in need.

### Step 5.   Exploration of Alternative Interventions and Services

Take each objective for every goal statement, and spell out the possible service or other intervention alternatives that might lead to achievement of those objectives. If the services or other interventions are clearly not feasible, eliminate them; *but don't be too quick* to eliminate possibilities. Premature decisions may rule out some alternatives that should have been considered. You can always eliminate them later.

In considering feasibility, the following might be important variables: public acceptance, costs in dollars or in personnel (paid or volunteer), possible sources of supply, needed facilities and equipment, the extent to which your agency might be able to conduct the program independently or the extent to which partners might be needed, the possibility of involving the right partners in the service. You might also want to consider the extent to which there might be opposition to the service from within the agency or elsewhere, and what might be needed to overcome resistance. To what extent are the service possibilities acceptable to potential service recipients? Will the answer vary for different segments of the potential consumer population?

*continued*

## EXERCISE 8-2 *continued*

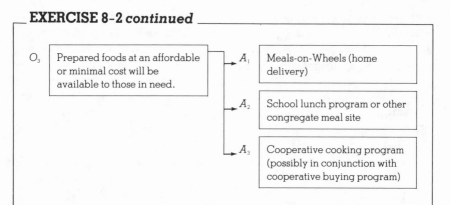

### Step 6.   *Identification of Required Intervention Components*

Each of these services requires sets of activities that might be defined as intervention or service components and include complexes of activities and resources needed to put a service into operation. Spell out the components for each potential alternative intervention.

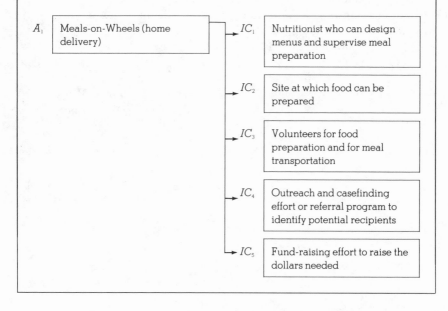

The branching tree program design exercise is a written *idea inventory* or *brainstorming* activity. It is a relatively simple procedure, although it may take quite some time to carry out. Like other rational or normative models, it is best used to explore all of the possibilities before you. It starts with problem definition (something you are ready to do now that you've completed the first exercise), then breaks down each general problem into its component parts. For each subproblem, a goal is selected, and this goal is used to generate operational objectives. There may be a number of alternative interventions (like service programs) that can be used to achieve a given objective. Sometimes, several interventions in tandem may be necessary. Once you have identified these alternatives, the final step is to identify the components of each intervention (i.e., what has to be done or put into place in order to realize it).

Figure 8-1 is an example of a branching tree program design.

Space did not permit extending the branches. In looking over the example, you will find that the longest branch is $P_1$–$P_{1.2}$–$G_1$–$O_1$–$A_2$–$IC_1 + IC_2 + IC_3$. Had all the branches, starting with $P_1$ and $P_2$, been shown fully, we would have ended up with several hundred intervention components. You will need a great deal of writing space to do Exercise 8-2. Many people who have done this exercise have used blackboards or newsprint. Agency administrators and others involved in program planning tend to prefer newsprint. It can be saved for continued examination. The chalkboard, on the other hand, has the advantage of being easy to erase, so that branches or directions can be redesigned.

Before doing the exercise, look over the schematic guide (Fig. 8-2). Now read through the exercise, as I suggested earlier. Beginning with one or more of the problems you identified in Exercise 8-1, follow the instructions given. You may wish to complete the activity with others: members of the planning committee or action group, staff members in your work unit, the agency's executive committee, fellow students, etc. Many of the exercises in the book are most useful when done jointly with others. They

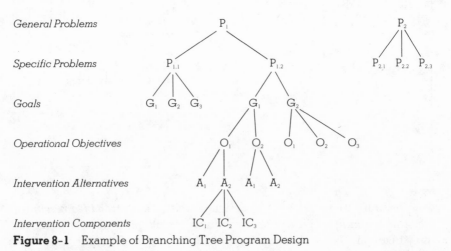

**Figure 8-1**   Example of Branching Tree Program Design

Adapted from Armand Lauffer, *Grantsmanship*, Sage Publications, Beverly Hills, Calif., 1984. Adapted by permission.

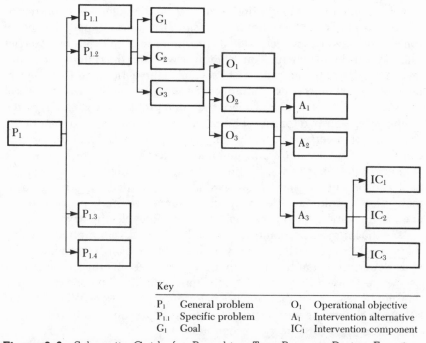

Key

| | | | |
|---|---|---|---|
| $P_1$ | General problem | $O_1$ | Operational objective |
| $P_{1.1}$ | Specific problem | $A_1$ | Intervention alternative |
| $G_1$ | Goal | $IC_1$ | Intervention component |

**Figure 8-2** Schematic Guide for Branching Tree Program Design Exercise. Using the sample track as a guide, design your own branching tree specifying all the choices possible. Note that space limitation does not permit tracking from more than one antecedent in each component or branch below.

are, after all, intended as intervention tools that can be used in the marketing process, and that process requires the involvement of many persons. Who should be involved with you in doing the exercise?

## Selecting from Among Alternatives

"Wow," you may be thinking, "on completing this exercise, we will have generated six or seven hundred alternative intervention components. How in the world will we choose among them?" You're quite right. There are many alternatives, but choosing from among them may not be so difficult. You may find the following judgment criteria to be useful: (1) frequency of appearance, (2) feasibility, (3) complementarity with organizational mission, (4) likelihood of contributing to goals and objectives without negative side effects or consequences, (5) acceptability to various publics, and (6) compatibility.

Almost all practitioners and students who have completed Exercise 8–2 have discovered an interesting phenomenon. Certain intervention components tend to appear frequently at the ends of different branches. On one tree, for example, you might find components—like counseling, outreach, transportation, volunteer training, or support groups—appearing many times. Any one of these components may appear at the ends of branches that have different origins. You might discover that the training of volunteers contributes to the conduct of several interventions, to the achievement of several objectives, perhaps even to the accomplishment of several goals and to the resolution of more than one problem. If you can, as the saying goes, "kill two [or more] birds with a single stone," why not do it? Training volunteers won't be the only thing that needs doing, but it may contribute to the accomplishment of many objectives.

*Feasibility* refers to the likelihood that a particular program component can be put in place. How available are needed resources such as money and credit, facilities, trained or committed staff, political influence, organizational and personnel time and energy, legitimacy?

Are the intervention components you have tentatively selected compatible with the organization's history and sense of *mission*? Or are they such wide departures from the norm that they are likely to either generate resistance or move the organization into new and untried paths for which it may not be ready? Are they functional for the organization? Will they contribute to achievement of its program missions? Its staff and board aspirations? Its need for resources and community support?

Some program components, although rated high on feasibility and frequency of appearance, may nonetheless contribute little to the achievement of program *goals* that are considered paramount. In such cases, they may divert the organization from investing its energies and other resources where they count the most. Even those that do contribute directly to the achievement of *objectives* may lead to undesired side effects or have unanticipated consequences: A one-time food distribution effort may generate such high demand that the agency may find itself permanently in the food business although that was never its intention. A volunteer program, once established, may place demands on the paid professional staff for support and ongoing training to such a degree that little time is left for staff to do what they prefer, work directly with clients.

There is also the question of *acceptability*. Are the program components acceptable to various key publics: agency funders, clients, board members? If not, are they likely to generate conflict or just indifference? Can you live with the indifference, deal with the conflict? Are other components so clearly acceptable that they will overcome disagreements over those that are not?

Finally, there is the question of the *compatibility* of one component to another. For example, in the Detroit freeway case, establishing a bus lane that reduces the lanes accessible to cars might be incompatible with widening or increasing the numbers of exit ramps. Clearly, some goals and some objectives may have to be put aside if others are to be adopted.

You may find Table 8–1 helpful in making decisions about intervention components. Should you find that a component is rarely present, and

**TABLE 8-1   Program-Component Decision-Making Guide**

|  | High | Somewhat | Low or Minimal |
|---|---|---|---|
| 1. Frequency of appearance |  |  |  |
| 2. Feasibility |  |  |  |
| 3. Complementarity with missions |  |  |  |
| 4. Contribution to goals/objectives |  |  |  |
| 5. Acceptability |  |  |  |
| 6. Compatibility |  |  |  |

judge it to be unfeasible and in any case not complementary to the organization's missions, you might eliminate it from consideration. If an item is rated high on all or almost all the variables, you might consider it seriously. When an item scores high on some, and zero or minimal on others, more careful examination will be necessary. An outreach program aimed at teen-age substance abusers may be right on target (*high*) on contributions to objectives and on feasibility; however, it may be *low* on complementarity, and it may be *low* on acceptability to some of the organizations' constituencies. What to do? There is no universal formula; personal value judgments, staff and board preferences, the availability of funds and other resources; all these may lead to a "go" or "no go" decision.

Choices are rarely easy to make. All program design efforts are influenced by the circumstances under which they take place. The branching tree exercise seems to imply that the options are unlimited. This is its advantage; it permits us to explore options we might otherwise have ignored or eliminated prematurely. Had you been involved in the analysis from which I abstracted items for Exercise 8–2, you would have concluded that there is a real need of a nutrition program for the elderly and that plentiful government funds are available for such a program. That does not mean that a community center serving the aged will be in a position to conduct the program. Its physical facility may not be very large, and the board of directors may feel strongly that all the agency's programs and services should be conducted within the building. Establishing a nutrition education program, Meals-on-Wheels, buying cooperatives, and other such activities may be considered too great a departure from the counseling and small-group activities that the center has conducted in the past. To be effective, the nutrition program may have to be so large as to require an allocation of staff time and other resources that would seriously jeopardize the agency's current programs and services.

Under these circumstances, the agency may have to decide to forgo the opportunity, to encourage others in the community to take on the responsibility, or to engage in a collaborative effort with others to establish a new agency that is capable of taking on the responsibility. It may also choose to delay action until such time as it is ready to assume some responsibility for one of these alternatives. On an interim basis, the agency might choose to continue studying the various possibilities and their ramifications for the organization, to promote public awareness for the need, or to engage in a promotional activity aimed at establishing an endowment fund that might provide the wherewithal for developing a nutrition program at some future date.

## Review

We began this chapter with a description and examination of what many call the rational or normative model of planning, and then we examined what its critics say about it. We also found that strategic marketing can accommodate rational planning, incrementalist, and transactive approaches. Much of the chapter was taken up with the branching tree program design model, which was introduced by an exercise intended to help you identify a problem to be addressed. It concluded with a set of variables that can be used to make choices between alternative intervention components.

If you have completed Exercises 8–1 and 8–2, and used the decision-making guide that followed, there is little need to review the chapter further. You may, however, find it interesting to examine a second example of a partially completed branching tree (Fig. 8–3). This one led to the design of a number of interagency linkages, rather than service components like the one in Exercise 8–2. Would you have taken off in the same direction had you started with a similar problem definition?

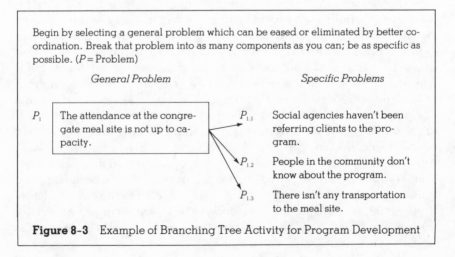

Begin by selecting a general problem which can be eased or eliminated by better coordination. Break that problem into as many components as you can; be as specific as possible. ($P$ = Problem)

|  | *General Problem* |  | *Specific Problems* |
|---|---|---|---|
| $P_1$ | The attendance at the congregate meal site is not up to capacity. | $P_{1.1}$ | Social agencies haven't been referring clients to the program. |
|  |  | $P_{1.2}$ | People in the community don't know about the program. |
|  |  | $P_{1.3}$ | There isn't any transportation to the meal site. |

**Figure 8-3**    Example of Branching Tree Activity for Program Development

Now translate the specific problems into objectives which would begin to alleviate the problem. ($G$ = Goal)

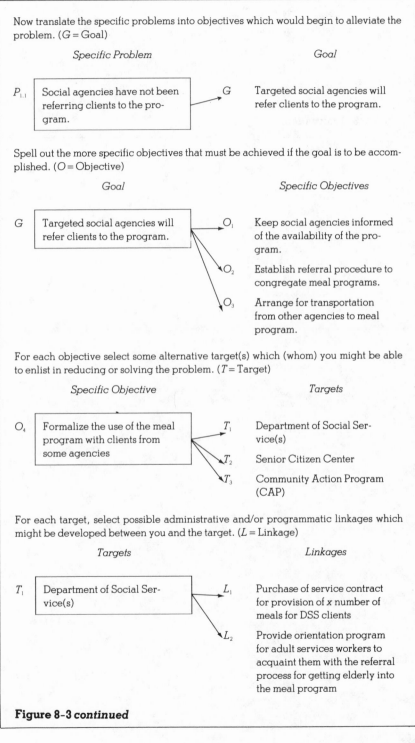

Specific Problem | Goal

$P_{1.1}$ | Social agencies have not been referring clients to the program. | $G$ | Targeted social agencies will refer clients to the program.

Spell out the more specific objectives that must be achieved if the goal is to be accomplished. ($O$ = Objective)

Goal | Specific Objectives

$G$ | Targeted social agencies will refer clients to the program.

$O_1$ Keep social agencies informed of the availability of the program.

$O_2$ Establish referral procedure to congregate meal programs.

$O_3$ Arrange for transportation from other agencies to meal program.

For each objective select some alternative target(s) which (whom) you might be able to enlist in reducing or solving the problem. ($T$ = Target)

Specific Objective | Targets

$O_4$ | Formalize the use of the meal program with clients from some agencies

$T_1$ Department of Social Service(s)

$T_2$ Senior Citizen Center

$T_3$ Community Action Program (CAP)

For each target, select possible administrative and/or programmatic linkages which might be developed between you and the target. ($L$ = Linkage)

Targets | Linkages

$T_1$ | Department of Social Service(s)

$L_1$ Purchase of service contract for provision of $x$ number of meals for DSS clients

$L_2$ Provide orientation program for adult services workers to acquaint them with the referral process for getting elderly into the meal program

**Figure 8-3 continued**

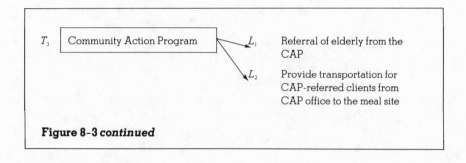

**Figure 8-3 *continued***

# 9  PRICING AND PLACING THE PROGRAM

THE COSTS of any service program are likely to be borne by many persons: funders, consumers, and providers. On the surface, it may be true that "he who pays the piper calls the tune." When we apply it to the human services, however, we soon discover that there may be as many payers as pipers and that the *financial* costs of a program may be the least important.

Some years back I attended the opening of a small branch library in a low-income neighborhood. The facilities were marvelous, as was the collection, and the librarians were carefully selected for their skill and sensitivity. A year later the branch closed. "We thought we were giving people a free service," one of the librarians explained. "We just didn't realize what else people would have to give up just to walk into this building. We could have been as far away as the moon." Some costs may just be too high, and some locations, though geographically accessible, may be as psychologically or culturally distant as the moon.

### Paying the Price

"You know," the director of a hospital outpatient clinic confided to a colleague of mine, "when we set up this program, we decided that low-income minorities deserved exactly the same quality of medical treatment as did upper-income folks. That's why we decided to locate the clinic right here, inside the housing project.

"Problem was, we just couldn't afford to put the latest equipment here after government funds became more scarce. No, that's not all there was to it. Truth is that some of our staff were afraid to come down here. And many of the local residents, although they come to the clinic regularly, don't seem to change their life-styles in such a way as to improve their health. The costs in dollars for health service to local residents were kept to a minimum. I guess we didn't recognize early enough that giving up native food preferences and customs does not come so easy. There are all kinds of prices we pay to change, and the benefits have to seem worth the cost."

## When Dollars Don't Count

When I first began my university studies, I attended a *small* East Coast liberal arts *college*. All male students were required to wear ties and jackets. Freshmen also had to wear "beanies." I know this may seem ludicrous to you now. It seemed so to me then. Even though I was working my way through school, I felt no misgivings about the financial outlay for books, tuition, transportation, and so on. But the psychological cost of wearing the tie and the beanie and of the many other regulations imposed on student behavior made the expense of attending that school beyond the benefits I hoped to gain. I withdrew and entered a *large* East Coast *university* where I paid twice as much tuition, but where no one seemed to care how I dressed.

Consumers pay all kinds of psychological costs for the services they receive. Unlike beanies, most of these costs are hidden from sight. Neither consumers nor providers may be fully aware of them. For example, coming to a family service agency may symbolize to the client an admission of inadequacy. Accepting help may be perceived as a loss of autonomy, as some responsibility for decision making is shifted temporarily to the worker or the agency. Entering a hospital may mean an even greater loss of control. It almost always means giving up one's familiar home surroundings and entering a rather alien environment. Minorities may respond much the same way when they enter a clinic that smells and sounds of white, "Anglo," middle-class America.

In addition to the psychological cost, there may also be social costs to pay. Attending an evening Yoga class may mean giving up the Thursday night bridge club. Going to night school in hopes of bettering one's social status may result in distancing oneself from former friends and family. There are also opportunity costs.

These are, in effect, opportunities lost, things one may not be able to do because one has already chosen to do something else. Going to an agency that uses behavioral modification techniques means that a consumer will probably not receive the other kinds of treatment provided at a different agency. Entering one occupation means that one has chosen not to pursue a different career, at least for the time being.

Psychological, social, and opportunity costs may be borne by nonconsumer publics as well. For example, when the United Way provides an award to one social service program, it has also determined to reduce awards to other petitioners. A social agency that accepts referrals from one organization may be unable to accept referrals from others. Social workers required to engage in fund raising or public relations cannot devote the time so allocated to providing direct services to clients. This may cost them dearly in terms of intrinsic satisfaction from client contact. Participating in a mandatory staff education program may require one to accept another's assessment that one is ignorant or unskilled.

The psychological costs of admitting inadequacy, or of putting oneself in the hands of another, may be too great for some people to bear. Nevertheless, the costs are frequently deemed acceptable when they are weighed against the promise of substantial reward. An agency administrator, who has decided to institute a management-by-objectives system, may be thinking ahead to greater worker productivity. The risks are (1) that decisions made at the lower levels of the organization may threaten upper management's authority and (2) that some of the agency's programs may be shifted in directions neither management nor the board may have anticipated. The possible benefits are precisely in those new directions.

Some costs and benefits are difficult to weigh against each other. A home for runaway teenagers was unable to get funding from the United Way or from the county community mental health board because it was perceived to be countercultural in its orientation. The more established agencies did not want to be tainted through association with the home. Only after a Catholic family service agency agreed to provide consultative and supervisory services to the center did funding became available, and then indirectly, through the family service agency. The family service agency was willing to pay the price of association in part because of the gratitude it received from other agencies just because it took them off the hook.

Nonfiscal costs may be the determining factors in the success of any marketing strategy. Unfortunately, they are almost impossible to measure and often poorly understood. Dollar costs, on the other hand, are relatively easy to measure and to understand.

## Setting the Price in Dollars

There are three principal methods for determining the monetary price of any product, such as a service, a book, a promotional campaign, or an intended outcome like a new skill or a degree: (1) demand (what people will be willing to pay), (2) the product's actual cost, and (3) competitive prices.

*Demand* determines what the market will bear. If demand is high, but services or products are limited, consumers may be willing to pay considerable amounts in dollars as well as in psychological, social, or opportunity costs. When demand falters, it may be necessary to adjust costs to attract consumers. If demand is irregular, it may be necessary to adjust costs on a seasonal basis. If there is no demand, or if there is indifference to the program or product, it may be necessary to reduce the costs or otherwise induce the public to buy.

The nature of the demand may depend not only on the product itself, but on the *place* where services are located and the *times* when services are provided. We will be discussing place and time later in this chapter. Because demand is likely to vary with different consumer markets, those markets can be segmented with prices set to the capacities of each product segment.

Some organizations charge different publics different prices for the same product. A local "Y" may charge a set course fee for nonmembers, but *discount* those courses for members. Health club members of a community center may pay a high membership fee, but receive all physical education courses at substantial discounts or free of charge, whereas general members who pay less up front may be charged substantial fees for the same activities. Some organizations' dues are set on a sliding scale, in accordance not only with *willingness* but with *ability* to pay.

Exercise 9–1 will help to clarify costs.

---

**EXERCISE 9-1**

**Identifying Costs**

1. Consider a service you have received from a human service organization or have considered applying for. In the space below, describe the service briefly, and identify the costs you might have had to incur.

   (a) *The Service:*


   (b) *The Costs*

   | *Psychological* | *Social* | *Opportunity* | *Financial* |
   | --- | --- | --- | --- |
   | | | | |

2. (a) Which of these costs were under the control of the service organization? Which were under your control? Which did no one seem to have any control over? List them below.

*continued*

---

**EXERCISE 9-1 continued**

| Agency Control | Your Control | No One's Control |
|---|---|---|
|  |  |  |

(b)  What could you have done to reduce the cost for yourself?

---

When price is set on the basis of *cost* rather than demand, the sponsoring agency begins by determining what the actual expenditures in providing a given service may be. These may be broken down into functional categories: a single counseling session, job training and job placement, or participation in summer camp. Fees are then set to recover all or part of the outlay. There are several weaknesses to basing the price on cost. First, it discriminates against those who cannot pay their full share. Second, it may not accommodate actual demand or willingness to pay.

Nevertheless, many agencies use this approach because of its relative simplicity. Some organizations charge on a "cost-plus" basis, using the income beyond cost to subsidize other programs or clients who may not be able to pay the full fee. Others prefer using markups to cost-plus calculations. Markup pricing refers to adding a predetermined sum for various goods and services that are more or less hidden. The markup is intended to cover hidden costs, like management or facility rental, that can generally be calculated accurately. In contrast, the "plus" in "cost-plus" generally refers to items that are difficult to cost out in advance. When a local agency agrees to conduct a conference for a federal bureau, it may charge the funder the actual cost plus 5 percent to cover unanticipated expenses. With cost, cost-plus, or markup pricing, the provider of a service does not take advantage of consumers when demand becomes acute. Nevertheless, the practice permits the provider to earn a fair return on investment.

*Competition-oriented fees* are based on imitative pricing. They are set by the "going rate." This approach works best where several organizations provide similar services at costs that are acceptable to the community at large. If other local agencies do not provide similar services, it is, nevertheless, possible to use a going-rate approach by comparing services in one community to comparable ones provided by similar agencies in other communities. When costs are difficult to measure, the going rate may represent the collective wisdom of others. Of all pricing systems, this one needs the least amount of interpretation to consumers.

With any of these three approaches, it is possible to *list-price* and then to *discount*. As noted, when people pay a general membership fee to an organization like a Y, they may receive a discount price (pay a lower fee) for a particular course or workshop. Families who send two or more children to a summer camp may receive a discount price for the second, third, or fourth child. Sometimes they are also charged customized prices: an additional fee if they wish the child to take a bus to camp or to have the camp assume responsibility for the delivery of the child's trunk and other baggage to the site. Families who can afford it may be "taxed" a surcharge to cover the cost of scholarships for those who are not able to pay the full fee.

These three approaches to price setting—demand, cost, or competition—may also figure in an agency's request to an allocating body. A grant application is generally made on the basis of costs or cost-plus. The "plus" is referred to as "indirect costs." If the demand for the agency's services is high, and no other organization seems capable of conducting the program that the funder wishes to put in motion, the agency may be able to demand a higher award. The additional funds permit it to do things that it wishes to do, in addition to those specified by the funder. Conversely, when competition for grants is high, an agency may be willing to provide a service at somewhat less than its cost in order to get the award or to stay in the good graces of the funding organization. It will then have to seek additional funds from other sources, such as fees, fund-raising efforts, gifts, or its own general fund appropriation, to make up the difference.


Changing the Price

These days, few prices remain stable for long. Your organization may find that it must frequently change the fees it charges or the funds it requests for performance of a service. There are generally four reasons, that economists call *price objectives*, why fees are set and/or changed: (1) cost recovery, (2) surplus generation, (3) increasing incentives to use services, and (4) decreasing incentives to use services. *Cost recovery* through fees is rarely an objective for human service agencies. The objective of recovering a reasonable portion of the cost of a service is somewhat more realistic.

We already know something about how prices are set (demand, cost, and competition). But who determines what portion of the price can reasonably be charged to the consumer and what part must be recovered from some other source? Frequently it will be the staff or the board of the organization, unless a major supporter like a government agency mandates certain fees or the recovery of a predetermined proportion of costs from fees charged. Medicare and Medicaid payments are good examples. Decision makers will also be influenced by tradition, public opinion, and potential competition—in short, by all manner of market factors.

Under some circumstances, human service organizations will attempt to go beyond recovery to the generation of a surplus, a "profit," so to speak. This may seem like a contradiction in terms for a not-for-profit organization. It isn't. Many organizations turn a profit on one program in order to support another. Generally, only certain events or services will be priced so as to generate optimum revenue. A Jewish community center at which I once did an internship, for example, charged heavy fees for health club membership. These were somewhat higher than fees set in the private sector, but considerably less than those charged by country clubs in the area. Nevertheless, the fees were roughly twice what it cost to the center to run the program. The surplus was used to support social services to senior citizens, from whom only minimal fees were sought; to provide summer camp scholarships for needy children; and to support various cultural events for which no fees were charged.

At what point is an adequate profit earned? This is a complex question, and it may require that you get some technical assistance from an accountant or a business economist. You can't always increase your profits by increasing the amount charged or the units of service delivered and sold (like number of health club memberships, or tickets to a benefit concert). At some point, the fees charged may be considered a *dis*incentive by potential consumers who may prefer to go elsewhere or who will refuse to participate in the service at all. Raising prices may reduce participation and ultimately income; increasing participation by reducing fees or in some other way inducing persons to join or to pay may also have an adverse effect. The loss of revenue incurred by lowering fees may not be offset by increased participation.

The cost of increasing service, particularly if this also incurs additions to the staff or to the facilities and the equipment necessary for the service, may actually reduce rather than increase net income. Moreover, it may impose on the organization a requirement to operate always at maximum capacity, even when the economy is poor or consumers are attracted to other suppliers. This can be risky indeed, as many social agencies learned during the recessions of the late 1970s and early 1980s. They might well have learned it from the automobile industry.

Outside the health field, there are almost no theoretical pricing models that can be used in pricing a human service program for profit. Economic models include various cost and demand equations that require relatively accurate estimates of cost and demand. These estimates are hard to come by. In many cases, services are themselves not standard, and experience with them may be minimal. Demand for particular human services is rather volatile. One may be able to estimate the numbers of people in a given geographic area that are likely to be in need of an organization's service, but whether or not the agency provides the service may be a function of whether the state legislature views the population in question favorably, or whether public opinion is behind the kind of service projected.

There may be times during which your organization will attempt to penetrate a particular consumer market rapidly. It will use all kinds of incentives to attract the greatest number of persons from a targeted segment. In India, for example, the government made contraceptives available at no cost and in some cases even paid people to use them or coupled contraceptive services with free medical help to a recipient's family. Price reduction or elimination may be in order when such a reduction is likely to attract many additional buyers or participants. It also makes good sense when the unit cost of program development and distribution drops with increased output. For example, in the child welfare training grant I described in the chapter on negotiations, we found that we could double the number of training modules with only a one-third increase in funds. In other words, if we could increase our income by 33⅓ percent, we could double our output.

Does your community movie theater provide a senior citizens' discount or a $1 movie night on Tuesdays? In Ann Arbor, "dollar Tuesdays" are always jam-packed. Regular nights, when the charge is $4, may see the theater only one-quarter full. Clearly, the theater managers are onto a good thing. At little or no cost, they generate a great deal of goodwill, and they don't do so badly on other nights, especially when those turned away on "dollar Tuesdays" are really motivated to see the movie that draws such crowds. Is there a parallel in your organization's operations? If so, consider two additional issues.

Will a reduction in price discourage competition and give your organization virtual control over the market? Is this desirable? Second, will a reduction in price actually serve as a disincentive? Will reducing the cost of camper fees because of market conditions signal the public that there has been a reduction in the quality of the service? Will parents hold out until the price gets even lower? Can reductions be defined as temporary so as to avoid this stigmatization? What would happen if, instead of reducing camper fees, the sponsoring organization provided a variety of markdowns? Examples might include a 50 percent reduction for the second session of camp or for the second child enrolled, or a free first day of camp for children who would like to test out the program. Can you think of others relevant to your organization?

Disincentivization may indeed be your goal. Disincentive pricing can be used to discourage persons from applying for service because the cost is simply too high. You may not, however, wish to discourage all segments of the organizations' consumer market; yet you are prohibited from charging different fees for the same services. What then are your options? Consider raising other costs: the social costs of offering the services at times that may be inconvenient to some groups, or of locating the service far from where consumers live and not convenient to transportation. Remember that there are psychological, social, and opportunity as well as fiscal costs to the consumer for participation.

## Price Elasticity

Changing prices once they have been operative for some time may not be all that easy. The equipment and other overhead items that must be used by a home-help program for the disabled require ongoing maintenance and continued bank payments. It might be difficult to defend discontinuance when so much has already been invested. Agencies tend to have rather substantial sunken costs. Nevertheless, when the price elasticity of demand is high, the agency may have more options to choose from.

In the last few pages, we've been discussing *price elasticity of demand*. This refers to the percentage of change in demand during a given period of time caused by a change in the price. For example, if sales rise (more children become enrolled in the day camp) by the same percentage as price falls (the amount charged for each camper per week is reduced) you have a price elasticity of $-1$.* Your total revenue is left unchanged. But if sales rise by *more* than the price falls in percentage terms, you have a price elasticity *greater* than $-1$ and total revenue rises. A price elasticity of *less* than $-1$ means that the percentage of sales rises by less than the percentage the price falls. In this case the total amount of revenue falls.

Some economists speak of long- and short-term elasticity. Parents may stay with the camp immediately after an initial sharp price increase because finding a new camp may be costly in terms of time and effort; however, they may start shopping around. In this case, demand would be elastic in the long run, though fairly steady in the short run. The opposite may happen: A sharp rise in the camp price may discourage parents from enrolling their children initially, only to see them return at a later time when they find that the camp's services cannot be properly duplicated anywhere else.

"But what if I'm the camp director and have to make a decision?" you might ask. "How do I make a decision to raise the fee or not?" There just is no easy answer. Even a 10 percent increase may be like the straw that broke the camel's back. It may be difficult to know the impact of a price change for at least one or two seasons.

To a large extent, the impact of price changes will have to be determined by trial and error. Nevertheless, there are some relatively systematic ways through which you can anticipate the extent of price or demand elasticity, and thereby decrease the risks of making a change. One is to do a

---

*Price elasticity of demand is defined as the ratio of the percentage change in demand (e.g., quantity sold per period) to the percentage change in price.

market test, checking whether or not an increase or reduction in price will have the desired effect. The test may be conducted for a few weeks, a few months, or even an entire season. Another approach is to use survey instruments or one or more of the other assessment tools we discussed in Chapter 7. Should you decide to use a survey, potential users might be polled to see whether they would increase [or decrease] their use of the service with a given rise [or drop] in the fee charged. It might also be possible to analyze the experience of organizations like your own in different communities. Consider evaluating the impact of price changes on similar services provided by others in your own community.

Try applying some of the same concepts to other sources of supply: funding agencies, individual donors, or staff members who may be expected to invest personal and professional energy at a level different than is currently demanded. Consider, also, costs in nonfiscal terms: Does a reduction in the length of the work week increase motivation and productivity? Does a new challenge increase independence and responsibility? Does it do so initially, only to result in slackened performance 3 months, 6 months, or a year after the changes are made? Like other exchange relationships, the benefits must always be perceived as outweighing the costs, and that presumption must be reinforced over time.

## Buy Now, Pay Later

When a private employment agency agrees to take on a client, it often charges a low initial fee for assessment purposes, but may charge the employer and/or future employee 5 percent of the first 6 months' wages after placement. The woman who bought only swimming when she purchased a membership in a community center soon discovered that much more was expected of membership than the payment of fees. Financial payments were required up front; they may even have been payable on a monthly or quarterly basis. But commitment to the organization, developing a shared identity with other community members, and sharing pool time with day campers were other costs; she had not initially bargained for these, and pool privileges might not be a sufficient reward for these costs.

What costs do your clients pay now? What will be expected of them later? What benefits will they receive? Can they be assured a net gain? If not, how well are they appraised of the risks?

Sometimes, we pay now, on the anticipation of benefiting later. Many federal agencies have done precisely that. For many years, the National Institute of Mental Health and the Children's Bureau provided fellowships to graduate students in social work as well as faculty development or employment grants to universities with MSW programs. Attached to these grants were requirements that schools add content on mental health or child welfare to their curricula and that students receiving stipends commit themselves to one year of employment in the selected field for each year of stipend. By paying now, these federal agencies were betting that the fields for which they were responsible would benefit later through an expanding pool of qualified personnel.

## From Price to Place: Locating the Program in Time and Space

Sometimes, providers or consumers may be willing to pay more for a service if its location is changed. Some years ago, I offered a number of workshops on marketing, budgeting, and management by objectives through the school of social work's continuing education program. The fees charged were, I thought, relatively low. The business school was offering similar workshops at four times our fees, but our workshops were undersubscribed whereas theirs were over-registered! Apparently there was a presumption on the part of consumers that the business school had the capacity to deliver and the school of social work did not. When we began cosponsored workshops with the business school, we were able to raise the price, increase the demand, and generate a net profit that could then be applied to subsidizing other activities. Through trial and error, we found out something else about consumers. Offering a workshop in Grand Rapids did not necessarily increase attendance by area participants more than offering the same workshop in Ann Arbor. In fact, people were willing to pay more to come to Ann Arbor. Clearly, the city and the campus made it an attractive location. The same service was devalued when it was offered closer to home.

*Location*, the time and place at which a service is offered, may be the determining factor in its acceptance and utilization. Location can be geographic, but it can also refer to the place in an organization's structure and its relationships to elements in the task environment. More important, perhaps, it can refer to the life spaces of the individuals and groups that make use of an organization's services or who contribute to the development and delivery of those services. The location of a university's regional campus near where you live may be of little interest if you are either unprepared to attend that university or if you don't have children or friends who are ready to attend. *Timing* then becomes a major issue. We've already discussed time as a cost to the consumer and others. In this section of the chapter, we'll examine the timing of service development and provision. But first, we'll examine some of the more traditional marketing concerns that focus on *geographic* location.

### Geographic Distribution

Let's assume, for the moment, that your agency is interested in providing counseling services to pregnant teenagers. Should those services be provided in the agency's downtown offices or in the local high school? Should they be provided directly by agency staff, or might it be better if they were provided by school personnel or young mothers under the staff's guidance or direction? These are questions of distribution policy. Distribution can be handled directly by agency staff in the agency's own facilities or by agency staff on location in a host setting. The agency may use a central office or satellites and branch offices. It may detach its workers (like group workers serving street gangs or organizers working with neighborhood block clubs). It may also work through others, by consulting with school personnel on behavior management or on substance abuse control; in effect, by providing indirect services. Finally, it may use a combination of these independently or in concert with other service providers.

These possibilities might be as depicted in Table 9–1.

**TABLE 9-1    Distribution of Services**

| Services Provided | Location | | | |
| --- | --- | --- | --- | --- |
| | Agency Central Location | Agency Branch | Premises of Other Host Agency | Natural Community Settings |
| Directly | 1a | 2a | 3a | 4a |
| Indirectly | 1b | 2b | 3b | 4b |

Now let's look at a few examples:

*Example*

*Discussion*

1. Women who have suffered spouse abuse receive service in the agency's safe house, where they can remain for a 30-day period. Subsequently, they can come to the First Unitarian Church on Tuesday evenings for participation in a women's support group. Agency staff also make home visits to families that have been reunited following a wife's return from the safe house.

In this example, services are provided directly by the agency in its central location (1a) and in its branch (2a), as well as in natural community settings (4a); three of the location types.

2. The public library offers its services in the following locations: central building, neighborhood branches, public schools, roving bookmobiles at neighborhood parks, and through volunteer readers who make home visits to the infirm or disabled.

Here services are also provided directly, but each type of location is used (1a, 2a, 3a, and 4a).

3. A training firm, following the design of an instructional package, trained trainers in locales throughout the United States. These trainers now conduct family-life education activities using the materials they purchase from the firm.

In this example, the firm provides its services indirectly by franchising them and permitting its franchises to operate relatively independently (3b and 4b).

Exercise 9–2 explains this concept further.

---

**EXERCISE 9-2**
**Locating Services**

1. Examine Table 9–1. Identify a program that falls into one of the boxes, one that fits three or more of the direct-service boxes, one that fits three or more of the indirect-service boxes, and one that fits three or more of the indirect- and direct-service boxes. Use a separate sheet of paper for each. You'll need the space.

2. Now take any one of those programs that already spread over several categories. What would the consequences be of extending it to one more category? Reducing the range of locations? Would either decision increase or lower the price to consumers? To other funders? Explain the reason for your answers.

---

Deciding Where to Locate the Service

Decisions about where to locate a service are generally made on the basis of efficiency and effectiveness. Efficiency considerations, unfortunately, are too often made on the basis of anticipated cost. It may cost more to establish satellite centers than to conduct a program out of a central location. It may be even less expensive to franchise out a service or to conduct it under the auspices of another organization. This is only half of the equation, however. Program designers must also consider the impact on agency income of alternative distribution patterns. Will distribution through other organizations remove your agency from view and thereby reduce its fund-raising capacity? Will opening up a highly visible storefront operation increase or decrease the likelihood of an effective fund-raising campaign? Will it attract grants from the government or private sector? Like any kind of investment, the costs associated with location must be examined against anticipated return.

There is a tendency to conclude that the closer or more accessible a service, the more likely it is to be effective. Frequently, this may be the case. But sometimes, as in the case of a library branch, all of an organization's resources cannot be brought to the public. Perhaps more important, some services are devalued when they are too close. Grand Rapids consumers of a university-based C.E. program, you will recall, preferred coming to Ann Arbor because of its reputation for academic excellence. A storefront family health clinic may cheapen the image of the service given. In both cases, atmosphere was of major concern.

Instruction offered in Grand Rapids, perhaps on the campus of a community college, did not provide the same learning atmosphere as Ann Arbor with its many university buildings, bookstores, and libraries. The storefront operation I have in mind was purposely designed to reflect consumer cultural patterns and preferences. Set up in a predominantly Hispanic neighborhood, it was decorated with Mexican artwork, used vivid colors on doors and windows, and included a lobby that looked more like someone's apartment than a medical clinic. The idea was to make people feel at home. Doctors and nurses wore everyday street clothing rather than uniforms or white hospital garb. The result? Neighborhood people did not take the clinic seriously. Doctors didn't look like doctors, and the informality of the clinic was taken to mean that the program's sponsors did not respect the local population. A neighborhood-based operation might have worked, but only if it looked as formidable and as formal as the hospital waiting room and the examination cubicles that residents were accustomed to.

## Timing and Life-Space Issues

Even if the storefront clinic had been fully acceptable, it would have been underused if people were not aware of its services or of their needs for it. Consumer readiness to take advantage of or to use a service will vary with age, education, residence, awareness, need, and so on. For some, participation may be its own reward. "It's been a long time since Charles died, but I still come to the group. These are my friends. I enjoy being with them." For others, participation may be more painful than it is rewarding; but participation is perceived to be useful not in and of itself, but for some other purpose or purposes. A person who decides to join a treatment group may reason as follows: "If I subject myself to a painful therapeutic encounter now, I will be able to save my marriage."

Agencies weigh similar considerations in determining their program priorities and distribution strategies. Approaching a federal agency for a grant may not be very productive if your organization has not properly positioned itself to get the grant by having demonstrated competence, commitment, or prior experience. The funder may agree that the work proposed needs doing, but if it does not fit into this year's priorities, a proposal is not likely to get much attention.

Although some organizations will plunge right in on a first fund-raising effort, others will prefer to get their feet wet by attracting small or medium-sized gifts for a year or two before going after larger contributions. "I knew there were bigger bucks out there," an administrator confided to me, "but if we went after the big donors right away and struck out, we could never have gotten as effective a fund-raising operation going. Our volunteers needed some experience and some success before we could set our sights higher." Donors, too, are likely to be more or less ready: "If we had approached Mrs. Glider last year, we would not even have gotten past the front door. Our good fortune was her bad fortune. It's too bad her concern with child safety had to be sparked by the accident." "I guess you could say Jack Belsen was feeling vulnerable. No one lives forever, and most of us would like to pass on a legacy of some sort. We've been talking to him for years. This year he seems ready."

Readiness may be a factor in the establishment of collaborative activities with other organizations as well. "We have been trying to place our staff at the senior citizens' center for 3 years. Suddenly their staff became aware of our existence. They not only want us there, but have suggested that some of their people come over to our operation to better inform us about the needs of the elderly. I guess it took a while for them to become aware that older people have substance abuse problems too. It took a few of the older persons, themselves, to push for information on drugs before the staff was willing to recognize the problem."

Clients, staff, donors, and even organizations have careers. They change over time, and those changes are likely to increase or decrease their readiness to fund, consume, redesign, or deliver services. Timing becomes of great strategic importance. An error in timing, a misperception about need or willingness to pay for a service or to collaborate on its delivery, is likely to yield an empty basket. Price, place (including timing), and product are clearly interrelated.

## Review

Costs, timing, and location are interrelated concepts; all have significant bearing on the success of an organization's marketing practice. Costs measured in dollars may be less significant than the psychological, social, and opportunity costs associated with service delivery. The fiscal costs, however, are easier to measure and so to plan around.

The price of a particular service is likely to be set on the basis of demand, cost to the agency, or competition. Each may have some impact on the service itself and on the relationship that an organization may have to establish with elements in its environment. Since fees rarely cover all the financial costs incurred, other sources of supply may be necessary.

Agencies sometimes manipulate their prices so as to increase or discourage demand. Price elasticity of demand refers to percentage of change in demand during a given period of time in response to a percentage change in the price attached to the service or product being provided. It can be used to determine whether net income is higher or lower in response to a change in price.

Price is only one of the factors influencing consumer use. The location of a service may be an even more significant factor. Services can be provided in a central location or through decentralized outlets. These outlets may be branch operations, the premises of another service provider, or natural community settings. Some agencies provide their services indirectly, through the intervention of those with whom they consult or whom they train. Issues of location and of responsibility for the provision of services are likely to affect cost and, in turn, be affected by the prices that participants are likely to be required to pay.

Timing refers to place in an individual's or organization's life space. Because readiness or need are so clearly tied to an individual's or organization's stage of development, timing can become the deciding factor in any decision regarding the placing or pricing of a program.

# 10 BUDGETING THE PROGRAM

LIKE PROGRAM PLANS, budgets are statements of intent. They are, in fact, program plans stated in fiscal terms. The budget is a planning tool and like any statement of intent, it can be used to guide your activities. But it must be a realistic guide.

### Budgets Can Be Tricky

"This budget should do the trick," said Margaret Petrocini. "It tells the Feds just what they're asking for and I think I followed the guidelines to a 'T.' What is your opinion?"

"You're both right and wrong," responded the associate director of the public health agency. "It does follow the guidelines. But it won't fly in Washington or in our accounting office or with some of your colleagues. It's not enough to follow instructions. It's just as important to understand the constraints imposed by others. Funders' instructions are important, but there are other things you did not consider.

"First of all, your use of paraprofessionals is going to create a problem; not only because we haven't used them before—we can handle that in a demonstration project—but because their salaries are too close to those of BA level professional staff already on board. Secondly, you're making an assumption that someone else is going to pick up the project when the federal bucks are gone. No one around here has made that kind of commitment.

"Then look at the line item for training manuals. It's very high. You may be justified in asking for that amount, but you don't explain your reasons for the request in the budget justification section, and the narrative description of the project only barely refers to their use. Seems to me you would have to have multiple use of such expensive materials to make them worth the investment. $10,500 for manuals to orient 60 staff members is likely to be considered out of line.

"Now look at. . . ."

Margaret was stunned. She had followed all the procedures, as she put it, "to a T," but the budget just wasn't right. It did not adequately reflect what had been written in the "program narrative," and while it took into account the funding agency's guidelines, it did not address the fiscal, the psychological, or the programmatic constraints in her own agency. Margaret had not fully grasped the essentials of budget making or of the strategic uses one can make of a budget.

Because the budget permits you to put down on paper what you propose to do and to spend, it provides you with an instrument for monitoring your activities in both programmatic and fiscal terms. This makes it a management tool: it provides the same opportunity to others. When used by suppliers who provide you with necessary financial resources to operate a program or project, it can be used as an instrument of fiscal control. We'll learn more about this aspect of the budget process when we examine auditing procedures in Chapter 15.

## Line-Item and Functional Budgets

In this chapter we will be discussing two broad categories of budgets: the *line-item* budget and the *functional* budget. Functional budgets are generally referred to as either *program* or *performance* budgets. Because all three are written in table form, they are sometimes referred to as tabular budgets. Each of these has its own distinct advantages and disadvantages. All three budget types can be used for programs that provide services to consumers, and all the illustrations in this chapter will have services as their focus. The same principles apply, however, for fund raising, promotion, or other marketing activities. One can hardly conceive of the marketing process without budgets. All marketing activities require budgets. All programs and services for which support is needed require budgets.

Let's start by looking at the line-item budget. You are probably already familiar with this form. Most funders and agency fiscal managers require that expenditures be detailed in line-item terms. Line items represent expenses just the way they are paid out. They tell you what you are spending money *on*, but not necessarily what *for*, and therein lies their drawback. Knowing that $100,000 is going to staff salaries, and $10,000 is going into equipment and supplies, does not tell you much about the cost of conducting activities like counseling or referral or about the cost of achieving program objectives such as placing a child in an adoptive home. For that reason, some funders want the justification for line items to be made in program or performance terms. Others will actually require performance or program budgets to be broken down into line items.

All of this may sound very complex. It really isn't. If you look over the sample budgets included in the chapter as you read the next few pages, I'm confident it will all become clear.

The performance budget projects the cost of *performing* a certain unit of work such as counseling, conducting a family-life education program, running the agency's information and referral service, or coordinating all these programs. Each of these performance areas can be costed out, permitting funders and other interested parties to compare the costs of similar activities, such as family counseling, in several agencies. The cost of counseling by agency staff could be compared to that of referring clients to other agencies from which counseling services are purchased. This budget also permits cost comparisons of different programs in a single agency.

A staff development and training office in a state agency, for example, could compare the costs of its workshop programs to the costs of its annual conferences. The problem with making such comparisons, however, is that it is a little bit like comparing apples and oranges, unless you can specify what you expect to accomplish with each of the programs being compared.

Program budgets make it possible to do just that. They categorize expenditures in relationship to the organization's objectives or to the objectives of a particular project. Costs are calculated for specific objectives such as placing someone on a job, increasing the reading-level performance of third graders, or doubling the number of clients who can live independently in the community. Clearly, the program's objectives must be quantifiable in measurable terms.

One advantage of the program budget is that it can be helpful in determining the size or scope of a program. If placing 100 workers through a job training program costs $1,200,000 ($12,000/per worker placed), but it costs only $1,800,000 to place 200 workers due to economies of scale, a funder may be induced to increase the job training agency's allocation.

It is not difficult to learn how to design or use each of these budgets. Because the line-item budget tells you exactly what you expect to spend your money on, it simplifies the process of monitoring your expenditures. It is a good device for tracking the outflow of funds, but it has several disadvantages. First, by focusing on expenditures rather than on the accomplishment of results, it does little to reflect the purpose of those expenditures. The line-item budget is primarily an accounting device. It's not very helpful in planning or evaluation.

A line-item budget for a "Special Needs Adoption" project appears in Table 10–1. Look it over before reading on. Refer back to it as you read the next section on designing line-item budgets.

**TABLE 10-1 Sample Line-Item Budget**

| Project: Special Needs Adoption | Total Budget $313,050 | Requested $217,500 | Donated $95,550 |
|---|---|---|---|
| I. Personnel | | | |
| A. Salaries and wages: | | | |
| Professional staff: | | | |
| 1. Project director @ $28,000/yr (0.25 F.T.E.)[a] | 7,000 | 7,000 | |
| 2. Caseworker @ $18,000–26,000/yr or average of $22,000 (5.0 F.T.E.s) | 110,000 | 88,000 | 22,000 |
| 3. Clinical psychologist @ $20,000/yr (0.50 F.T.E.) | 10,000 | | 10,000 |
| 4. Intake associate @ $18,000/yr (0.50 F.T.E.) | 9,000 | 9,000 | |
| Support staff: | | | |
| 5. Clerical @ $11,000/yr (1.5 F.T.E.) | 16,500 | 16,500 | |
| 6. Public relations coordinator $18,000/yr (0.5 F.T.E.) | 9,000 | 9,000 | |
| | $161,500 | $129,500 | $32,000 |
| B. Fringe benefits | | | |
| 1. Benefit package 22% of total salaries and wages not counting volunteer donations | $ 35,530 | $ 28,490 | $ 7,040 |
| | $ 35,530 | $ 28,490 | $ 7,040 |
| C. Consultants and contract services | | | |
| 1. Consultant on Spaulding Network Agency approaches 5 days @ $250/day plus travel (2 trips) and per diem of $50/day for 5 days | 13,250 | 13,250 | |
| 2. Legal services @ $400/day for 20 days (10 on a volunteer basis) | 8,000 | 4,000 | 4,000 |
| 3. Budgeting services @ $250/day for 10 days (volunteer) | 2,500 | | 2,500 |
| 4. 30 trainer days for family-life education programs @ $200 per trainer day (includes video consultant/trainer) | 6,000 | 6,000 | |
| 5. Editor, 20 days @ $200/day | 4,000 | 4,000 | |
| 6. Home advisors, tutors: volunteers working at tasks normally costing $10/hr for 3000 hr/yr | 30,000 | | 30,000 |
| | $ 63,750 | $ 27,250 | $36,500 |

[a]F.T.E. may be alternatively stated as: 25% for 12 months.

*continued*

**TABLE 10-1** *continued*

| Project: Special Needs Adoption | Total Budget $313,050 | Requested $217,500 | Donated $95,550 |
|---|---|---|---|
| II. Nonpersonnel | | | |
| A. Space cost | | | |
| 1. Office space, lease; 6 offices plus waiting and conference rooms × 12 months | 9,000 | | 9,000 |
| 2. Utilities for office space (heating, electricity, water) | 4,000 | | 4,000 |
| 3. Fire and theft and accident insurance | 200 | | 200 |
| 4. Maintenance @ $150/mo for 12 mo | 1,800 | | 1,800 |
| 5. Conference center rental for training programs, 10 times/yr @ $150 | 1,500 | 1,500 | |
| 6. TV studio rental, 5 days @ $200/day | 1,000 | 1,000 | |
| | $ 17,500 | $ 2,500 | $15,000 |
| B. Equipment | | | |
| 1. Desk @ $200 purchase[b] | 200 | 200 | |
| 2. Seven desks @ rental equivalent of $10 each/mo | 720 | | 720 |
| 3. 6 filing cabinets @ rental equivalent of $10 each/mo | 720 | | 720 |
| 4. 2 IBM Selectric IIIs leasing of $50/mo each | 1,200 | 1,200 | |
| 5. Word processor leased for $75/mo | 900 | 900 | |
| 6. Xerox and mimeo, shared time | 600 | | 600 |
| 7. Microcomputer time sharing lease arrangement based on 2 hr/wk @ $50 hr | 5,200 | 5,200 | |
| 8. Adding machine[b] | 50 | 50 | |
| 9. 6 waiting room chairs @ $200[b] | 1,200 | 1,200 | |
| 10. 12 office chairs @ rental equivalent of $5 each/mo | 720 | | 720 |
| | $ 11,510 | $ 8,750 | $ 2,760 |
| C. Office supplies (consumable) | | | |
| 1. Disposable supplies for professional staff ($50/yr each for 7 F.T.E.s) | 350 | 350 | |
| 2. Telephone, including installation cost for 3 new telephones and rental plus charges for 8 | 900 | 900 | |
| 3. Clerical supplies (mimeo, Xerox paper, typing supplies, and small equipment like staples) | 1,800 | 1,800 | |
| 4. Postage (all but that related to special mailings) @ $50/mo | 600 | 600 | |
| | $ 3,650 | $ 3,650 | |

[b]One-time purchases only.

*continued*

**TABLE 10-1** *continued*

| Project: Special Needs Adoption | Total Budget $313,050 | Requested $217,500 | Donated $95,550 |
|---|---|---|---|
| D. Program supplies (consumable) | | | |
|    1. Videotapes for prototype | 80 | 80 | |
|    2. Newsprint pads, poster board, markers, pens, and pencils for 20 family life educational workshops | 250 | 250 | |
|    3. Coffee for workshops (to be paid for by participants) | 250 | | 250 |
|    4. Brochure printing for workshops and other services | 1,000 | 1,000 | |
|    6. How-to-parent and how-to-adopt booklets, 5000 copies @ printing costs of $1 each, cost to be partially offset by sales | 5,000 | 3,000 | 2,000 |
|    7. Postage for mailing brochures 2000 @ $0.20 | 400 | 400 | |
| | $ 6,980 | $ 4,730 | $ 2,250 |
| E. Travel | | | |
|    1. Local | | | |
|       7 F.T.E. staff @ 402.5 mi/mo × 12 at $0.22/mi | 7,440 | 7,440 | |
|       Volunteer travel @ 300 mi/mo × 12 @ $0.22/mi | 790 | 790 | |
|    2. National professional meetings: project director plus 3 staff attend national meeting of Child Welfare League @ $400/trip (includes travel, per diem, and registration) for purposes of reporting the project in collaboration with representatives of other special needs adoption agencies | 1,200 | 1,200 | |
|    3. Attendance at regional CWLA conferences for 4 staff @ $200/trip (includes travel, per diem, and registration) | 800 | 800 | |
|    4. Out of town meetings with representatives of sister agencies for 2 staff @ $350 | 700 | 700 | |
| | $ 10,930 | $ 10,930 | |
| F. Other costs | | | |
|    1. Dues in professional organizations for the project (not for project | | | |

*continued*

**TABLE 10-1**    *continued*

| Project: Special Needs Adoption | Total Budget $313,050 | Requested $217,500 | Donated $95,550 |
|---|---|---|---|
| staff)—e.g., CWLA, FSSA | 500 | 500 | |
| 2. Library and journal subscriptions | 400 | 400 | |
| 3. Liability insurance for staff | 800 | 800 | |
| | $ 1,700 | $ 1,700 | |

*Note:* This budget does not need a section for "Indirect Costs" because these were virtually all reflected in the "Donated" column.

## Designing the Line-Item Budget

Line-item budgets are generally divided into two major categories: personnel and nonpersonnel items. These go onto the tabular budget, which is usually followed by a narrative *budget justification*. Budgets should be designed to communicate all relevant details to relevant audiences. If you are using a funder's guidelines, make sure that you follow those guidelines to the letter. If you are following the procedures generally used in your organization, make sure that you understand those procedures and that you use the categories considered standard for other programs.

Referring to the sample (Table 10–1), let's look at the anatomy of a fairly standard line-item presentation in tabular form. Notice that there are three columns: one for the *total* budget, one for the *requested* amount, and another for the *donated* amount. The "Total Budget" column projects what the program will actually cost, regardless of sources of income. The "Requested" column specifies the amount you are requesting from a particular source, say the United Way, the community mental health board, the city council, the federal Office of Human Development, the local Shriners' organization, or Litton Industries. The "Donated" column refers to all other sources.

For different audiences, you may wish to use different categories. Instead of the "Requested" and "Donated" categories, for example, you might prefer such designations as "Sponsor" or "Cost Sharing." If you have several sponsors, you might wish to subdivide the "Requested" column for each of the sponsors to whom you are submitting a proposal. If other suppliers have already committed funds, include a "Committed" column. In this case, the "Donated" column would reflect only your own organization's contributions. Should you be seeking funds primarily from the organization's General Fund, the columns might include General Fund Allocation, Fees from Clients, and Parents' Appeal Campaign. Clearly, there are many possibilities. Budgets are flexible tools. Design yours to communicate what is significant in your circumstances. The categories you decide to use should be determined by what you hope to convey to the different publics you are addressing.

The tabular budget must include as much information as possible, but no more than is needed. This may become clear when we examine each of the line items. Let's begin with "Personnel." The section on personnel generally includes three subsections: (1) salaries and wages, (2) fringe benefits, (3) consultants and contract services. You might wish to further subdivide salaries and wages into "Professional Personnel" and "Support Staff."

## Personnel

Indicating the specific salary allocated to a given staff member may be insufficient without designating the number of months that person will be working on the project or the percentage of work time allocated to that project. Assume that the project director's annual salary is $24,000, but she is assigned only quarter-time to the project. Assume further that you are asking the funding source to cover the full 25 percent of her time allocated to the project for the entire 12 months. Here is how you could communicate this as a line item.

|  | *Requested* | *Donated* |
|---|---|---|
| Project director @ $24,000 (25% × 12 months) | $6,000 | |

Suppose your project includes five caseworkers. The next line item might then read as follows:

|  | *Requested* | *Donated* |
|---|---|---|
| 5 caseworkers @ $20,000 (full time × 12 months) | $80,000 | $20,000 |

In this case, the agency or some other donor is contributing 20 percent of the salaries from some other source. If one of those workers is already on staff, this might be the agency's *in-kind* contribution. You may wish to explain this in the budget justification. But let's suppose things are a bit more complicated. The project may be slated to begin October 1, the beginning of the U.S. government fiscal year, but you know that it will take some time to bring all staff members on board. Moreover, some of the project's activities may not begin until you have completed a needs assessment. In this case, the casework line may read as follows:

|  | Requested | Donated |
|---|---|---|
| Caseworkers @ $20,000/year (2 full time × 12 months and 3 full time × 9 months) | $70,000 | $15,000 |

Again, the explanation for the request will appear in your budget justification. If you expect to be funded again the next year, this explanation may be crucial. How else can you justify moving up from 9 to 12 months employment during the second year? Some budget writers prefer to designate each item that is to be subsequently explained with an asterisk (*) or some other symbol; others prefer to use numbers[1] much as they might footnote a professional article; still others prefer no special designation, trusting that the reader will understand what is being communicated when reading the justification section.

The seasonal nature of some programs may require somewhat more complicated designations. For example,

|  | Requested | Donated |
|---|---|---|
| Camp director @ $20,000/year (3 months full time and 9 months @ 25%) | $8,750 | 0 |

The observant reader may have noticed that the sample line-item budget used the designation "F.T.E." instead of percentages (%). The F.T.E.* is a designation for *full-time equivalent* and should be defined and used in specific ways. For example, 1.00 F.T.E. is the amount of paid service equivalent to that of a single full-time employee for a full fiscal year (12 months). The fiscal year generally refers to 260 days of service (5 work days x 52 weeks) minus vacation time, legal holidays, and sick leave. A total of 2.00 F.T.E.s need not designate two full-time workers. It represents the *equivalent* of two-full-time workers and might be made up for four staff members each working half time. In effect, what you are saying for budgetary purposes is that the work output of four half-time workers is equivalent to that of two full-time employees over a 12-month period.

It doesn't matter how the work is divided or scheduled. One person may work full time for the full year. Another person may work half time for 6 months. Two other persons might work quarter time for the next six

*I am indebted to my colleague Robert Vinter for this material on F.T.E.s.

months. Any figure less than 1.00 F.T.E. always states the proportion of a 12-month full-time job for which a person or persons are being employed.

The F.T.E. provides a simple, uniform, and easily calculated measure of the personnel employed in an agency or program. The total number of F.T.E.s aggregates the paid service of all persons employed in all job classifications regardless of salary differences, part-time or full-time statuses, and so on. F.T.E.s are also generally comparable between programs in agencies allowing for differences such as in length of work week or vacation policy. The F.T.E. does not, however, reveal the numbers of particular individuals whose employment proportions are aggregated into the total. It does not reflect the changing numbers of staff who may be employed at different times during the 12-month period. Moreover, it doesn't reflect the departures and arrivals of individuals who succeed each other in the same job over a given period. It may be necessary for you to discuss these issues in the budget justification or in subsequent program and expenditure reports.

If you expect salaries to change due to union contracts or annual merit increments during a given or fiscal year, you will want to show this in the budget as well. Do so by designating that the project director will be paid for 3 months at $24,000 and 9 months at $26,000. This is how you might show it on your line-item budget:

| | Requested | Donated |
|---|---|---|
| Project director @ 25% of $24,000 for 3 months and 25% of $26,000 for 9 months | $6,375 | |

In F.T.E.s this would still amount to 0.25. It might be written as

$$0.25 \text{ F.T.E.} \left[ \frac{24,000}{4} + \frac{3(26,000)}{4} \right]$$

A similar procedure would be used for each of your professional and support staff (such as secretaries, clerical assistance, bus drivers, maintenance personnel, and accountants). Let's assume you have decided what work needs to be done and how many people it will take to do the job. Each job is given a title. So far so good; the trouble is, you're not sure how much each person should be paid. What to do? The first step is to find out what comparable programs, within your organization and outside, pay staff who have similar responsibilities. Is there a going rate in your agency and in your community for certain jobs? Pay rates on newly funded projects should neither exceed nor fall below pay rates for comparable positions elsewhere in your agency. This statement also holds true for pay raises and fringe benefits.

Before making a final decision, check local, state, and federal regulations in regard to pay rates, special licensing requirements, possible overtime requirements, and so on. If a local union is involved, or if a professional association sets minimum pay standards, find out what those standards are and what the union contract holds in store for the organization. Each of the agency's publics may, in its own way, influence the salary-determining process. In effect, the *market may determine what you can pay*, just as it shapes your decisions about what you are going to do and who will do it.

If some or all of the staff to be assigned to the project are new, you will have to make some guesses about where, on a range of possible salaries, each might be placed. Let's assume for a moment that the salary for a caseworker ranges from $18,000 at entry level to $28,000 per year for those at the upper end of the scale. If you estimate too low, say, close to the $18,000 beginning level, you won't be able to attract more experienced or expert staff persons. If you start too high, your funders are likely to be suspicious, fearing that you are padding the budget. As a rule of thumb, it is helpful to divide the salary range into six segments. In this case, it would be $18,000, $20,000, $22,000, $24,000, and $26,000, the upper limit being $28,000. You wouldn't want to hire all the staff at the upper level with no hope of advancement. Pick the anticipated salary level for the new employees somewhere at the middle or just above the middle range, say $22,000 or $23,000. This will be the figure you will use in your line-item budget. The reason for segmenting is that it indicates to the funder precisely why you chose to put the salary at the given figure. In Table 10–1, the sample line-item budget, we assumed a narrower range of $18,000 to $26,000, with a midpoint of $22,000, upon which the request was based.

## Fringe Benefits

Fringe benefits are generally calculated as a percentage of all *salaries and wages*. If you work for an established organization, chances are that these will account for about 22 to 26 percent of total salaries and wages for all professional and support staff. Note that the costs of fringe benefits have been rising annually along with rising costs of FICA (social security), health insurance, and other benefits. Executive officers may get higher fringe benefits with greater agency contributions to health, life insurance, or retirement benefits than other staff. Fringe benefits are likely to differ from organization to organization. Most voluntary and many state or local government social service agencies make mandatory payments into FICA. The size of both employer and employee contributions to FICA is governed by law. The agency may also be required to make payments to the state for disability insurance and unemployment compensation.

The fringe package may also include voluntary contributions to (1) health, mental health, and dental health insurance programs, (2) an annuity or retirement fund, (3) life insurance, or (4) some other benefit program. Some organizations also provide what have come to be known as "perks." These may include payment to attend training programs, memberships in professional associations, access to agency services and facilities, subsidized rent, or use of an agency vehicle.

If your organization has already developed a fringe package, use the standard percentage allocation in your budget. If you are starting up a new program, you'll have to design a package of your own. Consider what is mandated by law, what will be necessary to attract staff with the qualifications you desire, and what you can afford. Consider also when, in an employee's tenure, he or she will be eligible for certain benefits. Some organizations do not begin paying into a retirement fund until staff has been on board for 3 or more years. Some make a 100 percent contribution to health insurance, whereas others require their employees to pay all or part of the health insurance benefits that they have contracted for with an insurer. If you are not sure where to turn for help in developing your package, check with other comparable organizations such as the United Way, with the local municipality, or with other organizations similar to yours in other parts of the country. Look at the sample line-item budget (Table 10–1) to see how fringe benefits are generally designated. If your package is particularly high or especially low, in comparison to other organizations, you may have to explain the reasons in the budget justification.

## Consultant and Contract Services

Consultant and contract services are performed by people who are not regularly employed by the agency, although they may be involved on an ongoing basis with a particular project. They are generally people or organizations with expertise beyond that which you would normally expect from salaried staff. For example, on a training project, you might want to bring in a consultant on curriculum design or teaching methods to work with your trainers in an early stage of the project. You might also use outside trainers to conduct all the project's workshops, whereas salaried staff may be expected to do only planning, coordinating, and managing of activities and facilities. This section of the budget also includes contract services. Typically, organizations that are in the business of training or counseling contract out for certain supportive services, like transportation, rather than hiring their own bus drivers and purchasing their own equipment. Other contract costs that frequently appear on budgets include legal fees, accounting services, diagnostic or assessment services, information processing, and equipment repair.

Be especially careful to give details for consultant and contract costs. Funders are likely to be suspicious if the fees you pay are high. Here again, you will have to check on the going rate. Recognizing that some consultants demand much higher fees than others, your agency may have to establish an upper limit beyond which it will not go in paying consultants. In that case, you may find yourself unable to attract the specific person or persons you are interested in. In general, the funder will be interested in knowing what the consultant(s) can do for you that your salaried staff cannot. They will want to know that you have a well-developed set of criteria by which you make decisions about whom to employ as a consultant. These explanations go into the budget justification.

The reason why consultants are not listed in professional staff, under the "Salary and Wages" category, is that they do not receive fringe benefits. Generally, only those salaried employees on staff half time or more are likely to qualify for all fringe benefits. In most cases, the law does not require that you pay benefits to staff who are employed on an hourly or minimal part-time basis (such as club leaders and Sunday school teachers) or hourly secretaries who may work two or three mornings per week or type at home on call.

## Nonpersonnel Items

The nonpersonnel section of the budget includes such line items as facilities, equipment, consumable supplies (office and program), travel and per diem, and other expenses.

*Facilities* includes the space required by the program or project for all of its activities. This space may be leased, rented, purchased, or donated as an in-kind contribution. The facilities section may include such line items as lease or rental costs for office space and for conference facilities, insurance, utilities, maintenance (unless performed by salaried employees), remodeling and renovation (if appropriate), and other relevant items. Unusual items or unusual costs should be justified in the narrative. This is especially important if the funding period is only a year or two in length. It would be hard to justify major renovations or the purchase of a building for a one-year project. But if subsequent awards are anticipated from other sources during the project's second, third, and fourth years, and those contributions are dependent on an initial capital investment, you may have a good case.

It is not uncommon for organizations to lease *equipment* for a two- or three-year period, following an understanding with the leasing agency that the money paid in can be applied toward eventual purchase of that equipment. Check out the restrictions imposed by your potential funder. Sometimes funders will permit you to purchase equipment with the understanding that it is to be donated to another approved not-for-profit organization on completion of the program or project. That organization might even be the host agency in which your project is lodged. An explanation of the need for special or unusual pieces of equipment should appear in the budget justification. It should follow clearly from the longer narrative describing the program.

There are two categories of *consumable supplies*: those for *office* use and those for *program* use. Office consumables include disposables like stationery, paper clips, and commonly used items such as staplers and wastebaskets. They may also include laboratory and cleaning supplies. They don't usually include coffee or refreshments for staff!

Although some budgets show separate line items for telephone and mailing costs, when these are relatively modest they are included under consumable office supplies. In detailing telephone use, remember installation costs and justify any extensive out-of-town calling you expect to make. Look into alternative telephone services and low-cost long-distance plans.

Program consumables might include books and pamphlets for the professional staff, subscriptions, films and videotapes to be used in training, athletic equipment with a short life, and so on. Clearly, anything that appears on this line should be directly related to the program narrative and referred to in the budget justification.

*Travel expenses* are usually designated as *local* or *out-of-town*. You will have to be fairly explicit here as well. It is not sufficient to indicate how much money you need. On your line-item budget, you might want to specify the following under local travel:

| Local Travel | Requested | Donated |
|---|---|---|
| Project director @ 200 mi/mo<br>× 12 months × $0.22/mi | $  528.00 | |
| 5 caseworkers @ 500 mi/mo<br>× 9 mo × $0.22/mi | 4,950.00 | |

Better make sure those caseworkers have to be on the road in order to do their work. Someone reviewing your budget may just pick on this item to probe for excesses. Whatever is requested for travel must be reflected in the program narrative. If part of that program includes a transportation service for the elderly or for other clients, in contrast with the travel costs anticipated for staff, you would not include those costs on this line. Develop a separate line item called "Transportation Service" under program expenditure. That line might even include several sublines dealing with maintenance and repair, parking and garaging, and so on.

*Out-of-town travel* is often one of the most vulnerable sections of the budget. If you have a regional or statewide project, and that project requires that your staff travel to sites throughout the area, that travel will generally be considered local in nature because it deals with your program locality. Out-of-town travel refers only to the trips outside of the locality in which the organization provides its services. The reasons for such travel might include participating in professional conferences, meeting with staff of comparable or sister projects in other parts of the country, or attending staff training programs. These trips should be anticipated and planned for in advance, and they should be justified in the budget narrative.

There may also be an additional travel item, one that accounts for the people who are brought to your agency or your program locale. Travel and per diem expenses for consultants may be included here or located with proper explanation under "Consultant Expenses." There might be additional expenses for members of an advisory committee whose travel and per diem are to be covered by the project, or for trainees brought to your training site. Trainee per diem and travel costs are sometimes included under a special line item that deals with that part of the program.

There is no standard format for all budgets. A funding agency may have guidelines that specify where it thinks you should locate one or another item. If not, you will have to decide for yourself or build on agency tradition. In this case, common sense is the best rule. You may, however, need some ideas about how much and what may be included in per diem expenses. These are often spelled out in the application kits that precede federal or state contracts and grants, but are subject to modification depending on the locale. Obviously, it will be more expensive to pay for a hotel room and meals in New York City than it might be in Cody, Wyoming.

Nevertheless, some funding organizations may use a flat per diem rate regardless of the real expense incurred. In fact, they may not even require you to keep records of the expenditures so long as you don't spend more than the permissible upper limit. Check that out, too. Remember air fares are volatile. Pick what you anticipate will be the standard fare at the time the trip is planned for. Look for bargains later. No sense in being caught short.

"Other Costs" can be used as a catchall designation for a variety of items: (1) fire, theft, and liability insurance; (2) dues to professional organizations; and (3) items that don't seem to fit anywhere else. If, however, they are of central importance to the project, each should have its own category. Suppose you intend to design a series of how-to guides or videotapes for use in community education. This probably should have its own line with a number of subitems: typesetting, printing, binding, addressing, and mailing.

To be accurate in your estimate of many of these costs, it is a good idea to do some comparative shopping. Get estimates from different printers. Because current rates may change by the time you are ready to have the job done, pick one of the estimates that is nearer the high side.

## Indirect Costs

Now let's talk a little bit about one of the least understood aspects of the budgeting process: the request for indirect costs. Although the direct costs (those we have been discussing so far) may be easy to identify, they may not be so easy to specify. For example, if the project in question is located in an existing agency, new office space and equipment may not be necessary. Accordingly, there is no need to request line-item funds for space leasing, utilities, maintenance, and so on. These are costs typically incurred for common purposes in the operation of the total organization. The project, however, does use a percentage of the office space and equipment, and the expenses involved can be legitimately charged to the budget. If you just charge a percentage rate rather than the actual dollar amount for these benefits, they are called *indirect costs*.

Indirect costs can also reflect involvement of agency personnel not directly involved in the project. For example, adding a new project to an ongoing operation is likely to require at least minimal attention by the executive director. To indicate that the director is involved, say .05 F.T.E., or that the bookkeeper puts in 12 to 15 hours per year on the accounting procedures, would seem frivolous. All these expenses might better be lumped together in an estimated figure. This becomes part of the indirect cost of the project to the organization.

Universities, for example, typically establish institution-wide indirect cost rates for industrial sponsors of research and other rates for federal government sponsors. These are negotiated rates, agreed upon in advance for all projects that are likely to be submitted during a given fiscal year. Sometimes those rates are set by the sponsor. If the sponsor's rates do not meet the actual costs to the institution, the university may choose not to apply for research grants to that particular funding source. It is probably not unusual for a number of potential sponsors to be unwilling or unable to pay all the indirect costs associated with a project. I've known of more than one agency that nearly went broke because it was successful in getting projects funded, but the funds did not adequately cover the expenses involved.

If your organization is faced by that kind of choice, it will have to struggle with its decision. Are there legitimate reasons why it should absorb some of these costs in its own budget? Consider the extent to which the organization as a whole benefits from the project through gaining a contribution to the organization's missions or new opportunities to reach new populations or to secure other fiscal supports, establishing a relationship to a given sponsor, and so on. Make sure the benefits outweigh the costs.

Indirect costs do not represent a potential profit for your organization. If anything, they are likely not to be adequately recognized or thought through and may result in a net fiscal loss to the organization. You would be wise to account for them as closely as possible. It is important to know whether a project puts a drain on the rest of the organization's operation or whether it adds to the organization's capacity to do other work and expand into new areas. If the potential sponsor does not accept indirect cost as legitimate, you will have to go the route of detailing the actual expenditures for all the items involved.

Although the sponsor may not permit you to charge those costs off against the grant award (i.e., in the "Requested" column), you may be allowed to use indirect costs as part of your "cost sharing" or contributions to the project (in the "Donated" column). Some funders require the recipient of a grant to share the cost of a project by paying all indirect costs.

## Cost Sharing

Cost sharing is a new term for us to examine. It refers to a process in which an organization shares in the cost of a sponsored project by paying some part of the total, directly or indirectly. Almost all federally sponsored grants require some cost sharing. So do many foundation awards. The cost need not be shared by the organization itself. You may find another sponsor willing to share in the cost. You may use fees paid by consumers to offset some or all the cost-sharing requirements.

Cost sharing is not a new idea. What is relatively new is that most funders now require cost-sharing contributions to be documented and auditable and that such contributions must exceed specified percentages. Generally speaking, any real cost to the project, whether direct or indirect, may be counted in cost sharing. Examples include staff effort devoted to a project at no cost to the sponsor, facilities, equipment, supplies, and services (like maintenance).

In some cases, the time contributed to a project by volunteers can be used for cost-sharing purposes, but this is a bit tricky. You will have to check with your sponsor to find out if this is, in fact, permissible. When volunteer time is used, you will have to spell out the actual dollar value of the time contributed before you can locate it in your "Donated" column. There are generally two accepted ways of doing this. The first is to find out what the going rate would be for a comparable service purchased in the open market. Let's say the donated service is legal advice or bookkeeping. If the organization gets 20 hours of free legal advice, estimate the value of such advice on the basis of the going rate for similar services in your community. If a bookkeeper contributes 5 hours a month in time, find out what the going rate would be for such service if you had to purchase it, and locate it on your consultation line item as donated service.

The second way of calculating the value of volunteer time is to base it on what that volunteer would earn if he or she were doing the same work for pay elsewhere. A secretary may be employed elsewhere earning $8.50 per hour, but contributes 2 or 3 hours a week typing for your organization during her evenings or weekends. You would calculate the number of hours of such donated time anticipated during the life of the project before designating it in your "Donated" column.

If you are asking for federal dollars, you may not use, as your share of the costs, any percentage of the time of a staff member whose salary is derived from another federal source. Be aware of the dangers of padding your budget with volunteer donations. If your program is audited, as it may very well be, you will be held accountable as much for the time put in by volunteer staff as by paid staff.

## Making Changes in the Budget

At the beginning of this chapter, I indicated that budgets are flexible documents. They are not written in stone. Budgets are statements of intent. It is not uncommon for a new project to be 3 or 4 months into its first year before staff realize that many of their figures were inaccurate. Many costs may have skyrocketed. Alternatively, you may find yourselves underspending because staff were recruited late. You may be anticipating considerable savings on one or more of your personnel lines.

Most funders will permit you to make minor adaptations in your budget without demanding prior approval. Generally speaking, permission is not required to make adaptations of 10 percent, more or less, on any given line item or any line-item category (like professional personnel). Thus, if the project director's salary winds up lower than you anticipated, but a caseworker's salary turns out to be somewhat higher, and all this does not exceed the 10 percent limit, it will not be necessary for you to ask permission prior to appointing the person in question.

Changes that amount to more than 10 percent generally do require prior approval. Shifts from one line to another, say from personnel to equipment, likewise require approval if they are beyond the 10 percent limit. Note that a 3 or 4 percent reduction in personnel expenses, if those funds are shifted to consumable supplies, may result in a 25 or 30 percent raise in the amount of money allocated toward suppliers. You will need permission from the sponsor before making that change.

## From Line-Item to Performance and Program Budgets

Because line-item budgets tell you what you are spending money on, and not for what purposes, you will either have to justify your expenditures in performance or program terms or perhaps even reassemble the budget into a performance or program budget. For this reason, you should know how to design both a performance and a program budget. For this purpose, we will have to retrace our steps.

In the example that follows, the total budget figures that appeared in the previous line-item budget are listed first, and then the activities for which those funds are allocated are shown to the right. This is the *per-*

*formance budget,* which is used to spell out what it costs to conduct each activity within a project. The advantage of providing funders with a performance budget is that the funder can decide where cuts can be made, should the dollar request be too high. Cuts will generally be in those activities that the funder considers of less central concern.

That, of course, is a danger for the organization submitting the proposal. It puts some decisions in the funder's lap that the agency would prefer to keep in its jurisdiction. These disadvantages to an agency notwithstanding, program planners are likely to find the performance budget extraordinarily useful in program design. The performance budget permits the planners to cost out each of the activities they consider to be important and then to determine the proportion of funds that should be put into each of these activities.

The *program budget* permits you to go one step further. It focuses exclusively on the output or product of the project. It indicates the cost of achieving a given objective. Budget categories are developed around these objectives. In the next two illustrations, I've regrouped costs to compare line-item, performance, and program budgets.

It is unlikely that you will be required to submit only a program or performance budget. More than likely you will be required to submit a line-item budget, but you will have to explain or justify the reason for your expenditures in performance or program terms. On the other hand, for internal purposes, you may find the performance or program budget a sounder tool to use in program design, or even for identifying strategic input markets or publics from which to seek sources of financial aid and other resources. Should you start with either a performance or program budget format, you will have to identify the line items in each category so as to properly monitor the outflow of funds. You will now know not only *where* the money is going, but *how* it is being used and for *what* ends.

Exercise 10–1, following the sample budget (Table 10–2, p.202), will give you a better idea of how you might translate a line-item budget into a program or a performance format, for use in marketing your program with different supplier publics. Try it. You now know enough to complete it without further instructions.

## Fiscal Accounting and Audits

There are two additional terms that need some attention: "accounting" and "audits." *Fiscal accounting* refers to those ongoing activities involved in maintaining an updated and accurate record of the flow of income and expenses related to a project. Accounting is used to ascertain that income and expenses are in line with projections in the budget. The idea behind fiscal accounting is to make sure that money is spent not only as prescribed, but also at a rate of expected or available income. Unless the rates

**TABLE 10-2   Sample Combined Line-Item Budget Summary with Performance Budget (Costs Allocated to Components of Its Program Projected for the Current Year)**

| | Total Budget | General & Administration | Adoptions, Counseling, & Recruitment | Family-Life Education | Publications, Educational Materials |
|---|---|---|---|---|---|
| **I. Personnel** | | | | | |
| A. + B. Salaries, wages, and benefits | $197,030 | $20,000 | $130,000 | $ 7,000 | $40,030 |
| C.  Consultants | 63,750 | 6,500 | 17,250 | 4,000 | 16,000 |
| **II. Nonpersonnel** | | | | | |
| A. Office space | $ 15,000 | $ 5,000 | 10,000 | $ 1,500 | $ 1,000 |
|  Educational space | 2,500 | | | | |
| B. Equipment | 11,510 | 4,510 | 6,000 | 1,000 | |
| C. Office supplies | 3,650 | 2,000 | 1,050 | 600 | |
| D. Program supplies | 6,980 | | 460 | 500 | 6,020 |
| E. Travel | | | | | |
|  Local | 8,230 | 2,000 | 4,730 | 1,100 | 400 |
|  Out of town | 2,700 | | 2,000 | | 700 |
| F. Other costs | 1,700 | 1,700 | | | |
| Totals | $313,050 | $41,710 | $191,490 | $15,700 | $64,150 |

## EXERCISE 10-1
## Turning a Line-Item Budget into a Performance and Program Budget*

1. The Women's Opportunity Center (WOC) in Cantown (population 100,000) is a multiservice agency with three goals:
   a. To provide Cantown women with information about available services
   b. To educate women about topical issues of importance to them
   c. To assist women at risk in the community

   To these ends, WOC provides information/referral and short-term counseling, and also arranges seminars and retreats. While services are targeted at all women in Cantown, two groups figure prominently in WOC activities: victims of domestic violence and teens seeking contraceptive and related advice. (Document I describes WOC services.)

   WOC employs 4 full-time staff persons: a coordinator and 3 facilitators. WOC receives the bulk of its funds from the city of Cantown; The United Way supports the 3 facilitator positions. Document II is WOC's operating budget for FY 84 (the period beginning July 1, 1983 and ending June 30, 1984).

2. The city council election is fast approaching. Councilwoman Frieda Bart (Dem., 4th ward) faces stiff opposition in the form of Mrs. Matilda Spencer, who achieved prominence some years ago as leader of the Cantown "Stop the ERA" Coalition.

   WOC has emerged as the central issue of the campaign. Bart has been an ardent supporter of WOC during all of its budget hearings with the city; she feels it provides valuable services to women in her ward (which has high rates of domestic violence and teen-age pregnancies). Mrs. Spencer has announced that her first priority as councilman [sic] will be to have city funding of that "divorce and abortion center" rescinded.

   Bart asks the WOC staff to provide her with information about the use of staff time, in order to rebutt Matty's charges. The coordinator charts staff activities according to three functional areas and costs them out. (see Document III)

   *TASK 1:* This information is fine; but it only includes costs in terms of staff salaries. *Your task, as Bart's campaign manager, is to prepare a performance budget.* (Worksheet 1 is provided for this purpose.)

3. Matty Spencer is still hot on Bart's campaign trail. The performance budget she released to the press doesn't indicate the extent of

*continued*

## EXERCISE 10-1 *continued*

WOC's activities in programmatic terms. Matty asserts that all WOC activities are centered on abortion and divorce; this budget proves just how expensive it really is. She contends that WOC is a subversive force in the community, and repeats her pledge to have city funding rescinded.

Bart is frantic—the Cantown *Daily News* is eating this up, and the election is only a week away. She needs to prove that she isn't antimotherhood. What can be done to get her some good press, and salvage the campaign?

*TASK 2:* As a quick-thinking campaign manager, you know you need to show the *objectives* of WOC services. *Your task, then, is to prepare a program budget.* (Worksheet 2 is provided for this purpose.)

### Document I    WOC Service Information

- 50 women call the WOC Opportunity Line each week requesting information about community services and activities.
- 5 calls per week are from women seeking crisis intervention; they receive counseling (short-term) in the form of follow-up calls or visits to the center.
- 3 requests per week are from women who are victims of domestic violence in need of emergency shelter. These women are referred to volunteers' homes.
- 5 "battered wives" per week are provided with "transitional guidance" (e.g., counseling related to divorce, marriage, jobs, child care, etc.)
- 10 women per week receive information related to medical care from the WOC Family Planning/Health Information Service.
- 2 women per week request abortion counseling.
- 10 teenagers receive contraceptive education at the weekly WOC Teen Clinic.
- 6 weekend retreats, for about 20 women, are conducted for purposes of training on such topics as women and the law, self-awareness, and math anxiety.
- WOC staff are available on request for talks with local clubs. The center usually receives 2 requests per month, from groups of about 25 persons.
- The WOC coordinator supervises these activities and attends to the administrative tasks of the center.
- WOC employs one 3/4-time secretary. A bookkeeper is available on a 1/4-time basis.

*continued*

**EXERCISE 10-1 continued**

- WOC is located on the first floor of the Century Building, 592 Main Street, Cantown.

## Document II   WOC Operating Budget (Fiscal Year 1984)

|  | Amount and Source | | |
| --- | --- | --- | --- |
| Item | Cantown | United Way | Total |
| Personnel | | | |
| Coordinator | $18,500 | | $ 18,500 |
| Facilitator | | | |
| (3@$15,500) | | $46,500 | 46,500 |
| Secretary | | | |
| (.75 F.T.E.) | 8,000 | | 8,000 |
| Bookkeeper | | | |
| (.25 F.T.E.) | 3,500 | | 3,500 |
| Personnel subtotal | 30,000 | 46,500 | 76,500 |
| Fringe benefits | | | |
| (22% salary) | 6,600 | 10,230 | 16,830 |
| Personnel total | 36,600 | 56,730 | 93,330 |
| Equipment | 2,790 | | 2,790 |
| Consumables | 2,340 | | 2,340 |
| Travel | 500 | | 500 |
| Shelter | 8,400 | | 8,400 |
| Telephone/communication | 2,134 | | 2,134 |
| Direct costs total | 52,764 | 56,730 | 109,494 |
| Indirect costs | | | |
| (20% salaries and wages) | 7,320 | 11,346 | 18,666 |
| Grand total | $60,084 | $68,076 | $128,160 |

## Document III   WOC Monthly Summary *(Case Volume, Service Staff Proportions, and Cost Data by Method of Service)*

|  | Counseling | | | Referral | | | Community Education | | | Administration | Total |
| --- | --- | --- | --- | --- | --- | --- | --- | --- | --- | --- | --- |
|  | | # | % | | # | % | | # | % | | |
| Case data | VDV[a] | 20 | 42 | VDV | 12 | 05 | WAR | 10 | 10 | | |
|  | OLCI | 20 | 42 | FPHI | 40 | 16 | WAL | 50 | 50 | | |
|  | FPHI | 8 | 16 | OLG | 200 | 79 | FPHI | 40 | 40 | | |
| a.   Number of cases | | 48 | | | 252 | | | 100 | | N/A | 400 |

[a]VDV = victims of domestic violence; OLG/CI = opportunity line, general, or crisis intervention; FPHI = family planning/health information services (includes Teen Clinic and counseling related to abortions); WAR/L = women's awareness retreat, lectures

*continued*

## EXERCISE 10-1 *continued*

### Document III  *continued*

| | Counseling | | Referral | | Community Education | | Administration | Total |
|---|---|---|---|---|---|---|---|---|
| | # | % | # | % | # | % | | |
| b. Percentage of total case service units[b] | 12 | | 63 | | 25 | | N/A | 100 |
| Staff time/ service data: | | | | | | | | |
| c. Percentage of staff time by method | 30 | | 40 | | 20 | | 10 | 100 |
| Cost data | | | | | | | | |
| d. Staff cost/ service method | $2,330.50 | | $3,107.32 | | $1,553.66 | | $776.83 | $7,768.30[c] |
| e. Service unit cost/staff- time costs | $48.55 | | $12.33 | | $15.54 | | N/A | N/A |

[b]Service unit = number of cases handled in each method.
[c]$7,768 = monthly salaries (coordinator, 3 facilitators, secretary, bookkeeper) + fringe @ 22%.

### Worksheet 1   Performance Budget

As Ms. Bart's campaign manager, you want to determine the total costs—including the total cost to the city of Cantown—of each service method (activity). You have at your disposal two items which contain all necessary information:

- Document II: contains total city, United Way, and grand total costs
- Document III: indicates (line c.) percentage of staff time per service method

Remember that, in a performance budget, physical outlays are subsumed by each functional activity: costs (for shelter, consumables, etc.) are spread across activities according to the *percent of staff time per service method.*

| | Amount and Source[a] | | |
|---|---|---|---|
| Activity | City | United Way | Total |
| Counseling (48 cases per month) | | | |

*continued*

**EXERCISE 10-1 continued**

|  | Amount and Source[a] | | |
|---|---|---|---|
| Activity | City | United Way | Total |
| Referral (252 cases per month) | | | |
| Community education (100 cases per month) | | | |
| General administration | | | |
| Grand total | | | |

[a]Based on FY 1984 operating budget.

**Worksheet 2    Program Budget**

You now need to determine the cost of each *program* administered by WOC. This budget will indicate the *purpose* of each activity. The performance budget which you prepared (and which gave the Cantown *Daily News* grist for its misogynist mill) gives the *total cost of each activity* (by source of funding).

Document III (line a) indicates the *percentage of each activity per program* (e.g., 42 % of all counseling is directed at victims of domestic violence). These two figures (total cost of activity and percentage of activity/program) will yield the cost of each program.

|  | Amount and Source | | |
|---|---|---|---|
| Program | City | United Way | Total |
| Opportunity line a. Counseling | | | |
| b. Referral | | | |
| 1. Total | | | |
| Victims of domestic violence a. Counseling | | | |
| b. Referral | | | |
| 2. Total | | | |

*continued*

**EXERCISE 10-1** *continued*

| Program | Amount and Source | | |
|---|---|---|---|
| | City | United Way | Total |
| Family planning/ health information | | | |
| a. Counseling | | | |
| b. Referral | | | |
| c. Community education | | | |
| 3. Total | | | |
| Women's awareness | | | |
| 4. Total | | | |
| General administration | | | |
| 5. Total | | | |
| Grand total | | | |

*This exercise was developed by two former students, Deborah Caskes and Robert LaPorte.

of expenditure and of income are in balance, or in favor of income rather than expenditure, the program may find itself in considerable trouble.

*Fiscal audits* refers to periodic examinations of the financial records involved to see whether or not income and expenditures go according to plan (the budget). The auditor considers whether or not the amounts expended on specified items were proper, whether the sources from which money was drawn were proper, whether the timing was appropriate, and whether documentation of each of these was proper. Audits may be conducted internally or externally.

Internal audits are generally conducted by an accountant or other staff within the organization itself. External audits may be conducted by the sponsor or funder or by an outside agent acting on behalf of the sponsor. Audits are sometimes conducted several years after a project has concluded its activities. Thus, it is not only important to maintain good records, but to keep them for a minimum of 3 to 5 years.

## Checking Your Budget

The checklist includes items that are often used by potential funders in examining your budget and determining whether or not there is a strong argument in favor of funding the project. The same issues are also considered in the audit process.

*Budget Check*

1.  All budget items are justified in the text of the proposal narrative and in the budget justification.
2.  Each figure is properly explained unless it is clearly self-explanatory.
3.  The budget designates *requested* and *donated* sums, or uses some other designation to convey what is required of the funder and of the recipient.
4.  The budget is broken down into logical segments such as personnel, non-personnel items, and indirect costs.
5.  Budget figures are realistic. For example, fringe benefits are not out of line. Salaries are compatible with local standards.
6.  The proposal is tailored to the funder and follows the guidelines or procedures and forms required by the funder.
7.  The total size of the budget is appropriate to the project itself.
8.  The costs are reasonable and in relationship to concerns for efficiency.
9.  Line items represent not only reasonable estimates of current cost, but include estimates of future costs, taking into account inflation or changes in salary rates.
10. Extraordinary costs (such as high telephone or travel costs) are fully explained in the budget justification.
11. No important items have been left out of the budget.
12. Figures total properly. The writers know their arithmetic.

There are additional issues that should be considered. First, what will happen if the sponsor is not willing to fund the project—in part or in total? Are there other sources of supply? Will the organization be willing to start the project if less than the amount requested is provided? Under what circumstances might it be possible to pull the project off with a more limited appropriation? If this is not possible, be clear about it. If it is, do you have a fallback position? I have found it useful to discuss alternative budgets with funders prior to submitting a final proposal. But be careful. Being too candid can result in too small an allocation.

Second, have you considered what happens when the project period ends? Have arrangements been made for continued support of the project from the agency's general fund allocation or from some other source? Has time been allocated to seeking newer or alternative sources of funding, (perhaps even from fees) to maintain the project beyond the period for which the request has been made? What is the process by which such funds will be sought? Who will take responsibility for the required activities?

These are questions that must be answered not only for the potential funder, but for others in the organization who may be called upon to shoulder all or part of the responsibility for maintaining a program or for seeking alternative sources of support for it.

## Review

The budget is a program, management, and fiscal document. It can be used to plan programs and services, anticipate cash income and outflow, monitor the flow of cash, and hold the organization accountable for what it sets out to do. It is not an immutable document, however, and should be changed in relation to changed circumstances or modified program objectives.

There are a number of formats used in budget making. The format you choose should accommodate to the requirements of a potential funding source and/or to the standardized ways in which your organization develops its other budgets. The most common budget categorizes all of its expenditures into line items. These items are generally divided into two major categories: personnel and nonpersonnel. Personnel items may include salaries and wages for professional and other personnel, the fringe benefits they receive, and fees for service from consultants and outside contractors. Other, nonpersonnel, items include rental, leasing, and related expenses; disposable office supplies; program supplies; and equipment. A number of programs or projects may also include travel and per diem expenses for staff, board members, trainees, and others. Telephone expenses are generally, but not necessarily, included under consumable office supplies. Other nonpersonnel items may be included that are directly relevant to the program or project. When it is not possible to detail all expenditures, a percentage figure may be used and labeled as "indirect costs."

All line items must be consistent with the program narrative in a project plan or proposal (as when a project application is submitted to an outside funding source). Items may need to be further explained in a "budget justification" section that generally follows the tabular budget. This justification is generally couched in program or performance terms.

The entire budget, in fact, can be written in program or performance terms. Such a budget is referred to as "functional." Performance budgets describe the cost of performing certain program activities and are generally related to the functions or work of distinct operational units. They are most useful in describing the work planned or authorized, and are useful management devices. Program budgets focus more directly on the purposes of an operation: the goals and objectives to be reached. For this reason they are most useful as planning tools and for purposes of program evaluation. Although the line-item budget's disadvantages are that it is not much more than an accounting device, that is also its strength. It can be used to monitor the flow of cash into and out of the organization. Because it focuses on what the money is being spent on and according to what timetable, it is the easiest to design and to use. It cannot, however, document the reasons for spending the money in terms of purpose or function.

The accounting process is aimed at tracking funds into and out of an organization or program as well as checking on whether the rate of income is adequate to cover the rate of expenditures. The auditing process is used periodically to determine whether the expenditures are proper and according to plan.

# 11 GETTING ON THE CHARTS

LIKE BUDGETS, charts are also statements of intent. They describe in visual terms what will be done, in what sequence, and frequently by whom or when. Funders have been known to place as much emphasis on the time frame in a project proposal as on the budget. More than one marketing effort or program and resource-development activity has been known to go off course because of poor navigation.

## Trip-Tics

"We were great at generating ideas," a health care planner involved in a national preventive intervention effort confided to me recently. "We were clearly onto a major concern of both the medical community and the general public. But once we got into operations? Man! A bunch of competent racing car professionals were turned into a mob of angry commuters at rush hour. We knew where we wanted to go, but our timing was off. And it looked like some of us might never make it. There just was no system to the way we were moving. Some of us should have been sharing rides instead of going our own ways. Some of us should have started from different places at different times if we wanted to meet up at an agreed upon time and place."

"The drivers, in this analogy," I responded to my colleague, "might have been helped by having available to them AAA *trip-tics* that not only routed them to their destinations, but indicated the amount of time it might take to get from one place to another." But once having uttered it, I knew that the analogy seemed a bit off. We don't deal with individual drivers in most agencies. We deal with different players, each with a specific responsibility. Unlike a driving team, or a rac-

ing team in which the entire group wins when individuals score highly, agencies
might better be compared to a football team. Since you know I'm from Michigan,
you will indulge me on this. A good coach is concerned that each of his or her
players perform as well as possible. But in a game like football or basketball, one
player's success is very much bound up with the way in which other players perform. Each play has to be carefully orchestrated, and the orchestration process
includes planning, sequencing, and monitoring actions so as to make necessary
on-course corrections.

Charts are used for these purposes both in football and in program
planning and strategic marketing. The types of charts that we'll be exploring together are widely used in the analysis, planning, and control of complex action processes. We'll begin with flow-charting and learn how to use
the international symbols for sequencing decisions, activities, and events.
From there we'll move on to PERT and other examples of the use of *critical path* methods. Finally, we'll examine the use of relatively nontechnical
*Gantt charts* and timetables.

The design of charts, such as those we will be working on, is often a requirement by funding and monitoring organizations. Basic charting skills
will help you get grants and prepare required reports. But even more important, they will help you to orchestrate the complex process involved in
program design, fund raising and promotional campaigns, and other aspects of strategic marketing. Getting on the charts may be the key to your
success and to your organization's survival in an increasingly turbulent and
difficult-to-predict environment.

## Flow Charts

Flow charts are schematic diagrams that indicate the components and the
boundaries of sequences of both activities and events and their functional
interrelations. The design of a chart requires the delineation of processes
and events in such a manner that all major actions and decision points are
clearly identified and located in what is sometimes called a *precedence
network* (precedence, because some activities, events, or decisions precede
others, and network because the chart shows the connections between
them). You can use a flow chart for analytic purposes, portraying an existing program or program structure, or you can use it to plan a new program
or project. You might use one to depict your agency's current budget development process, as shown in one of the following examples, or you may
use it to design your organization's emerging strategic marketing plan.

As you begin the process of chart design, you will find that by breaking
down processes and events into their sequential operations, you will better
understand how events take place or how they should take place, and you
will be able to share your understanding with others. As in any analytic

process, you will have to make choices about how much detail to include or to eliminate. Too much detail may obscure the larger process, whereas too little limits how much we see. In effect, you will have to chart your way between the forest and the trees.

Before we try our hand at flow-charting, you should review the following international conventions or rules that are currently used by its practitioners.

### Rules for Flow-Charting

1. The sequence of activities and events should move from top to bottom or left to right; exceptions such as feedback loops are possible, but these must be clearly indicated as representing a separate or subprogression.

2. Although any symbol may be used to denote different types of activities and events, each symbol must be used consistently.

   Symbols used should be keyed (explained) somewhere on the chart or prior to its presentation, unless they conform to the established meanings of *International Standardized Symbols* developed by IBM or some other readily recognized convention.

3. Lines are used to denote relations or directions, not events, decisions, activities, or roles. The *main line* of any process must be determined and drawn as either a vertical (top-down) or horizontal (left-to-right) double or heavy line. This main line represents the central sequence of activities and events that involve designated agency staff with those publics associated with those activities or events. If that public is a consumer population, the main line could show the interaction between clients and the service system (e.g., a client-careers flow chart) or the staff activities associated with a given service sequence. If the public were a resource provider, the chart might depict the steps required to locate potential funders, assess their interest, make contact, submit proposals, and so on.

4. Subactivities or events that occur in relation to one of these main-line processes (but are not of the process itself) should be shown to one side of the main line, in their own sequence, and in proper sequence with other subactivities and events. Thus, there may be several flow charts, and each of these must be ordered or sequenced according to the time at which the activities in it are performed or according to some other logic (complexity or difficulty) which must be clearly spelled out. Its relation to the main line must be equally clear. The temporal or action boundaries of each program or process must be determined, defined, and designated on the chart in some way as to be easily recognizable (by locating each separately, by drawing a line around it, by color-coding or shading it, etc.).

5.　Loop-back or *recycle sequences* are shown by lines and arrows that return from one activity or event to some antecedent activity or event. Dotted lines are sometimes used to designate "contingent" sequences, those activities and events that are uncertain even though they may be likely.

6.　The location of events and activities along the main line is always determined by its temporal sequence; the major activities being clearly delineated from the minor, auxiliary, interconnecting activities.

7.　All charts should be clearly titled and all identifying notations should be as brief as possible. One of the reasons for designing the chart, after all, is to simplify presentation, and this requires the least amount of narrative that you can get away with while still conveying your message.

## Universal Flow-Chart Symbols

Let's try building a simple flow chart together. First, it is important that we understand the language of flow charts. Figure 11–1 shows international standardized flow-chart symbols that can be purchased in any stationery store as Prestype (pages of rub-off symbols), or on plastic, protractor-type stencils for guiding your drawing. First look at the symbols in Figure 11–1.

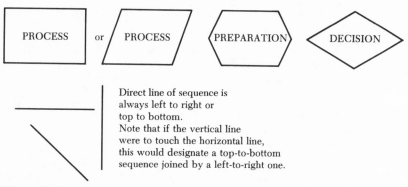

**Figure 11-1.**

Assume, for a moment, that your agency wishes to promote a workshop for adults who are managing one-parent families. Figure 11–2 shows how a

**Figure 11-2.**

simple flow chart might look from the identification of potential consumer populations through the preparation of promotional materials.

Obviously, the process is more complicated than this, and you may wish to express that complexity through the addition of other steps and symbols. Since the process will not end with the preparation of promotional materials, and since there may be no more room on one page to continue the chart, you might want to show that the chart continues to another page. Use the page connector symbol (Figure 11-3). Other important symbols include those in Figure 11-4.

Figure 11-3.

Networking or interaction between people looks much like Figure 11-5. Figure 11-6 shows a subset of activities that take place along the main line.

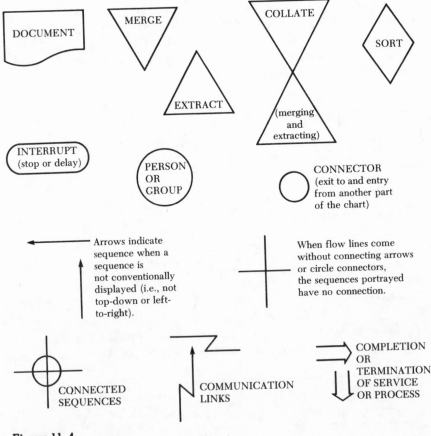

Figure 11-4.

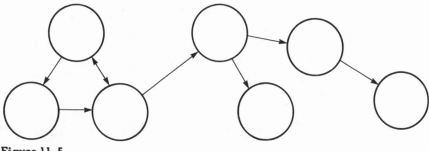

**Figure 11-5.**

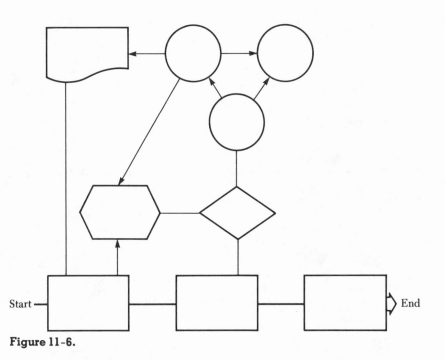

**Figure 11-6.**

The two sample flow charts (Figures 11–7 and 11–8) demonstrate more complex or comprehensive processes. I have chosen to include them as exemplars only, recognizing that they are borrowed from more comprehensive documents and that this may cause the reader some grief. Flow charts are rarely self-explanatory. They help to clarify a process that would be more difficult to visualize if only narrative materials were used. On the other hand, without the narrative, the flow chart will present incomplete information. Nevertheless, I include them because they are good examples of the use to which flow charts can be put. The design-and-use process will become more clear to you as you design your own flow chart according to the instructions in Exercise 11–1.

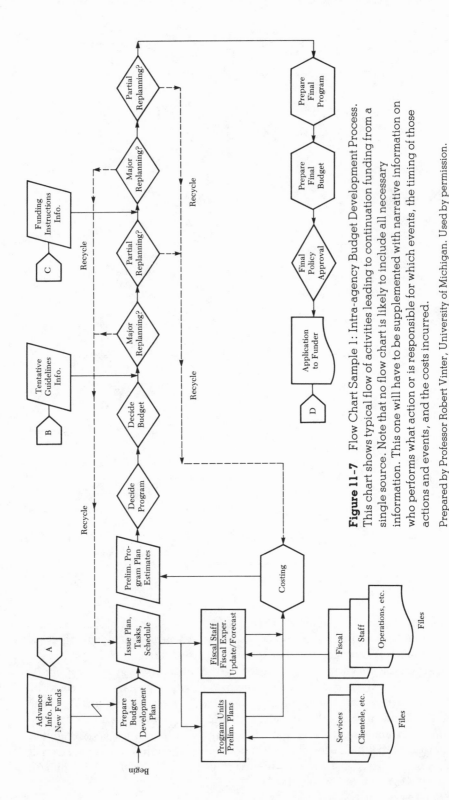

**Figure 11-7** Flow Chart Sample 1: Intra-agency Budget Development Process. This chart shows typical flow of activities leading to continuation funding from a single source. Note that no flow chart is likely to include all necessary information. This one will have to be supplemented with narrative information on who performs what action or is responsible for which events, the timing of those actions and events, and the costs incurred.

Prepared by Professor Robert Vinter, University of Michigan. Used by permission.

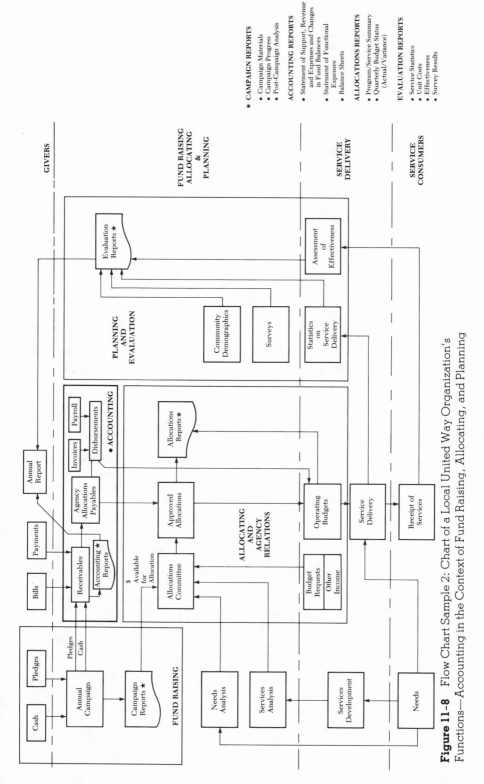

**Figure 11-8**  Flow Chart Sample 2: Chart of a Local United Way Organization's Functions—Accounting in the Context of Fund Raising, Allocating, and Planning

## EXERCISE 11-1
## Designing Your Own Flow Chart

Now it's your turn. Design a flow chart of some process in your organization that will help you and others to engage in strategic marketing. What follows are some suggestions. You and others on staff, with whom you may wish to complete this exercise, may have additional ideas.

| Publics | Processes to Chart |
|---|---|
| Consumers | Client careers through the service system <br> Worker-directed case-management activities <br> Agency-managed, recruitment, intake, throughput, and termination processes |
| Suppliers | Fund-raising campaign <br> Grant-seeking and grant-application process <br> Funding and allocating processes |
| Collaborators | Initiating and negotiating interagency linkages <br> Combining efforts to produce a new program or public relations campaign <br> Establishing, managing, and evaluating a joint client-information system |
| Auspice providers | Preparing an annual report <br> Political campaign to influence regulations <br> Recruitment and selection of board members |
| Internal (staff) publics | Recruitment, selection, orientation, and assignment of volunteers <br> Planning, conducting, and evaluating in-service training <br> Developing the annual budget with input from all departments |

To do the exercise:

1. Select a process that you wish to understand better through its breakdown and sequencing, or one that you wish to put into effect.
2. Review the symbols that are conventionally used in flowcharting and the way they are used. Look over Figures 11-1 through 11-6.
3. Be clear about the items that follow each other temporally along the main line. Consider the subprocesses that would also have to be conducted as a consequence of or as an antecedent to events and activities on the main line.
4. Draw up the chart.

Just as there are many ways to structure a report or a lecture, there are many ways to structure a flow chart. Experiment. Check your work with colleagues and others familiar with the process you are describing or planning. Ask them if your chart is clear and if it is valid; that is, if it presents the appropriate information accurately. You may find that you have included too much detail or too little. Experiment some more. You will find yourself developing skill with experience. Let's turn now to another, more specialized, form of sequencing activities and events. It is variously called "backward chaining," the "critical path" method, or PERT.

## PERT and the Critical Path Method

PERT, as the *Program Review and Evaluation Technique* has come to be known, is a special form of charting. It does not use as many symbols as flow-charting, but it does follow the convention of moving from left to right and sometimes from the top down. As you will see, however, the design process may begin at the right, even though the order of events starts at the left. The main line need not be identified or diagrammed. What PERT designers call the *critical path* has little to do with the centrality of a sequence of events, but it has everything to do with the length of time it takes to get from one point (the beginning) of a process to another (the end). This will become clear as we examine the construction of a PERT network.

The critical path is the most important one on the PERT chart. It indicates which part of a project requires the most time in getting from the initial event to the final event. Any event on the critical path that consumes extra time will cause the final event to fall behind by the same amount of time.

To decide how much time to allot to a project, the planner can choose to find the critical path by backward chaining or by forward chaining. Backward chaining requires that you being with the final event, the date when the project or activity complex is to be completed. In forward chaining you start with the date on which the project begins. The choice between the two methods depends on whether or not a fixed date for the final event is established. If you know that a conference must take place at the end of August, backward chaining will enable you to determine the latest possible date on which the planning process must begin. Forward chaining would begin with today's date and yield information on the earliest time the conference could be conducted, given all the activities and/or subevents that would have to occur first. In some complex situations, one might combine both approaches. An example of this technique will be given shortly.

PERT first received national attention when it was used to schedule and to monitor events leading to the construction and launching of the first

Polaris submarine. Prior to that, it had been used frequently by the Allied Command during World War II for planning large-scale military operations that required massive movements of men and supplies. Since then, it has been modified for application in a variety of business and human service settings. One of the first applications of PERT to social service delivery occurred in the early days of President Johnson's War on Poverty. Planners and managers of community action programs, and later of Model Cities agencies, used PERT for planning community-based services and for the coordination of work by social agencies at the local level.

PERT is a management technique. A PERT network is nothing more than a visual representation of a logical and temporal sequence of activities. It can be used by the program planner to increase administrative control over the use of time, staff, and other resources. Used properly, it can provide the planner with a guide—a map through time—that specifies what is expected by whom, and permits the planner to monitor progress as it is being made. It can also be used to identify areas where shifts in personnel or in emphasis can lead to more efficiency or a greater likelihood of success.

While PERT cannot be used in defining objectives (since these must be defined in advance), it can be used to:

1.  Chart the activities that are required to accomplish those objectives
2.  Coordinate those activities in an effective and efficient manner
3.  Estimate the time necessary to perform those activities and to accomplish a project's overall objectives (in some cases actually to minimize the time required)
4.  Communicate in a precise and visual manner the activities that must be performed in successive steps so that all those who are engaged in the planning activity can see where their contributions fit in
5.  Monitor activities and impose necessary correctives or controls

*Events* on the schematic diagram (Figure 11–9) have been numbered 1 through 4. This time, we are forward-chaining. An event represents the start or completion of a task. Examples of events include the following: a

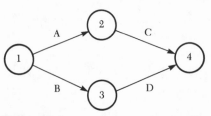

Figure 11-9.

piece of legislation has been passed; a public hearing has been held; the first in a series of task force meetings has been scheduled. The event is not the actual performance of a task. It can be thought of as a significant step along the way toward achieving an objective. In PERT terms, some events may be identified as *milestones*, particularly significant events which must be encountered, but which themselves do not consume time or resources. Most events are shown as circles; milestone events are generally depicted as squares or as circles within squares.

Both time and resources are consumed in *activities*. An activity is the actual performance of a series of tasks required to move from one event to another. On the chart, activities are represented by the lines A, B, C, and D (Figure 11–9). They could just as easily be designated 1–2 (A), 1–3 (B), 2–4 (C), and 3–4 (D). To occur, activities may require materials, space, and personnel. For an activity to be completed, personnel must perform certain *tasks*, jobs that require time.

Events are connected by activities in the design of a PERT network. The events that immediately follow another event are called *successor* events. Thus 2 is a successor event to 1, and 4 is a successor to 2. *Predecessor* events come immediately before another event. Thus 2 and 3 are both predecessors of 4, and 1 is a predecessor of both 2 and 3.

Once events and activities have been charted on a PERT network, it becomes possible to estimate the amount of time required to perform each of the activities that lead from event to event. This would give the planner some notion as to how much time it might take to complete an entire project.

Having designated a PERT network to indicate the interrelationships between events and activities, the planner now makes a time estimate for each activity and enters that value on the PERT chart near the appropriate activity line. For example, if the *estimated* *time* for Activity A in Figure 11–9 is 6 days, you would write $t_e = 6$ next to A. If $B$ $(t_e = 5)$, $C$ $(t_e = 8)$, and $D$ $(t_e = 4)$, which is the critical path? $A + C$ of course! Why include the $e$ after the $t$? Because some complex PERT charts also show $t_o$ (optimistic time), $t_{ml}$ (most likely time), $t_{mp}$ (most pessimistic time), and so forth.

You should now be ready to design your own PERT network. Review the instructions and terminology in this section of the chapter and then go over the list of potential processes to chart suggested on the instructions for the flow-charting exercise. Not all of these lend themselves to PERTing. Which ones do? What other events and activities are you currently engaged in for which a PERT chart might be helpful? Would you use it for planning purposes; for monitoring a sequence of events and activities? What is the final event you are aiming for? Go to it! Work individually or with a colleague using the instructions in Exercise 11–2. Make sure you use a large enough piece of paper or a blackboard so that you have both enough room and the possibility of making frequent adjustments and corrections.

## EXERCISE 11-2
## PERTing Your Way to Success

Now it's your turn again. Select a project with a clear-cut objective and a specific time frame. For example, a first-time PERT experience might deal with preparations for a staff meeting or for a workshop on strategic marketing.

1. Begin by listing all the events you can think of. Be sure these are actually events and not activities. Examine for completeness or redundancies.
2. Should other events be added? Some eliminated?
3. Try to arrange the events in some reasonable chronological order; determine which are predecessor or successor events.
4. Decide whether you are going to seek the critical path by forward-chaining or backward-chaining. Then begin with either your last or your first event. Remember that these are milestones. Are there going to be any other milestone events on your chart?
5. Locate all the successor and predecessor events on your chart between the beginning and ending milestones. Chart the events with lines. Use as many branches or paths as are necessary. Remember to use interconnecting lines should two or more successor events flow from more than one predecessor. Note Figure 11–10 below.

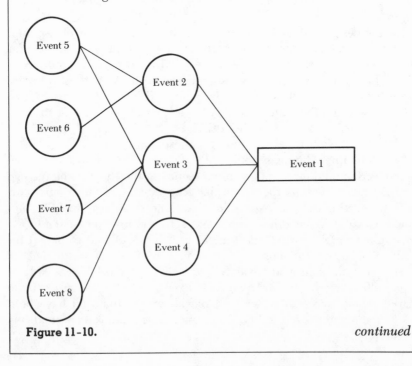

**Figure 11-10.**                                                    *continued*

___ **EXERCISE 11-2 continued** _____

6. Your network having been designed, estimate the time needed
   to move from one event to another. Note this as $t_e$ on each line.
7. Finally, determine the critical path by adding the times required to move from the first to the last event along each conceivable path.

## Gantt Charts

Now that you've mastered the branching tree, flow-charting, and PERT-
ing, Gantt charts and timetables will seem like duck soup. Unlike PERT,
*Gantt* is not an abbreviation or acronym. It refers to its originator, Henry
Gantt, one of the early pioneers of scientific management. Around the
turn of the century, Gantt, an industrialist, began experimenting with
time-and-motion studies. He discovered that proper worker motivation
and clear scheduling guidelines by plant managers resulted in improving
both effectiveness and efficiency. Because of its relative simplicity, what
has come to be known as the Gantt chart continues to be a favorite management and planning tool. Funders frequently require grantees to spell
out their timetables on a Gantt chart, and will then use the chart as a way
of monitoring progress at given periods throughout the grant period. In
the example that follows, I will share with you a Gantt chart prepared by
staff on a training project I directed some years back.

Horizontal lines are drawn under calendar dates. Their lengths are
proportional to the duration of the activity. Progress on the completion of
these activities can be monitored by the drawing of parallel lines adjacent
to the activity lines themselves. An example of the Gantt chart for a project
funded by the "Rufus" Foundation is found in Figures 11–11 and 11–12.

The Gantt chart only describes activities. It does not indicate events as
in the PERT network, nor does it graphically describe the interconnections
between activities and events. The Gantt technique is used only in the forward direction; backward chaining, which is often employed in the PERT
technique, is not possible. The weaknesses of the Gantt technique are obvious: It is almost impossible to reflect slack; interrelationships among activities cannot be illustrated, nor can coordinating functions or precedent
relationships be adequately shown. Conversely, it is a relatively simple
method that can prove invaluable in planning less complex projects.

Notice how neatly this process fits the functional-budgeting approach
we discussed in Chapter 10. Funders frequently require both to be used in
a grant application. The nice thing about using them in tandem is that it
enables you to articulate your expenditures time frame with your programmatic time frame.

Another instrument, called the Sched-U-Graph, was designed by Rem-
ington Rand and is similar to the Gantt chart. In its original form, it was

THE RUFUS FOUNDATION
ACTIVITY SCHEDULE AS OF Sept. 23 1983

ORGANIZATION Kamp Steel    PROJECT TITLE Salesmanship    GRANT START DATE February 1, 1983

| MAJOR OBJECTIVES | | ACTIVITIES | | DURATION | | | | | | | | | | EXPECTED RESULTS | GRANTEE COMMENTS ON STATUS | EMCF USE ONLY |
|---|---|---|---|---|---|---|---|---|---|---|---|---|---|---|---|---|
| | | | | 1st QTR. | 2nd QTR. | 3rd QTR. | 4th QTR. | 5th QTR. | 6th QTR. | 7th QTR. | 8th QTR. | 3rd YEAR 1 2 3 4 | | | | |
| 1.0 | | Certificate Program II | Plan / Status | | | | | | | | | | | | |
| | 1.1 | Selection of trainees | Plan / Status | | | | | | | | | | | | |
| | 1.2 | Curriculum/materials prep. | Plan / Status | | | | | | | | | | | | |
| | 1.3 | Conduct training | Plan / Status | | | | | | | | | | Cohort of 30 trained | | |
| | 1.4 | Evaluation/follow-up | Plan / Status | | | | | | | | | | | | |
| 2.0 | | Certificate Program III | Plan / Status | | | | | | | | | | | | |
| | 2.1 | Selection of trainees | Plan / Status | | | | | | | | | | | | |
| | 2.2 | Curriculum/materials prep. | Plan / Status | | | | | | | | | | | | |
| | 2.3 | Conduct training | Plan / Status | | | | | | | | | | Cohort of 30 trained | | |
| | 2.4 | Evaluation/follow-up | Plan / Status | | | | | | | | | | | | |
| 3.0 | | Social Work Education | Plan / Status | | | | | | | | | | | | |
| | 3.1 | Workshop #1 | Plan / Status | | | | | | | | | | | | |
| | 3.11 | Recruitment/selection | Plan / Status | | | | | | | | | | | | |
| | 3.12 | Develop overall strategy | Plan / Status | | | | | | | | | | | | |
| | 3.13 | Develop workshop plan | Plan / Status | | | | | | | | | | | | |
| | 3.14 | Complete materials | Plan / Status | | | | | | | | | | | | |
| | 3.15 | Conduct workshop | Plan / Status | | | | | | | | | | Cohort of 20 trained & curriculum/course plans developed | | |
| | 3.16 | Evaluation/follow-up | Plan / Status | | | | | | | | | | | | |
| | | | Plan / Status | | | | | | | | | | | | |
| | | | Plan / Status | | | | | | | | | | | | |

NOTE:
• Planned duration indicated with horizontal line covering respective time periods.
• Actual status indicated below planned duration with horizontal line. (up-dated for each reporting period)
• The original plan is duplicated by the Foundation in quantity needed for all quarterly progress reports.

**Figure 11-11.**

THE RUFUS FOUNDATION

ACTIVITY SCHEDULE AS OF _____

ORGANIZATION _____  PROJECT TITLE _____

| MAJOR OBJECTIVES | ACTIVITIES | | DURATION | | | | | | | | | 3rd YEAR | | | | EXPECTED RESULTS | GRANTEE COMMENTS ON STATUS | EMCF USE ONLY |
|---|---|---|---|---|---|---|---|---|---|---|---|---|---|---|---|---|---|---|
| | | | 1st QTR. | 2nd QTR. | 3rd QTR. | 4th QTR. | 5th QTR. | 6th QTR. | 7th QTR. | 8th QTR. | | 1 | 2 | 3 | 4 | | | |
| 3.2 | Workshop # 2 | Plan / Status | | | | | | | | | | | | | | | | |
| 3.21 | Recruitment/selection | Plan / Status | | | | | | | | | | | | | | | | |
| 3.22 | Develop workshop plan | Plan / Status | | | | | | | | | | | | | | | | |
| 3.23 | Prepare materials | Plan / Status | | | | | | | | | | | | | | | | |
| 3.24 | Conduct workshop | Plan / Status | | | | | | | | | | | | | Cohort of 20 trained & | | |
| 3.25 | Evaluation/follow-up | Plan / Status | | | | | | | | | | | | | curriculum/course plans developed | | |
| 3.3 | Sch. of Social Work Graduate Course | Plan / Status | | | | | | | | | | | | | | | | |
| 3.310 | Course offered, term 3A '77 | Plan / Status | | | | | | | | | | | | | | | | |
| 3.311 | Develop course plan | Plan / Status | | | | | | | | | | | | | | | | |
| 3.312 | Include curriculum course | Plan / Status | | | | | | | | | | | | | | | | |
| 3.313 | Develop course outline | Plan / Status | | | | | | | | | | | | | | | | |
| 3.314 | Teach course | Plan / Status | | | | | | | | | | | | | | | | |
| 3.315 | Evaluate | Plan / Status | | | | | | | | | | | | | | | | |
| 3.320 | Course offered, Winter '78 | Plan / Status | | | | | | | | | | | | | | | | |
| 3.321 | Modify above plan based on evaluation | Plan / Status | | | | | | | | | | | | | | | | |
| 3.322 | Teach course | Plan / Status | | | | | | | | | | | | | | | | |
| 3.323 | Evaluate/plan continuation | Plan / Status | | | | | | | | | | | | | Course developed, established & included in SSW curriculum | | |
| 3.4 | Spring/Summer Symposium Workshop | Plan / Status | | | | | | | | | | | | | | | | |
| 3.41 | Develop workshop plan | Plan / Status | | | | | | | | | | | | | | | | |
| 3.42 | Conduct workshop | Plan / Status | | | | | | | | | | | | | Cohort of 35 trained | | |
| 3.43 | Evaluate workshop | Plan / Status | | | | | | | | | | | | | | | | |

NOTE:
• Planned duration indicated with horizontal line covering respective time periods.
• Actual status indicated below planned duration with horizontal line. (up-dated for each reporting period)
• The original plan is duplicated by the Foundation in quantity needed for all quarterly progress reports.

**Figure 11-12.**

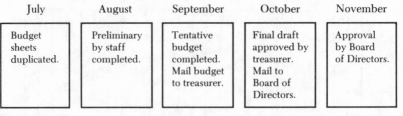

**Figure 11-13.**

designed on a 24 × 42-in. chart containing pockets in which to insert 3 × 5-in. cards. The horizontal portion of the chart is labeled by months near the top. Specific activities or tasks to be performed are typed on 3 × 5-in. cards and inserted in appropriate slots on the chart. For example, if a planner were preparing a budget for presentation to an agency's board of directors, the sequence of activities might be identified as shown in Figure 11-13.

The weaknesses in the Sched-U-Graph are similar to those described for the Gantt chart. It is difficult to determine the time needed to complete the required tasks; since more than one task is generally scheduled for a particular day, week, or month, it becomes increasingly difficult to show the relationships between these tasks and completed events. Exercise 11-3 will illustrate this.

---

**EXERCISE 11-3**
**Gantt Charting**

1. Try your hand at designing a Gantt chart or a Sched-U-Graph. Consider redoing the PERT chart you recently completed or design a Gantt chart around another program or project.

2. Note the advantages and disadvantages of this method over PERT. When would you use one rather than the other?

---

### Timetables

An even simpler way of aggregating this information is on a timetable. Timetables are sometimes used as predecessors or warm-ups for the design of more complex and detailed schedules such as those shown on Gantt charts and PERT networks. In this system, the day, week, month, or quarter is listed in a column at the left of a page, and the activities and events that are to occur during a given time period are written at the right. You've undoubtedly written or used timetables in your work before. Figure 11-14, borrowed from Mary Hall's book on proposal writing, will look familiar.

| Month | Activity |
|-------|----------|
| March | Idea identified. Preliminary discussions held with colleagues to determine their interest; contact made with colleagues in other states to determine the regional or national significance of the idea. Preliminary discussion held with agency administrators and board chairperson. |
| April | Planning group appointed by agency director. Feasibility assessment begun. Inquiries submitted to national information systems to determine if similar idea has already been tried, to get names of communities or agencies with related experience and to identify related research. Data collected to support statement of need. Potential funding sources identified. |
| May–June | Various approaches to implement idea discussed in planning group. Best approach chosen after contacts made with other local agencies, state agencies, etc. Approval to proceed with development of project obtained from agency director. Planning group puts preliminary plan to paper. First draft of idea in project form discussed with agency administrators, potential population to be served, and other groups necessary to local support. |
| | Preliminary outline sent to funding sources to determine interest in the project and to acquire necessary application information. |
| July | Project idea modified by input received during previous months. Continued communication with potential funding sources. Second draft completed and circulated for review to agency administrators and any local or state group involved in a clearance procedure. |
| August | Funding source chosen by planning committee. Final draft prepared based on source's forms or requirements. Official clearance received from local administrators. Review and clearance sought as necessary from any local or state agencies. |
| September | Proposal submitted to funding source. Receipt card with processing number received in return. |
| October–November | Alternative arrangements considered if project is fully funded, if it is rejected, or if it is funded below request. |
| February | Approval or rejection received. In either case comments of reviewers should be sought. |
| March | Authorization for expenditure received. |
| April | Recruitment of personnel. Modifications started on facilities, if necessary. |
| May–June | Plans developed for staff training. Materials prepared. |
| July | Personnel salaried and project started. Staff training initiated. Detailed management plan outlined. Assignments and responsibilities clarified. |
| October | Refunding application prepared and submitted. |

**Figure 11-14**   Timetable for Proposal Development

Adapted from Mary Hall, *Developing Skills in Proposal Writing* (2d ed.), University of Oregon Continuing Education Publications, Portland, Ore., 1979, p. 363.

While its advantage is simplicity, and that's no mean advantage, clearly the timetable suffers from the inadequacies of the Gantt chart and the Sched-U-Graph, and to a greater degree. Nevertheless, it is easy to draw up, requires no technical skill, and communicates its intentions directly. If you've already completed a PERT or Gantt chart, try reassembling the activities and events on a timetable. How much detail is lost? What is gained? If you've not yet worked on one of the more sophisticated scheduling charts, work on a timetable first, then try the Gantt or PERT chart.

Which of these methods do you prefer? Why? From which would you anticipate the most resistance by fellow workers at the agency? Which would generate the most support and involvement? Why?

## Review

Charts are used for planning, scheduling, and coordinating purposes. They can show, at a glance, what a process is, how much time is involved in completing tasks, and, in some cases, who is responsible for those tasks. They can also be used to monitor, evaluate, or correct a process.

Flow charts show the sequencing of activities, decision points, and potential revision points of a process. Typical flow-chart applications focus on client or resource flow through a service system, program planning and project design, and the sequencing of issues to be addressed and decisions to be made. The major advantage of flow charts is in the breaking down of complex processes and procedures.

PERT charts show the complex interrelationships between events and the activities that occur between them. Predecessor and successor events and their linkages to each other are clearly identified. PERT can be used to communicate, in a condensed and precise manner, who is responsible for what and within what period of time.

Gantt charts and Sched-U-Graphs also display major activities and tasks in relation to a specific time frame, but tend to condense them, without detailed attention to the network aspects of event-event or activity-event relationships. Gantt charts parallel functional budgeting or programming processes.

Timetables condense data even further; they are sometimes useful devices for getting started on more detailed charts and networks.

Each type of chart has its own diagram or symbol conventions.

# 12 EVALUATING PROGRAM OUTCOMES

EVALUATION QUESTIONS are focused on what happened and whether it should have happened. Evaluation, as I will be using the term, focuses on outcomes. Some people also refer to "input evaluations." This is what I have called "assessment." You will recall, from Chapter 7, that assessment focuses on what is, what is likely to be, and what ought to be. The two sets of questions are interrelated, integral components to the program-design process and to all aspects of strategic marketing. There is another set of questions that focus on throughputs, how things happen or happened. These will be examined in Chapter 16 when we discuss the marketing audit.

The perceptive reader will have recognized that many assessment tools can also be used for evaluation (e.g., questionnaires used in surveys and in the Delphi method, or structured discussions like NGT). Sometimes assessment data are used as base lines against which outcomes are measured. We have also seen how assessment provides the information needed to establish program goals and operational objectives. In this chapter, we will be learning how to use one particular tool, goal attainment scales (GAS), to evaluate the extent to which goals have been attained. Again, the perceptive reader will see how GAS can also be used to clarify and to set goals early in an intervention process.

I have chosen to limit most of the discussion to GAS because I find it a very effective program-design tool and because a more exhaustive treatment of evaluation tools is beyond the scope of this book. There is another reason as well. In profit-making organizations, money spent, when subtracted from money earned, is often used to measure success. This hardly is an adequate measure for not-for-profit organizations. Other criteria are necessary for determining the extent to which human service interventions are successful. GAS provides you with the means for specifying those criteria. The chapter references at the end of the book will guide you to a growing body of literature that deals with many additional aspects of program evaluation. The following vignette illustrates how goal attainment scales can be used.

### Cooking with GAS

Some years ago I was involved in a training program in which one of the goals was to increase the marketing skills of agency personnel. As is often the case, we had general goals, but we had not broken them down into measurable performance objectives. We, the trainers, were kind of winging it, assuming that those objectives would shake themselves out as we and our trainees became more realistic about possibilities. Frankly, we were a bit troubled by this. Since we were located at a university, and many of us were social scientists, we recognized the importance of having clear-cut objectives and evaluating the achievement of those objectives. Besides, the funder would hold us accountable. (Incidentally, that is sometimes a good reason to keep your objectives fuzzy; the more ambiguous they are, the more difficult it will be for anyone to fault you for not achieving them.) Nevertheless, we were not maintaining a defensive posture at this point. We really *did* want to know what we were achieving.

Unfortunately, we were not 100 percent clear about what our trainees should or could be doing after they completed the program. We were also unable to predict with any certainty those external variables that were likely to influence their achievements. Accordingly, we hit on the strategy of involving our consumers (the trainees) in the design of their own performance objectives.

This required identifying what was feasible and desirable in each person's case. Staff met with each trainee individually to help clarify personal objectives and to scale them in some ordinal fashion. We discovered that this process had a side benefit, one which we had not fully anticipated. It permitted us to individualize the training program, and it helped trainees to think in performance terms about putting what they were learning into practice.

For example, one trainee set her objectives as managing media and promotional committees more effectively. We then helped her specify, in operational terms, what "more effective committee management" meant. Here is how the conversation went.

*Staffer:* How will you know that the committee process is working effectively?
*Trainee:* When members are participating to my satisfaction.
*Staffer:* Too vague, let's try again. How will you know that participation has increased to some level you consider acceptable?

*Trainee:* When at least half of the members take an active role in decision making, and everybody takes a position when it is time to vote.

*Staffer:* That's an acceptable objective. Now let's find out what might make you even more pleased.

*Trainee:* Well, it would be great if some of the members of the staff would take responsibility for key agenda items, so that I wouldn't have to be at the center of the discussion all the time.

*Staffer:* And what would you consider to be a superior achievement?

*Trainee:* If half or more of the staff contributed to the design of the agenda, and at least one or two took responsibility for presenting items on the agenda and leading discussions on those items.

*Staffer:* Good, now let's figure out what would be somewhat less than acceptable.

*Trainee:* If everyone came to the meeting, at least aware of what was going to be on the agenda, even if less than half participated fully.

*Staffer:* And hardly acceptable at all?

*Trainee:* If most of the people showed up, and at least paid attention, instead of disrupting as they usually do.

*Staffer:* Great. Now you are really "cooking with GAS."

## Scaling Your Goals

I'm certain you are aware that we just witnessed the design of a five-point scale using words instead of numbers. The scale spelled out in some detail how the trainee would be able to measure the achievement of the objective. Using a more traditional numerical summary, the scale might have looked like Figure 12–1.

The trainee was left to decide when the objective was to be accomplished. Let's assume that the trainee decided to aim for the achievement of her objective within 3 months of the completion of the course. At that time, we would ask her to describe what she had achieved in the committee-management process. Using the measures that she had developed in advance, we would now be able to determine not only whether the trainee achieved her objective, but the degree or extent to which it had been achieved, on a five-point scale.

| 5 | 4 | 3 | 2 | 1 |
|---|---|---|---|---|
| Highly acceptable | More than acceptable | Acceptable accomplishment | Somewhat less than acceptable | Hardly acceptable |

**Figure 12-1.**

## Designing Goal Attainment Scales

There are a great many ways of designing goal attainment scales. In the next few pages I will introduce you to four fairly standard approaches. In Figure 12–2, you will find an approach that follows a format almost identical to the one we've just witnessed.

Figure 12–2 is a personalized scale developed by an agency worker who was given the responsibility for planning a fund-raising project. Note the way the scale is designed. It identifies a target date "within three months," at which point the worker can check to see how well she is doing. Exercise 12–1 contains a blank form (Table 12–1). Use it to design your own personalized goal attainment scale (GAS) for a single, measurable objective. If you wish, substitute another set of words for those used in the sample and in the exercise. I used "expectations" and "acceptable." What will you use? It is possible that, due to unforeseen circumstances, the objective was temporarily shelved, or deemed no longer reachable or relevant. This does not

Name of trainee:   *Olive Cline*

Objective:   *Within three months of* today, I want to be able to design *a plan for* fund raising in my agency.

The scale of acceptable results is as follows:

| | |
|---|---|
| Barely acceptable | *I will know what goes into a plan and will be able to work out all the steps that need to be followed to get it designed and implemented.* |
| Somewhat acceptable | *I will have completed most of the plan and gotten some directions from colleagues about where to take it next.* |
| Acceptable | *The plan will be fully designed and submitted to those who can act upon it.* |
| Somewhat better than expected | *Many people will have been involved in the plan design or will have reacted to it favorably.* |
| Much better than expected | *The plan will actually be implemented, perhaps with some modifications, or be well on the way to implementation.* |

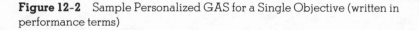

**Figure 12-2**   Sample Personalized GAS for a Single Objective (written in performance terms)

invalidate either the process or the form (Table 12–1). The form will force you and others to confront those possibilities and to reassess the appropriateness of objectives in light of what is possible. It may also lead you to identify the reasons why an objective was not reached, thereby generating new program activities or staff arrangements.

Let's try another approach. In this one, objectives are rank-ordered according to such criteria as importance, complexity, impact, or whatever is relevant. The order in which objectives are listed indicates where they fit on the scale. They are, in fact, the scale. Figure 12–3 illustrates a goal attainment hierarchy designed by an agency in which middle-management personnel were being groomed for participation in agency-wide policy making and planning. Note that three sets of objectives are designated, in effect *rating* them by groups, in addition to their individual rankings.

## EXERCISE 12-1

### Instructions for Designing a Personalized GAS

1. Write the objective in as concrete terms as you can. The objective may be a personal one related to your job or career aspirations. This is the way you would use the exercise in working with trainees or supervisees, or with clients whom you may be involving in goal specification around their own needs or interests. Alternatively, the objective may flow from one of the agency's program goals. It might be related to service delivery, interagency linkages, resource development and orchestration, etc. Refer to the discussion of objectives earlier in this chapter and in Chapter 8 on program design. Give yourself a target date to shoot for: the time when the progress toward the objective will be evaluated.

2. Now "scale" the criteria by which you will know how well you did when the time for evaluation comes around. If you are developing a personalized scale, you might want to discuss these performance criteria with a supervisor or instructor. If you are working on an objective that was drawn from a program or marketing goal, you might want to consult with persons who are responsible for program design and implementation to be sure that the criteria are realistic.

3. At the end of the period of time you set for yourself, you will examine the extent to which the objective was achieved in relation to the performance criteria. To score the achievement, use the numerical ranking scale at the bottom of Table 12–1.

*continued*

__ EXERCISE 12-1 continued _____

**TABLE 12-1   Form for Personalized or Program GAS on a Single Objective (written in performance terms)**

Name of trainee:_____

Objective:_____

_____

_____

_____

The scale of results is as follows:

| | |
|---|---|
| 5  Way beyond my expectations | |
| 4  Somewhat above my expectations | |
| 3  Right on target (acceptable) | |
| 2  Not as high as I want it to be | |
| 1  Not acceptable or satisfactory | |

*Numerical ranking→Scale*

My achievement level at the end of _____ months:

| 5 | 4 | 3 | 2 | 1 |
|---|---|---|---|---|
| Way beyond my expectations | Somewhat above my expectations | Right on target | Not as high | Not satisfactory |

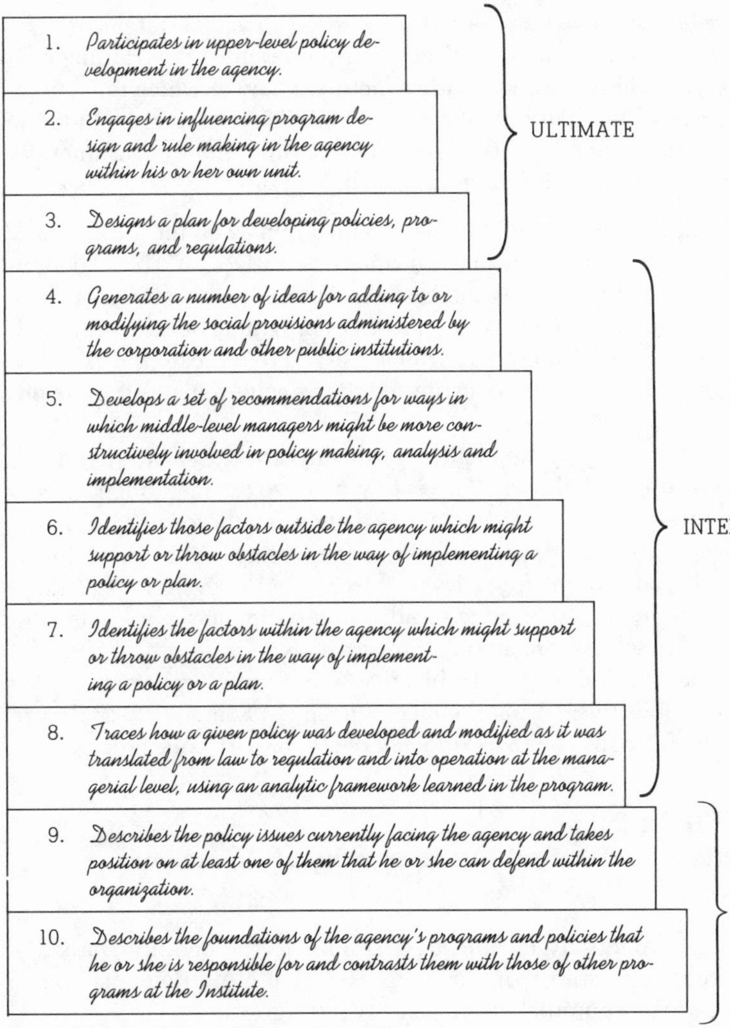

1. Participates in upper-level policy development in the agency.

2. Engages in influencing program design and rule making in the agency within his or her own unit.

3. Designs a plan for developing policies, programs, and regulations.

} ULTIMATE

4. Generates a number of ideas for adding to or modifying the social provisions administered by the corporation and other public institutions.

5. Develops a set of recommendations for ways in which middle-level managers might be more constructively involved in policy making, analysis and implementation.

6. Identifies those factors outside the agency which might support or throw obstacles in the way of implementing a policy or plan.

7. Identifies the factors within the agency which might support or throw obstacles in the way of implementing a policy or a plan.

8. Traces how a given policy was developed and modified as it was translated from law to regulation and into operation at the managerial level, using an analytic framework learned in the program.

} INTERMEDIATE

9. Describes the policy issues currently facing the agency and takes position on at least one of them that he or she can defend within the organization.

10. Describes the foundations of the agency's programs and policies that he or she is responsible for and contrasts them with those of other programs at the Institute.

} IMMEDIATE

**Figure 12-3** Sample Hierarchy of Objectives

*Immediate objectives* are those that are attainable during the grooming program itself, or shortly thereafter.

*Intermediate objectives* are those that participants are expected to achieve within a designated period. A time period of 6 or 12 months might be selected, after which trainees will be polled to see if these objectives were met. In general, self-reporting on the part of the trainee is sufficient to ascertain if these objectives have been met, although supervisor reports and feedback from colleagues might also be used.

*Ultimate objectives* are as close as one can get to a goal statement. The achievement of ultimate objectives is the result of the training program in combination with other factors, many of which may be totally out of the hands of those involved. These factors include the opportunities available due to expanding programs or consumer demand, cutbacks in funding, and so on.

The program's success might be determined in part on the basis of how many participants achieve any of the ultimate objectives, and how soon, in comparison to a similar population that did not undergo training or some other form of grooming. The program's success might be bolstered by feedback from participants and others who are asked to indicate the extent to which the grooming program contributed to the achievement of those objectives.

Notice that the step-by-step nature of the hierarchy is illustrated in the way that Figure 12–3 is drawn. This is to symbolize the fact that each successive step requires some achievement at a preceding or lower step. In actual practice, it may be possible for someone to skip one or more lower steps and still achieve an upper-level objective. Moreover, not all these steps will be of equal importance to all the participants, who should, in fact, be helped to select from among those objectives.

Try designing a hierarchy of objectives from some organizational or personal set of objectives, using the model given. In Exercise 12–2, Figure 12–4 is a blank form for you to use independently or with colleagues.

---

## EXERCISE 12-2

### Instructions for Designing a Hierarchy of Objectives for GAS

1. Prepare a hierarchy of objectives similar to the one illustrated, based either on staff work or on involvement of participants in a procedure like nominal group priority setting.

2. Introduce the hierarchy to those who may be involved in an intervention process (e.g., volunteers, program staff, fund-raisers) pointing out the differences between those that are immediate, intermediate, and ultimate. Indicate that each of these objectives may be of greater or lesser importance and that it is not expected that each participant will achieve exactly the same objectives by the end of the program.

3. Ask participants to place a check ($\nu$)next to each of the objectives they wish to achieve, and to be prepared to discuss these with an advisor, instructor, or program staff.

*continued*

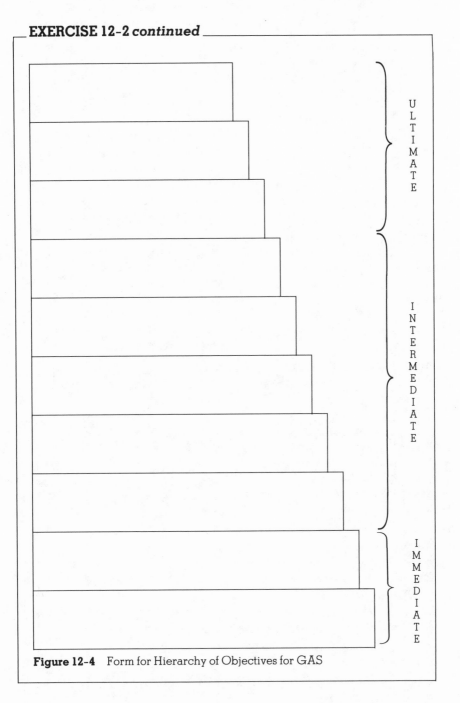

**Figure 12-4**   Form for Hierarchy of Objectives for GAS

**TABLE 12-2  Goal-Planning Worksheet Using Verbal Descriptions**

| Goal attainment scale for period beginning Sept. 1 and ending Nov. 30 | Managing people's relationships: Importance 1-②-3 | Managing work flow: Importance 1-2-③ | Defining tasks and describing jobs: Importance 1-2-③ | Reducing errors: Importance 1-②-3 |
|---|---|---|---|---|
| Results much worse than expected (What are the worst outcomes you can imagine?) | Staff will avoid any out-and-out conflicts that are disruptive to their work and the workplace. | Members of the staff are aware that I am concerned about work-flow problems and are willing to learn more. | Staff understand what task analysis is all about, but they are resistant as hell! | Work-related error will be identified and have base-line data gathered. |
| Results somewhat less than expected (What outcomes would be slightly below your expected results?) | Staff members will stop bad-mouthing each other. | Members of the staff recognize that there is a work-flow problem and agree to work on it. | The task-analysis process will have begun, with little or no staff resistance. | Each staff member will determine the extent to which he or she will reduce error. |
| Expected results (What will you probably accomplish?) | People in my work unit will treat each other with civility. | Everyone in my unit understands the procedures each is to perform. | Task descriptions will be prepared for all staff in my unit. | Errors will be reduced by 25% for the entire unit. |
| Results somewhat better than expected (What outcomes would be slightly above your expected results?) | Staff will cooperate willingly and in good spirits. | Staff understand the procedures to be used by others with whom they must interact. | All staff will have been involved in the task-analysis process. | Errors will be reduced by 50% and a plan will be set in motion for 100% reduction. |
| Results much better than expected (What are the best outcomes you can imagine?) | Staff will really enjoy working together and cooperating on work-related tasks. | Input and output work flows between staff are moving smoothly. | Staff will not only have been involved, but will be really committed to using task analysis in job redesign. | Errors will be reduced by 75%, with a program under way toward total reduction. |

*Note:* Major objectives appear in the top row of each column.

**TABLE 12-3  Form for Goal-Planning Worksheet Using Verbal Descriptions**

| Goal attainment scale for period beginning _____ 1984, and ending _____ | Importance 1-2-3 | Importance 1-2-3 | Importance 1-2-3 | Importance 1-2-3 |
|---|---|---|---|---|
| Results much worse than expected (What are the worst outcomes you can imagine?) | | | | |
| Results somewhat less than expected (What outcomes would be slightly below your expected results?) | | | | |
| Expected results (What will you probably accomplish?) | | | | |
| Results somewhat better than expected (What outcomes would be slightly above your expected results?) | | | | |
| Results much better than expected (What are the best outcomes you can imagine?) | | | | |

Since it is likely that not all of you will be working toward each objective, you may wish to take those you have checked and develop specific performance or outcome criteria for those you have selected following the guidelines for Exercise 12–1. Alternatively, the program staff may wish to design such criteria for each of the objectives on the hierarchy. Note that once such criteria have been determined, it makes sense to re-examine some of the earlier intervention or action decisions made. If you or the staff have used the branching-tree exercise described in Chapter 8 for planning purposes, go back over your earlier decisions and make the necessary adjustments. You have now begun the process of using an evaluative procedure for program design.

There is still a third GAS approach you may find equally useful. It has the advantage of including several goals or objectives on a single page. Table 12–2 will show you how it is done. If you have completed Exercise 12–1, you should have no difficulty in completing the form for Exercise

---

**EXERCISE 12-3**
**Goal-Planning Worksheet**

1. Use the exercise form in Table 12–3 and place major objectives areas in the top row. "Major objectives" refers to the key areas in which you hope action will take place.

2. Distribute a form to each person at an appropriate time (e.g., right after solicitor orientation at the start of a fund-raising campaign, or during an early session of an interagency task force looking into expanded collaborative efforts). I have found that a practice run with GAS helps before the form is finalized.

3. Give the participants instructions for completing the scale. You might say something like the following:

   "Look at the four boxes in the top row. Each box represents an area that we have discussed. This exercise will help you in your goal planning for these four areas.

   "In each of the boxes in the top row, write a goal that you would like to accomplish for that area. Your goal should be something that you could realistically accomplish during the specified time period (say 3 months). Please write only one goal in each box.

   "Not all goals are of equal importance. In order to think through your priorities, use the following numbers to rate the importance of each goal. This is *not* a rank ordering of the four goals. You may use the same number for more than one goal.
   3 = extremely important to you
   2 = not as important as 3, but more important than 1
   1 = fairly important to you"

12–3 (Table 12–3). The instructions in Exercise 12–3 suggest how you might guide a staff group in completing a form similar to Table 12–3.

Some evaluators may find it a bit difficult to use verbal measures in grouping their data, or to analyze the meanings of their findings. In Table 12–4, objectives are listed in a column along the left-hand side of the page. In this form of GAS, respondents (trainees, program designers, clients, and so on) are asked to rate each objective on the basis of importance at the start of a program or intervention activity. Altogether, a total of 100 points (equivalent to 100 percent of importance) can be allocated.

Notice that the respondent in Table 12–4 considered only items 1, 3, 5, and 6 as being important. This is a *ranking* procedure. Column C is completed at the end of an intervention effort. The respondent scores each of the objectives he or she considers important, with a score of 0 (no fulfillment) to 10 (total fulfillment). This is a *rating* procedure. Next, the respondent completes the instructions for column D. The degree of importance is multiplied by the degree of fulfillment, yielding an "index of objective-fulfillment."

Finally, the scores in column D are added up, yielding a composite index of fulfillment of all the objectives in column A. In the case illustrated, they total 655. The maximum possible score is 1000. This would have been achieved if each of the objectives were fully reached (i.e., each had scored a 10). The beauty of this approach is in its ability to reduce relatively complex data to numbers that can be used to summarize and compare results.

First, let's come to some agreement about the meaning of the numbers in column C. Let's assume the following:

    0 = no fulfillment
    1–2 = poor or unsatisfactory fulfillment
    3–4 = below average fulfillment
    5 = average
    6–7 = above average fulfillment (or above expectations)
    8–9 = very good
    10 = totally fulfilled

When these are multiplied by importance, and a *composite index of objective fulfillment* is calculated for each participant, it is possible to compare participant scores, one to another; or to compare different cohorts of participants. When one is comparing achievement of objectives in a marketing or in any other intervention program, it is possible to calculate indices of importance and achievement. These, in turn, can be used to determine whether or not to continue in a given direction or to invest resources in an area that is considered to have greater payoff. Payoff is measured in the terms of the GAS ratio. A ratio of 655/1000 (which might be shown as 0.655 or 65.5 percent on the *importance fulfillment* scale) would be considered more effective than a score of 450/1000 (45 percent) and less effective than 800/1000 (80 percent). Low scores suggest that there are

**TABLE 12-4   Sample Goal Attainment Scale Using Scoring Index**

Name_____

| A.   Objectives:<br><br>Check the objectives that are important to you.<br><br>All supervisors will be able to | B.   Degree of importance:<br><br>On a scale of 1–100 weigh the importance to you of each checked objective. You must allocate 100 points among all checked items.[a] | C.   Degree of fulfillment:<br><br>On a scale of 0–10 weigh each objective that you checked to indicate how well it was fulfilled by the workshop. | D.   Index of objective fulfillment:<br><br>Calculate the index by multiplying Columns B and C. |
|---|---|---|---|
| 1.  *Conduct a staff meeting in which all members participate.*   ✔ | 20 | 1 | 20 |
| 2.  *Conduct a task analysis of all the jobs performed in my work unit.* | | | |
| 3.  *Identify all those factors which lead to low productivity in my work unit.*   ✔ | 15 | 9 | 135 |
| 4.  *Develop a map of resources in the community of importance to my agency's clients.* | | | |
| 5.  *Use three new consultation techniques in my work with staff of other departments.*   ✔ | 5 | 8 | 40 |
| 6.  *Design a new information flow system for the organization.*   ✔ | 60 | 8 | 480 |
| | Total: *100* | | Total GAS: *655* |
| | | | GAS Ratio:<br>655/1000 |

[a]If you checked 1 objective, you should allocate 100 points to it. If you checked 4 objectives, divide the 100 points 4 ways.

components of the intervention process that might be modified, that the objective is not desirable, or that it should be modified. High scores might suggest that no one should tamper with success.

Thus it becomes apparent that one can use GAS as both a formative or a summative evaluation tool. Now it's your turn to try this format for GAS. Do Exercise 12–4.

## Some Criticisms of Goal-Focused Evaluations

Now that you may be convinced about the utility of goal attainment scales, let me make some cautionary remarks. Because GAS depends heavily on personal reporting rather than on observations, it can yield less than valid information. This may be less of a defect than it seems. Goals are not always all that clear, and even the best-designed performance objectives may be difficult to measure.

Moreover, objectives change as a program is implemented and as circumstances that led to the original program design change. This is, perhaps, the more important criticism of goal-focused evaluations; by focusing exclusively on goals, evaluators and program staff may impose premature closure on those goals, particularly when circumstances may suggest other, more appropriate interventions. Excessive focus on stated goals is likely to eliminate unanticipated outcomes from consideration. For this reason, some program evaluators have suggested that it may be more appropriate to engage in "goal-free" evaluations. These are generally grouped under what has come to be known as the "systems model" of program evaluation.

The systems model focuses on the interaction of the program and the key elements in its internal and external environment. It recognizes that a program may perform functions for the organization that are unrelated to its stated or formal objectives: Whatever its stated goals, an agency may really engage in an intervention effort in order to increase its credibility with the public, or to secure new funds and other resources which will enable it to expand its operations or even "survive." Program efforts may be designed to increase the staff's opportunities for professional development or occupational mobility, or to provide a funding agency with a setting for discharging its public obligations. These purposes may have little to do with the stated goals and operational objectives of the project itself.

Evaluators who follow the systems model look at how the program relates to the various forces in its own environment and in the environment of the host organization. They examine the way in which a program might penetrate other systems, and may be penetrated by those systems in return. They recognize that failure to achieve specific objectives may actually lead to successes in other areas. Unlike the goal model which tends to use precise measurements, the systems approach may use more process-oriented methods, such as case studies or comparative examinations. The reason why it is sometimes called goal-free is that it does not begin by an examination of stated goals.

The systems model may infer those goals from an examination of the processes and activities that take place during the course of a project, particularly those that relate to resource recruitment, mobilization, and allo-

## EXERCISE 12-4

## Instructions for Designing a GAS Using a Scoring Index

1. Determine what program goal you wish to evaluate on the basis of importance and fulfillment.

2. Design a goal attainment scale specifying the objectives to be reached, or use the blank form (Table 12-5) as your guide.

3. Decide who should complete the form (e.g., agency staff, funders, clients) and administer the form. Have it completed.

4. Compute the results and use them for formative or summative purposes.

### TABLE 12-5  Form for Goal Attainment Scale Using Scoring Index

| A. Objectives:<br><br>Check the objectives that are important to you. (Write them in below.) Be able to: | B. Degree of importance:<br><br>On a scale of 1–100 weigh the importance to you of each checked objective. You must allocate 100 points among all checked items. | C. Degree of fulfillment:<br><br>On a scale of 0–10 weigh each objective that you checked to indicate how well it was fulfilled by the workshop. | D. Index of objective fulfillment:<br><br>Calculate the index by multiplying Columns B and C. |
|---|---|---|---|
| | | | |

Total: 100              Index:
                        out of a
                        possible: 1000

cation. Thus, it is freer to examine the unintended consequences of an intervention effort or the functionality of a program with regard to the agency's survival and the interests of its various publics.

These strengths are also the weaknesses of the systems approach. By not focusing on the outcome goals specifically, it may be less than helpful in shaping those goals or in holding the staff and the agency involved accountable for achieving the goals specified.

## Overcoming Resistance to Program Evaluation

Whatever the approach used, you're likely to uncover some resistance to an evaluation on the part of managers, program staff, and even consumers or supplier publics. People don't like to be graded. They may see the evaluation as a diversion from the real task, from the job to be done. Some practitioners and others may fear exposure and the loss of self-esteem or the respect of others.

The processes that an evaluator uses may seem alien to agency practices. They may take time away from other more cherished or valued activities. They may create disruptions, and in turn these disruptions may be perceived of as a devaluation of the staff's current knowledge, skill, experience, and even connections. The results of an evaluation may challenge long-held beliefs.

Evaluators may have different ideas of who or what should be studied than do others involved in the program; they may be concerned with the impact of a given intervention and may wish the intervention methods to be tested on a number of different targets. Evaluators may accuse the professional staff of "creaming," selecting only clients that are most likely to succeed on the basis of the intervention method used.

Friction can be reduced if others are involved in specifying the data that are to be collected, in collecting the data, and in analyzing and interpreting the findings. When evaluators are outsiders, staff and other representatives of key publics should be involved, at the very least, in an evaluation planning committee, or perhaps in an advisory group from which the evaluators get guidance.

This committee might be charged with formulation of recommendations for modifications or changes in some aspect of the program based on the evaluation findings. It also helps to schedule informal meetings between evaluators and those persons whose activities may be evaluated. These meetings provide opportunities for the expression of doubt and the clarification of expectations. The implications of findings should be discussed before they emerge, so that the key participants will understand how these findings are likely to affect them. Finally, staff and others should be rewarded for their participation, encouraged, and given recognition for their efforts, such as time off and perhaps even specialized training aimed at increasing their competence and skill.

## Review

Evaluation, as we use the term, focuses on outcomes. When goals are transformed into operational objectives, these objectives can provide the framework within which achievement can be measured. Goal attainment scales can be used for such measurement. Four approaches to the use of GAS were presented. One of the dangers in an exclusive focus on goal attainment, however, is that it may limit the evaluator's perspective to preconceived outcomes. Goals change during the course of an intervention effort. Whatever the stated goals, these are likely to change over time, and whatever the goals, programs frequently perform other anticipated and unanticipated functions that may remain unstated. The performance of such functions may be as important or more so to key publics than the stated goals and objectives.

# PART IV

# Resource Development

# 13 THE PROFITABLE WAY TO RAISE MONEY

DEVOTEES OF Winnie the Pooh remember their introduction to Edward Bear, coming down the stairs "bump, bump, bump, on the back of his head, behind Christopher Robin. It is, as far as he knows, the only way of coming downstairs, but sometimes he feels that there really is another way, if only he could stop bumping for a moment and think of it."* Most of us are much the same, being pulled ahead by momentum or habit, so full of the experience as to not be able to stop and think of how we might manage it better. This is especially true when it comes to fund raising from individuals and the general public. Sometimes predicaments provide us with just those opportunities we need to take stock and consider new directions. But, unlike Edward Bear, we can take the initiative rather than just reflect on it. Let me share an example with you.

## Getting Fired Up

About a year ago, a dynamic and rapidly growing health advocacy institute found itself in deep difficulty. Not only was its growth threatened by cuts in federal and state grants and by reduced access to philanthropic foundations, but its very survival as an advocacy center was in danger. The problems were not of its own making. Shifts in national and regional spending priorities and a lagging economy had conspired to define its services as nonessential. The staff of the organization was not about to accept that definition. If the problem were not of its own making, the solution would be.

---

*A.A. Milne, *Winnie-the-Pooh*, E.P. Dutton & Co., New York, 1926, p. 1.

One of its major concerns was the prevention of disabling, disfiguring, and life-threatening burns. "It is precisely when times are bad that we have to get our act together," the executive director began a staff meeting. "Cuts or no cuts, this is the time when public awareness and prevention activities are all the more important." "Clearly we can't do it all alone," a planning associate added. "Up to now we depended on others for grants and contracts. We're still going to have to depend on others for financial resources, but we are going to have to find new ways of getting the money we need. Let's make a list of those groups and organizations in the community that might care as much about burn prevention as we do."

The list generated by staff included firefighters; the police; public health officials; individual physicians, nurses, and other health-care professionals; public housing officials; landlords; and a number of other easily definable publics. "Okay," continued the planner, "let's figure out which of these are to be targets of our intervention, and which ones are potential partners in that intervention." Staff members discussed each public. Clearly some, like landlords, were both targets and potential collaborators. But landlords were not likely to put money out or engage in a fund raiser on behalf of the Institute. Health-care providers might be individually concerned with prevention and with treatment, but were also not likely to be actively engaged in fund-raising activities. Firefighters, on the other hand, seemed to be a good bet for involvement as partners in raising the public's consciousness as well as suppliers of needed financial resources.

"When I first approached one of the firefighters' associations, I was surprised at the warmth with which they greeted me," explained the planning associate a year and a half later. "I've never really known firemen. Let me tell you. They know their business and they care. They depend on each other in emergencies, they develop a real camaraderie and esprit de corps. And they have no trouble including other people in their inner circles. That's why they are so outgoing and friendly toward schoolkids when they come to visit the firehouse. And, most of all, they know what getting burned means.

"The first thing we did was to provide them with some of our written material on the prevention of fires, handouts that they could use in schools and public presentations. Then we coached them on how to work with the local radio station and the newspapers. But we also leveled with them about our own financial needs. We couldn't continue providing materials of this sort or consult with them without some financial support from the community. I really wasn't expecting it, but the first fund-raising effort took place at their annual picnic last May. Firefighters and their families, other city officials, and, interestingly, people who had been helped by the fire department at one time or another, were all there. The chief got up and made a speech, then he introduced me. I spoke for about 5 minutes about how we all need to work together and I described some of the serious consequences of burns to individuals and their families. The chief came back to the mike and told everybody about the importance of the work of our Institute and asked everybody to dig in. They collected over $500. The firefighters were ecstatic.

"When I met with them a few weeks later, they felt proud of themselves, but as one of the guys put it, 'We really can do better but we don't know much about fund raising.' That was my opportunity. Together we mapped out a campaign that included the involvement of parent-teacher organizations, the same PTOs with which the firefighters worked when schools sent children to visit the fire stations in the community. And it included involving burn victims as well as people who had suffered property damage but not bodily harm through fires. They went to work on fund-raising committees. It took only about 3 months of organizing to put everything in place. The annual picnic is now seen as a fund-raising event. There is a semiannual letter-writing campaign. The firefighters' wives auxiliary has opened up a thrift shop (and would you believe, it got its first major donation from what was left over in a clothing store after a fire).

"This year we expect about $2,500 in gifts from that community, but that is not the entire point. By involving people in fund-raising efforts, we have actually involved them in a process of *consciousness raising* and prevention. I've spent about 20 working days in that community, and I suppose for a fund-raising effort that wouldn't be cost-effective. Not the first time around. But it will get more cost-effective as the community is able to take more and more responsibility for fund raising on its own behalf. And as we get more experienced with these approaches, we will be able to replicate them in communities throughout the country. We couldn't have found better partners than the firefighters."

## Principles on Which to Design Your Fund Raising

Out of the staff's experience, the health institute had evolved a number of practice principles that have come to underlie its fund-raising approaches. I highly recommend them to any organization. First among these is to *broaden your base of support* so as to minimize your dependence on one or two sources. When foundation grants become scarce, for example, it may make more sense to seek support from industry or the general public, rather than from another foundation. Second, *find another partner or partners*, persons and organizations that will be as concerned as you about raising the necessary funds; partners who may even take on fund raising for your organization as a major commitment. Third, *use fund-raising activities in such a way as to complement other organizational programs* and services. In some cases, fund-raising activities may themselves become essential services, particularly when they increase public awareness and involve the public in programs of self-help. Fourth, *articulate fund-raising efforts with other sources of support* like general-fund allocations, regular appropriations, and so on.

As you read through this chapter, you will identify a number of other practice principles that will fit your organization and its fund-raising style.

Here's a beginning inventory, which, when added to the four above, will give you an even dozen principles to start with:

Boost, don't boast. Involve people in the cause, a concern for a population in need or a commitment to a service program. Don't push yourself or your organization.

Reward those who are involved in the fund-raising effort. Although involvement itself may be a reward, the benefits of participation may be insufficient to overcome the costs in time and emotional energy.

Treat all donors as prospects, but recognize that all prospects are not necessarily donors. That someone contributed money or other goods in previous years does not mean that he or she is going to be willing to contribute this year.

Contributors rarely reach their maximums. Most people can give more and/or can be induced to solicit others.

Don't build a campaign around the hope of finding a sugar daddy who will bail the organization out. Broaden the base of the fund-raising effort to include large, medium, and small givers.

Let donors know that they and their contributions are needed. But don't build a fund-raising effort exclusively on guilt. Involve people in the sharing of the responsibility.

Don't ignore persons who have been irritated by a solicitation or bypass those who refuse to contribute at this time. Build on their concerns, establish relationships, and cultivate them for the next round.

Although campaigns and events may be seasonal, fund-raising strategies should be planned the year round. They should be articulated not only with the organization's service programs, but also with its supportive public relations and community-education activities.

Got those under your belt? Good, now let's examine the kinds of fund-raising activities your organization might engage in.

## Fund-Raising Activities Defined

In this chapter, we will be focusing our attention on special events, campaigns, bequests, and development funds. In the next chapter we will turn our attention to presenting the agency's case for ongoing appropriations, grants, and contracts. *Special events* are, as the name implies, unusual occurrences such as dinner-dances, concerts, picnics, or rallies. They may be annual, seasonal, or ad hoc in nature. They don't generally require a separate organizational structure, although they do often depend on well-managed committees or task groups of staff and volunteers. Money is raised by participation in the event rather than through individual pledges and gifts.

*Campaigns*, on the other hand, do require separate and often complex organizational structures. Campaigns aim at generating support from individuals or organizations without the promise of a tangible product or service (such as a banquet meal, a concert, or rummage sale items). There are many kinds of campaigns: Capital or building-fund campaigns aim at construction, expansion, or modification of facilities or at the purchase of needed equipment. General-support campaigns can be distinguished from these or from those aimed at supporting specific programs or projects. *Endowments* can be used to make investments that generate funds to be used to provide support in the future. Campaigns may be one-time only events, or regularly scheduled, perhaps on an annual or seasonal basis.

*Bequests* are gifts that the organization does not generally receive until the donor has passed on. Although most are built into a will or a trust fund, some can be designed so as to provide support for the agency during the donor's lifetime. *Development funds* are earmarked for new or special programs the agency hopes to establish in the future, or for ongoing programs that require expansion or modification. All but special events require lists of actual and prospective donors. They may also require door-to-door interactions, letters, the targeted use of annual reports, and related public relation activities. You are now ready for Exercise 13–1.

---

## EXERCISE 13-1
### Identifying Practice Principles

1. Look over the 12 practice principles stated earlier in this chapter. Which do you agree with? Which do you have some questions about? Why? Which are you in agreement over, but uncomfortable with? Why?

2. Add five or more additional practice principles from your own experience in fund raising (even if you have to go back to Cub Scouts or Campfire Girls).

3. Now add as many more as you can find in this chapter. Is there some logical way to group or cluster them, for example, around issues that relate to different publics or to types of fund-raising activities.

4. Now review the list. If you substituted the term "programming" or "serving" or "promoting" for "fund raising" or "soliciting," would you have to make many other changes in each principle as it is written?

Consider doing the exercise with colleagues, perhaps those with whom you will be engaging in fund-raising activities.

## Special Events

We've all participated in and many of us have planned special events as fund-raising activities. These can be divided into (1) sales and (2) socials. Sales often include the contribution of merchandise as well as its purchase. "Treasures for trash" type sales begin with contributions of used household furniture and family clothing. These are then resold through bazaars, garage sales, white elephant sales, rummage sales, auctions, gift shops, and at-home sales like Tupperware parties. Making useful items available at low cost to low-income populations, as do Salvation Army thrift shops, is in itself an important agency service.

Such activities require little cash investment on the part of the sponsor. But they do require considerable investment in time and energy on the part of staff or volunteers. Sales events can be destructive of normal agency operations if paid staff are too heavily involved. Volunteers, on the other hand, may find bazaars or thrift shops and even yard sales to be rewarding in terms of the social relationships established, the recognition received, and the sense of achievement and accomplishment gained from having completed the work on behalf of others in need. They may benefit as much from these social exchanges as do the consumers of other agency services.

Some agencies, in fact, view their volunteers as both consumers and partners, and in many cases purposefully involve clients in such activities. "If the kids wanted to keep using the facilities," we reasoned, "they would have to raise some of the funds for rent and renovations. Within two years, they raised money for additional use by senior citizens. They are now feeling fully committed to the purposes of the agency."

In some cases, the agency's services may be organized around production and sales, as in the case of Goodwill Industries and other sheltered workshop or home industries programs.

The items or services donated by corporations, such as a lease or a discount on an automobile, office equipment, a free concert, or theater tickets, may be resold by the agency directly or at an auction. Art and antique auctions have become increasingly popular over the years. They can be organized around items donated, for which the giver receives a tax benefit, or may include merchandise obtained on consignment. An organization I volunteer my time with contracts with a commercial auction gallery each year. It is the organization's responsibility to advertise and bring people to the auction. It is the gallery's responsibility to bring the artworks and to conduct the auction, for which the agency receives 20 percent of the proceeds.

Purchasers also receive a tax benefit for their purchases and frequently are able to purchase items at considerably below regular gallery prices. Art auction galleries frequently make their own purchases in large quantities, sometimes early in an artist's career. They also keep overhead low. For this reason, they make money while passing on considerable savings to the consumer. Works of art, antiques, and other collectibles can be certified as genuine by the gallery, thus further inducing the purchase as a sound investment.

## Examples of Special Sales

Works of art, oriental rugs, or valuable handcrafted articles need not be sold only through auctions. A Boston gallery, with which I have worked over the years, provides local sponsors with an attractive package that includes artwork selected to reflect the consumers' interest and pocketbook. The sponsor receives a complete kit of instructions for the opening night. It includes a slide show about the exhibit, instructions for conducting a wine and cheese party, and flyers and announcements for distribution prior to the opening which describe in pictures and words many of the items to be offered for sale. Sample press releases are also included.

The sale items arrive with instructions for display and for repackaging and shipping to the next destination. Costs can be covered in advance through the sale of an "ad book" or recruitment of sponsors who, through gifts of $25 to $50, are listed on the program or invitation to the sale. This initial gift can be applied toward the purchase of any item in the exhibit. Thus, the donor has the satisfaction of sponsoring the exhibit, receives recognition for his or her contribution, is assured a discount at the sale, and, of course, acquires a tax benefit.

Some organizations have done very well with "discount days" arranged through local merchants. It is not uncommon for large food chains to provide charitable organizations with discount days. The organization's members, on presenting the cashier with a coupon, can have 5 percent of their total purchase allocated to the organization. Information on the organization, along with discount coupons, may be made available at the door.

Clothing and hardware stores, bookstores, and record shops may also be induced to allocate 5 or 10 percent of sales in any given day, week, or month to a charitable organization or cause. What kinds of arrangements are possible in your community? Should such arrangements be negotiated on a store-by-store basis, or might it make more sense to involve members of the downtown merchants' association or shopping mall associates in planning such an event?

Sales may also be aimed at people at home. For example, Hadassah, a Jewish women's organization, sponsors a "lox box" as an annual event in many American communities. People who purchase the box in advance are assured delivery on a given Sunday morning of a breakfast box that includes lox, cream cheese, bagels, and coffeecake. The activity not only invigorates the organization's members and other volunteers, but makes all the participants feel that they are engaged in the community-wide event without ever having to leave their homes. Besides, it tastes good! Jewish organizations and other religious groups have frequently used a "pushke," or home contribution box, in which family members deposit loose change. The box is collected at specific dates and the family involved is often provided with a certificate or a gift of some modest value in return for its contributions.

Discount books that provide the purchaser with reduced prices for dinners, movies, or merchandise are popular with merchants and individual purchasers, both of whom expect financial benefit and possibly a tax benefit. Ad books, which may include coupons, provide similar benefits to the donors. They can be given away at a special event or sold like discount books. Now try Exercise 13-2.

---

**EXERCISE 13-2**

## Designing Sales and Special Events

1. In four pages or less, outline a special event or sale-type fund-raising activity. Be sure to specify

   Overall goals
   Target objectives
   Organizational structure needed to conduct it
   Composition of the team that will be managing or conducting the activity
   Special instructional needs the fund-raisers may have and how they will be met
   Overall promotional activities
   The timetable

2. What are the dangers involved if you don't meet your dollar goal? Are there other benefits, besides dollars, that may overshadow a poor financial showing?

3. If your design specifies that an outside person or organization, or a specially designated group, is responsible for the event or activity, why so? If not, why not?

4. Do your answers to these questions articulate with the practice principles you identified in Exercise 13–1? Explain.

---

Social Events

Socials are special events that don't require the sale of goods or services. Participation by payment for admission to the event constitutes the donor's gift. Common forms of special events include bingo or Las Vegas nights, dinner dances, fun nights, hay rides or barn dances, carnivals, theater parties, mystery bus rides, and endurance races such as bike-a-thons, walk-a-thons, and marathons.

Special events require well-thought-out objectives. Typically, these include (1) raising a targeted amount of money, (2) creating a sense of shared commitment, and/or (3) raising public awareness. Although the funds raised can be substantial and well worth the investment in time and effort, the income from an event may be relatively inconsequential, but the activity is considered worth the investment because of its public relations value to the organization. Involvement of volunteers in fund-raising events may lead to their participation in agency programs and services. In the example, involvement of the firefighters and others was seen as raising the community's consciousness.

## Campaigns

Campaigns are of a much different order. Religious or ethnic organizations (such as the Catholic archdiocese, the Urban League, Lutheran Social Services, and Jewish Welfare Federations) and nonsectarian organizations (such as college alumni associations or the United Way) run highly professional annual campaigns. Your organization may be a great deal smaller, but there is no reason why its campaign should be any less professionally run. Some advice: if you are new to the campaign business, get some technical assistance. You may wish to employ a professional fundraiser. The United Way agency may be able to steer you to several fundraisers in your community or to get you started in thinking through your own campaign strategy. Other places to go for help are colleges, churches, or cultural institutions with which your organization may be linked or in whose campaigns members of your staff or board may have participated. There are many aspects to a successful campaign.

Some of these aspects include clarifying the goals and objectives, building a campaign structure, managing volunteers, establishing a timetable and keeping to it, and institutionalizing the campaign process. Let's look at each of these separately. The first order of business for the sponsoring organization is to clarify its *goals*. Are they to raise money and nothing more, or do they also include activating one or more of the organization's publics, increasing public awareness, or building a cadre of volunteers who might become involved in other aspects of the agency's program? How are these goals to be translated into operational objectives?

Goals should be clarified by key members of the executive staff in collaboration with lay leaders who have a stake in the organization and who may be required to take primary responsibility for aspects of the campaign. Put the goals on paper. Determine which are compatible and which may be diverting from other organizational commitments. Let's assume that the major goal is to raise money for the organization. How much money? What is your target goal in dollar terms? Is that sum to be reached this year? Or is the target to be reached over a 2-, 3-, or 5-year period? If so, what proportion is to be reached this year? Are those funds to be raised from a relatively small number of individuals and organizations (such as local corporations and businesses)? Will targeting your campaign to certain publics generate distrust among other publics? Should it include big, medium, and small givers? Is this to be an annual campaign, or is it to be a one-time-only campaign, oriented toward capital giving or the establishment of an endowment fund? Once these decisions have been tentatively made, you will have to build a campaign structure and determine its format.

## The Campaign Structure

Although campaign structures must be tailored to each organization's circumstances, a number of structural elements have proved themselves in a wide variety of settings. First among these is a separate governing board, often called the "campaign cabinet." A general chairperson will work with a small steering committee, often made up of the heads of the cabinet's subcommittees or task forces. Typically, task forces may be assigned to (1) soliciting initial or special gifts, (2) general solicitation, (3) prospects development, (4) public relations, and (5) various administrative functions.

The current wisdom among experienced campaign managers is that 20 to 25 percent of the funds to be raised during a given year should be solicited from a pacesetter group during the early phases of the campaign, or even before it's officially kicked off. It is the responsibility of the *initial* or *special gifts group* to solicit persons who have regularly pledged the largest sums in previous years. Pacesetters need not be the wealthiest members of the community; they must, however, have confidence both in the persons soliciting and in the organization. They must believe that the funds that they contribute will achieve what the organization has promised and that other donors will be induced by their examples to contribute sufficient sums to reach the targeted goal. Like all donors, pacesetters may require some recognition for their contributions. Although some prefer to remain anonymous, others will appreciate having their names appear on campaign stationery. This has the added strategic value of legitimizing the organization to other potential donors.

The *general solicitation committee* will aim its efforts at these other donors, those who give medium and smaller-sized gifts. Depending on the scope of the campaign, the general solicitation committee may be further divided into a number of groups, each with its own captain. These groups may be organized around categories of publics: corporations, individuals who give medium-sized gifts, etc. Or they may be organized around peer groups: doctors, lawyers, other professionals, small business owners, corporate executives, homemakers, and so on. Households may be divided geographically by neighborhood, by size, or along ethnic and religious lines. A special category may include former consumers of an agency's service: families that have adopted children, persons who have used the hospital's services, alumni, or parents of students at the university.

The *prospects committee* locates individuals that should be added to the list of those to be solicited. A good way to begin a prospect list is to ask for names from board and committee members of the organization, current and former givers, former recipients of service, even agency "partners" like firefighters and their publics—parents of schoolchildren who have visited the fire station. These lists require continual updating as new prospects are identified. Names may be coded according to size of gift anticipated and the history of the prospective donor's relationship to the agency.

The *public relations (PR) committee* is not concerned with fund raising per se, but it is concerned with setting the scene for effective fund raising. It may issue periodic press releases, arrange for feature articles in the paper, and work with the local radio and television people interpreting the campaign and the services that it is intended to finance. Typical PR activities include arranging for

Orchestrated letter-writing campaigns to the local newspaper
Printed handouts—posters, bulletins, etc.
Special articles or features for the general press or the house organs of business corporations, unions, churches, and civic associations
Displays in public places such as shopping centers and concert halls
Speakers who present information to community groups prior to their solicitation

*Administrative groups* provide necessary supportive services without which the campaign could not proceed. Their services include recruiting and training solicitors, auditing and clerical assistance, preparation of reports on the campaign, or monitoring the campaign structure and the activities of its component units.

## Campaign Leaders and Campaign Workers

"To win at horse-racing," a colleague explained, "you not only need horses that *can* run, but those that *will* run." The same can be said of campaign workers. Numbers are not enough. They need the competence, the skill, and the motivation to win. Like donors to the campaign, solicitors and others must be convinced that the endeavor is important and that the efforts they put in will have payoff. But like any other human service endeavor, campaigns can be slow in starting, and the results can be disappointing. Good leadership can do much to overcome difficulties.

Some leaders will have developed their capacities to solve problems or to motivate others over the course of many previous campaigns. Others may start fresh with your organization, drawing on professional and occupational skills or on volunteer experiences with other organizations. If you are the campaign staffer, you may want a balanced leadership group, composed of persons who may have been trained through your organization and others who were recruited or borrowed from other organizations and who can bring relevant experiences to the campaign.

Most new solicitors and other volunteers will need some instruction. The following activities might be considered:

*Orientation sessions* that include written and spoken materials and that introduce the worker to the procedures to be used, the campaign structure and its key actors, the targets to be reached, and the purposes for which funds will be used

*Campaign literature* that is designed for solicitors or other volunteers, and other literature that can be mailed or given to prospective donors

*Solicitor training*, which may include films, role-play, and practice experiences

*On-the-job supervision and coaching*, which may include observation of more experienced solicitors, followed by joint solicitations and eventual solo flights

*Small group feedback sessions* at which solicitors and others can be informed of how the campaign is faring, get reinforcement from sharing experiences with others, and so on

Volunteers may need ongoing support and recognition. Many will need to get over inhibitions about requesting funds; others will need to become more realistic about what can be achieved, yet continue to be sufficiently committed to go beyond the expected. Some organizations have routine ways of recognizing outstanding solicitors. These include awards and special recognition ceremonies, prizes, or feature articles in the organization's newsletter or in the general press.

## Making the Pitch

The solicitor's pitch should emphasize those features in the agency's program or campaign objectives that the prospect is most likely to be interested in, those things the prospect values: religious concerns, the survival of an ethnic group, caring for needy children, fairness for the elderly, opportunities for his or her children to attend college, the survival of a species or the cleanup of the environment. The prospect may wish to know how the money given is to be used, what proportion of the budget raised will be allocated to one or another aspect of the program, and, perhaps, how much is being used for the administration of the campaign.

The prospective donor may also want to know who else is being solicited and the average size of peer contributions. If the prospective contributor gave in the previous year, it may be helpful to recall the amount and to indicate the general target for upgrading contributions this year. If the solicited individual gave a minimal amount in previous years, it may be time to try to upgrade the gift to a more adequate amount.

In general, it is not wise to try to move people up too rapidly. A solicitor might try one of the following approaches, "Last year you gave $10; this year we'd like you to put aside 50¢ a week. It's not necessary for you to give the full amount all at once; you can pay off your pledge in quarterly payments." Or, "I'd like to see you move up to what I'm giving. Last year I gave $500, but I know it's not easy to make that jump from $100 all at once. Why not consider $200 this year and perhaps moving to $300 or $400 next year?" Or, "Your gift is so close to what our pacesetters give, why not consider jumping from $750 to $1000? I know it's a strain in today's economy, but your previous gifts clearly show your commitment, and you are a well-respected member of our community. You really should be among the pacesetters. You've given so much in other ways."

Most donors will require receipts for tax purposes. Quoting the tax advantages of giving is no small motivator, but tax receipts do not substitute for acknowledgments.

Let me say a few words about tax advantages. They are not as big as they used to be. Until 1982, big givers might have had to pay only $3,000 for every $10,000 donated. Those in the 70 percent tax bracket could have received 70 percent of their donation back from the IRS. Reagan's tax reforms dropped the upper tax limit to 50 percent. It will now cost a big giver $5,000 to donate $10,000. Keep your eye on other tax changes as well as on local and state laws that may increase or decrease motivation to be generous.

Donors should receive thank-you letters, even if they are not personalized. On the other hand, a personal phone call or a handwritten note, in particular to a donor who has made a large initial pledge or who has made a large jump from previous years, may be essential to maintaining that level of giving or to raising it in the future.

## Deferred Giving: Developing a Bequest Program

When I asked a colleague of mine, an attorney who manages a number of family trusts, for suggestions about what to include in this section of the chapter, he was forthright. "There are three things you need to remember: (1) where there's a will, there's a way; (2) most bequeathers have gray hair; and (3) deep down inside, all of us strive after immortality. All the rest is commentary." So here comes the commentary.

Although many people *do* strive after immortality, others know better. Their reward will come in the *here and now* rather than in the hereafter. But they may also be concerned with the future—with those who will come after they've gone. They may have a concern with security, not necessarily for themselves but for those who will live in the future. Their concerns may be for the survival of an ethnic group or a cultural inheritance. They may be concerned about the security of others with whom they've identified in the past. Perhaps some are trying to work out a balance in their lives, overcoming a long-buried sense of loss through an act of expurgating guilt.

I recently asked an elderly woman, who had made a bequest to an organization with which I'm affiliated, what had compelled her to contribute to the agency. "When I was young, there wasn't a place like this for me. But if I were young now, this is the kind of place I would want to come to. I feel toward it almost the way I do toward my warmest childhood memories. When I think about this place it generates a nostalgia for my youth." "And besides," she continued, "I always think about Rabbi Zusya. He was a Talmudic scholar, but he wasn't a saint, and I certainly haven't been. 'When I go to Heaven,' Zusya said, 'no one will ask me why I wasn't Moses. They'll ask me why I wasn't Zusya.' A lot of things I've done in the past, that wasn't the real me. Being a part of your organization, that's who I really am."

Another Talmudic quotation comes to mind. It comes from a small book observant Jews frequently read on Sabbath afternoons, *The Sayings of the Fathers*. "It's not your task to complete the job, nor are you free to desist from it." People who make bequests often do so because they feel obliged to make a contribution, even if that contribution only starts up a process that they will not live to see. It is that belief in the future and the desire to contribute to the future that characterizes many bequests. Perhaps there is in their commitment a share in immortality.

Successful fund-raisers are masters at tapping such motivations. I say "tap" instead of "capitalize on" because I believe that's exactly what the process is all about. There is, in all of us, an untapped reservoir of unselfishness and a desire to do good. But many of us do not know how or where to make our contributions, so we go with the institutions that have proven themselves: those with successful track records. That is why most bequests tend to go to the more successful institutions. They'll go to Harvard more rapidly than they will to a smaller, less-known, and much more needy school in a mid-western state. But the mission or purpose of that small college may be much more in keeping with the interests of a prospective bequeather if he or she only knew of it. For this reason, a successful bequest program may require even more planning and organization than does any other kind of campaign.

Most bequest programs include the following ingredients:

1.  A bequest committee, or task group, that plans and manages the program
2.  A booklet, or other descriptive material, that spells out details of the bequest program: how it will be used, and for what purpose; the types of gifts that might be given; how the gift will be built upon; how taxes favor the individual that gives, or his trust or other beneficiaries; and other useful information
3.  A list of prospective givers
4.  A list of others who might be appropriate solicitors
5.  A set of procedures used to canvass the list of prospects and to target certain individuals at the appropriate time

In addition to money, other types of properties may also be contributed: real estate, equipment, works of art, furniture, and so on. In many cases it is not necessary for the donor to pass on before the agency benefits from a bequest. It is possible for the bequest to be made in the form of a life-insurance policy, an annuity, or some other income-generating investment from which the agency draws now and from which it will receive a larger indemnity or death benefit in the future. It is also possible to establish a life-income annuity plan for the donor, with the larger sum going to your organization at a later time. These are sometimes known as "delayed gifts."

A not inconsequential inducement is the tax benefit that may accrue to the donor's estate. Because the laws on inheritance and on estates change rapidly at both the national and state level, it makes sense for anyone embarking on a bequest program to consult a tax attorney or an estate planner. Banks, attorneys, or trustee organizations in your community will be available to consult with you. Becoming familiar with such people is not a bad idea for other reasons. As you get to know them, they will get to know you. And they will be able to advise their clients about the tax and other advantages of bequeathing money to your organization.

The better professional trustees know your organization, its programs, and its missions the more likely they will be to suggest just such a bequest when the time is appropriate. In effect, then, these people become your partners in the development of a bequest program. They may be as anxious to find you, so as to serve their clients better, as you are to find them and their clients. Making a bequest puts one among the community's elite; facilitating one may be next best.

## Bricks-and-Mortar Campaigns, Development Programs, and Other Activities

Bricks-and-mortar campaigns (building funds) have characteristics of their own. First, they require consensus on the kind of building desired. On other programmatic issues, nonprofessionals (the fund-raising volunteers) may be happy to refer decisions to the professionals. But almost everyone has an idea about what makes a building beautiful or functional. Some members of churches and synagogues have been accused of having an "edifice" complex, being more interested in the pretentiousness of a new building than in its uses. But if a more modest building would not be sufficient motivation to generate community giving, there may be something to be said for pretentiousness.

When working on the basic structure of the building, the campaign committee should also consider its landscaping, equipment, and upkeep. It may not be sufficient just to raise enough money to "burn the mortgage," it may also be necessary to raise enough to establish a special fund to pay the additional costs that the new or modified structure may require. A mortgage may be helpful to start the construction process early. But remember, not-for-profit organizations gain no tax advantage for mortgages. The faster the mortgage can be paid off, the less drain there will be on the organization's ongoing operations.

Build upkeep and fuel costs into the building-fund target. When fuel prices skyrocketed a few years back, I saw several organizations close at least some of their doors.

With the exception of upkeep, capital campaigns must be clearly separated from concerns over operating budgets or ongoing programs. They are time-limited, generally 2 weeks to 4 years in duration; they are aimed at construction of a new building, the modification of an existing facility, or at the purchase of equipment. Such equipment may include electronic data-processing systems, items for a physical-education plant, art facilities, or other items necessary for the programmatic or administrative functioning of the organization.

As the nomenclature suggests, *development programs* are aimed at the expansion or development in some depth of an existing program or the establishment of a new program or service. Funds are not raised for ongoing operations but for purposes of generating a new approach or reaching a new population. Development funds are generally long-term in their orientation. In lieu of a campaign cabinet, a development program may have a "development council" made up of staff, board of trustees members, and others. It may include capital gifts and a special alumni fund, and will generally be given a title that is easily identifiable: "the golden age fund," the "minority opportunities fund," etc.

Development funds also require a careful cultivation of various publics long before they're asked to contribute. In addition to individual donors, contributors to development may include business corporations and philanthropic foundations. The appeal to different publics may have to be around special concerns: school lunches, increasing environmental esthetics, the installation of playground equipment or park benches, or providing support to the disabled or the aging.

Unlike bricks-and-mortar campaigns, development campaigns are not one-shot affairs. Although special funds may be raised for a specific program, this is done as part of an ongoing process. Former donors may be tapped again and new prospects identified. Like other programs, campaigns of various kinds can be collaboratively sponsored by several human service agencies or by industrial and civic organizations working in concert on behalf of a single agency or a target population.

Now try Exercise 13–3.

---

**EXERCISE 13-3**

### Designing a Campaign

1. In four pages or less, outline a campaign (general solicitation, bricks-and-mortar, development fund, or bequest program) activity:

   Overall goals
   Target objectives
   Organizational structure needed to conduct it
   Composition of the team that will be managing or conducting the activity
   Special instructional needs the fund raisers may have and how they will be met
   Overall promotional activities
   The timetable

2. What are the dangers involved if you don't meet your dollar goal? Are there other benefits, besides dollars, that may overshadow a poor financial showing?

3. If your design specifies that an outside person or organization, or a specially designated group, is responsible for the event or activity, why so? If not, why not?

4. Do your answers to these questions articulate with the practice principles you identified in Exercise 13–1? Explain.

5. How did your answers to these questions differ from those to similar questions in Exercise 13–2? Explain the reasons for the differences.

---

Organizations develop their own campaign styles over time. Some will appeal directly to the public, whereas others will work through second and third parties. Some develop special membership groups for the express purpose of fund raising. While some use the postal service, others may go door-to-door, and still others may use a payroll-deduction plan. Some do all their solicitation in person, whereas others use a combination of telephone and in-person interviews. Some consolidate all their fund raising in a single "tag day," marathon, or "Super Sunday." Some use individuals to approach groups, and some use groups to approach individuals.

## Big Givers

At one time or another, we've probably all had fantasies of a big giver bailing us or our organization out of a bind we may have found ourselves in. But big givers, like heroes, are made—not born. It may take a long time to cultivate a donor. A gift, too, grows over time. In most communities, and around most issues, there will be some persons who are able and willing to contribute handsomely. Some, a few, may seek you out directly or through an intermediary such as a tax attorney or a trust officer. You can locate the potential contributor through the same third parties or by checking with colleagues in the human services. They may know of someone who is not interested in their organization but who may be interested in yours.

Don't overlook the press. A feature article may lead you to an individual or an organization that will eventually fall into your big donor category. Keep newspaper clippings and other bits of information for future reference. Once a potential big giver is identified, some organizations keep a dossier on the person which includes the size and frequency of contributions, personal interests and community involvements, and information on family and friends.

Big givers may not be interested in any involvement with your organization beyond the gift. Others will want to be involved in the campaign at a level that is commensurate with their gifts. Be careful not to move people up the leadership structure unless they have paid their dues in more than money alone. It is easy to demoralize other committed volunteers who may have worked their way slowly into positions of leadership. Some big givers think only their contribution is special. In contrast with others, or with their ability to give, it may actually be very small.

The following story may seem apocryphal, but it is nonetheless true. The executive director of a sectarian welfare council recalls how a few years back the associate chairman of the campaign burst into his office, ecstatic that he'd received a check for $10,000 from an industrialist. "This is the first time he's ever given us a penny," he exclaimed. The executive took the check and looked at it calmly. "This will never do," he replied. Together, the two of them made an appointment to see the industrialist who assumed that he was to be thanked for his generosity.

"Sorry," the director of the council told the industrialist, "we can't accept this check. It doesn't befit your dignity, nor does it properly address the needs in this community. We want you to be among those who pay their fair share. Twenty-five thousand dollars would more closely approximate what your peers are giving." He got the new check.

But be careful! Grandstanding of this sort is risky business. It can alienate unless you know your prospect well—what he or she is capable of—and if others who value that prospect also know. Remember the big tipper we spoke about in Chapter 2. He may not be trying to impress the waiter; he may very well be impressing others at the table with him.

## A Few Words About Lists

Throughout this chapter, I have spoken about lists of prospective donors. If you haven't already developed lists of your own, you may be able to find appropriate lists from other sources. First, you should know that there are list brokers available in most metropolitan communities. They can either design or locate the appropriate list for you. For example, there are lists of music lovers, people who buy diet books or classical records, attorneys, business executives, psychiatric nurses, members of certain clubs, alumni of universities and colleges, contributors to other organizations.

You may not need to go to a list broker. Your local librarian may be able to help you locate the appropriate reference book in which you'll uncover lists of lists. For example, *Standard and Poor's Register* or *Dun and Bradstreet*, or the *Directory of Directors* publishes lists of companies nationwide, arranged geographically, with designations of the kinds of business they are in. Such lists can be used to locate industries that may have interests that complement those of your organization. Thomas' *Register of American Manufacturers* indicates the kinds of products produced by most manufacturing concerns in this country. Moody's *Industrial Manual* lists corporations, the names of their officers, plant locations, the names of trustees, and the names of the corporation's attorneys and accountants. People contribute most when it is in areas of their strength or interest. These lists can yield names and companies in your area that you may not have thought about as prospects for involvement in fund raising or in providing in-kind contributions like equipment and facilities. With these names in mind, some checking around with colleagues, or careful monitoring of the local press, is likely to yield additional information on who may be interested in the disabled, in the elderly, or in other areas of concern.

If you did not know where else to go, you might consider the telephone directory or the local newspaper. Telephone directories frequently list professionals in the community by occupation. Some cities publish a "reverse telephone directory" which can be purchased directly from the telephone company by any subscriber. Streets are listed by neighborhood alphabetically, house numbers are then given, and the names of residents in each of the buildings with their telephone numbers appear last. This is an excellent source for a neighborhood canvassing program, and it permits you to target specific neighborhoods in the community. Local newspapers are too often ignored. Staff members or volunteers might be assigned the task of clipping feature articles on wealthy people, those with special interests or life experiences, obituaries, birth announcements, and as one professional fund raiser told me, "even robberies which sometimes include the size of the home and provide a clue to the donor's interests."

## Some Final Thoughts

As you get into fund raising, you'll have additional questions. There are many experienced fund raisers from whom you can learn. Some earn their living at it, and others, among the more talented, do it as volunteers. But you can also learn from your own experiences. Like anything else, it requires that you keep careful records of what you do; for example, how many letters were mailed, the average size of a gift, who might be cultivated for a larger gift next year. It may require conducting a market audit before deciding to aim a campaign at a certain population or opening up a used clothing store in a given neighborhood.

It often requires trial and error, with adaptations as you gain experience about what is both feasible and cost-efficient. And remember, your fund-raising efforts, though they may require a separate structure, should never be done in isolation from the agency's other programs, resource development, or promotional activities. The more integral fund-raising activities are to your other programs and services, the more likely they are to be productive.

## Review

A number of principles were enunciated upon which you might develop a fund-raising strategy. Foremost among them were the exhortation to broaden the resource base, to develop a cadre of devoted staff or volunteers who will demonstrate a deep and ongoing commitment in seeking support for the organization and to build the fund-raising efforts into other ongoing programmatic concerns. Several kinds of fund-raising approaches were discussed. Special events include sales and socials. The range of sale possibilities is relatively unlimited. Typical sale activities include bazaars, thrift shops, auctions, chances or raffles, the sale of donated services, and store discount days. Social events might include walk-a-thons, dances, film and theater nights, banquets, and so on.

Campaigns were defined as being of a different order. They tend to have their own structures, often composed of a cabinet, steering committee, and a number of working groups or task forces. Solicitors often train or work in groups under the leadership of a team captain. Campaign leaders and workers both need ongoing training and support. Campaigns may target certain individuals for large gifts, or otherwise segment the populations at which they aim (e.g., by occupational groups, by services received).

Deferred giving programs and other forms of bequests are a special form of campaign, often appealing to the deepest and most important sentiments a donor can express. They often reflect the donor's concerns with the here and now no more than his or her commitment to the future. Building funds and development programs each have their own characteristics and require rather different designs. Building funds are short-term in duration, the organization making a rather large push over a limited period. Development programs have a much more long-term perspective.

# 14 INCREASING YOUR GRANTS, CONTRACTS, AND ALLOCATIONS POWER

FEW AGENCIES or agency programs could long survive without the infusion of at least some funds. Even those agencies that have successfully cut back expenditures through program reduction or through the substitution of other resources, like borrowed facilities or volunteer staff, are on the constant lookout for new sources of dollars. The lookout can be a lonely place, however, when successes are rare and far between. Your organization's fiscal strategy can be improved if you treat potential funders as a market to be developed and penetrated, much as you would a consumer market.

The fiscal market includes government bodies, foundations, voluntary agencies like the United Way, and the private sector that is composed of business and industrial concerns. As in other marketing strategies, these markets must be carefully segmented and their interests kept clearly in mind. It does not help to approach a foundation interested in children's issues if you are looking for a grant that deals with the aging. That may seem self-evident; what may be less evident is that the foundation may be interested in only some children or in some children's issues, or may be open to collaboration with only some social agencies and citizens' groups. An understanding of these differences is central to development of a winning marketing strategy aimed at generating financial support.

### Lose a Few, Win a Few

A couple of years back, I began looking seriously for funds to support a neighborhood study in a foreign country. Quite certain that federal funding would not be available, I turned to foundations. The search began with a review of the *Founda-*

*tion Grants Index*. There are thousands of foundations in this country, and I knew I had to begin with a realistic list of prospects. The *Index* is published by the Foundation Center, an association of the largest foundations in the country, which also publishes the *Foundation Center News*.

The *Index* lists the awards made by foundations in sums of $5,000 or more by title, foundation name, or category, and indicates in which issues of the *Foundation Center News* more information can be obtained. It is a quick way to get a handle on who is funding what, and for how much. I kept my eyes open for grants that dealt with neighborhoods, ethnicity, socialization, urban problems, and of course the city and country I was interested in doing my work in. I also looked for grants to photographers; much of my data-gathering methods were to include generating photographic records of neighborhood structures and their impact on resident interactions. Having located 67 likely prospects, I sent them each a two-page letter describing briefly the project and asking whether or not they might be interested. The letter, I might say, was textbook perfect. It even included a photocopy of a photograph as an eye-catcher. I got 65 responses, all turndowns, most of them on mimeographed postcards. "So why is this guy telling us about it?" you might ask. Because we all make mistakes, particularly when we are convinced that something we are doing will be as interesting to others as it is to us. Unfortunately, that is not the reason why the grants, allocations, and contracts are made. It's really the other way around. We are more likely to get an award if what we are willing to do is what others are interested in funding.

Funders are not particularly concerned about us, our professional interests, or our agencies' needs. They are concerned primarily with their own agendas. If they perceive us as potential partners in the addressing of those agendas, we stand a fair chance of getting funding.

While the approach I used to uncover prospective funders was systematic, it was not complete. The first mistake I made was to limit myself to foundations, in particular to the larger ones that tend to have their awards listed in the *Index* and the *News*.

Foundations provide less than 5 percent of the nonpublic amount of support given to voluntary services and even less to the social sciences. Corporations give about the same amount, and some, I should have realized, were interested both in photography and in the country where I planned to do my research. Last year, individual donors provided 86 percent of the nongovernment funds that went to universities and voluntary agencies. I should have used a wide-angle instead of a telephoto lens in my search.

I made another big mistake. I neglected to use personal contacts. These can be either direct or indirect. I have worked with some foundations before, so a telephone call to a foundation executive might have yielded a referral to another foundation. Moreover, I know of other social scientists who have studied neighborhoods, and some use photographic methods in those studies. I should have approached them for ideas about where to turn. I am actually referring to using a networking approach not only to discover leads, but to find proper persons who might vouch for me or for the project. Fortunately, I do not always strike out, or it would not have been easy to write this chapter. Let me give you another, more successful example.

Within a few days of having spotted the announcement of new funds available for training in child welfare, in the *Congressional Record*, I received a phone call from a colleague in the State Department of Social Services. "Are you interested in working on this one with us, Armand?" he asked. "I have already written to Washington for the application package," I replied. "If you've got one on hand, why not photocopy it and ship it out to me?" The phone call was not unusual. We had spoken many times about collaborating on some project of mutual interest. I knew the state agency needed the resources of the university, and we needed access to their staff in order to be able to do the training. Moreover, we had positioned ourselves pretty effectively to get this or any other child welfare training grant that might be coming down the pike. Ann Arbor and Lansing newspapers had recently featured public interest articles on training activities the School of Social Work was conducting for child welfare workers, indicating the school's capability to do work in this area. Several of the faculty were engaged in ongoing consultation to child welfare agencies throughout the state.

You already know the ending of this story. We got the grant. You read all about it in Chapter 6 where I described the negotiating process that led to the school's being awarded $320,000, not far from an original target of $360,000. For this example, clearly the funder (a federal agency) was in the market for projects that would achieve objectives compatible with the funder's mandate. We were able to design such a project. And the state agency served as our sponsor, providing the references we needed to defend our claims to competence and dependability.

## Identifying Sources of Funding

Perhaps we're moving too fast. Let's come back to the first step: identifying potential sources of funding. We'll look at foundations first and then move on to corporate, voluntary-sector (e.g., United Way agencies and sectarian foundations), and government sources.

### Foundations: What They Are and How They Work

There are a number of different types of foundations, each with its own characteristics. *Private foundations* have broad charters and often rather large endowments. Some have what they call in the trade "general" purposes whereas others may focus on very specific concerns, like minority youth employment. Most of the large independent foundations are professionally staffed, and many specialize in particular areas of interest. Many independent foundations will support only pioneering or innovative programs and will be reluctant to support projects or organizations for long periods of time. Although, in times of emergency, some have been known to bail out a supplicant, they are more apt to see themselves as responsible for providing seed money to launch programs that will in time become self-supporting. Examples include the Ford Foundation, the Mott Foundation, the Rockefeller Brothers Fund, and the Edna McConnel Clark Foundation. Although the foundations are no longer connected with industry, many of their initial donors were large industrialists. Thus the Clark Foundation's portfolio began with large bequests from Avon Products, and the Mott Foundation built its portfolio around a donation of General Motors stock.

These foundations, however, operate fully autonomously, independent of the businesses and even the individuals who founded them. That is why they are called *independent foundations*. They have their own boards of directors who ultimately make the decisions on any grants to be made. However, the key people in the grants process are the staff members responsible for given areas of concern (e.g., child welfare, job training, community education). They are the ones with whom you will have contact, and they are the persons who will screen proposals before any are to be submitted to the board. They also recommend whether or not a grant is to be made and how large the award should be. Such foundations are often national or even international in the scope of their interests.

In contrast, *community foundations* are set up to serve a specific geographic area, usually a city and sometimes adjacent townships. Initially established to ensure proper stewardship of trusts and bequests, community foundations now actively seek funds from individual and corporate donors who prefer to have their philanthropic responsibilities administered by professional foundation managers.

Community foundations are concerned primarily with local needs. At one time, they tended to sponsor cultural programs, like the local philharmonic or a summer "concert in the park" series. Today, they are increasingly involved in human service and community-development activities. These include downtown reconstruction, the building of pocket parks, and the support of social services for which other funds may not be readily available. Community foundations frequently use their funds as "venture capital" that may attract other grants, possibly from government or industrial sources.

Their trustees include prominent citizens who make all final decisions. Some make genuine efforts to include trustees who represent all segments of the population. As in the case of private foundations, staff are both gatekeepers and the primary decision makers. Your success as a fund raiser will be much improved if they are knowledgeable about your agency's services and the needs of the populations you are concerned about. Although many trustees and staff may be savvy about local needs, they may also need to be educated. It may take a while before you can properly position your organization to make applications. Your promotional strategy need not be direct. Media and public-awareness campaigns that indirectly educate community foundation staff and trustees may increase your chances considerably.

*Family foundations* make up by far the largest numbers of foundations in the United States. They vary greatly in size and areas of interest. Their endowments generally are under $5 million, and many may be in the $10,000 to $200,000 range. Although some have boards, the preferences of family members who make major contributions generally prevail. Some family foundations are administered by trustees. The trustee may be a private attorney, a local banker, or a trust corporation. Few have professional staffs.

Some family foundations are clearly tax shelters. The goal may be to provide scholarships to universities and colleges, but recipients may be limited to friends and relatives of the family. Many have religious purposes, and a few are connected with social agencies, serving as the primary supporters of endowment programs for specific projects in those organizations. Family foundations are sometimes on the lookout for good prospects: people and organizations to fund. Once you are on a family foundation's list, you may remain on it indefinitely; but getting on that list is another matter. It may require knowing someone in the family or knowing someone who knows someone. Because most family foundations do not have professional staff, they may not know how to deal with unsolicited proposals; some will not even acknowledge receipt of your inquiry.

Recent concern with corporate America's social responsibilities has focused attention on *company-sponsored foundations*. You are probably aware that corporations are permitted to make charitable contributions of up to 10 percent of their pretax earnings, and frequently they establish foundations which provide them with tax benefits in order to administer those funds. Like the others, corporate foundations are tax-exempt and not-for-profit entities. Although they are separated from their parent companies, their boards tend to consist almost exclusively of company officers.

Historically, corporations have given less than 1 percent of their earnings to charitable organizations although they can legally give up to 10 percent and reap tax benefits. When they do give, the funds tend to be confined to communities where the parent company has its offices or plants. In general, they make grants to support institutions or agencies that benefit the company's employees, its stockholders, or others with whom it has business relationships.

Many corporations have used their foundation to enhance their corporate reputation or public image through their sponsorship of cultural and other programs. In some communities, corporation executives have banded together to attempt to increase the size of their giving programs. The Ford Foundation, in fact, has encouraged corporations in cities throughout the United States to increase their giving by offering matching funds that deal exclusively with economic development at the grass-roots level. In San Francisco, several executives have organized a "2% Club" that is actively involved in the recruiting of corporations and inducing them to contribute more than 1 percent to the local community.

Finally, a growing number of *operating foundations* exist; these solicit funds for their own purposes and give those funds to pet projects and organizations or to programs they themselves sponsor. It is unlikely that these foundations would be receptive to your organization's interests, unless they clearly further those of the foundation.

## Private-Sector Financing

Increasingly, corporations and other businesses are financing human service programs directly. But such financing must clearly fit in with the interests of the sponsor. A local industrial plant, for example, may be willing to contract with your agency to do drug counseling in the plant or establish a preventive intervention program aimed at reducing absenteeism. It actually may be looking to organizations like yours to provide a service to employees. The little-noticed growth area for the human services is the contracting-out by companies to agencies that conduct employee-assistance programs. In such situations, the company views itself as the prime beneficiary. Its need may provide your organization with an opportunity to expand services to a population that may currently be poorly served or under-served.

That same corporation may subsequently be willing to fund a pilot or demonstration project aimed at preventing substance abuse in the schools where many of its employees' children are enrolled. Chances are this will be a seed grant, and you will be expected to seek new and additional sources of support when the demonstration project is completed; those sources may include the board of education. Corporate executives who may be actively involved in parent–teacher associations or in the school board can be expected to support efforts to institutionalize the program you have begun.

Although much corporate giving is presented as philanthropic, it is, in fact, often in the direct self-interest of the corporation. In Boston, Pittsburgh, and Cleveland, for example, insurance companies have been among the largest supporters of community organizational efforts. On first examination this may seem incongruous; but, on closer examination, it seems quite obvious. The organizers in question are primarily involved in neighborhoods in transition, unstable neighborhoods.

If these can be stabilized, the reasoning goes, crime might be reduced. There would tend to be fewer fires in houses and apartment buildings and fewer arson-based business fires. The incidences of mental illness and other health problems are a good deal lower in stable communities in which citizens network effectively and support each other. Clearly, stable neighborhoods could save the insurance companies from making payments for fire, theft, health, accident, and death benefits.

Look around at your community. Check the corporate annual reports of the major businesses in your area. Which of these might have needs that your agency could respond to? How might these businesses benefit from an exchange relationship with your agency? What changes in the way in which your organization provides services, or in those services themselves, might be required if new and effective partnership relations might be established? Do you already have relationships with some corporations, albeit indirectly, through members of your board of directors or through others who may have been involved in a fund-raising campaign on behalf of the agency or one of its programs?

Midway between the private sector and the voluntary sector are the many *civic associations* that are not normally considered sources of funds. Most of them already have their pet projects, and the amounts of funds they can raise may be limited. We are talking about fraternal organizations like the Junior Chamber of Commerce (Jaycees), the Fraternal Order of the Eagles, the Elks Lodge, the Masonic Temple, the Knights of Columbus, and the Loyal Order of Moose. You will find them listed in the Yellow Pages.*

You will also find churches, synagogues, and religious organizations listed, as well as boosters' clubs, educational organizations, and advocacy groups. Which of these are likely partners in fund raising? From which are you likely to get grants or allocations on an occasional or regular basis? Through which of these could you make connections with larger corporate givers?

Industrial unions are a not unlikely source of support. Even in times of high unemployment, when unions are themselves hard pressed for money, they invest considerable sums in social services for their members, for retired members, and for former members who may be currently unemployed. Unions also have large trust funds through which they sometimes make modest, but nevertheless significant gifts, particularly if these gifts result in benefits to the union's members.

How could your agency's services increase a union's bargaining position during its next round of negotiations with industry? When unions were first considering negotiating for mental health benefits, they were in desperate need of service providers with whom they could contract on an experimental basis to test out alternative ways in which those benefits might be structured. What are the hot issues today in your community?

---

*Often listed under the following headings: *Clubs, Associations, Fraternal Associations, Social Service Organizations* (although most under this last listing will be social agencies that provide professional services to the public).

Funding Through the Voluntary Sector

The *voluntary sector* continues to fund a substantial portion of the social services delivered at the local level; only "entitlement" programs are almost entirely financed by the public sector. Entitlements comprise public welfare grants, social security, Medicare and Medicaid, unemployment insurance, and so on. Some programs, like job training, may be supported by public, private, and voluntary sources, as in the case of Goodwill Industries or the Salvation Army. Although public programs dwarf all others in amounts of money spent, voluntary sources of support are nevertheless the lifeblood of many agencies.

The United Way is by far the largest and most ubiquitous of the voluntary fund-raising organizations in the United States and Canada. Loosely confederated but operating independently at the local level, United Way agencies conduct their own fund-raising programs with well-trained professional staffs. In addition to campaign cabinets and staff, most also have a planning or community-development division which is responsible for setting standards for its member agencies, assessing needs, determining priorities, and allocating funds to recipient organizations, most of which are considered to be "member agencies."

United Ways are federated structures that include member agencies and departments or divisions responsible for fund raising and allocations. In addition to the United Way, which raises most of its funds through individual solicitations (many of which are made through payroll-deduction plans) or through corporate gifts, many communities support other federated structures as well. They may include councils on aging, Jewish Welfare Federations, community health or hospital federations, Lutheran Social Services, and Catholic Charities. They are all relatively similar in their allocation procedures.

"Councils" or "divisions" are set up to deal with specific areas of interest: cultural and educational programs, social services, health programs, and so on. Each council is made up of volunteers who may have undergone some training before being appointed to the council, or who may have worked on a variety of tasks and on subcommittees prior to their appointment. Volunteers receive technical assistance from one or more professional staff members. The staff also works with *petitioner organizations*, those member agencies who will be requesting allocations.

In general, only member agencies can expect to receive an appropriation, and this appropriation is made on an annual basis. Member agencies come to expect regular appropriations, generally at the same level as the sums received in the previous year, adjusted for inflation. They are held accountable for the way in which those funds are spent, must report on their programs, and must spell out the details if their current requests diverge in any way from the previous year's. It is difficult for nonmember organizations to receive allocations.

Nevertheless, such allocations are sometimes made, especially when the community faces a particularly pressing problem and none of the member agencies is prepared or willing to take on responsibility. A grant or allocation to a nonmember organization may also be made on a tentative basis if that organization is being tested for possible full inclusion as a member of the federation. In addition to their regular allocations, member organizations may submit requests for the financing of special, innovative projects. Sometimes, the funds requested are designated as seed money and are intended to attract funds from other sources. In a period when the available supply of funds seems to be outdistanced by need, federated agencies are examining their traditional allocation patterns very closely. In some cases, it has become as difficult for old-time member organizations to receive allocations as it is for new organizations that are more responsive to current needs.

## Public Sources of Support

Government programs are so varied in size, scope, and style that they could be the subject of another book. In fact, they have been the subject of many books. A good one for you to begin your search with is the *Catalogue of Federal Domestic Assistance*. It is available from the Superintendent of Documents each May and has semiannual or quarterly supplements. Its price has been relatively low in recent years, but as is the case with other government publications, it is likely to skyrocket over the next decade. It is available, however, in most libraries and in the library or bookstore of your local Federal Building. It provides a profile of every federal funding source available. It tells you which federal agency sponsors which programs, the legislation under which they are established, the criteria of eligibility for applicants, the deadlines for application, and the funding levels; it also provides contact names and, often, the telephone numbers of key officials who can provide you with additional information.

Federal agencies issue awards in the form of both contracts and grants. Despite President Reagan's first-term efforts to distribute domestic assistance funds directly to the states in the form of block grants, most funds are still administered through categorical programs; that is, there are specific categories of funds available to deal with the needs and problems of various populations and regions of the country. They may be categorized according to populations, like the aging, children, or adolescents. Within those categories they may be further subdivided into children with health needs, developmental disabilities, or a need for permanent placement.

These categories sometimes overlap problem areas such as mental health, substance abuse, chronic mental illness, or hypertension. Sometimes the categories deal with service arenas like primary or secondary education or community development. To apply for funds, you do not need to understand the entire system. You need to know only which category fits the kinds of programs or services your agency is interested in. For that, the index to the *Catalogue* will be most helpful.

I have used a number of terms throughout the chapter that may be unfamiliar to you. I will be using still others as we move along. This is as good a time as any to define them.

### Let's Get the Terms Straight

*Agreements*: Exchanges between two or more groups or organizations for a variety of commodities and actions. "Purchase of service" agreements are essentially contracts for specific services that the contracting agency is mandated to perform but finds more effective or efficient to contract out.

*Annual appropriation*: Regular allocation of funds for ongoing budget or program, generally from the same source to the same recipient; sometimes modified to reflect inflation, program growth, or program cutback.

*Application kit*: Information provided by the potential funder about what is desired and the procedures that must be followed; often includes abstracts or summaries of grants given out in previous years.

*Award*: The sum of money given by a contracting or granting agency to cover all or part of the sponsored project's costs.

*Contract*: An award given for a specific activity in which the funder has specified all the terms (e.g., who can apply; exactly what is to be done and how, at what cost, and by whom).

*Funders*: Organizations that give grants and award contracts.

*Grant*: A type of award that is supportive in character, given for a specific purpose, yet permitting the recipient considerable latitude in determining what is to be done, for whom, when, how much, and, within limits, at what cost.

*Grantee*: The individual, group, or organization that is the recipient of a contract or grant award.

*Grantor or contractor*: The individual or organization making a specific award.

*Guidelines*: General information on how to complete a proposal and specifications of the issues that must be addressed in a grant application (proposal). Frequently these are found in the application kit. Guidelines must be meticulously followed; improperly submitted or improperly written proposals, especially those that go to government and foundation sources, are likely to be disregarded.

*Proposal*: A plan of action (always in writing when applying for a grant or contract) describing what is to be done, for what purpose, how, by whom, and at what cost.

*RFP*: Request for Proposals, generally communicated in writing and sometimes posted in public documents like the *Commerce Business Daily* or the local press. The term RFP was once used exclusively to refer to requests for contract proposals, but it is now increasingly used to refer to grants as well.

*Solicited proposal*: One that is requested by a potential funding source (grantor or contractor) that has originated the ideas for the program or project, often through an RFP.

*Sponsored project*: A specific complex of activities, or program, financed by funds other than those of the regular budget of the group or organization (sometimes the individual) administering the project. For example, if your agency regularly provides services to the disabled through allocations from the United Fund, but receives a special additional subvention from the United Fund to establish a home-based program, or receives a grant from a government agency to do so, this is considered to be a sponsored project because funds outside the normal allocations of the organization are used for the project.

*Unsolicited proposal*: One in which the idea for the project clearly originated with the proposal writer or submitting agency (potential recipient).

### Types of Grants

1. *Block grants*: Awards are made to a unit of government (state, regional, or local) for broad purposes like housing or employment, as authorized by legislation or administrative policy. Recipients have great flexibility in distribution of those funds and may themselves become grantors or funders within the broad purposes of the grant according to the criteria established by the original grantor.

2. *Categorical grants*: Funds are expended for specific purposes, generally by the recipient, unless used by the recipient for the purchase of a service that can be provided better or cheaper by a third party.

3. *Formula grants*: Awards are provided to specified grantees on the basis of a specific formula prescribed by legislation or regulation, rather than on the basis of individual project review. Formulas may be set on the basis of such factors as population, per capita income, or age. The Administration on Aging may use a formula that includes the proportion of the elderly in the population, the number of those people who fall below the poverty line, the square mileage of the area, and the extent to which it is urban or rural, in

determining how much money is available to each state or to sub-regions within states.

4. *Discretionary funds*: Awards are made in which the funding agency or its chief officer has considerable latitude in deciding who can receive funds and for what amount, so long as it falls within the general policies or guidelines governing the funding source.

*Grants can be given for* organizing, coordinating, and managing; for components of an overall program or project budget such as travel, books, or staffing; for provision of a service or services; for research, and so forth.

### Types of Contracts

1. *Sole-source*: Only one party is asked to apply, because of the source's specific and unique qualification.
2. *Open-bid*: Anyone meeting the general qualifications for a particular type of contract can bid for it; RFPs are generally posted and information on them distributed broadly.
3. *Fixed-price*: The size of the award is fixed at start. No cost overruns may be allowed.
4. *Cost-reimbursement*: The grantee's costs are fully reimbursed; a maximal limit may be set, but this is subject to review in relation to changes in prices, problems in technology, and so forth.
5. *Cost-sharing*: Two or more organizations (one of which may be the recipient) share in the cost of the project.

*Contracts are made for* the conduct of specific services like program evaluation (instead of a more general research project) and other tasks that are clearly defined by the funders.

## Who Should Be Funded and for What Purpose

The extent to which your agency is likely to receive needed appropriations and awards will depend a great deal on its successful claim to a particular domain. The domain is that aspect of the human service system over which it claims a special role or responsibility. This domain includes (1) the social problems or needs covered; (2) the populations it serves; (3) the services rendered. For example, an agency may deal with the problems of joblessness (1) among black residents under the age of twenty in a particular section of the city (2). Its services (3) may include counseling, job training, job development, and job placement.

Your agency may make exclusive claim to a particular domain; that is, it may claim that only it can provide those services adequately or that it has the legitimacy with consumers and others to provide those services. Or the agency may share parts of the domain, for example, the problem covered, but may make a particular claim on the population targeted for services.

What your agency actually does constitutes its *de facto* domain, although it may also make claims for expanded domain over other problems, populations, or services in the future. That is, it may position itself to take advantage of changing public awareness or emerging problems in a given area of service.

The extent to which your agency is likely to receive funding for maintaining partial or absolute ownership over its particular turf will depend on the consensus by other relevant publics that its claim is a legitimate one. Funders must agree that your organization's claim is appropriate and that it has the capacity to perform adequately. Consumers must consider your organization to be the right address to which to apply for service. Collaborating organizations must be willing to work with your organization, even if there may be some competition between your agency and those collaborators over one or more aspects of your claim.

Domain consensus defines and sets the boundaries and the jurisdiction of your organization within the larger human services community. It includes formal agreements between your organization and others as well as informal expectations that services will be provided in an acceptable manner. Consensus over your organization's domain continues so long as the agency fulfills the functions judged to be appropriate to it and adheres to generally agreed-upon norms regarding standards of quality.

For funders to agree that your organization is worthy of support, they will also need to know something about the severity of the problems to be addressed. They must agree that the population to be served is legitimately in need of those services and that the services rendered are appropriate to those needs. Effective claims to domain reflect the credibility an agency has achieved with its input and output publics. Some agencies may be regarded with mistrust, not because of anything they may or may not have done, but because some of their other publics may be mistrusted. Thus a client may mistrust a social agency because it receives support from a government source he or she does not trust. Some government agencies may not trust a service organization that provides services to consumers that may be considered somehow nonlegitimate.

An organization's credibility often depends on the credentials of the staff. The way in which these credentials are established will vary from one constituent group to another. Reports the director of an agency,

> When I meet with government officials, I establish my identity through formal credentials. I interpret the functions of my agency and let them know what my responsibilities are. They can't care a hoot about who I am personally, but they do care who I represent and what my and the agency's past record is. It also helps that I have a Ph.D. It's only after we get to working together that we develop personal relations, mutual obligations that I may be able to capitalize on.

But it's different when I meet with representatives of self-help groups and other community people. They don't want to know about my position in the bureaucracy. They want to know what I stand for personally; who I am as a person. With low-income people, in particular, I have found formal credentials don't mean a thing. They even get in the way.

This may be especially true in work with minority populations whose increased militance or self-awareness often results in the mistrust of formal credentials. Some consumers may be more concerned with the authenticity that an agency representative projects. In some areas in particular, like working with substance abusers and ex-offenders, agency staff with backgrounds similar to clients' may be able to project understanding; they have "been there."

In the long run, however, credibility is bound up in achievement, in an individual's or an agency's track record. The track record may not be known by potential funding sources; you may have to inform them. If your agency is new, or new to its claim for a particular mandate, it may have to create a track record by showing how effective it has been in other areas or how qualified its staff are on the basis of things they have done in the past. Where a track record does not exist, collaboration with other agencies that do have well-established reputations and endorsements from representatives of key publics may be necessary. Just the way it helps to have a sponsor, someone who knows you and whose reputation is good, when you are applying for a job, it is good to have credible sponsors when applying for funds. Who might your agency's sponsors be? What kinds of relationships with them already exist, and what kinds of relationships must be cultivated?

## Making the First Contact

First contacts with the funder may be made formally or informally, directly or indirectly. It is sometimes important to position your agency to get needed support through indirect contacts. These include public education campaigns and public awareness activities that highlight the problems you seek to deal with, the population in need, or the services that you provide. The press, radio, and television are good places to begin. So are public-speaking engagements in schools, churches, and civic associations. Brief stories, vignettes, and announcements in corporate or house organs are other ways of becoming known. Board members and other volunteers associated with your agency can also be enlisted in spreading the word or interpreting the work of your organization.

Direct contacts might begin informally. They may be made through attendance at conferences where potential funders will also be participating. Leaders in the business community often join groups and clubs in order to make contacts. There is no reason why not-for-profit agency personnel could not do the same. Potential funders may be invited to visit your agency or to attend a special function it sponsors. Board members may be encouraged to invite other potential suppliers to special dinners or parties. Once an interest in your organization has been generated, it may be helpful to send those persons notes or information about the organization or relevant issues in which they may be interested. Send them articles you have written, public relations information releases that you have sent to the press, annual reports, and, where appropriate, endorsement letters from satisfied consumers and others.

Seek advice from potential funders before you seek funds. Ask them to comment or suggest improvements in the program design. Ask them to refer you to others they know who may have expertise in that area. Involve them as members of a project advisory committee. Ask them to refer you to other funders. As they come to know your organization, ask them to provide you with written endorsements when you approach those other funders. Involve them on the podium at a press conference, as co-authors of a paper at a professional meeting. Invite them to chair committees or to become involved in community-wide programs of which your agency perhaps is only one part.

When you are ready to approach a funder directly, even if you do not know anyone in the funding organization, you should do a number of things. Let us assume, for the moment, that your first contact will be by telephone.

Prepare a list of questions that you would like answered once you reach the right party. Do not call a funder with a general question like "What are you folks interested in?" If you are not sure what to ask, begin with a request for written information on what the organization funds, who is eligible for those funds, the size of the grants, and the schedule of when applications must be received and allocation decisions are made. Even before calling, you should try to locate the name of the appropriate project officer, and then ask for that person by name. If you do not have that name, call the organization the day before and get it from the receptionist who answers the telephone. Then call back, asking for the person by name. Sometimes, the receptionist may not be sure of what you want or whom you are looking for. Be prepared to give the receptionist a description of your project in a dozen words or less.

When you do reach the desired person, introduce yourself and the organization briefly. For example: "I am Morgan Johnson, coordinator of the home-help program for the disabled at the Developmental Disabilities Center in Milwaukee." Tell the funder how you got its name or who referred you (i.e., a professional colleague, someone who received a grant from the same agency, a congressman, a member of your board).

Tell the person why you are calling, and try to keep it down to one or two sentences. Check to see if what you are thinking about is on target. If it is close, but not right on, say something like, "That's interesting, we've been considering just that approach." If it is way off target, ask whether someone else at the funding source might be interested in your idea or what other funding sources might be more appropriate.

Assuming you reach the right person, and interest is there, be prepared to discuss your project more fully. Begin by briefly outlining the need you want to address. State the anticipated benefits to those who will be helped. Say something about the capacity of your organization and its track record. Point out who else cares. *Above all*, spell out clearly how this project fits into the priorities or interests of the potential funder.

During the conversation, check periodically to see if your program or idea seems to be on target. If you are getting a mixed reaction, ask if there is some way in which the project might be adapted to fit the funder's priorities. If the conversation seems to be moving along well, indicate the methods and procedures you intend to use in dealing with the problem or meeting the needs identified. Be prepared to answer questions on such items as the length of your project, when your project might start and how long it will run, the size of the staff needed, who your other partners or collaborators might be, the amount of money you would need this year and in subsequent years, where you will seek regular or ongoing funding when the grant monies are spent, or whether you will need continued and ongoing appropriations.

Assuming things are still going well, ask the person with whom you are speaking whether he or she thinks it is appropriate for you to submit a proposal. Find out what the preferred format is and if there are any written materials or guidelines that you should be following. End the conversation by summarizing your understanding and by outlining the next steps you will be following. Ask if you can call when you have additional questions, and find out the best times to call and whether there are other persons you should also be in touch with.

On completion of your call, check your notes. Make sure that everything of importance to your project is fully recorded. Go over the steps or activities that you have committed yourself to. Think through who else should be involved at this point. Make a tentative timetable for yourself.

Do not leave the matter at this point. Drop a note to the potential funder, summarizing the conversation and indicating what you intend to do next. If there were key points of understanding, spell them out. If some points have to be clarified, ask whether or not these steps are appropriate or if your understanding is correct.

A similar format might be followed in making an office call. You may, in fact, prefer to go no further than introducing yourself, your organization, and your interests in a telephone conversation, and then ask for an appointment. "I'll be in the state capitol next week. Would it be possible for me to drop in on Wednesday morning or in the early afternoon?" "I understand you'll be visiting Chicago next week. Sally Marcus told me you would be at the downtown center. Our offices are close by. Would you have some time for me to visit with you for about 20 or 30 minutes? I think we are on to something you might also be interested in. I'll send you a two-page summary." Exercise 14–1 should increase your understanding of the technique.

---

**EXERCISE 14-1**
**Making Initial Contact**

1. Contact a potential funding source by telephone. Before beginning, review the suggestions in this chapter. Make yourself a checklist of things you want to find out on the telephone and of additional information you may wish the funder to send you.

   Be clear about how you will identify yourself, your organization, and the program or project you are seeking funding for.

   Try out the phone call on a colleague first. Then do it for real. You may wish to look over Exercise 14–2 for some further tips on what kinds of information may be useful to record during and right after your conversation.

2. Write a one-page letter to a funder, identifying your organization and the kind of project you are seeking funds for. Include relevant questions and requests for further information.

   Test the letter out on a colleague first. Modify it. Send it.

---

If you are new at this sort of thing, practice, perhaps telephoning a colleague in the next office. If you decided to make your first contact through a letter, you might consider one of two approaches. In the first, you simply request information on funding priorities or on how organizations can apply for membership or for grants. You need say nothing about your own program or project, but might say something about your organization, at least listing its name and its primary areas of interest. In the second, include a brief statement of the proposed project. Specify what your organization intends to do, for whom, where, over what period of time. Be clear about the problem to be addressed and how it fits into your agency's domain. In both types of letter, make sure it is on the official letterhead and a telephone number is included.

## Getting and Updating Information

If you expect to seek appropriations, contracts, grants, and other awards from a variety of sources and on a regular basis, you will need an updated information system. Develop a file and keep it up to date.

Your file should include information on the following:

1.  To what kind of organizations and for what purposes does the funder make awards? Is the funder's range of choices limited by law? Assuming that the funder is limited to a particular field of service such as adoptions of hard-to-place children, medical care for the aging, or education for minority populations, are there other limits? Will the funder support ongoing projects or only demonstration or time-limited ones? Will the funder award grants for service-delivery programs, research, and training, or for only one of the three?

2.  What criteria does the funder use in determining eligibility for an award? Are grants awarded only to public institutions or can they be awarded to sectarian social agencies, private hospitals, and others? Are awards limited to domestic projects, to international ones, to certain sections of the country? If so, what percentage of the grant is the recipient required to match? Must the applicant meet certain staffing qualifications to obtain support? What is the probable duration of grant support?

3.  What kind of management controls is the funder likely to exercise over the recipient of an appropriation, a grant, or an award? Does the funder tend to view the proposal as a binding contract or as a statement of intent? Does the funder presume the right of direct intervention in the activity it supports? What latitude will the funder allow the recipient in administering a grant award budget? What types and frequency of progress reporting are required?

You will save yourself a good deal of time and aggravation if you get answers to those questions before submitting a proposal. If you find that a funder's requirements are unacceptable to your agency, forget it and move on to the next funder.

It may not be all that easy to get updated information on all funding sources. Although federal agencies have been traditionally the most likely to have complete and thorough information, changes in priorities, cutbacks, and the seesaw impact of allocating responsibilities to the states only to have the states turn back those responsibilities to the federal government, have resulted in considerable confusion. A number of federal agencies have begun to earmark certain funds for discretionary allocation, and decisions about how those funds are to be allocated are likely to change considerably from year to year. Thus, last year's guidelines and priorities are not necessarily adequate clues to what to expect for this year. The situation is even more confusing in many state agencies. Efforts by some states to allocate block grants to local agencies have generated such frustration that some potential recipients have judged the cost to be greater than the potential rewards. Most states are not properly structured to do the planning necessary for allocating the large masses of funds that have traditionally come from the federal government.

It may be even more difficult to get accurate information directly from medium- and small-sized foundations, particularly family and company foundations. The potential funders targeted may not have clear funding priorities, and even when they do, these are frequently not published or made generally available to the public. Nevertheless, information is available.

Much of it is available in many of the reference guides described in the extensive annotated bibliography at the end of the book. Second, more personalized information will be available from colleagues and other agencies in your own community or from similar agencies in other communities which have dealt with the funder. Third, much of it will be available through your own independent contacts with potential funders. Information is also available from government publications like the *Federal Register* and the *Commerce Business Daily*. Announcements about new programs will frequently be made through news releases in the *Washington Post*, *The New York Times*, your state capitol newspapers, or the local press. Additional information may be available through the *Grantsmanship Center News* and other newsletters aimed at specific agencies or service sectors. If all these sources prove inadequate, or if your staff is not prepared to make adequate use of them, you have two other options.

First, you can go to a private consultant. In larger metropolitan areas many consultants may be available to help you with all aspects of your grantsmanship or fund-raising endeavors. Some consultants may be known to the national organization with which your local agency may be affiliated (like the Child Welfare League of America or the National Association of Settlements). In smaller communities, a university development office professional, the community development staff at the local community college, or community educators affiliated with the intermediate school district may be available to consult with you as a public service or for a modest fee.

Second, you may choose to subscribe to a search service. Capitol Publications, at 2430 Pennsylvania Avenue, N.W., Washington, DC 20037, for example, publishes *Education Daily* and *Health Grants and Contracts Weekly*, each of which does the legwork of finding out where grants and contracts may be available for organizations concerned with either providing education or health-care services. Morris Associates at 1346 Connecticut Avenue, N.W., Washington, DC 20036, publishes a weekly, *Health Systems Report*. The ARIS Funding Messenger, at 2330 Clay Street, San Francisco, CA 94115, publishes several periodic newsletters including a *Creative Arts and Humanities Report*, a *Medical Sciences Report*, and a *Social and Natural Sciences Report*. The ORYX Press, at 3930 East Camelback Road, Phoenix, AZ 85018, deals with higher education and related issues. It publishes an annual volume with monthly updates. For a fee, it will also conduct a computer search of organizations that may have funding available for agencies like yours. Exercise 14-2 should consolidate your knowledge of data gathering.

## EXERCISE 14-2
### Developing a Resource File

1. Decide what you want to include in a master file on funder possibilities. Look over the Funding Source Information Worksheet (Table 14-1). Is this information adequate? How might you add to it or otherwise modify it? Make the changes.

2. Create a smaller locator file, perhaps on index cards that will lead you to the right information worksheet. Use such descriptors as private, public, local, state, federal, child welfare, or whatever other categories are appropriate to your needs.

3. Now get the information you need on at least:

   3 federal allocating sources
   3 voluntary sources
   3 private-sector sources

   You may have to seek the information in one or more of the books and guides discussed in this chapter, by telephone calls or personal interviews, or through correspondence. To really get a handle on the process, it might help to try each approach. Append useful information provided by the source itself.

4. Share the information with a colleague and get some feedback. Is it complete enough? What information is missing? Make the corrections.

**TABLE 14-1   Funding Source Information Worksheet**

1. Name of source:_____     Title:_____

_____     4. Assets: $_____

2. Street_____     As of _____(year)

   City_____     5. # of grants:_____

   State_____Zip_____     in _____(year)

   Phone (    )_____     # of applicants that year:

3. Name of contact person:     _____

_____

*continued*

## EXERCISE 14-2 continued

### TABLE 14-1    continued

Average grant size:

$_____

Dollar range of grants:

$_____to_____

6. Funding cycle:_____

_____

_____

7. Restrictions:_____

_____

_____

8. Matching funds
   requirement: _____Yes _____No

   Spell out _____

_____

9. Names of all decision makers,
   trustees, reviewers, etc., in
   funding organization:

_____

_____

_____

_____

_____

_____

_____

10. Geographical area of grants:_____

_____

_____

_____

_____

11. Kinds of support given:

   _____ Categorical grants

_____ Formula grants

_____ Block grants

_____ Contracts

_____ Others _____

_____

_____

12. Types of grants:

   _____ Research

   _____ Program/service

   _____ Staffing

   _____ Education

   _____ Capital improvement

   _____ Demonstration

   _____ Others _____

_____

_____

13. Due times for proposals:

_____

_____

14. Names of decision making or pro-
    gram persons in our organization
    that should be involved in pro-

    posals to this source: _____

_____

_____

_____

_____

_____

15. Recent grants in an area of in-
    terest:

    a. Grant_____

*continued*

**EXERCISE 14-2 continued**

**TABLE 14-1** *continued*

| | |
|---|---|
| Org._____ | 16. Actions (to be) taken: |
| Project dir._____ | a. Phone contacts_____ |
| Address_____ | _____ |
| b. Grant_____ | _____ |
| Org._____ | _____ |
| Project dir._____ | b. Written contacts_____ |
| Address_____ | _____ |
| c. Grant_____ | _____ |
| Org._____ | _____ |
| Project dir._____ | c. Interviews or meetings_____ |
| Address_____ | _____ |
| d. Grant_____ | _____ |
| Org._____ | _____ |
| Project dir._____ | d. Proposal(s) submitted_____ |
| Address_____ | _____ |

## Developing Your Grants, Contracts, and Allocations Strategy

Back when I was heavily involved in the continuing education business, I spent a lot of time on the road consulting with trainers and managers of staff-development programs. Many of my conversations still remain clear in my mind. You may find the following vignette instructive.

### Lost Opportunities

"It makes me sick to think of the opportunities lost. Except for orientation training for new workers, the State Department of Social Services has been nickel-and-diming staff-development and training activities for years. The budget for this is over $3 billion per year. Public welfare is big business these days. But we don't think of human resource development the way big business does.

"I agreed to become chief of the state office training bureau only when it became clear that new funding patterns were possible. The agency had just received $60,000 from the Office of Child Development [OCD] and another $70,000 from the Social and Rehabilitation Service [SRS] of the Department of Health, Education, and Welfare for training in child welfare, and Title XX funds were still open-ended as far as training was concerned. All we needed was a state plan that articulated training with service delivery and the Feds would reimburse us $75 for every $25 we put up for training.

"And that's where the shocker came and why I'm feeling so sick. Would you believe that the word 'training' never once appears in our service plan for the coming year? And would you believe that the two training proposals submitted to OCD and SRS are both totally unrelated to our Title XX service plan? Here we are stuck with two small grants that don't serve the agency's program priorities and a set of program priorities that don't take staffing needs into account and include no plans for staff development!"

I decided to share this statement with you because it is all too typical of the way in which many agencies pursue grants or other funding without first developing a well-thought-through, agency-wide funding strategy. This is a serious shortcoming. If your organization is without such a strategy, you may sometimes find yourselves with more money than you need, but more often with an inadequate financial basis upon which to build and to deliver effective services. You may find yourselves responding to a funder's priorities regardless of whether they fit those of your organization. No well-managed social agency should be without a funding strategy that articulates well with a broader marketing strategy and that is so designed as to give it the financial wherewithal to operate. In developing a funding strategy, consider your current and potential funding sources as well as your agency's long-term goals and the limits imposed on achieving those goals, and the supports necessary to find the necessary funds to achieve those goals.

We have already discussed the range of funding sources at least potentially available. They include regular appropriations, project grant awards, and contracts. In Chapter 13, we discussed a variety of fund-raising approaches aimed at individual donors through campaigns, sales, and socials. There are four other sources of support you should consider in the development of your funding strategy. These include (1) fees or tuition, (2) investment, (3) reserve funds, and (4) in-kind contributions.

Fees or tuition payments are generally made by individuals who enroll in an instructional activity, seek a particular service from the agency, or join the organization. These are sometimes set by tradition; they are frequently determined on the basis of what the market will bear, and in turn, this is determined on the basis of previous experience or on what similar organizations are charging. You will recall, from Chapters 9 and 10, that they sometimes are set on the basis of the actual cost of the service or program. How are your fees set? Are they arranged on a sliding scale, adjusted to the ability of consumers to pay?

Some agencies, including publicly supported organizations like universities and hospitals, have rather extensive *investment portfolios*. You cannot use money from a grant or contract for investment purposes, but you are often permitted to use money earned from fees or through individual solicitations in campaigns for the establishment of endowment funds and other kinds of investments. The income generated by these investments, in stocks, land, or other properties, is then used to support general-fund expenditures or special projects for which they may be earmarked. Most agencies seek outside advice from investment firms, banks, or knowledgeable individuals in the development of an investment portfolio. The portfolio may be managed by an outside organization or individual.

Where permitted, funds can be held in *reserve* through the accumulation of income from a particular activity or throughout the activity year or from a variety of sources. They can be drawn upon to cover unanticipated deficits or for the ongoing maintenance of the organization and its operations. Some agencies have rather active reserve fund accounts. These accounts permit the recycling of funds, allowing the organization to take risks and permitting the provision of subsidies to new endeavors. Some organizations are more conservative in the use of their reserve funds, holding them as a last resort in case all other sources of support become unavailable.

Although not often considered an element of the funding strategy, *in-kind services* or the contribution of goods and equipment can provide substantial underpinning for an agency's programs. In-kind services may be as diverse as the loan of facilities or equipment to be used by the agency, the assignment of staff from other agencies to particular tasks within your organization, or the provision of supportive services such as bookkeeping, mailing, the registration of participants.

This might be a good time for you to take stock of your current or potential funding sources. Try Exercise 14–3.

---

**EXERCISE 14-3**

### Current and Potential Funding Sources

On the exercise form (Table 14–2), check those funding sources your organization drew upon last year (Column A). If you know how much of your income came from each of those sources, indicate the total amount. Use approximate figures if necessary. Now go back and figure out what percentage of your income came from each source. Under appropriations, for example, you may have received $250,000 from regular sources like the United Way, but an additional $25,000 of discretionary funds from a special kitty established by the United Way to permit your agency to expand its ongoing programs. Indicate how much you received from project awards, contracts, fees, and so on. You may have to estimate the value of in-kind services or contributions in dollar terms. Now go to Column B.

*continued*

## EXERCISE 14-3 continued

Can you anticipate your income potential for next year? If you do not know how much or what proportion of your income will come from each of the funding sources, just put a check in the box to indicate those sources that are probable. You are now ready for Column C. Check all those funding sources that you think might be desirable for the future, say 3 to 5 years from now. Do not be put off by the fact that some of these may not seem realistic to you at the moment. You are projecting that which you think is desirable. Later, we will examine why some of these sources may be more feasible than others.

**TABLE 14-2    Inventory of Current and Potential Funding Sources**

| Funding Source | A<br>Sources<br>Last Year | B<br>Probable<br>Sources<br>Next Year | C<br>Desirable<br>Sources for<br>the Future |
|---|---|---|---|
| 1. Appropriations | | | |
|   a. Regular | | | |
|   b. Discretionary | | | |
| 2. Project awards | | | |
| 3. Contracts | | | |
| 4. Fees or tuition | | | |
| 5. Sales | | | |
| 6. Gifts, campaigns | | | |
| 7. Investments | | | |
| 8. Reserve funds | | | |
| 9. In-kind services<br>  or contributions | | | |

A decision to pursue one funding source or more will be determined in part by the extent to which your agency operates autonomously, and that to which it may be regulated by others. Some public agencies are limited only to appropriations from public sources. It is sometimes possible, however, to get around these limitations by establishing a voluntary group of interested citizens who constitute a "friends of the agency" organization that raises funds for specific programs or services above and beyond those which are mandated by your public auspice provider.

It is frequently possible for individual units, within a larger organization, to seek independent sources of funding for certain activities. For example, a family-life education department in a family service agency may charge fees for its courses and workshops and may sell booklets, pamphlets, toys, and other materials to its consumers. The staff-development unit in a public agency, although it almost always receives the bulk of its funds from the central administration, may seek outside sources of funding as well.

Because its general-fund allocation may be fully earmarked for salaries of the training staff, very little may be left over for discretionary disbursements like the purchase of consultation or of outside trainers. Although the staff-development unit may be required to provide services internally, it may not be prohibited from offering continuing education to nonemployees whose effectiveness is important to the agency's clientele. When educational services are offered to nonemployees, those consumers or their employing organizations may be charged fees. What kinds of fiscal constraints are imposed in your organization? Which funding sources are totally out of the question for you?

Look over Column C in the exercise. Are any of these nine types of funding sources totally off limits for your agency or for your unit within that organization? Cross out or erase these. Which of these sources are possible, but unlikely without some change in your agency's policies or procedures? Circle these. What will be necessary if you were to go about trying to create those changes?

## Making the Pitch for Greater Allocations from Internal Sources

You are now ready to think through your overall agency or departmental funding strategy. This strategy should be carefully articulated with the sources of support, both actual and potential, and with your agency's overall missions and those of its subunits. If the agency's primary mission is the provision of services to specified populations, then your department's efforts to raise funds must be carefully articulated with that mission. An argument for allocating funds to your unit must be made within the overall concerns of the agency.

If rapid growth in support for your particular unit or project outdistances the growth of other programs, you might have to argue for a shift in the mission or direction of the agency. In a tight money market, arguments about mission may be ineffective unless they are supported by an equally vigorous pitch for the utility of those activities in achieving the organization's maintenance goals. Sometimes this argument has to be made in long-range terms.

An argument might be made, for example, that by increasing the competence of foster-care workers or expanding the foster-care department for a short period, the agency will reduce the number of children who must be maintained in foster homes, and increase the likelihood of permanent placements at a reduced cost to the agency and to the state in the near future. Sometimes, an investment in a particular activity may be made on the assumption that it will either generate net savings in the future or so increase the organization's capacities as to position it properly for increased support from individual donors or funding organizations in the future.

## Timing

The timing of your efforts to secure funding must take into account your agency's readiness on the one hand and the funder's timetables on the other. You may have a good idea that no one in the agency is ready to listen to. The agency's priorities may be focused on a particular program area, or a population in need, or on its very survival. Your idea may be considered a frill. If the agency does not have a long-term strategy, it may be difficult to be heard or to generate interest in your idea, even should funds be available.

On the other hand, when others' attentions are focused elsewhere, that may be just the opportunity to jump into the breach and to do a little creative programming. In the long run, however, your fund-raising strategy must be clearly articulated with the agency's program and marketing strategies. Funding sources should be viewed as supplier publics, and relationships to those publics must be considered in light of the organization's need to relate to other publics as well. Your agency's desire to serve a given client public may be related to a supplier's interest in promoting services to that population.

To a large extent, then, timing is related to opportunities, but those opportunities go unrecognized and are frequently allowed to slip by. Recognizing opportunities requires knowing where one wants to go and being prepared to go there when the opportunity arises. It means having your bags packed and being on the lookout for a ride. You may have to be prepared to detour occasionally so long as you know where your journey will ultimately take you. You must also avoid permanent detours unless you are willing to substantially readjust your goals.

## Gearing Up to Writing a Proposal

You have to develop an idea long before you can commit it to paper. The idea for a modified, expanded, or amended program, or for a new program, may be the result of a systematic needs assessment conducted either by your agency or by someone else. It may be a response to a demand by one or more of your external or internal publics. To what extent have you discussed the idea with your colleagues and the agency, as well as with others in potentially collaborating organizations to see whether or not they are interested? How about the administration? Do they perceive the idea as fitting into the agency's programmatic or overall marketing strategy?

If the idea seems to fit the organization, the next step is to research it. Who else has conducted a similar project or grappled with the same issue?

How have they handled it? Are there experiences on which you can draw locally or nationally? Sometimes information can be gleaned from the annual reports of agencies that received grants from funders you are interested in. Funders will be quick to tell you if someone else is working in your area, particularly if they are pleased with the progress being made or the approach used. Have you checked the scientific literature to locate data which support your assumptions or concepts which can be used to help shape your intervention approach?

It is often essential to discuss your ideas with potential participants whose opinions about a particular service or program will help set it on the right track. It is also important to meet with relevant influential individuals in the community and with representatives of other agencies or community groups, to see whether they are interested in participating in the project and to solicit their support for its goals. We've already noted that their endorsements may be essential when you are ready to submit a request for financial support. A two- or three-page summary of your program or project might be circulated among some of these people in order to elicit further ideas. That same summary, modified by their suggestions, may later be used in communicating with the funder.

## What If You Get Funded, and What If You Don't?

If your marketing strategy is in place, if you have established relations with the appropriate external publics, and if you have worked the internal system properly, getting the grant or new appropriations should be no problem at all. Unfortunately, some agencies are less than systematic in preparing for a new or expanded program. It is not unusual to hear administrators say: "Let's see if we get the money first. Then we'll figure out what we have to do." or "Let's get the money, and then we'll run with it." Sometimes that works. Frequently it does not.

That approach creates such disjunctures that it can cause serious harm to other units of the agency. Moreover, it may delay start-up of your project by 2, 3, or sometimes even 4 or 5 months, as you are putting the administrative structure in place, recruiting staff, or working out the necessary exchange agreements with other organizations. If the project is funded for a limited period, say 12 months, much of your fiscal year may have gone by before you even begin. You may not be permitted to carry over funds into the next fiscal year.

What if you do not get the award? If the agency or particular program you have in mind is heavily dependent on the funds, you may be in serious trouble. If you have made contingency plans, if you are ready to seek other sources of support, or if you can delay start-up, you may be far ahead of the game. If the application process itself has helped you and the agency clarify its objectives and think through a new and needed service, it may have put you well on the road to success on the next round.

Sometimes, a turndown is the result of poor or inadequate preparation on your part. Sometimes, it is the effect of the funders not having sufficient money to allocate to worthy projects. Often, funders suggest that applicants resubmit, particularly if an idea is good or if it needs only minor adjustments. If that is the case, you will be well prepared for the next round. A well-thought-through idea with adequate local support can be put on hold for a while. There are, after all, many potential sources of support.

You may discover that the same program can be conducted without additional funds. It may require other resources that can well substitute for those funds: volunteers, loaner staff from other agencies, in-kind contributions like facilities and equipment. If you have prepared well for this round, you will be even better prepared for the next.

## Review

There are many sources of information on grants, contracts, and other awards. Many are located in the chapter references at the back of the book. Of particular interest are the *Catalogue of Domestic Federal Assistance, The Foundation Directory*, and other publications of the Foundation Center. A good general-purpose newsletter is the *Grantmanship Center News*.

Sources of support may be located in federal or state government agencies or in local government departments or block grant organizations. Other funds may be available from general-purpose, community, industrial, family, and operating foundations. Private-sector funds may be available from local companies, particularly if the service your organization provides articulates with a corporate need. Civic associations and religious groups are a potentially useful, but too often neglected source of support. The voluntary sector, particularly federated fund-raising and allocating organizations such as the United Way, are the major sources of support for many agencies.

Your organization's ability to gain support from funders will depend to a great deal on the funders' needs and how well you market your ideas. It will also depend on the kind of consensus that exists about your organization's domain, its claim to competence in providing certain services to targeted populations. To what extent is domain consensus present? What must be done to increase the legitimacy of your claim? Endorsements from other funders, from consumers, and from collaborating social agencies may be important.

Initial contact with a potential funding source must be carefully planned. You will need to know what you are looking for and what to tell the funder about your organization. You will also need a well-thought-through inventory of questions to ask. Contacts can be made through correspondence, by telephone, or in person.

Agencies should keep two kinds of funder information resource files: a relatively complete and periodically updated master file (see Exercise 14–3), and a locator file that indexes the master.

A grants or contracts strategy should be articulated with the agency's broader marketing program and funding strategies. Other sources of income to be considered are fees and tuition, investments, reserve funds, endowments, gifts, and in-kind contributions. In making a pitch for internal allocations to your department, consider these other sources and how investment in your program might put the agency in a better position to capitalize on them. How else will investment in your idea benefit the overall agency (not just the clients it is intended to serve)?

A well-articulated idea and a well-designed proposal are rarely wasted efforts. If you get funded, you will be able to gear up quickly when the funds arrive. If you don't, you will have established contacts and positioned yourself to be more competitive the next time around. You may even discover that you can conduct all or part of the project without additional outside funding.

# 15

# PROMOTIONS: A STRATEGIC COMMUNICATIONS APPROACH

FROM A MARKETING PERSPECTIVE, which of the following definitions of the verb "promote" do you find most on target?

To move forward.
To advance in station or rank or from one grade to another.
To help bring into being; to launch an enterprise.
To present (merchandise or services) to public attention.
To further public awareness and acceptance, or to sell through advertisement and publicity.

If you checked each of the above, you were right on every count. Human service organizations are involved in promotions every time they work at heightening public awareness or consciousness of a problem to be addressed or of a population in need. They promote when they launch a fund-raising campaign or an effort to engage collaborating agencies in new linkages. Agencies promote ideas, services, action programs, resource-development activities, and themselves.

## Targeting Promotional Activities

Unfortunately, promotional activities are not always as targeted as they might be. Some social workers and others may mistake promotional activities for what they consider a crass sales approach, giving evidence of the debilitating bias discussed in the Introduction. Others may be unaware of what they might accomplish through a more strategic approach to communicating with the general public or with targeted publics within it. By *strategic* I mean a carefully planned and orchestrated set of activities aimed at achieving a goal or goals. By *communications* I mean the transmission of information or the exchange of messages. Many of the psychotherapy methods we use are strategic communications approaches. So are promotional activities, or at least they would be if we were skilled and knowledgeable in their use. Let me share an example with you.

Some years ago, I interviewed planners concerned with the needs of the elderly throughout the United States and Canada. I think you will find the following vignette, excerpted from one of those interviews, instructive:

### Ombudsman on the Air

"While the survey was in progress, I arranged with the local cable TV station to do a weekly show on the city's retired people and the social services available to them. One of our retired school principals became the moderator. He was well-liked in the community, and had all the wit and charm you can imagine. I played a behind-the-scenes role, working with an advisory committee of other older people on the selection program content, how it would be presented, and so on. There were three parts to the show. Each week we interviewed an agency administrator. At first we picked only the best agencies: the ones that had good, well-delivered services for older people. We wanted to highlight these services. Then we began to pick service agencies which had a variety of deficiencies. Instead of just probing at the deficiencies, we invited a panel of older people to make suggestions on how services might be improved. The idea was to get people talking, thinking, and acting.

"By the third week, we were getting a tremendous amount of fan mail, mostly from older people who had additional questions they wanted answered, and from others who had strong opinions about what was being said on the show. Some letters came from younger people who wanted to know how to handle problems with parents or older relatives. Some even came from professionals and from agency people. That's when we decided to add a third part to the program. We began taking a limited number of telephone calls at the studio and asking our agency guest and our panelists to respond to them.

"We still couldn't handle all the phone calls and letters we were getting. It was obvious that we needed something in the nature of an action line or an ombudsman. After only two or three months, the show was so well established that it didn't take very much to get a small grant from a local family foundation to hire a Geri-Action reporter. Together with a group of volunteers recruited from various organizations, this person began following up on the kinds of problems people were having, and reporting them on the show. We had an ombudsman who reported successes and failures on the air!"

In this example, the problems of the elderly were highlighted and interpreted to the general community, effective and responsive social agency programs were promoted, and some of the weaker or less responsive programs were identified, as were new needs and interests. The stage was set for a subsequent community-wide planning effort in which task forces were established to deal with a wide variety of needs. Thus service programs, the needs and interest of a particular population, and a planning process were all promoted through a television program.

The planner knew precisely what he was aiming for and TV might be a useful adjunct of his overall strategy. Effective promotional efforts require clarity of goals, targeted publics, and the means to get to where we want to be.

Typically, these goals might include:

A general public that is informed about the needs of a particular population

Heightened awareness or sensitivity to the capacities of that population

Increased self-confidence on the part of those who may need to become more assertive as individuals or as collectivities

Dissemination of information on available services to populations in need

Shared information on the impact of alternative policies or service programs on the disadvantaged

Increased demand for a particular service or product

Commitment to or willingness to contribute money or time to support an agency's programs

The targets of a promotional effort might include all residents in a given community, potential employers of the hard-to-employ, families who have the capacity to but may never have considered adopting a special-needs child, decision makers in social agencies that are not currently providing service on a coordinated basis to a population in need, self-help groups that may not be aware of the potential benefits of collaborative relationships to a particular agency, or potential funders not aware of a particular agency's capacities to provide a given service or its willingness to modify its services in a desired direction. In deciding on your targets, use the same approach you used to segment your markets. Consider geography, demographics, psychographics, and function. Review the exercises in Chapter 3.

## Image Building

Many of our promotional efforts might be aimed at improving the public's understanding of social work and of the agencies that provide social services. Consider for a moment how the general public in your community views social work and other human service professions and how it perceives the agencies that provide social and related human services. Is the public image the same as your agency's own self-image? Is there a difference between the actual image held and the ideal image that you would like to promote? Do different publics hold different images, and how do those images affect the kind of support you're likely to engender or the demands for services you wish to promote?

Is there an image problem? Do people hold stereotypic views of social workers, of your agency, of its clients, or of their needs? Are these stereotypes necessarily negative? Should you wish to challenge some of those stereotypes, your professional association may be able to help you. In 1981, the National Association of Social Workers produced the *NASW Publicity Kit* and a *Public Relations Manual*. Both are available from the Washington office. If your agency belongs to a national organization of "like-agencies" (e.g., the Association of Community Mental Health Centers or the National Jewish Welfare Board), that organization, too, will have available promotional materials that can be adapted for local use.

It is difficult, however, to change a long-held image overnight. How long might it take your organization to change its image or to modify the public image of a vulnerable consumer population?

In image building, symbols can be very important. In the United States, "welfare" tends to take on a negative connotation. To many, it means "cheating," "dependency," or a "drain on the taxpayers' resources." But no one is against the "deserving poor." In a recessionary economy, who can be against "laid-off" workers, in contrast with the "unemployed," some of whom, at least, are blamed for their situation. Some people may be turned off by the term "runaway kids" but not by "troubled teens." People may be against the high cost of Medicare or Medicaid, but they won't be against serving crippled children or good health care for impoverished senior citizens. They may be against welfare, but they are not against feeding hungry children.

Getting the right message across means using the right words: those that are most likely to generate sympathy or support.

Promotional activities can be conducted on an interpersonal basis, formally or through word of mouth, on a one-to-one basis, or through public appearances. They can also be conducted through the media: the press, radio, television, and myriads of subcommunity or organization-linked newsletters published nearly everywhere.

## Working with and Through the Media

Unfortunately, the media haven't been our closest allies, nor are we theirs. We frequently accuse the media of being too superficial and sensationalist. Scandals, unfortunately, tend to be more newsworthy than the everyday efforts of dedicated practitioners. By focusing on problems, we complain, the media frequently convince the public that social programs do not work. We sometimes find ourselves being pushed into defensive postures. And therein lies our biggest mistake.

We assume too much. We assume that because we know that we do important work or that all people in need are worthy, others will not only agree but will dig up the facts to prove our contentions.

Too often we play catch-up ball, responding defensively rather than taking the initiative. Taking the initiative requires giving accurate information, not just when a scandal breaks, but on an ongoing basis. Media professionals—journalists and others—are professionals, but they are not human service professionals. They, too, play catch-up ball, and they depend on whatever is available to them to put their message across. If we want their message to be our message, we must build effective and ongoing relations with them.

For some of us, this won't be easy. Most of us don't know much about how the media work. We may not even be sure about whom to communicate with or how to find this information. We are, perhaps, overawed by the same media we criticize, dazzled by them. Interestingly, we seem to have been effectively blocked from achieving our potential with the media by debilitating attitudes, lack of knowledge, or insufficient skill—precisely the faults we find in the media and precisely those providing the basis on which we organize services aimed at other populations in need.

## Organizing a Media Campaign or Broader Promotional Effort

To compensate for past omissions, why not organize in much the same way as you might in establishing any kind of campaign structure? We saw that in a fund-raising campaign it is fairly standard to establish a campaign cabinet. In planning a media campaign, it might make sense to establish a media committee or perhaps a more comprehensive promotions committee that includes a media task group.

The committee might be made up of key staff and board members, representatives of other agencies with which you will be coordinating a promotional effort, consumer representatives, and technical experts such as journalists or faculty and students from a nearby university's journalism department. The scope and focus of the group's efforts will require some clarification. Should it coordinate with the agency's fund-raising campaign or grantsmanship efforts? Should it aim at generating support from unions, the business community, the general citizenry? Should it focus on the agency as an organization, its programs and services, the recruitment of volunteers, the needs of vulnerable populations, the community's interest in improving the quality of life for all of its residents?

Through which vehicles should promotional activities be transmitted? Even word-of-mouth campaigns require careful preparation and management. A personal-appearance program will require decisions about who is to make those personal appearances: current or former clients, agency staff, board members, or other expert parties? Where are those appearances to take place: at public meetings, in the school, in other agency settings, or at meetings of fraternal, church, and civic associations?

## Getting to Know Media People: Working with Them

An important component of any promotional strategy is the establishment of effective relationships with representatives of the media and the other organizations through which promotional efforts are likely to take place. Make appointments with these people, perhaps at first only for exploratory purposes. Find out how they work in their organizations and what their interests are.

Promotion specialists I have interviewed suggest development of a basic media kit that you might present at a first meeting. It could include general information on your organization and its programs or on the population and issues about which you are concerned. It might be made up of brochures, fact sheets, annual reports or their summaries, selected news releases, or examples of features and news stories that may have appeared elsewhere. It should be possible to update the media kit; you may wish to expand it by regularly sending in information that can be added to the kit.

Your relationship with the media must be built on both mutual respect and mutual need. Most media people struggle to meet deadlines. They are either overworked and overstimulated, or overworked and understimulated, by newsworthy events. Some may have to invent events or write about nonevents. Real pros don't like doing this any more than real pros in social work like to fill meaningless quotas. But there may be little news available and even less time to dig it up. Time is the journalists' greatest enemy.

Don't give them extra work. Reduce their workloads by leading them to interesting items, to new story angles; by giving them the material on which they can base a story or a column. Some journalists may be putting themselves on the line by working with you. To make it worth the risks, their interests must coincide with yours.

Trust, an accompaniment to mutual respect, comes from ongoing experiences. You will expect media people to follow through; they will expect the same from you. Follow-up is equally important. The simplest follow-up is a thank you stated personally; it is much better when followed by a letter. Letters to the editor, some of which may be published in columns or read over the radio and television, not only support an individual journalist's effort but support the work of the paper or station. Those letters can come from you or from your promotional committee members. They may also come from others who you may have stimulated to write, reinforcing the work done by the media.

Remember that in order to raise the consciousness of the general public or of targeted segments, you will first have to raise the consciousness of media professionals. It may also be necessary to raise the "media consciousness" of your own staff and other interested publics. Have the staff and others scan the local press, listen to the radio, or spot appropriate programs and messages on television. Discuss these at a committee or staff meeting. If faulty images are projected about your programs, the populations you are concerned about, or the issues you wish to promote, how can they be corrected? Make this a regular item on your staff meeting agenda, on the board's agenda.

A next step might be to become thoroughly familiar with selected print or airwave media. The patterns of operations in newspapers are relatively similar in most communities; the same holds true for radio and television.


## Working with Local Newspapers

Most local newspapers carry stories about human services and social policy issues with some regularity. These stories not only inform the public, but they shape public opinion. Large metropolitan papers generally have special supplements on particular days of the week that include features on life-styles, daily living, or the family. Both big-city and small-town newspapers include community calendars and announcements of special events. Make sure your activities are listed, but don't limit yourself to general newspapers.

Consider also weekly neighborhood papers, advertiser-supported "shoppers," weekly or monthly community magazines, underground publications. Don't ignore union bulletins, the newsletters of civic associations like the League of Women Voters, employee newspapers put out by industry or business groups, tenants' newsletters. These reach specially targeted populations, often reaching them on a more personal level than the general press.

Consider the following kinds of coverage: weekly press releases; an occasional news story or feature article; a regular column, perhaps one written by a member of your staff or board; letters to the editor in which staff members, board members, and clients speak up. *News releases* should focus on current or anticipated events; issues or problems of importance to the community; information on activities or persons; changes in an organization's services or location of those services; the results of an activity such as a survey, a successful membership drive, or the completion of a funding campaign; the displacement of special-needs children in adoptive families. The message should be one to which people will respond favorably.

If, in the past, you've felt news coverage to be biased and uninformed, use every opportunity to use agency news releases. Don't slant the news. Releases should inform; they should be objective and accurate. News releases can publicize events, interpret them, and promote community understanding. If they are accurate and unbiased, they must also be verifiable; otherwise the paper will not take the risk of publishing your release a second time.

*Feature articles* permit fuller treatment of an issue. They may not require immediate release, so can be held for a time when the paper may have less current news to report. Feature articles, in contrast to news stories, may include opinions; if they do, they should be by-lined. You, or individuals with whom you work, may wish to write the feature article; alternatively, you may wish to provide story ideas and supporting materials to journalists. Features may appear one time only or be serialized.

Like feature articles, *columns* are also by-lined. Some may describe programs and services or discuss issues. Others may aim to provide direct help to people in need. Advice columns written by local agency personnel have become regular features in newspapers throughout the country. Some speak to teenagers, others to their parents, still others to parents with young children or to people with health problems. Some are aimed at the elderly, some at the unemployed, others at ethnic populations. They may be written in English, in Spanish, or in another language. Foreign-language columns have begun to appear as regular features in some English-language dailies.

## Tips for Increasing Your Press Appeal

You can add to the appeal of a written message by including photographs, but be sure to caption them to identify the people shown. Candid shots tend to do better than posed pictures. Most papers will accept only black-and-white glossy prints that are 5 x 7 or 8 x 10 in size. Check the requirements with your local paper. If you want the pictures back, provide a mailing envelope; if you want to protect your photos, sandwich them between pieces of cardboard. If you can't include photographs, be sure to use words that describe your image graphically. Include as many names of local people and organizations as possible.

Your article or feature is likely to be received more positively if you follow these rules:

1.  All submissions should be typed, double-spaced, on 8½ x 11 in. sheets of white paper.
2.  They should have wide margins, at least an inch or an inch and a quarter in size (editors make corrections in the margins).
3.  Don't carry over paragraphs from one page to the next.
4.  Keep the sentences in your paragraphs short.
5.  If you must include technical terms, define them.
6.  Type on one side of the page only and *never* send carbons or poor-quality photocopies.

7. At the top of your first page, include your name and the name and address of the organization or its contact person from whom additional information might be sought.

8. Indicate whether the item is for immediate release or whether it is a feature item. If you wish it to appear on a given day, in a given section of the paper, so indicate.

9. On each subsequent page, type the name of the organization or your name at the top in the right-hand corner or along with the page number.

10. End the article with the word "end" or the symbols "-30-" or "***."

It is not necessary for you to develop your own copy. You may wish to submit prepared or "canned" copy. If you do, let the newspaper know. Include some cover explanation indicating its source or for what purpose it was developed. For example, the Alcohol and Drug Abuse and Mental Health Administration (ADAMHA) sponsors an Information and Feature Service as part of its Office of Public Affairs. The ADAMHA staff prepares a series of reproducible columns under the titles "Understanding Mental Health" and "Understanding Drug Abuse." Copies are available free to human service organizations and local newspapers. They can be ordered from the NIMH Office of Public Affairs, 5600 Fishers Lane, Rockville, MD 20857. The National Clearing House for Alcohol Information also has a "feature service." Its articles can be ordered from the National Clearing House at P.O. Box 2345, Rockville, MD 20852.

Other features can be lifted, or borrowed, from the newsletters of national associations with which your agency might be affiliated. They can be used verbatim or adapted for your own local press. You might wish to supplement them with information about your agency and its services or about the problems in your own local community. Whether you use these or other information sources, be available to local reporters to answer questions and to correct misinformation in advance rather than after the fact. It is easier to get the news right the first time than to publish retractions or to correct faulty impressions when they have been published. You are now ready for Exercise 15–1.

Figure 15–1 is a guide for collecting useful information on the print media in your local community. It may help you uncover what a particular paper or journal features and who its key officials and reporters might be. If you are not sure where to start in getting the information, consider getting help from a friendly journalist you may have met or whom a colleague knows, the public library, or from others who regularly work with journalists. These may include promotions specialists from the United Way, the League of Women Voters, the NAACP, and other civic-minded organizations. Your contacts may be able to tell you who the managing editors, news and feature editors, or key reporters are. If all else fails, call the paper. It is, after all, in the information business!

## EXERCISE 15-1
## Profile of a Local Newspaper

Get to know a local newspaper. It might be a general-purpose daily or a highly targeted weekly or monthly newsletter.

1. Look over the Sample Data Sheet: Local Print Media (Figure 15-1). Complete the information in such a manner as to make it communicable to others in your organization; be both complete and accurate.

   From whom will you get this information? How?

2. Share your findings with colleagues in the agency or organization. Ask them to indicate what might be left out or confusing. Make the necessary adaptation in the Data Sheet and gather the missing information.

3. Who else should be involved in a similar process? What other news or print media should be listed? If you don't know, how can you find out?

4. Design a plan for getting the information; include who will be getting it and from where. By when? For what purposes?

Name of print medium:_____
Address:_____
Telephone:_____     Category of print medium:
Executive editor:_____     _____Newspaper
Other relevant editors and their titles:             _____In-house newsletter
_____     _____"Shopper" guide
_____     _____Neighborhood newspaper
_____     _____Community magazine
_____     Other_____

Reporters:                    Phone #        Areas of special interest
_____   _____   _____
_____   _____   _____
_____   _____   _____
_____   _____   _____

Photographers:

_____   _____

Other contact persons:

_____   _____   _____
_____   _____   _____
_____   _____   _____

Areas covered:
  •Geographic_____
  •Ethnic or interest groups_____
  •Special characteristics_____
Circulation:_____
_____Daily  _____Weekly  _____Monthly  _____Other (describe)_____

**Figure 15-1**   Sample Data Sheet: Local Print Media

*continued*

## EXERCISE 15-1 *continued*

Types of coverage                                                        Deadlines

_____News items, press releases                                    _____
_____Calendars (specify)    _____    _____
                                            _____    _____
_____Feature articles         _____    _____
(specify sections)              _____    _____
                                            _____    _____
                                            _____    _____
_____Special issues           _____    _____
(specify)                          _____    _____
                                            _____    _____
                                            _____    _____
_____Advertisements, clsfd. _____    _____
                                            _____    _____
Special requirements           _____
_____
_____

Persons at the agency who have special relationships to the media or are designated with special
responsibility (specify):_____
_____
_____

Other information:_____
_____
_____

**Figure 15-1    continued**

## Getting on the Air: Working with the Radio

I do a lot of driving, and that means that I do a lot of radio listening. In addition to music, I listen to a constant stream of news about local, regional, national, and international situations. I also listen to talk shows and to call-in programs. Now you might ask yourself, "What is a university professor doing listening in to talk shows?" I listen precisely because I am a university professor. I am interested in knowing what is on people's minds.

Many talk shows reach large and faithful audiences. They draw on a wide range of interests and concerns. Some have become *de facto* forums for the expression of opinions and the exchange of information. Many serve as outlets for the lonely and the isolated. In some communities, a trained social worker, nurse, psychologist, or physician may be available to provide crisis counseling or to refer callers to professional care givers and community-based self-help groups.

Recognizing their potential to serve large numbers of people in need, some agencies have undertaken the responsibility for conducting daily or weekly talk shows. A typical format might begin with brief presentations or interviews with experts, go on to respond to phoned-in questions, and then to the establishment of a dialogue between telephone callers. When the radio is thus used, as a way of promoting well-being, it complements your agency's other service efforts, and it adds to the promotion of general well-being and public understanding and perhaps to the promotion of other agency services. You may decide to conduct such a show or to participate regularly as a panelist or consultant.

But this may be more than you or the organization is prepared to do. Getting on the air need not require long-term commitments, or for that matter, extensive preparation. For example, on a call-in program, all you have to do is dial the station, wait your turn, and then ask your question or make your point. Many radio shows provide opportunities for local people to make guest editorials, to air tapes of special events, to provide coverage on meetings, or to feature speakers whom your organization has brought to town.

Although many stations carry news stories about their communities, most local newsrooms are notoriously understaffed. News reporters have a great need to supplement their meager resources. As with the local print media, you can provide the station with news releases and perhaps prerecorded or prewritten messages that will be aired when there is time. If local reporters know you are available, they can use you as a resource person. If they don't know you, you won't be used.

The accessibility of the airwaves is a matter of public policy. Under the Federal Communications Act, the airwaves were designated as public property. Broadcasters are required to use them in the public interest. The Federal Communications Commission has established a fairness doctrine that is subject to periodic review and change and that obligates stations to facilitate public debate and information. Opportunities for local self-expression are encouraged, although stations are not under any obligation to grant time to any specific group. Nevertheless, they are under the gun to fulfill the legal requirements to maintain licensure. Frequently they do so by making public service announcements. PSAs can be read either by the station announcer or by you. They can be prerecorded in 10-, 20-, 30-, or 60-second spots. The regulations on PSAs have changed recently. They may change again. Traditions also vary with locales. Keep informed.

Just as a number of traditions have arisen regarding the print media, in preparing written material for news or other radio coverage, certain forms should be observed. As with news releases for the press, your radio communication should also be clearly identified at the top of the first page and on all subsequent pages. Be clear about whether this is a news release, an editorial comment, or a public service announcement.

You will have to be very careful in your use of language. The listener will have to understand what you are attempting to communicate the first time around; it is not possible to go back and reread a paragraph for future clarification.

The radio announcer must also be able to read your material without difficulty. Triple-space rather than double-space. Keep sentences and paragraphs very short. Do not carry over paragraphs to the next page. It is better to end with a great deal of white space on a page than to take the chance that the thought may not be fully communicated on the air.

Remember that it is not just *what* you get on the air, but *when*. The best-contrived PSA and the most valuable lecture are not likely to be heard by many people if aired at 4 A.M. Time is not the only factor that determines who is listening. Different populations will listen to different stations. If you are trying to reach people who listen to rock stations, that is where your message should be heard. If you are trying to reach people who listen to classical music, let common sense direct you to a different station. Consider also who the announcer is and what his or her audience might be interested in.

## Getting on the Tube

Just as the radio station that you selected will be important, so will the television channel. Will you be using VHF, UHF, or CATV? VHF channels (2–13) include the national networks and their local affiliates plus a number of local, commercial, and noncommercial channels. They have strong signals and generally reach populations in a relatively wide area. UHF channels (14–83) have weaker signals, and therefore have smaller, but perhaps more targeted, audiences.

Unlike the VHF channels, which include many first-run programs, UHF channels tend to broadcast old movies and reruns. But they may be more strongly committed to local and community issues than the VHF channels. They frequently seek ideas for local programming from their viewing public. This is also true of cable television.

Although much of CATV programming originates far from the local community, as a condition of being granted a license most local communities require their cable companies to provide access channels to local individuals and organizations. The Geri-Action Reporter vignette that I shared with you at the beginning of this chapter is a good example of one organization's strategic use of cable television.

Less ambitious efforts might include a slide show about hunger in the community; a prerecorded lecture by a well-known therapist; live coverage of an open meeting of a self-help group; interviews with experts on drug abuse; a live demonstration of family therapy followed by called-in questions from the audience; or announcements about, or requests for, foster homes or Big Brothers and Sisters, perhaps accompanied by testimonials from children and adults who have participated in such programs. Such activities involve little if any financial outlay on the part of the agency. Even the equipment required for prerecording announcements, stories, or meetings is generally available from the cable operator. And cable staff may be available to consult with you on how to use the equipment or may even record the event for you.

In preparing news releases or feature stories that someone else may read on public or commercial television, use the same guidelines as in preparing items for the radio. But remember that television is a visual medium; include photos or illustrations. Charts that highlight your message may be most helpful. Be aware that your story or idea may not be aired on the day that you present it to the station. Be clear about the timeliness of the material; if it is aired after an event, or after an issue has been resolved, it will do you no good and the station will look bad. Try to be available to station personnel to answer questions, to provide additional background material, or to appear in an interview.

Exercise 15–2 contains a Sample Data Sheet on Radio and Television (Figure 15–2) similar to the Data Sheet you completed on a local newspaper for Exercise 15–1. Read the instructions and complete the form for Exercise 15–2.

---

**EXERCISE 15-2**

**Profile of a Local Television or Radio Station**

Get to know a local radio or television station. If television, it might be VHF, UHF, or cable. If radio, it might be a general-purpose station, an all-music or all-news station, or a station that focuses primarily on talk shows.

1. Look over the Sample Data Sheet: Radio and Television (Figure 15–2). Complete the information in such a manner as to make it communicable to others in your organization; be both complete and accurate.

   From whom will you get this information? How?

2. Share your findings with colleagues in the agency or organization. Ask them to indicate what might be left out or confusing. Make the necessary adaptation in the Data Sheet and gather the missing information.

3. Who else should be involved in a similar process? What other airwave media should be listed?

4. Design a plan for getting the information; include who will be getting it and from where. By when? For what purposes?

Name of station:_____ Letters and number:_____

Address:_____ Telephone:_____

| Radio category | | TV category | |
|---|---|---|---|
| _____AM | _____Private | _____VHF | _____Private |
| _____FM | _____Public | _____UHF | _____Public |
| Other_____ | | _____CATV  Other_____ | |

**Figure 15-2**   Sample Data Sheet: Radio and Television

*continued*

Station manager:_____ Phone:_____
News director:_____ Phone:_____
Public affairs coord.:_____ Phone:_____
Other contact persons:_____ Phone:_____
_____ Phone:_____
_____ Phone:_____
Viewing or listening area:_____ Population:_____

Audience characteristics:
_____Urban _____Children _____Minority (specify):_____
_____Rural _____Teens _____
_____Suburb. _____Adults Socioeconomic characteristics:_____
_____Seniors _____

Station format
Television | Radio

_____National network programs | _____News _____Classical
_____Local programs | _____Features _____Easy listening
_____Movies and reruns | _____Drama _____Rock
_____Public access | _____Talk _____Country
Other_____ | Other_____ _____Jazz

| Program opportunities | Contact persons | Day/Times |
| --- | --- | --- |
| News | | |
| | | |
| | | |
| | | |
| PSAs | | |
| | | |
| Commercials | | |
| | | |
| Editorials | | |
| | | |
| Talk or | | |
| interview | | |
| shows | | |
| | | |
| | | |
| | | |
| | | |
| Special | | |
| programs | | |

Persons at the agency who have special relationships to the station or are designated with special
responsibility (specify):_____
_____
_____

Other information:_____
_____
_____

**Figure 15-2   continued**

## Community-Service Projects

It is not unusual for radio and television stations to engage in community-service projects. If you have been successful in engaging a local station in working with you on the promotion of a cause or on educating the community to a certain problem or service potential, be prepared to provide commentators and editorial staff with all the support they will need to provide you with the coverage that you need.

Remember that a radio or television community-service project requires a great deal of investment in the station staff's time and effort. Working with you means they probably can't be working with another organization at the same time. Dealing with your issue means that they must downgrade or ignore other issues. Be sure to show appreciation. Thank you letters from your board or your agency executive may not be enough. Supportive letters from the public may be even more important if you wish to encourage the station to work with you again in the future.

Should you be invited to go on the air or appear on television, prepare yourself properly. Be sure of what you are going to say. Be ready to be vigorous in stating your position on a given issue, but be moderate in tone. Try to maintain a sense of humor.

It is a good idea to find out in advance what you are likely to be asked. This will permit you to prepare properly and to avoid overstating or restating your position too often. If others are going to appear with you, find out who those persons are and what their affiliations are. Prepare for what they will be saying, so that you can rebut it or complement their positions as the situation may call for.

## Advertising

Unlike the promotional efforts we've been examining, when we speak about advertising, we refer to *paid* presentations of ideas, goods, or service by an identified sponsor. Agencies and other organizations can advertise through television and the radio, in magazines, journals, newspapers, and newsletters. They can also advertise on outdoor billboards and on supermarket bulletin boards. They can use novelty items like calendars, recipe cards, and matchbooks for advertising. And they can advertise in reference guides like the Yellow Pages, a United Way Community Agency Directory, or a local health services directory. Advertising is also done through circulars and brochures that are handed out at meetings or distributed directly through the mail.

Advertising requires a financial investment, and most investments are made in anticipation of a return. That return may be in clients that come to the agency or in money that is raised through various appeals. It may be in the achievement of goals like increased hiring of the disabled, placement of special-needs children, improved diets for the elderly, or completed screenings for hypertension.

Advertising can be linked strategically to other promotional activities. For example, on the same day that a paid ad appears in a local newspaper for your agency's summer day camp, a feature item describing the camp's new site or next week's special program might appear, possibly (and preferably) on the same page. Knowing the reporter who handles the story helps. A fund-raising campaign frequently uses advertisements as a way of reaching a wide public. "You may have seen our ad in this morning's paper," a telephone solicitor might say. "Let me tell you a little bit more about the disabled people we are serving and why we need your contribution."

## Public Appearances and Personal Contacts

Media and print exposure are important. So are personal contacts. Sometimes the best way to sell an idea or to demystify a process is to discuss it in person, where you, as an organizational representative, can be measured along with the message itself. Appearing directly and interacting with people makes it possible to tailor the message to different audiences. By interacting with people you can learn from them just as they are learning from you. Agency staff, clients, and board members may be dispatched to various publics: members of service organizations and civic groups, the downtown business association, the local association of accountants, or the state chapter of the American Nursing Association. Personal contacts can be followed up by more formal presentations.

There is a wide range of formats and approaches that can be used in making presentations. Lectures have the advantage of compressing a lot of information in a small amount of time. You can use a lecture to reach a large audience, presenting the message in a clear, concise, and ordered manner. Unfortunately, some lecturers are dull. Even when they are not, the format requires that the audience be relatively passive. Some of these deficiencies can be corrected by including visual aides (charts, illustrations magnified by an overhead projector, slides, and so on).

The audience may be involved through periodic "buzz group sessions" in which participants turn to each other to discuss a particular issue or to respond to a point made by the speaker. Members of the audience may also be encouraged to ask questions. Other presentation methods may be integrated with lectures or may substitute for them.

Demonstrations are sometimes used to demystify a process or to teach a particular skill. For example, a family-treatment session conducted on the stage may help a group of potential consumers understand what to expect when they seek service or refer others to that service. A film or a tape of a therapy session may do the same, particularly when it is followed by a brief presentation by a trained therapist or a question-and-answer period.

Sometimes, audiovisual aids are used less to demonstrate than to elicit response and clarify feelings and attitudes. The University of Michigan has long been a pioneer in the development of trigger films. Let me describe one to you.

An elderly woman enters a local supermarket. There is pleasant, up-beat music in the background. She is tastefully dressed, although clearly her clothing belongs to another era. She wheels an empty shopping cart to the meat counter. The packages seem big, heavy for her. She picks one up, looks at the price of a package of lamb chops, and returns it. She does the same to a pound of chopped meat, hesitates, and returns it.

Moving on to the fruit section, she pulls two bananas off a larger bunch; takes one orange. She then gets a pint of milk, detaches a half-dozen eggs and puts them in her basket. On her way back to the meat counter, she stops for two rolls from the day-old bread counter. As she is about to reach down for the hamburger meat, a young mother, her basket full and with two children trailing behind, swoops down and grabs the hamburger, oblivious to the older woman.

Our heroine shrugs her shoulders and wheels her nearly empty basket to the checkout counter. Removing the wallet from her purse, she takes out a card and a couple of dollars. Up to now, not a single word has been spoken. Suddenly we hear the clerk shout, "Hey, Marg, what do you do with food stamps?" The camera focuses in on the older woman's face.

It is a powerful image, and it takes only 2 minutes to present. How could you use a similar technique in your public presentations?

Consider also panels, interviews, and public forums. Panels have the advantage of presenting several points of view and of soliciting opinions and information from more than a single expert. They also have the feel of spontaneity. Panelists may be asked to present for 3 or 4 minutes, and then to engage in a dialogue with each other or to respond to questions from the audience. If you are coordinating a panel, be sure that you are up to date on the issues so that you can probe or stimulate when things slow down. Select the right panelists. They may include subject-matter experts, consumers, funders, and others.

An interesting variation is the *expanding panel*. Members of the audience may be invited to come in and sit in on the panel for part of its discussion. Their involvement increases the entire audience's sense of participation. Another approach is to use a reactor panel that follows a lecture or film. A disadvantage of panels is that all the information you may deem important may not be presented. Other information may be presented in a haphazard rather than systematic manner.

The *interview* may also have this disadvantage. In this presentation arrangement, one or more persons considered to be experts, on the basis of experience or technical knowledge and training, may be interviewed in front of a larger audience. Like panel presentations, interviews have the feel of spontaneity and so tend to hold the audience's attention. However, important issues may be left out or poorly handled; there is no way of fully anticipating what may come out in an interview, unless it is well rehearsed, and this may result in loss of the spontaneity you may be looking for.

The *public forum* is even more spontaneous. Although the subject matter is generally determined in advance, the discussion is much more open. Everyone can participate from the floor or from the stage. The microphone may be located on-stage or may be available at different locations throughout the meeting hall. Forums are usually useful for generating interest or getting the issues on the table. They often require follow-up with other information-giving or promotional activities: the distribution of brochures or pamphlets, lectures, interviews, and workshops.

More informal contacts can also be used in promotional efforts. Staff who are out-stationed in other agency settings, those who are involved in case conferences or case-management activities, volunteers who recruit other volunteers for your agency, they, too, are potential promoters of ideas, services, and programs. When their activities are not perceived as part of the agency's overall or promotional efforts, they may yield only partial results. If not consciously planned, promotional activities may be ineffective and sometimes even counterproductive. This is especially true when messages are only partially complete or if they have reached some audiences and not others. Remember: communication is strategic when it is goal-oriented and well targeted.

## Staging Events

Promotional activities, as we have seen, frequently are staged through events: public appearances, concerts, shows, marathons, and so on. And these activities often serve multiple purposes. They can be used for fund raising and for involvement of clients and volunteers. They raise critical consciousness, and they provide for a sense of involvement and participation. These multiple purposes can become confused, one with the other. More significant, one goal, perhaps a minor one, can take on such force as to overshadow the others. Thus, an effort aimed primarily at raising the public's awareness of the needs of the aging, the disabled, or neglected children may require an extraordinary and unexpected demand on staff to support and coordinate the work of volunteers. The volunteers, because of the pressures on them, may focus more on the event and its organizational demands than on the purposes for which the event was intended. Poor organization can result in frazzled nerves, burnout, and displacement or even abandonment of original goals.

Proper planning can do much to avoid some of these pitfalls. Before staging an event, reread the chapters on program planning, budgeting, and scheduling. Be clear about your primary and secondary or complementary objectives. Determine who your publics, internal and external, will be. Who is to assume responsibility and for what? Do some market segmentation. Determine which publics are to be involved and for what purpose, in reference to your objectives. To what extent will demographic, psychographic, functional, or geographic characteristics influence your choice of publics? Consider issues of *price* (cost to whom, what costs) and *place* (location in time and space).

I used the term "staging events" consciously. It implies both a stage and a performance. It requires performers and an audience. And it suggests the need for a script, a libretto, or a score. Must you write the script yourself or can you borrow one from a national organization? Might the performers have their own script? To what extent must the script be prepared in advance in contrast to improvisation by the performers as they interact with each other and their audience? To what extent must you direct the performers and the performance? To what extent must you warm up or prepare the audience for what they are about to experience? Is the audience expected to be relatively passive during the event, and only later to take action (as in making a financial contribution or becoming a volunteer), or are they expected to be full participants in the event itself?

Let me repeat: Communication is strategic when it is goal-oriented and well targeted. But its success depends on its staging.

## Review

Unlike previous review sections, this one will be combined with an exercise.

---

### EXERCISE 15-3
**Promotions Checklist**

Look over the checklist (Table 15-1). It summarizes much of Chapter 15 and can be used to design an agency's promotions strategy.

1. Consider the promotional activities your organization has engaged in during the past year. Check the appropriate items in Column 1. If you are not certain, consult with colleagues or complete the exercise with them.
2. Go through the entire inventory starting with "goals" and ending with "presentations." Indicate whether your organization's current efforts are high (1); moderate (2); or rare and perhaps nonexistent (3), using the first column.
3. Now think through the components of a desired promotional

*continued*

## EXERCISE 15-3 *continued*

campaign. To make it work, i.e., to make certain that it is both strategic and effective, what are the *required* components? Check these off in the second column.

4. Before moving on to the next chapter, reconsider the exchange concepts we discussed early on in this book. How can benefits be shown by more effective collaborations with media representatives, with staff of other agencies? Who else should be involved?

You are now ready to design a promotions campaign much as you might design a fund-raising campaign, service program, or action system. Good luck!

**TABLE 15-1    Promotions Checklist**

|  | Current Efforts[a] (1) | Required Efforts (2) |
|---|---|---|
| Goals of promotional activities: | | |
| 1. Information dissemination on | | |
|    a. problems or needs | _____ | _____ |
|    b. policies | _____ | _____ |
|    c. programs | _____ | _____ |
|    d. organizations | _____ | _____ |
| 2. Attitude change regarding | _____ | _____ |
|    a. resource allocation | _____ | _____ |
|    b. getting service | _____ | _____ |
|    c. general support | _____ | _____ |
| 3. Improved competence in | _____ | _____ |
|    a. resource allocation | _____ | _____ |
|    b. getting service | _____ | _____ |
|    c. providing help | _____ | _____ |
| Targets of promotional activities: | | |
| 1. The community at large | _____ | _____ |
| 2. Funders and other resource suppliers | _____ | _____ |
| 3. Potential volunteers | _____ | _____ |
| 4. Potential consumers | _____ | _____ |
| 5. Other human-service providers | _____ | _____ |
| 6. Natural helpers | _____ | _____ |
| 7. The media and potential collaborators | _____ | _____ |
| Media and personal appearances: | | |
| 1. The press | | |
|    a. daily newspapers | _____ | _____ |

*continued*

## EXERCISE 15-3 continued

### TABLE 15-1    continued

| | Current Efforts[a] (1) | Required Efforts (2) |
|---|---|---|
| b. weekly newspaper | | |
| c. monthly newspaper | | |
| d. shoppers advertisers | | |
| e. company or union magazine | | |
| f. agency newsletter | | |
| g. civic association newsletter | | |
| h. underground or alternative press | | |
| i. other special interest publication | | |
| **Format** | | |
| a. news releases and articles | | |
| b. features; occasional or regular | | |
| c. columns and opinion pieces | | |
| d. reader advice columns | | |
| e. calendar announcements | | |
| f. letters to the editor | | |
| **2. Radio** | | |
| a. FM | | |
| b. AM | | |
| c. general audience | | |
| d. easy listening | | |
| e. all news | | |
| f. country | | |
| g. rock | | |
| h. classical | | |
| i. church or ethnic | | |
| **Format** | | |
| a. news release or interview | | |
| b. talk show hosting or advising | | |
| c. talk show interview | | |
| d. editorial | | |
| e. PSA | | |
| **3. Television** | | |
| a. VHF | | |
| b. UHF | | |
| c. cable | | |
| d. educational | | |
| e. public channel | | |
| f. community access channel | | |

*continued*

## EXERCISE 15-3 *continued*

**TABLE 15-1** *continued*

| | Current Efforts[a] (1) | Required Efforts (2) |
|---|---|---|
| Format | | |
| a. news release or interview | | |
| b. talk show hosting or advising | | |
| c. talk show interview | | |
| d. editorial | | |
| e. PSA | | |
| f. agency-sponsored film or TV show | | |
| 4. Advertising | | |
| a. the press | | |
| b. radio | | |
| c. TV | | |
| d. public displays | | |
| e. novelty items | | |
| 5. Personal appearances and presentations | | |
| a. lectures | | |
| b. demonstrations | | |
| c. panels | | |
| d. interviews | | |
| e. out-stationing and other interorganizational linkages | | |

[a]Code: 1 = high; 2 = moderate; 3 = rare or none

# 16 THE MARKETING AUDIT

AGENCY ADMINISTRATORS, planners, and program personnel are familiar with the terms "assessment" and "evaluation." We've discussed them in Chapters 7 and 12. Another term, "audit," is used in the marketing literature. To audit is to review, to examine, to verify. It adds the notion of *monitoring* to assessment and evaluation. The marketing audit is an effort to *examine* an organization's total marketing effort, to *verify* that the effort made leads to the gains intended at a cost that yields a net benefit. In standard marketing language, the marketing audit includes *review* of (1) the marketing environment; (2) the products and product lines developed, promoted, and distributed; and (3) the marketing system itself. In short, it's what we often call "taking stock."

In our examination of what goes into the auditing process, we'll turn back to what we have already learned about assessment and evaluation and we'll reexamine much of what we have discussed about other aspects of the marketing process in previous chapters. Some readers may find here reminders of what they have explored elsewhere. Others will find this chapter a useful base upon which to build a win strategy when engaging in a marketing activity for real, or for exploratory and planning purposes, as suggested in COMPACTS II: The Collaborative, Marketing, Planning, and Action Simulation found in the Appendix. Let's begin by examining an experience in taking stock.

## Taking Stock

"We started as a *hot line*, giving emergency advice when people called about family problems and referring people to other social agencies when that seemed appropriate. Then when unemployment devastated the region a few years back, we found ourselves responding to a new set of circumstances. Almost 18 percent of the population was out of work; unemployment benefits were running out, and many of the families most badly hit were not eligible for welfare. People couldn't pay their electric or heating bills. Even worse, some folks didn't have food. It's hard to believe, but here, in America of the 1980s, people were hungry; I mean really hungry.

"We worked with the churches, arranging for free food distribution, and referred people in need. But it wasn't enough. To do the job right, we organized a task group of agency and church and civic association people, in order to coordinate distribution efforts and to get the contributions needed to keep the system going. Before we knew it, we were in the food distribution business ourselves. And then we got into setting up workshops on nutrition and smart buying for families that needed the help. It went on like this for about 2 years, when we decided we just had to take stock.

"And we had a lot of stock. Not just food. We had a whole new image and a new set of relationships to people in the community and to those agencies we traditionally related to. The United Way saw us in a new light, and so did those churches and fraternal organizations whose efforts we had coordinated. And we had a new clientele that expected direct face-to-face counseling and advice, some education on a regular basis, even job referral when we could give it. It required of us a new and better trained corps of volunteers, many of them from among the unemployed themselves. And it required money, lots more than we ever thought our small agency would need."

New demands, changed circumstances, unanticipated opportunities, altered expectations—these all affect service and other programs and provide the impetus to take stock. Sometimes external organizations compel the stock taking. The administrator of the hot-line crisis center quoted later revealed that the United Way was concerned about how his agency had changed its direction without first clearing those changes with the United Way and without getting assurance that continued funding would be available for food distribution, family-life education, and so on.

Many of us take stock when our lives or our circumstances undergo major changes. So do many organizations. How much better might it be to take stock on a more regular basis so that we could have more control over those changes and their consequences, more choice in what we do and when. This, after all, is what many social agencies attempt to enable their consumers to do. Stock taking is precisely what the marketing audit is concerned with. It often begins with a look at the environment.

## Assessing the Marketing Environment

The *marketing-environment review* examines an organization's relationships to each of its key external and internal publics. The major segments of each public are identified, and the present and expected future size or other characteristics of each of those "markets" are determined. The markets include consumers, auspice providers, suppliers, competitors, and collaborators or partners. The marketing-environment audit may also examine the larger community or societal environment we have called the *consensus environment*. In the vignette, there was clearly consensus about the desirability of feeding the hungry. Later, there may have been some concern about whose responsibility it was, where the resources might come from, and whether other, perhaps ancillary agency programs were appropriate. Similar concerns were reflected in our discussions about market segmentation (Chapter 3), exchanges with collaborating service providers (Chapter 4), with consumers and natural helpers (Chapter 5), with suppliers who contribute money or other resources (Chapters 13 and 14), and with the publics at which promotional activities are aimed (Chapter 15).

An environment audit conducted by or on the crisis center involved in food distribution might examine the needs of consumers, the readiness of various community groups to respond to those needs, and the availability of resources to provide required services. Although the program described seemed to evolve in response to a crisis situation, and such responses rarely permit careful and reasoned considerations of alternatives (witness a community's response to a flood or some other crisis situation), stock taking permits us to reexamine the situation that led to our responses. It permits us to examine what was or what is, what is likely to be, and what ought to be. You will recognize these concerns from our discussions of interactive assessment techniques, in Chapter 7. Assessment questions are generally asked about people, about programs and resources, and about how these are all linked together.

When focusing on people, the assessor's concern may be with the extent to which they are informed, are constrained by debilitating attitudes, or possess the requisite skills to act in desired ways. For example, consumers such as the unemployed and hungry may not *know* about an agency, its services, or the benefits these services might provide. Concerned citizens might not know about how to refer persons in need or where to make contributions. An indifferent public may not even be aware that a problem is severe or that anything can be done about it. Funders may be unaware of the agency's capacities or of a newly developed service approach.

*Debilitating attitudes* such as prejudices about a population in need or a negative attitude toward certain kinds of services must be identified and overcome if consumer, provider, and supplier behavior is to be changed. Sometimes a debilitating attitude is self-directed, as when potential consumers have given up on themselves and on their capacities to change or to control events. Neighborhood organizing, organizational development, and counseling are often directed at overcoming such attitudes as part of a larger strategy of empowerment. Promotional activities may be aimed at

changing the attitudes or strengthening the convictions of individual donors, of institutional funders, or of the general public.

Key publics may also lack the *necessary competence or skill* to perform
in what may be considered a desirable manner. It may not be enough to
recognize that one has a problem, to know where one might go for help, or
to want to go for such help. It may be just as necessary to know how to define one's problem so that it is understood, or how to maneuver through a
complex system of fragmented services. The desire to raise funds for a worthy cause may yield little in terms of new resources if those expressing commitment do not have the skills to organize and manage a campaign effectively.

When the focus is on programs and resources, the assessor/auditor may
focus on the total program or on components of it. The assessor may look
at the extent to which the component programs are accessible and to
whom, the mechanisms used to make agency personnel accountable and to
whom, and personnel effectiveness and efficiency. The information gathered can then be used as a base line (where things are at the starting point)
against which outcomes might be evaluated. The way in which outcomes
are defined, however, may vary considerably. I'll get back to this point in
a moment.

The assessor may also wish to focus on the relationships between publics and programs: who receives services or provides resources; how programs are linked to each other so as to increase effectiveness, comprehensiveness, efficiency, or continuity; what mechanisms are used to link
persons, organizations, and resources. These data, too, can serve as base-
lines for product audits or what is more generally referred to in social
agencies as program evaluations.

## The Product Audit

The assessor/auditor concentrates on the nature of the problem to be
solved, as well as its proper location in one or more of the various relevant
publics, thereby defining the issues to be addressed and laying the foundation for establishing action goals and subsequent intervention activities.
These goals, along with other baseline data collected during the assessment
process, make it possible to evaluate products and product lines. A human
service agency's products generally comprise the services it provides and/or
the outcomes of those services. Since it is also engaged in resource development and in a wide variety of other marketing activities, its products also
may include those activities and their outcomes (e.g., a fund-raising campaign plus the dollars raised): specifically, those activities that together
form a program and its results. The inclusion of such activities as "products" can cause some confusion which may, in turn, result in conflicts between the program staff and the auditors or evaluators.

The first reason for confusion is that few organizations have only a single product. They may group several products together into a product line, and they may have several product lines. A community mental health center may sponsor a drug-abuse prevention program that includes several services: consultation to teachers and school officials; counseling and family-life education, provided through churches and community centers; outreach to teen-agers and preteens in the schools. These services may compose a product line. A wide variety of other activities may be grouped into a drug-treatment product line. Evaluators must be clear about whether they are examining an entire line, a single product within it, or parts of several product lines, as must staff and others who may be interested in the findings of the auditor/evaluators.

Second, whereas some of the concerned parties may be interested primarily in an overview of these services—what they are, how they are distributed, what they cost, and how they are working—others may be more concerned with their outcomes—whether drug abuse has been prevented, to what extent, and for whom, or the extent to which it has been reduced or modified. To a large extent, the way in which products are evaluated will depend on how they and the goals that created them are defined. Consider the differences between the following three statements of objectives, each flowing from the former hot-line agency's commitment to dealing with hunger: By the end of the year

1.  hunger will have been eliminated in the Melville/Slausen area.
2.  emergency food services will be provided by volunteers on a round-the-clock basis in response to needs as they arise, and food distribution centers will be established in all sections of the community served.
3.  sixty-five volunteers will have been recruited, trained, and assigned to four distribution centers, to emergency food delivery, to fund-raising and donations procurement, and to promotional tasks.

The first of these is what might be termed an *outcome objective* similar to those discussed in Chapter 12. The extent to which this objective has been reached at the end of a year can be scaled in relation to the extent to which hunger has been reduced or to the proportion of the hungry served. The second is what some program evaluators call an *operations objective*: it spells out the major services provided by the organization. These, too, can be evaluated on some scale in relation to degree of accomplishment. The third is an *activity objective*; it spells out all the activities that must be performed if the operations are to take place and the desired outcomes achieved. This objective is more properly left to the marketing-*system* review.

Assuming clarity regarding whether a single product or a total product line is to be evaluated, and assuming agreement about the type of objective to be evaluated, a third source of confusion arises when "intervening" and "antecedent" variables are ignored. *Antecedent variables* are independent of the program or product, but provide the opportunities and constraints within which it operates. In the example we have been using, antecedent variables might include public commitment to the needy and the hungry, the state of the economy, the willingness of the United Way to provide at least temporary support, and the agency staff's flexibility.

*Intervening* variables are those that may potentially influence outcomes. For example, changes in the employment picture or in the welfare benefits available from public sources during the year in question may considerably affect the outcome objective. It may be reached without any effort on the part of the agency we are examining. Decisions on the part of supermarkets to provide free food to the unemployed may obviate the necessity of the agency's programs. Conversely, an increase in the number of unemployed may so overwhelm the agency as to reduce its capacity to achieve the objectives specified. Sixty-five volunteers or four distribution centers may prove totally inadequate to the achievement of the outcome objective. Without careful regard to both antecedent and intervening variables, any conclusion about the program and its outcomes is likely to be spurious at best and misleading at worst.

A fourth area of confusion may lie in the inability to distinguish between products and the operations that go into establishing the overall marketing system. The marketing-system audit is used to review the organization of resource procurement and programming efforts, the allocation of responsibilities for specified tasks, and the extent to which key actors perform requisite tasks willingly, competently, and efficiently.

## The Marketing-System Audit

One way of doing a marketing-system audit is to look at each of the individual components of the system: the key internal and external publics; the tasks performed by key actors (e.g., resource procurement, assessment, goal formulation, program design, decision making about location and price, market segmentation, promotions, and so on); or the sequences of activities and events that may lead to changes in program design and product development.

Typically, in a marketing-system audit, the auditor will look for congruence or "fit" between the persons who are the principal actors in the marketing process, the organizational units to which they are attached, the larger organizational structure, and the environmental units that impinge on that structure. Assuming that you and others in your organization have been engaged for some time in a marketing strategy based in part on suggestions in this book, it is likely that your activities have included public relations and community education, fund raising and grant seeking, the establishment and management of interorganizational linking mechanisms, and market segmentation and penetration.

The success of these activities will be affected in part by the fit between the staff involved and the organizational demands on them. This fit will include such variables as (1) the individual's reward value-hierarchy and the capacities of the agency to provide the desired rewards while attaining the level of productivity desired, (2) the individual's skills and capacities and the technical requirements of the job, and (3) the individual's personal style and the organizational management style. I'll give you an example of item 3.

Some organizations are highly rule-governed with few degrees of freedom given to workers performing assigned tasks. But marketing activities often require innovative departures from the normal ways of doing things. Thus, we start off with a potentially poor fit between the organization's general concern with standardization and control and the marketing function, which requires greater flexibility. Assign to the marketing function an individual whose personal style tends toward dependence and compliance, and the fit with the organization's management style may be good; however, with this particular marketing assignment, the fit may not be good at all. On the other hand, assign to the marketing function a person who by personality and temperament tends to be independent, comfortable with ambiguity, and self-directing, and you may have a good fit between that person and his or her assigned tasks but a poor fit with the organization's general management style. If other agency staff are permitted little latitude in what they do and how they do it, those associated with marketing may find themselves out of sync with their colleagues on whom they depend for effective collaboration. Equally significant, they may find managers reining them in and putting roadblocks in their way at every turn. By focusing on this issue, the marketing audit may help each key actor make those adjustments that are important to make the fit better. This situation is clear when we examine the fit between what the individuals involved in marketing know or can do and what is required of them to be successful at marketing.

The technical requirements of the job may perhaps include negotiating skills, knowledge of the larger service system in the community, and competence in fund raising. If the individuals involved possess the requisite knowledge and skills, the fit is likely to be good. If they do not, they may be frustrated in their work, resentful of it, and poorly motivated. In such cases, it may be necessary to provide them with special training and other supports. If the individuals involved value the rewards associated with marketing (external contacts with publics, opportunities to try untried approaches, and the recognition that may come with success), and if they can live with the frustrations of occasional failure or with the possible hostility of colleagues who resent their rapid movement up the organizational ladder, then the fit is likely to be good. But if career movement and other valued rewards are not available, the fit is likely to be poor.

One way of improving the fit, particularly in large organizations, is to set up a special marketing department or division whose functions and operating style are clearly defined. Even in a small agency, those individuals involved in marketing may be located in a specialized unit in the agency, such as a planning or resource development department with a clearly defined mandate that is acceptable to other units in the organization (such as the child welfare department and the family-life education service); then there is likely to be congruity between the various organizational units. But if the child welfare department sees itself as more knowledgeable than the planning department about its needs or about the resources that should be tapped to respond to those needs, there is likely to be conflict that may adversely affect planning and resource development efforts.

Thus far, we have been examining the fit between individuals responsible for the marketing process and the organization that employs them. These persons are involved in the agency's "throughput system." We can ask similar questions about the closeness of fit between the agency and other elements in its external environment: its input and output publics. Earlier in this book, we spoke about segmenting the market according to geographic, demographic, functional, and psychographic characteristics. An agency that is inaccessible because of location would not be wise to attempt to market its product to people in a broad geographic area. An agency that makes demands on its clients that may be resisted by a particular ethnic or residential community (psychographics) might do well to consider marketing activities aimed at different populations or new methods or mechanisms for more effectively communicating with the populations in question. This might also be said about looking for the proper fit between an agency and the various publics from which it hopes to generate financial support or recruit other resources like personnel, materials, and facilities.

These, then, are the issues of concern to the persons involved in marketing-system audits. Properly used, such audits are a key to programming success and often to agency survival. They are the principal tools by which an organization becomes self correcting in its operations. They pinpoint those operations that require expansion, reduction, elimination, or some other modification. They can be used as the starting point of strategic marketing rather than as an end point.

Unfortunately, agencies and resource providers too often misuse audits or abuse the process. There are a number of reasons for this. First, people develop vested interests in what they do and how they do it. They are therefore reluctant to change, still less to admit to error. The purpose of an audit should be to abandon wasteful, counterproductive activities; but abandoning cherished ideas and their concomitant programs can be extremely difficult. Staff, in such a situation, often find themselves on the defensive. They become more defensive when the findings of an audit are used by various publics for their own purposes.

Thus, clients may argue that a particular service or program reaches the wrong population. A group of active volunteers may feel that their involvement in fund raising has generated results that are not commensurate with the effort invested. External funding agencies may point out that the objectives of a particular service program were barely achieved. The agency's staff, on the other hand, may point out that the involvement of volunteers has heightened and raised community consciousness, that the proper processes and procedures were used, and that external variables may have affected outcomes.

There is a second reason why system audits are sometimes poorly conducted or misused. The organization and its staff, as suggested earlier, may not have the knowledge or competence to conduct the audit. Key agency staff may not know *what* should be examined or *how* it can be examined. More aware of the dangers of poorly conducted audits than of the promise of effective auditing procedures, staff may even subvert the process. Under such circumstances, it frequently makes sense to search outside the organization for an auditor or evaluator who can be both helpful and objective.

Outsiders not only may have the requisite technical competence, but may be more objective, less committed to ongoing operations, and more able to examine alternatives. Their lack of familiarity with operations, however, can be a drawback. For this reason, it is often advisable to establish audit committees or task groups that include both insiders and outsiders. Of whom should the group be composed: management; operating personnel responsible for each aspect of the operations being examined; or representatives of external publics like clients, auspice providers, resource suppliers? Should different groups examine different operations, perhaps in relation to different points in the marketing process?

Perhaps it is fitting that we conclude this chapter with a set of questions. I've raised other issues throughout the book. If you have completed the exercises in Parts I, II, III, and IV, you already have answered many questions of your own and you may have written almost as many or even more pages than I have. In that case, this has been a collaborative effort. It has included many parties: the author, the publisher and the bookseller, the reader/doer, and the others with whom you engaged in doing some of the exercises or in various marketing activities.

The collaboration and exchange process is not yet over. Turn now to the Appendix. In it you will find COMPACTS II, a *CO*llaborative *M*arketing, *P*lanning, and *ACT*ion Simulation. Don't just read it. Play it. It will take you and your colleagues a step further in development of competence in strategic marketing and, as you will discover, it can be used in the program and resource development process itself.

## Review

Auditing is a way of taking stock of what we are doing and how we are doing it. Broadly defined, it includes a review of the marketing environment, an examination of the agency's products and product lines, and a verification of the effectiveness of the marketing system itself. It includes assessment of what is, what ought to be, and what is likely to be. It also includes an evaluation of programs and their outputs, and it provides the wherewithal to monitor activities and to make corrections where they may be needed.

# APPENDIX

# THE COLLABORATIVE MARKETING, PLANNING, AND ACTION SIMULATION

If you've completed most of the exercises as you read this book, you already will be well into the marketing process. By using the Appendix, you'll have the opportunity of pulling it all together and putting what you've learned into practice. Unlike the preceding chapters, however, you won't learn much from reading it. This is a *doing* Appendix. It is composed of two sets of instructions: one for participants in a gamed simulation of the marketing process and one for the convenor.

Participants will have the opportunity to represent various publics: social agency or other not-for-profit organization staff members, consumer groups, funders and resource suppliers, auspice providers, and influential representatives of the general public. They will be involved in a variety of market exchanges that include the orchestration of resources and the establishment of interorganizational linkages. Players will do problem assessment and analysis, program design, fund raising, and grantsmanship. Their efforts will be evaluated on the basis of feasibility, relevance, and acceptability.

## Making Believe for Real

As they play COMPACTS II players will be making believe *for real, if not for keeps*. COMPACTS II, like other simulation games, reveals real-world processes. These processes unfold as participants make decisions, exchange resources, put strategies into action, and test their results. As in the real world, players do not start off with the same resources or with the same levels of skill. Rewards may also be variable. To a large extent, they will depend on the predicaments that players find themselves in and the intelligence with which they turn those predicaments into opportunities, independently or in partnerships. Strategies may result in competitive efforts, in collaborative and cooperative arrangements, in direct and indirect payoffs, and sometimes in outright competition.

Players who know something about marketing may have an advantage over other players, who may wish to finish reading this book or selections from it before they play the game. But it does not require advanced or specialized knowledge to play. Anyone who has worked in a social agency or in another not-for-profit organization as a paid staff member, a student, or a volunteer will have little difficulty in understanding the rules. If misunderstandings occur, other players will explain fast enough. As in any role-related activity, other members in the role-set will instruct uncertain role performers on what is expected, how, and when.

The game can be used as an introduction to strategic marketing by itself or as part of an instructional program. It might also be used on conclusion of the instructional program, to test what people have learned or to give them a chance to put what they know into practice. COMPACTS II is both a *priming mechanism* and a *frame game*.

As a priming mechanism it provides an opportunity to learn and to begin the strategic marketing process. People learn as they play. Players face predicaments that may be fortuitous or that may have been anticipated and even planned. These predicaments may become obstacles to individuals or to groups of players, or they may become opportunities by which players negotiate an advantage for themselves, for some constituency, or for the service system in its entirety. Players are constantly forced to make decisions, to establish priorities, and to change them when things do not go as planned.

Each decision and action may have consequences for subsequent decisions and actions. Environmental factors outside the control of the players may conspire to upset player strategies or to bolster players' efforts to achieve goals and objectives. Those processes will affect the equilibrium or imbalance of the system, and it is in this state of flux that opportunities for effective marketing occur. Those players who do succeed will learn from their successes; other players will confirm the appropriateness of their actions. Those players who do not succeed or who don't play according to the rules will soon learn from other players what is expected. Some of this learning occurs during the course of play. A great deal more occurs during the postplay discussion period.

Thus players are primed to learn. But COMPACTS II can do more. It can also be used to begin the design of a marketing strategy, to test out that strategy in a *make-believe* setting as if it were *real*, without the risks attendant when the play is "for keeps." On the basis of their simulation experience, the game plan can be modified or improved for application in real-world settings.

I mentioned earlier that COMPACTS II is a frame game. By that I mean that the basic frame simulates a social structure or process. The internal components of the game can be modified, however, to approximate reality more fully. Thus, you should feel free to change the cast of characters and to raise or lower the numbers of resources allocated to players. In fact, you might find it interesting and instructive to do that with the players.

Start with the game as it is. Following play and postplay discussion, redesign it with the participants so as to reflect the realities in your own community. The new game, then, might be played in an effort to test out various marketing strategies in a simulated environment that more closely approximates your real-life situation.

COMPACTS II has gone through scores of such iterations. It was first published as COMPACTS: the *COM*munity *P*lanning and *ACT*ion Simulation for use in training people in the grantsmanship process. Later, it was published by the Rehabilitation Service Administration of the Department of Health and Human Services as the Rehabilitation Planning Game for training state planners. Shortly thereafter, it became *Turn-On* (*T*apping *U*ntapped *R*esources, *N*ow *O*r *N*ever), a game designed for use by area agencies on aging to involve local decision makers in the design of area plans. You will find versions of it in several of the books listed for this chapter in the Reference section at the end of the book.\* Feel free to make your own adaptations of COMPACTS II or to duplicate the player instructions in this chapter for your own use. But beware! Publishers protect their copyrights. You may use the game, not republish it in some other version. The following is a general guide to the time that might be allotted to each of three sets of activities.

| | |
|---|---|
| 30–40 minutes | Introduction, reading instructions |
| 60–80 minutes | Playing round (1 fiscal year) |
| 30–60 minutes | Postplay discussion |
| 2–3 hours | |

---

\*For example, "R.F.P." in *Resources for Child Placement*.

# Convenor's Guide for COMPACTS II

Before proceeding, skim the entire Appendix. Pay particular attention to those sections that may be duplicated for distribution to participants. Decide whether or not you will use the game as found here. If so, follow the instructions given. If you prefer to modify the game by changing the roles, the procedures, or the forms, feel free to do so. Guidance for game modification or redesign is given under "Suggestions for Postplay Activities."

## Preparing the Game for Play

1. Draw up a *role badge* for each player (stick-on tape will do). Use the Inventory of Players' Roles and Resources (Table A–1) as a guide. You may find that play proceeds more smoothly if all the social agency administrators wear role badges drawn up in red, the consumer groups wear black badges, and so on. Whatever roles you choose, we think you will find that color coding will help players locate each other during play.

**TABLE A-1  Inventory of Players' Roles and Resources**

| | | Resources at Their Disposal | | |
|---|---|---|---|---|
| *Groups and Individuals* | *Money* | *Personal and Organizational Energy (blue)* | *Political Influence (white)* | *Expertise (red)* |
| **Agency administrators:** | | | | |
| Community mental health center | — | 5 | 5 | 10 |
| Rehabilitation workshop | — | 5 | 5 | 10 |
| Senior center | — | 10 | 10 | 5 |
| Family service agency | — | 5 | 5 | 10 |
| Community public library | — | 5 | 5 | 10 |
| Legal Aid Society | — | 5 | 5 | 10 |
| Urban League | — | 5 | 10 | 10 |
| Neighborhood health clinic association | — | 5 | 10 | 10 |
| Child guidance clinic | — | 5 | 5 | 10 |
| Public welfare department | — | 5 | 10 | 5 |
| Substance abuse project | — | 5 | — | 5 |
| Safe house and shelter | — | — | 5 | 5 |
| Independent living services | — | — | 0 | 5 |
| **Funding organizations:** | | | | |
| Department of Health and Human Development | $250,000 | — | — | — |
| Community foundation | $100,000 | — | — | — |

**TABLE A-1**   *Continued*

| | | Resources at Their Disposal | | |
| --- | --- | --- | --- | --- |
| *Groups and Individuals* | *Money* | *Personal and Organizational Energy (blue)* | *Political Influence (white)* | *Expertise (red)* |
| Consolidated Industries Foundation | $100,000 | — | — | — |
| State human resources agency | $250,000 | — | — | — |
| United Way | $150,000 | — | — | — |
| **Consumer and self-help groups:** | | | | |
| Neighborhood association | $ 10,000 | 10 | 10 | 5 |
| Parents of Retarded Children | $ 10,000 | 10 | 5 | 5 |
| Grey Panthers | $ 10,000 | 10 | 10 | 5 |
| Going Straight | — | 5 | — | 5 |
| Minority rights group | $  5,000 | 10 | 10 | 5 |
| **Community influentials:** | | | | |
| University expert in services planning | — | 5 | 10 | 20 |
| Union leader | $ 50,000 | 10 | 10 | 5 |
| Church leader | $ 50,000 | 10 | 10 | 5 |
| City council activist | $ 50,000 | 10 | 20 | — |
| Civic association president | $ 50,000 | 5 | 10 | — |
| Newspaper or magazine editor | — | — | 15 | 5 |
| TV anchorperson | — | — | 15 | 5 |
| **Staff members of the Marketing Organization** (3–5 persons) | — | — | — | 30 |

Feel free to add or subtract roles so as to accommodate the number of players you anticipate. Consider three or four players for the Marketing Organization. By making up more badges than you need, you will be prepared for extra players. If you run short, you can always add process observers, nonplayers who can be assigned the task of observing during play and reporting on their observations during the postplay discussion.

COMPACTS II can be played with as few as 16 or 17 players and as many as 60. You will have to decide which roles to keep and which to drop or add.

2.   Place each role badge in a plastic bag of its own, and add the appropriate  number of *strategic resource chips*. To designate the different resources used in the game you can use any small colored objects. These can be poker chips, bits of colored paper, Lego blocks, and so on. For each type of strategic resource you will need a different color. Any set of colors might work. To remind players what each chip represents, you might want to draw up a wall chart or poster that looks like Figure A–1.

| | |
|---|---|
| Money | = Checks |
| Personal and organizational energy | = Blue |
| Political influence | = White |
| Expertise | = Red |

**Figure A-1**   Strategic Resources Wall Chart

3. Use the sample checks (Table A–2) to make up your own COM-PACTS II checks. Give each funder or other player with access to money a small number of checks—say 5 to 10—and remind those players that the Inventory of Players' Roles and Resources tells them how much they can spend.

   Use Table A–1 for determining how many resource chips go into each plastic bag. If you add roles, use your own judgment about the number of resource chips for these roles. Remember that different categories of roles have access to different amounts of resource chips (from 0 to 10). Try not to let any player have more than 30 chips of all kinds or less than 10. But life is not always fair; some players will not have the same access to strategic resources as others will have.

4. You are now ready to prepare the room for play. Set up tables so that each player sits at a table with other players in the same category. On the appropriate tables lay out the plastic bags with the name badges and resource chips or checkbooks, one by each chair. A typical setup might appear as in Figure A–2.

   Put up the wall chart (Fig. A–1) telling people which color is used to designate each strategic resource and (if you find it helpful) other charts summarizing the rules of play. Have sufficient chairs at the tables. Have extra newsprint or boards and chalk available for players to work on.

   Some game leaders prefer that players seat themselves randomly. It is not essential that you group players according to types of roles they are to perform (see Fig. A–2), but you may find that doing so will reduce the likelihood that they will form coalitions only with others at their table. Players will quickly discover that coalitions made up of only agency administrators or consumers are not likely to be as effective as those more broadly constituted. Marketing, after all, requires collaborative exchanges with many publics.

5. If you wish, duplicate copies of the pages that spell out *player in-*

**TABLE A-2   COMPACTS II Checks**[a]

| Player_____ | COMPACTS II Check |
|---|---|
| $ available prior to writing check   $_____ | To_____ |
| Amount of check  $_____ | Amount_____ $_____ |
| Payable to:_____ | From_____ |
| _____ | Stipulations or conditions_____ |
| Balance         $_____ | |
| Carry forward to next check: | _____ |
| _____ | *cut on line* |
| Player_____ | COMPACTS II Check |
| $ available prior to writing check   $_____ | To_____ |
| Amount of check  $_____ | Amount_____ $_____ |
| Payable to:_____ | From_____ |
| _____ | Stipulations or conditions_____ |
| Balance         $_____ | |
| Carry forward to next check: | _____ |
| _____ | *cut on line* |
| Player_____ | COMPACTS II Check |
| $ available prior to writing check   $_____ | To_____ |
| Amount of check  $_____ | Amount_____ $_____ |
| Payable to:_____ | From_____ |
| _____ | Stipulations or conditions_____ |
| Balance         $_____ | |
| Carry forward to next check: | _____ |
| _____ | |

[a]Checks may be duplicated and stapled together as checkbooks for funders and community influentials who have access to money. Fill in the amount each player has available to allocate.

*structions* for the game and that list the *order of play*. If you do not duplicate these pages for distribution, communicate their content verbally when giving participants instructions prior to play. One way of helping players remember what you tell them is to summarize some of the information on wall charts or posters.

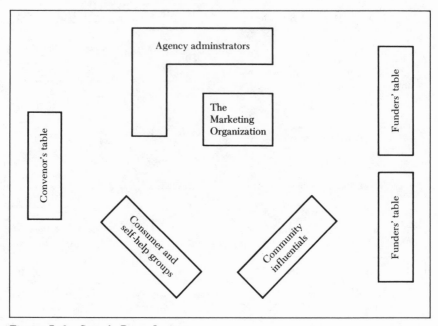

**Figure A-2**   Sample Room Layout

6.  Duplicate sufficient copies of the COMPACTS II Proposal Form (Table A–3) to assure that they are easily accessible to all players. Leave a stack of 10 or so at the funders' table(s) and some at each of the other tables. Between 5 and 10 at each table should do. Do the same for the Fund-Raising Action Plan (Table A–4). Duplicate several copies of the Funding Priorities Form (Table A–5). Make them available to the funders.

7.  *That's it; you're ready to introduce players to the game!* The following activities are suggested:

    a.  Welcome participants. Ask them to find a place to sit that includes a bag with a badge representing the role they might like to play. Ask the players to pin their badges on. If you have duplicated materials and located them at each table, ask the players to look over the materials as they wait for the rest of the participants to come into the room.

    b.  When everyone is settled, explain that you will be playing the COMPACTS II game and what the purpose of play will be (to simulate the collaborative marketing process, to learn something about the proposal development and grantsmanship processes, or whatever other purpose you may have in mind).

    Ask players to stand up one at a time, table by table, and tell the group who they will be (for the purpose of the game, i.e., their roles).

**TABLE A-3   Proposal Form for Grants and Contracts**[a]

GENERAL INFORMATION

Sponsorship
1. Name(s) of the sponsoring organization(s) or group(s)

_____

_____

2. Who is to be on the project's advisory panel or board of directors?

_____     _____
_____     _____
_____     _____

3. Total amount requested   $_____          Project or budget period
   Total budget              $_____          _____

PROGRAM NARRATIVE

4. The problem(s) to be addressed (Specify who is affected and how.)

5. Goals and/or operational objectives (Specify the anticipated outcomes.)

6. Action or service plan (Describe how the outcomes are to be reached.)

7. If interorganizational linkages or other forms of collaboration are required, describe.

[a]The whole form may be duplicated for player convenience.

**TABLE A-3 continued**

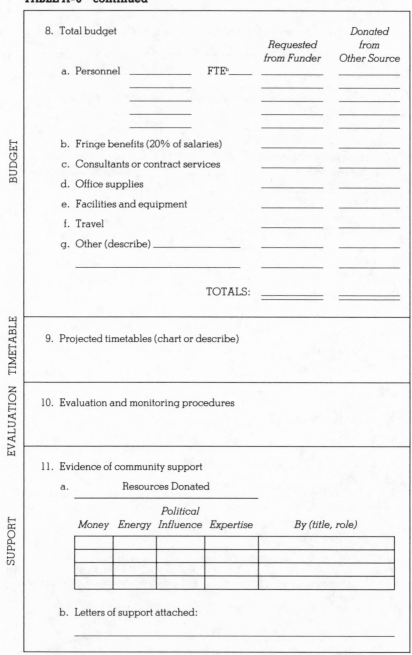

BUDGET

8. Total budget

|  |  | Requested from Funder | Donated from Other Source |
|---|---|---|---|
| a. Personnel _____ FTE[b] ____ | | _____ | _____ |
| | | _____ | _____ |
| | | _____ | _____ |
| | | _____ | _____ |
| b. Fringe benefits (20% of salaries) | | _____ | _____ |
| c. Consultants or contract services | | _____ | _____ |
| d. Office supplies | | _____ | _____ |
| e. Facilities and equipment | | _____ | _____ |
| f. Travel | | _____ | _____ |
| g. Other (describe) _____ | | _____ | _____ |
| _____ | | _____ | _____ |
| TOTALS: | | _____ | _____ |

TIMETABLE

9. Projected timetables (chart or describe)

EVALUATION

10. Evaluation and monitoring procedures

SUPPORT

11. Evidence of community support

a. _____ Resources Donated _____

| Money | Energy | Political Influence | Expertise | By (title, role) |
|---|---|---|---|---|
|  |  |  |  |  |
|  |  |  |  |  |
|  |  |  |  |  |
|  |  |  |  |  |

b. Letters of support attached:

_____

[b]FTE = Full-time equivalent or percent time.

## TABLE A-4  Fund-Raising Action Plan

1. Sponsors (groups or organizations) _____

2. Target publics (from whom funds
   are to be solicited)                  _____

3. Target amount (to be raised)          _____

4. Types of fund-raising activities (Check all that apply.)

   | *Campaigns* | *Sales* | *Special Events* |
   |---|---|---|
   | ____General solicitation | ____Thrift shop | ____Marathon |
   | ____Bricks and mortar | ____Auction | ____Dinner/dance |
   | ____Endowment | ____Garage sales | ____Benefit performance |
   | ____Other (specify) | ____Other (specify) | ____Other (specify) |
   | _____ | _____ | _____ |
   | _____ | _____ | _____ |
   | _____ | _____ | _____ |

5. Planning and management structure (Describe committees, cabinets, task
   groups.)

6. Timetable (Show major events and activities on a chart below.)

7. Over-all funding strategy (Describe how this set of activities and the funds
   anticipated complement your organization's other funding efforts such as
   grants, contracts, and fees for services.)

8. Expertise allocation

   | *From Whom* | *Number of Chips* | *From Whom* | *Number of Chips* |
   |---|---|---|---|
   | _____ | _____ | _____ | _____ |
   | _____ | _____ | _____ | _____ |

9. Signature and promises (Key parties involved in this effort and their
   constituent group or organization.)

   | | | | |
   |---|---|---|---|
   | 1._____ | $_____ | 4._____ | $_____ |
   | 2._____ | $_____ | 5._____ | $_____ |
   | 3._____ | $_____ | 6._____ | $_____ |

Amount actually raised $_____
(Flip coin five times, multiply needs × money listed in box 8.)

**TABLE A-5   Funding Priorities Form**[a]

---

1. Name of funder_____

2. Total amount of money and credit available_____

   Percentages of (local) matching funds required_____%

3. Issues that receive highest priority

   _____

   _____

3. Other issues that will receive consideration

   _____

   _____

4. Client populations most concerned about:

5. Operations that will receive preference

   _____

   _____

   _____

   Operations that will be considered

   _____

   _____

   _____

6. Requirements for citizen support, consumer involvement, interagency
   cooperation
   (*if* any)

---

[a]This form may be duplicated for funders' usage. All funders should fill in items 1 through 4. Others are
optional.

   c. Tell participants how the game is to be played. Go over the information on the orientation sheets.

   d. Show them how the Proposal Form is to be filled out. Do the same for the Funding Priorities Form and Fund-Raising Action Plan.

   e. Tell them when the fiscal year begins. They can now begin the planning and negotiation processes. It is not necessary for you (the game leader) to play an active role in the game. Be available to coach players and to help them over the hurdles.

      Get the process observers together (if you decide to use non-playing roles) and help them decide what to look at. Some may wish to study the coalition-forming process, the way in which funding decisions are arrived at, the extent to which leadership emerges at the local level, differences in behavior of agency representatives and consumer-group representatives, and so forth. Process observers should be prepared to report on what they observe at the end of the fiscal year. Consider giving them such titles as "program evaluator," "social psychologist," or "economist." Process observers may be seated at any table.

8. The fiscal year generally takes 1 hour, although you may find that a slightly shorter or longer period does just as well. Whatever amount of time you choose, let the players know. From time to time, inform them of how much time has gone by. For example, if F.Y. = 60, then 5 minutes of play is equal to 1 month. Stop play at the end of the fiscal year.

## Suggestions for Postplay Activities

1. The first thing to do after the play of COMPACTS II is to debrief, or to discuss and evaluate the experience. Participants will be anxious to talk over what happened. You might want to focus on some or all of the following:

   a. Which proposals were funded and which ones were not? Why? Ask players who worked on a successful proposal to explain why things worked out the way they did. Ask the same questions of those who were not successful. Probe for real-life parallels and for principles that might be applied in practice. Do the same for fund-raising plans and activities.

   b. Whose plans or proposals were best? Why? Because of their thoroughness? Their objectives? The support they engendered? Would such a project work in your (the participants') communities?

   c. Did you feel each actor played his or her role appropriately? Focus on certain actors, perhaps a funder, a representative of a consumer group, an agency administrator, or staff members of the Marketing Organization. Find principles that participants might use in trying to "make friends and influence people" in a real situation.

One way to make certain that all pertinent aspects of the playing session are discussed is to ask the process observers to begin the debriefing session by reporting what they observed. Of course, they should be asked to prepare for this in advance.

2. Consider redesigning the game. This can be done by you alone, or by the entire group following a playing session. Have participants
   a. Identify a set of issues that concern them or that reflect local realities.
   b. Identify the local community people who might be involved in a real-life version of COMPACTS II—those who would tend to be concerned with the issues identified.
   c. Allocate resources to those persons.
   d. Change or modify the rules or any of the forms used to play COMPACTS II so that it conforms more closely with shared perceptions of how the "marketing game" really works.

3. Use the game in another situation to accomplish one or more of the following:
   a. Assessment of issues and testing of alternative marketing intervention strategies.
   b. Development of real marketing activities and permanent coalitions of persons and organizations with interests in common.

Any Other Ideas?

# COMPACTS II: The COllaborative
# Marketing, Planning, and ACTion Simulation

## Instructions*

*All players* are concerned with improvements in service delivery and with the marketing of service innovations to key publics. *Agency administrators* may decide to engage in fund-raising efforts or to design new programs for which they will seek funding through contracts and/or grants. *Funding organizations* seek to promote interest in their priorities and may allocate funds to organizations or consortia that submit acceptable proposals. *Consumer and self-help groups* can choose to seek their own funding, but are more likely to attempt to influence funding and service organizations to ensure that their interests and those of their constituents are met. *Community influentials* represent larger constituencies and have access to private and voluntary sector funds and energy. The *Marketing Organization* is a service organization's service organization. Its staff can be helpful in the design of a marketing strategy. All players have direct access to money, personal and organizational energy, political influence and legitimacy, marketing expertise, or some of each of these resources.

Participants decide on their objectives and seek support from other players. Coalitions may be formed, projects designed, proposals submitted. Action coalitions made up of any combination of players may decide to pool their resources in efforts to develop new service programs and to engage in fund-raising activities.

*Pin on the badge* that describes a role you wish to play. You will notice that there are resource chips in the bag in which your badge was located. These represent the resources that you will have at your disposal during the game.

If you are a funder, you will have money available to allocate to worthwhile projects. Use your checkbook to make those allocations. Consumer and self-help groups and community influentials may also have checkbooks. These do not represent money in the bank right now, but the potential sums that could become available through successful fund-raising efforts. These efforts will require the design of an effective and approved fund-raising plan.

Many players will also have blue energy chips, white political influence and legitimacy chips, and red expertise chips. They can be used effectively in the marketing and planning processes. They represent what you are willing to commit to a program design or fund-raising effort. Funders and others will check to see if you have allocated these resources to plans and proposals and if you were successful in orchestrating the resources of others in a goal-oriented manner.

*The instructions that appear on pp. 349–354 and Tables A–3, A–4, and A–5 may be duplicated for single plays of COMPACTS II. They may not be republished, redistributed, or used for any other purpose.

Look over Table A–1. It will give you an idea of who has access to which resources. Then read the instructions for your role and for those of other players. It is important to know not only what you can do, but also what others in the community might be concerned with.

In designing programs, in raising funds, or in making allocations, it is important that you remain true to your role, to your constituents, and to those who may depend on your for programs and services. Set your goals and priorities accordingly. Only you know best what may be needed in the community. If you are not sure, check with others. They may have ideas as well as resources that they are willing to share.

## "Tips" for COMPACTS II Players

### Agency Administrators

Agency administrators are concerned with promoting the interests of their organizations and the populations in need that fall within their service mandates. Administrators are always on the lookout for general support. Determine your general goals and those of your organization. You may then seek support through a fund-raising activity aimed at the general public, or you may decide to submit a proposal to one of the *funding organizations*. If you do, check out the organization's priorities and be clear about whether the award will be in the form of a contract or a grant (different expectations will be attached to each). Then design a program to meet those priorities, alone or collaboratively with other service organizations, *consumer groups*, and community influentials.

Complete the Proposal Form (Table A–3), making certain all sections are properly filled out. Check with the funder periodically to see if your proposal, as it is evolving, is on target. Get as much support as you can in the community, and record that support on your Proposal Form (box 8 under the "Donated" column and box 11). Service organizations sometimes form coalitions for purposes of proposal submission or establish extensive linking mechanisms for the coordination of services or service administration. Record these where appropriate on the Proposal. Submit the Proposal before the end of the fiscal year.

If you decide to engage in other fund-raising efforts, follow the guidelines on the Fund-Raising Action Plan (Table A–4). Check your plan with an expert in the *Marketing Organization*. If he or she checks it out and gives you the go-ahead, you are on your way. If the fund-raiser suggests some modifications, make them until the plan looks right.

To raise *money*, go to any of the *consumer and self-help groups* or *community influentials* who have access to constituents who might make contributions. They may have already committed their funds to pet projects, so keep on the lookout for interest, or modify your programs to serve their needs as well. To find out whether or not your campaign was successful, flip a coin five times. Five tails means you got nothing toward your goal; one head means you are 20 percent toward your goal, two heads means 40 percent—up to five "heads," which means 100 percent. Good luck. A successful campaign sometimes needs the right environment and a lot of luck, not only good planning! Once you know the percentage raised, ask the target groups for their checks for the appropriate amount.

What kind of help can you get from the *marketing organization?*

## Funding Organizations

Agency administrators and other players will soon be approaching you with requests to fund their projects. Funders should establish clear priorities and guidelines within the first 15 minutes of playing time. Priorities should be posted at the *funder's table.* Use the Funding Priorities Form (Table A–5). Some funders prefer to keep their priorities flexible, responding to proposals that interest them as they come in; others are influenced more by who submits the proposal than by its content.

Your funds may be allocated in the form of grants or contracts. Grants are general awards to do something that fits your priorities, but the idea and the approach used are developed by the applicant organization. Contracts are specific pieces of business you wish to see completed on behalf of target populations in need. *Funders* specify all the terms of contracts and award them to those best able to perform the work.

*Funders* may go aggressively into the community to seek the kind of proposals they are interested in. Some demand matching funds from other state, federal, local, voluntary, or private agencies. In evaluating COMPACTS II Proposal Forms for the grants and contracts, check them over for consistency, accuracy, and closeness of fit with your criteria or priorities. Check also to see if the applicant organization has gathered support in the community for the proposal (box 8 and box 11). While you may not be able to fund all the proposals submitted to you, there is no reason to turn down proposals for which you have the funds. You must spend all your money before the end of the fiscal year. Issue COMPACTS II Checks and keep careful records.

## Consumer and Self-Help Groups

This is the consumer age. *Consumers* sometimes take matters into their own hands and seek funding for their own self-help activities. You may follow the same procedures as suggested for *agency administrators.* Alternatively, you may wish to work collaboratively with one or more agencies in efforts to bolster your organization's fund-raising or grants and contract-award efforts, thereby ensuring appropriate services to your constituents. Since *funders* sometimes require evidence of *consumer* inputs on agency-submitted proposals, you may be in a relatively powerful position—the more so if agencies need the resources you have at your disposal.

Should you decide to fund-raise, you may already have a potential of $5,000 to $10,000 from your own constituency. But you will need a fund-raising plan and you will have to use the "coin flip" method to determine how much you actually raised. You may also try to raise funds from other self-help groups or pool resources with them. Finally, you may involve *community influentials* in your fund-raising efforts.

Seek help, as appropriate, from the *Marketing Organization*.

## Community Influentials

Community influentials are concerned about the welfare of the community. They are also concerned about maintaining their own influence through successful efforts to promote programs. While there is no final score in this game, influentials measure their success by the number of coalitions they joined and the number of proposals submitted by each coalition that were approved by the funder. Unsuccessful coalitions or unsuccessful attempts to block other projects reduce their influence.

Most influentials have access to *funds* from their constituents. These can be allocated only if raised. Follow the same procedures for fund raising as suggested for agency administrators and for consumer groups. Use the Fund-Raising Action Plan (Table A–4) as your guide, and use the coin-flipping device to determine how successful you were. You may also commit some of your "access" to other groups and organizations trying to raise funds from your constituents. In this case, you will have to agree in advance to their requests to approach your constitutents. But you write the check only after the other fund-raisers tell you how successful they were in their efforts. Seek help, as appropriate, from the *Marketing Organization*.

## The Marketing Organization

Your only resources are *energy* and *expertise*. Your objective is to use your expertise in helping others achieve their objectives. If you are successful, you actually increase your expertise with each success. Allocate responsibilities internally. You may decide that each person will be a generalist, or that individual staff will specialize in grantsmanship, fund raising, promotions, budgeting, and so on.

It is your job to market your expertise. Your success, like that of any consultation firm, is measured in the successes of those whom you help. If they are successful, you can double the number of "expertise" chips you invested in their projects. This would be the number you would start with if we played a second round.

## Order of Play

### Getting Started

Check your resources. How many of each do you have? Which are you interested in? Who else seems to be interested? Do they have the kind of resources that complement your own? What resources are needed to develop a program you are interested in? Do you expect anyone to block your efforts to design a proposal or fund-raising plan around this issue? If you are a *funder*, you must complete your Priorities Form (Table A–5) and post it on your table within the first 15 minutes of play. Other players would do well to discover what the funders' priorities are.

### Forming Coalitions

You may choose to form or join an action coalition working for or against the resolution of any particular issue. Coalition members (1) determine their own program objectives, (2) recruit additional coalition members with necessary resources, (3) manage the resources (stacking them up on the resources board and graph), (4) write the proposal or fund-raising plan. Funders do not join coalitions but may attempt to influence their composition or the projects they are working on. The Marketing Organization may be helpful.

### Preparing a Proposal for Submission

Be certain all parts of the Proposal Form (Table A–3) are completed. Did you specify the issue or issues to be addressed? Are your program objectives clearly spelled out? Do they match the criteria established by the funder(s) to whom you will be submitting your proposal? Has agreement been reached on auspices and sponsorship? Is your statement on resources complete? Be careful: Poorly designed or incomplete proposals may not be accepted by funders. Completed proposals require supportive documentation. Funders may want to see how much support (in the form of resource chips) you've got backing your proposal. There is space on the proposal form to keep your records. How can the marketing organization help?

### Submitting Proposals

To determine whether they fit the guidelines or priorities of the funding agencies, discuss your proposals with the funders prior to final submission. Try to submit proposals to funders that are not inundated with requests or that have sufficient financial resources. Early submissions may have a better chance than last-minute submissions. *No proposals may be submitted after the close of the fiscal year.*

If your proposal is rejected, you may take your resource chips back and use them for another project, or resubmit your proposal to another funder —time permitting.

### Reviewing Proposals

Funders may review proposals on the spot (if they are submitted early enough and the funder has time) or hold them until the end of the fiscal year. In reviewing proposals, the funder should ascertain that (1) all sections have been clearly filled out, (2) there is evidence of community support through a resource committee, (3) the applicant has commitment of local matching funds (if required), and (4) the proposal fits the funder's priorities. A funder who does not have sufficient funds to approve all proposals will have to make a choice among those submitted.

### Fund Raising

If you decide to engage in a fund-raising effort as a complement to or substitute for trying to get a contract or grant award, design your fund-raising strategy. Consider involving collaborators here, too. Check your completed Fund-Raising Action Plan (Table A–4) with a member of the Marketing Organization staff. If it looks OK and if you have the commitment of your constituency or someone else's to engage in fund raising, check to see how successful your efforts were. Flip a coin five times. Each time you get a head on the coin, you are 20 percent of the way toward your goal. You may reach all or none of your goal or somewhere in between. If the funds were to have been raised from someone else's constituents, go to that player and get a check (Table A–2) for the amount you actually raised (e.g., 0, 20, 40, 60, 80, or 100 percent of your goal).

# REFERENCES

Chapter 1    The Strategic Marketing Approach

ANDREASEN, ALAN R. "Nonprofits: Check Your Attention to Customers." *Harvard Business Review*, Vol. 60, No. 3, 1982.

CRAVES, DAVID. *Strategic Marketing*. Homewood, Ill.: Richard C. Irwin, 1982.

GELB, BETSY and GABRIAL GELB. *Marketing Is Everybody's Business*. 3rd Ed. Glenview, Ill.: Scott, Foresman, 1980.

GOEDEKE, RALPH. *Marketing in Private and Nonprofit Organizations: Perspectives and Illustrations*. Glenview, Ill.: Scott, Foresman, 1977.

KOTLER, PHILIP. *Marketing for Nonprofit Organizations*. 2d Ed. Englewood Cliffs, N.J.: Prentice-Hall, 1982.

KOTLER, PHILIP, et al. (Eds.). *Cases and Readings for Marketing for Nonprofit Organizations*. Englewood Cliffs, N.J.: Prentice-Hall, 1982.

LAUFFER, ARMAND. *Doing Continuing Education and Staff Development*. New York: McGraw-Hill, 1978, pp. 90–103.

LAUFFER, ARMAND and EDWARD NEWMAN. "From the 1980s to Century 21." In Lauffer and Newman (Eds.), *Community Organization for the 1980s*. Special double issue of *Social Development Issues*, Vol. 5, Nos. 2 and 3, Summer-Fall 1981.

McCARTHY, JAMES E. *Basic Marketing: A Managerial Approach*. Homewood, Ill.: Irwin-Dorsey, 1968.

MACSTRAVIC, ROBIN S. *Marketing by Objectives for Hospitals*. Rockville, Md.: Aspen Systems, 1980.

RADUS, DAVID L. *Marketing for Non-Profit Organizations*. New York: Auburn House, 1981.

RATHMELL, JOHN M. *Marketing in the Service Sector*. Boston: Little, Brown, 1974.

ROBIN, DONALD. *Marketing: Basic Concepts for Decision Making*. New York: Harper and Row, 1978.

RUBRIGHT, BOB and DAN MACDONALD. *Marketing Health and Human Services*. Rockville, Md.: Aspen Systems, 1981.

WEBB, STANLEY G. *Marketing and Strategic Planning for Professional Service Firms*. New York: American Management, 1982.

WILSON, A. *Marketing of Professional Services*. New York: McGraw-Hill, 1972.

## Chapter 2   Exchange and Other Concepts That Underlie Strategic Marketing

BLAU, PETER. *Exchange and Power in Social Life*. New York: Wiley, 1964.

BLUMER, HERBERT. "Society as Symbolic Interaction." In Arnold Rose (Ed.), *Human Behavior and Social Process*. Boston: Houghton Mifflin, 1962.

COOLEY, CHARLES H. *Social Organization*. New York: The Free Press, 1956.

DAHRENDORF, RALPH. *Class and Social Conflict in an Industrial Society*. Stanford, Calif.: Stanford University Press, 1959.

DOWNS, ANTHONY. *Inside Bureacracy*. Boston: Little, Brown, 1967.

EVAN, WILLIAM. "The Organization-Set: Toward a Theory of Interorganizational Relationships." In James D. Thompson (Ed.), *Approaches to Organizational Design*. Pittsburgh: University of Pittsburgh Press, 1966.

GALASKIEWICZ, JOSEPH A. *Exchange Networks and Community Politics*. Beverly Hills: Sage Publications, 1979.

HAWLEY, AMOS. *Human Ecology*. New York: Ronald Press, 1950.

_____. *Urban Society: An Ecological Approach*. New York: Wiley, 1981.

HOMANS, GEORGE C. "Social Behavior as an Exchange." *The American Journal of Sociology*, May 1958.

KATZ, DANIEL and ROBERT KAHN. *The Social Psychology of Organizations*. New York: Wiley, 1966.

LAUFFER, ARMAND. "Where It's At: The Use of Mapping Tools." In *Assessment Tools for Practitioners, Managers and Trainers*. Beverly Hills: Sage Publications, 1982.

_____. *Understanding Your Social Agency*. 2d Ed. Beverly Hills: Sage Publications, 1984.

LEVINE, SOL and PAUL E. WHITE. "Exchange As a Conceptual Framework for the Study of Interorganizational Relationships." *Administration Science Quarterly*, March 1961.

LITWAK, EUGENE and JACK ROTHMAN. "Toward the Theory and Practice of Coordination Between Formal Organizations." In William R. Rosengren and Mark

Lefton (Eds.), *Organizations and Clients: Essays on the Sociology of Service.* Columbus, Ohio: Bobbs-Merrill, 1970.

## Chapter 3    Finding Your Program's Niche in the Market

GOTTLIEB, MAURICE. "Segmentation by Personality Types." In Lynn H. Stockman (Ed.), *Advanced Marketing.* Chicago: American Marketing Association, 1959.

GREEN, PAUL E. and VITHALA RAO. *Applied Multidimensional Scaling.* New York: Holt, Rinehart, 1972.

KOTLER, PHILIP. *Marketing for Non-Profit Organizations.* 2d Ed. Englewood Cliffs, N.J.: Prentice-Hall, 1982, chap. 6.

WARREN, ROLAND L. *Truth, Love and Social Change.* Chicago: Rand McNally, 1971, chap. 3.

Review also marketing references for Chapter 1

## Chapter 4    Exchanges with Other Service Providers

AIKEN, MICHAEL, et al. *Coordination of Services for the Mentally Retarded.* Madison: The University of Wisconsin, 1972. Available from Project Share, U.S. Government Printing Office, Rockville, MD 20857.

BROSKOWSKI, ANTHONY, et al. (Eds.). *Linking Health and Mental Health: Coordinating Care in the Community.* Beverly Hills: Sage Publications, 1981.

EVAN, WILLIAM. "The Organization Set: Toward a Theory of Interorganizational Relations." In James D. Thompson (Ed.), *Approaches to Organizational Design.* Pittsburgh: The University of Pittsburgh Press, 1966.

GANS, SHELDON P. and GERALD T. HORTON. *Integrating Human Services,* New York: Praeger, 1975.

HORTON, GERALD T., VICTORIA M. E. CARR, and GEORGE J. CORCORAN. *Illustrating Services Integration From Categorical Bases.* Human Service Monograph Series, No. 3. Washington, D.C.: Project Share, Department of Health, Education, and Welfare, 1976.

*Integration of Human Services in HEW: An Evaluation of Service Integration Projects.* Vol. L. Washington, D.C.: Department of Health, Education, and Welfare, Social Rehabilitation Services, 1972.

LAUFFER, ARMAND. *Social Planning at the Community Level.* Englewood Cliffs, N.J.: Prentice-Hall, 1978, pp. 187–221.

_____. *Getting the Resources You Need.* Beverly Hills: Sage Publications, 1982, pp. 47–67.

LITWAK, EUGENE and JACK ROTHMAN. "Toward the Theory and Practice of Coordination Between Formal Organizations." In William R. Rosengren and Mark Lefton (Eds.), *Organizations and Clients: Essays on the Sociology of Service.* Columbus, Ohio: Bobbs-Merrill, 1970.

PEARL G. and D. H. BAR. "Agencies Advocating Together," *Social Casework*, Vol. 57, 1976, pp. 611–618.

*Pooled Funding as a Method of Achieving Human Services Coordination.* Hartford, Conn.: Community Life Association, 1975.

ROSSI, ROBERT J., KEVIN J. GILMARTIN, and CHARLES W. DAYTON. *Agencies Working Together: A Guide to Coordination and Planning.* Beverly Hills: Sage Publications, 1982.

SAMPSON, BARBARA C. *Services Integration* (Parts I and II). Cambridge, Mass.: Abt Associates, 1975.

THOMPSON, JAMES D. and WILLIAM J. McEWEN. "Organizational Goals and Environment: Goal-setting as an Interaction Process." *American Sociological Review*, February 1958. (Reprinted in Mayer Zald, *Social Welfare Institutions.* New York: Wiley, 1957.)

## Chapter 5   Exchanges with Consumers and Natural Helpers

ABRAMS, PAUL. "Social Change, Social Networks, and Neighborhood Care." *Social Work*, Vol. 22, 1980, pp. 12–23.

ANDREWS, PAUL and D. NORTON. *Neighborhood Self Help Project.* Chicago: Chicago Commons Association, 1979.

BERGER, P. and R. NEWHAUS. *To Empower People: The Role of Mediating Institutions.* Washington, D.C.: American Enterprise Institute for Public Policy Research, 1977.

COLLINS, ARLENE and DIANE PANCOAST. *Natural Helping Networks: A Strategy for Prevention.* Washington, D.C.: National Association of Social Workers, 1976.

FELLIN, PHILLIP and EUGENE LITWAK. "The Neighborhood and Urban American Society." *Social Work*, Vol. 13, No. 4, July 1968, pp. 72–80.

FROLAND, CHARLES, et al. *Helping Networks and Human Services.* Beverly Hills: Sage Publications, 1981.

HASENFELD, YEHESKEL. "Client-Organization Relations: 4 Systems Perspective." In Rosemary C. Sarri and Yeheskel Hasenfeld (Eds.), *The Management of Human Services.* New York: Columbia University Press, 1978.

LAUFFER, ARMAND. *Getting the Resources You Need.* Beverly Hills: Sage Publications, 1982.

LEFTON, MARK and WILLIAM ROSENGREN. "Organizations and Clients: Lateral and Longitudinal Dimensions." *American Sociological Review*, December, 1966.

LITWAK, EUGENE and LYDIA F. HYLTON. "Inter-Organizational Analysis." *Administrative Science Quarterly*, Vol. 6, No. 4, March 1962, pp. 395–420.

LITWAK, EUGENE and HENRY J. MEYER. "A Balance Theory of Coordination Between Bureaucratic Organizations and Community Primary Groups." *Administrative Science Quarterly*, Vol. 11, June 1966, pp. 31–58.

_____. *School, Family and Neighborhood: The Theory and Practice of School-Community Relations.* New York: Columbia University Press, 1974.

LITWAK, EUGENE and JACK ROTHMAN. "Toward the Theory and Practice of Coordination Between Formal Organizations." In William R. Rosengren and Mark Lefton (Eds.), *Organizations and Clients*. Columbus, Ohio: Merrill, 1970.

MATTHEWS, R. MARK and STEVEN B. FAWCETT. *Matching Clients and Services*. Beverly Hills: Sage Publications, 1981.

REISSMAN, FRANK. "How Does Self Help Work?" *Social Policy*, Vol. 7, 1976, pp. 41–46.

SCHINDLER-RAINMAN, EVA and RONALD LIPPITT. *The Volunteer Community: Creative Uses of Human Resources* (2d Ed.). La Jolla, Calif.: California University Associates, 1975.

SILVERMAN, PHYLLIS R. *Mutual Help Groups*. Beverly Hills: Sage Publications, 1971.

_____. "The Widow As a Caregiver in a Program on Preventive Intervention with Other Widows," *Mental Hygiene*, Vol. 54, No. 5, 1970.

WARREN, RACHELLE B. and DONALD I. WARREN. *The Neighborhood Organizer's Handbook*. Notre Dame, Ind.: Notre Dame Press, 1977.

WELLMAN, BARRY, et al. *Community Ties and Support Systems*. University of Toronto Research Paper No. 11. Toronto: Center for Urban and Community Studies, July 1972.

## Chapter 6   Negotiating Your Way to New Partnerships

ALINSKY, SAUL D. *Rules for Radicals: A Practical Primer for Realistic Radicals*. New York: Vintage Press, 1971.

American Federation of State, County and Municipal Employees, Education Department. *Getting Help to People*. Chicago: The Midwest Academy, 1973.

BACHARACH, SAMUEL B. and J. LAWLER (Eds.). *Bargaining: Power, Tactics and Outcomes*. San Francisco: Jossey-Bass, 1981.

CHALMERS, WILLIAM E. and GERALD W. CORMICK. *Collective Bargaining in Racial Disputes*. Ann Arbor: Institute of Labor and Industrial Relations, The University of Michigan, 1970.

COFFIN, ROBERT. *The Negotiator*. New York: Barnes and Noble, 1973.

FAGAN, HARRY. *Empowerment*. New York: Paulist Press, 1979.

FISHER, ROGER and WILLIAM URY. *Getting to Yes: Negotiating Agreement Without Giving In*. Boston: Houghton-Mifflin, 1981.

KARRAS, CHESTER L. *The Negotiating Game*. New York: T. Y. Crowell, 1970.

MASLOW, ABRAHAM. "A Theory of Motivation." *Psychological Bulletin*, Vol. 50, July 1943, pp. 370–396.

NIERENBERG, GERALD I. *The Art of Negotiating*. 2d Ed. New York: Hawthorn Books, 1982.

_____. *Creative Business Negotiating: Skills and Successful Strategies*. New York: Hawthorn Books, 1971.

RUBIN, JEFFREY Z. and BERT R. BROWN. *The Social Psychology of Bargaining and Negotiations*. New York: Academic Press, 1975.

STRAUSS, ANSELM L. *Negotiations: Varieties, Contexts and Social Order*. San Francisco: Jossey-Bass, 1978.

## Chapter 7 Interactive Assessment Techniques

BRAGER, GEORGE and STEPHEN HOLLOWAY. *Changing Human Service Organizations*. New York: The Free Press, 1978.

DALKEY, NORMAN C., D. I. ROURKE, R. LEWIS, and D. SNYDER. *Studies in the Quality of Life: Delphi and Decision Making*. Lexington, Mass.: Lexington Books, 1972.

DEBLOOIS, MICHAEL and RAYMOND C. MELTON. *Functional Task Analysis: The Training Module*. Tallahassee, Florida: Department of Education, 1974.

DELBECQ, ANDRE L. and ANDREW H. VAN DE VEN. "A Group Process Model for Problem Identification and Program Planning." In Neil Gilbert and Harry Specht (Eds.), *Planning for Social Welfare: Issues, Models, and Tasks*. Englewood Cliffs, N.J.: Prentice-Hall, 1977.

DELBECQ, ANDRE L., ANDREW VAN DE VEN, and DAVID H. GUSTAFSON. *Group Techniques for Program Planning: A Guide to Nominal and Delphi Processes*. Glenview, Ill.: Scott, Foresman, 1976.

EPSTEIN, IRWIN and TONY TRIPODI. *Research Techniques for Program Planning, Monitoring and Evaluation*. New York: Columbia University Press, 1977.

FINE, SYDNEY and WRETHA W. WILEY. *An Introduction to Functional Job Analysis*. Kalamazoo, Mich.: W. E. Upjohn Institute for Employment Research, 1971.

HARVEY, DONALD F. and DONALD R. BROWN. *An Experimental Approach to Organizational Development*. (2d Ed.). Englewood Cliffs, N.J.: Prentice-Hall, 1981.

LAUFFER, ARMAND. *Assessment Tools for Practitioners, Managers and Trainers*. Beverly Hills: Sage Publications, 1982.

LINSTONE, HAROLD and MURRAY TUROFF. *The Delphi Method: Techniques and Applications*. Reading, Mass.: Addison-Wesley, 1975.

TUROFF, MURRAY. "The Design of a Policy Delphi." *Technological Forecasting and Social Change*, No. 2, 1970, pp. 140–171.

## Chapter 8 Designing the Program

ABELS, PAUL and M. J. MURPHY. *Administration in the Human Services: A Normative Systems Approach*. Englewood Cliffs, N.J.: Prentice-Hall, 1981.

BRODY, RALPH. *Problem Solving, Concepts and Methods for Community Organizations*. New York: Human Sciences Press, 1982.

BLAKELY, E. J. "Goal Setting for Community Development—Case of Yuba City, California." *Rural Sociality*, Vol. 44, No. 2, 1979, pp. 434–436.

COHN, A. J. "Definition of the Task: Facts Projections and Inventories," In N. Gilbert and H. Specht (Eds.), *Planning for Social Welfare*. Englewood Cliffs, N.J.: 1977.

CRAIG, DOROTHY. *Hip Pocket Guide to Planning and Evaluation.* Austin, Texas: Learning Concepts Publications, 1976.

DALE, D. and MITIGUI, N. *Planning for a Change.* Amherst, Mass.: Citizen Involvement Training Project, 1978.

DELBCEQ, ANDRE and A. H. VAN DE VEN. "A Group Process Model for Problem Identification and Program Planning." *Journal of Applied and Behavioral Science*, Vol. 7, 1971, pp. 466–492.

ERVING, DAVID. "Discovering Your Problem-Solving Style." *Psychology Today*, Vol. 11, December 1977, pp. 69–74.

ETZIONI, AMITAI. "Mixed-Scanning: A Third Approach to Decision Making." *Publication Review*, Vol. 1, December 1967, pp. 385–392. (Reprinted in Neil Gilbert and Harry Specht (Eds.), *Planning for Social Welfare.* Englewood Cliffs, N.J.: Prentice-Hall, 1977.)

FRIEDMANN, JOHN. *Retracking America: A Theory of Transactive Planning.* New York: Anchor Books, 1973.

GLIDEWELL, JOHN C. *Choice Points.* Cambridge, Mass.: The MIT Press, 1976.

HUDSON, BARCLAY M. "Comparison of Current Planning Theories: Counterparts and Contradictions." In Ralph M. Kramer and Harry Specht (Eds.), *Readings and Community Organization Practice* (3d Ed.). Englewood Cliffs, N.J.: Prentice-Hall, 1983.

KILMANN, RALPH H., LOUIS R. PONDY, and DENNIS P. SLEVEN (Eds.). *The Management of Organization Design: Strategies and Implementation.* New York: North-Holland, 1976. (See especially articles by Jay W. Lorsch, "Contingency Theory and Organization Design," and Charles E. Summer, "Strategies for Organization and Design.")

LAUFFER, ARMAND. *Grantsmanship.* Beverly Hills: Sage Publications, 1983.

———. *Social Planning at the Community Level.* Englewood Cliffs, N.J.: Prentice-Hall, 1978.

LINDLBLOM, CHARLES E. "The Science of Muddling Through." *Public Administration Review*, Vol. 19, Spring 1959, pp. 79–88. (Reprinted in A. Gilbert and H. Specht (Eds.), *Planning for Social Welfare.* Englewood Cliffs, N.J.: Prentice-Hall, 1977.)

LIPPITT, RONALD, JEANNE WATSON, and B. WESTLEY. *The Dynamics of Planned Change.* New York: Harcourt, Brace, 1958.

MAGER, JOHN. "Decision Trees for Decision Making." *Harvard Business Review*, July-August, 1964, pp. 126–138.

MAGER, ROBERT. *Goal Analysis.* Belmont, Calif.: Fearon Publishers, 1972.

MANN, FLOYD C. and F. W. NEFF. *Managing Major Change in Organizations.* Ann Arbor: Foundation for Research on Human Behavior, 1961.

McCORMICK, M. *The New York Times Guide to Reference Materials.* New York: Popular Library, 1971.

NIEHOFF, A. H. "The Process of Innovation," In A. H. Niehoff (Ed.), *Handbook of Social Change.* Chicago: Aldine, 1966.

PARNES, SIDNEY, J., et al. *Guide to Creative Action.* New York: Scribner, 1977.

REIN, MARTIN and ROBERT MORRIS. "Goals, Structures and Strategies for Community Change." In Ralph Kramer and Harry Specht (Eds.), *Readings in Com-*

*munities Organization Practice* (2d Ed.). Englewood Cliffs, N.J.: Prentice-Hall, 1983.

RESNICK, HYMAN and RINO PATTI (Eds.). *Change from Within: Humanizing Social Welfare Organizations.* Philadelphia, Temple University Press, 1980. (See especially articles by Patti, "Organizational Resistance and Change," Robert Morris and Robert Bienstock, "Organizational Resistance to Planning Goals," and Joanne Hage and Michael Aiken, "Program Change and Organizational Properties.")

YOUNG, R. C. "Goal and Goal Setting." *Journal of the American Institute of Planners,* Vol. 32, March 1966, pp. 76–85.

ZANDER, ALVIN. "Resistance to Change: Its Analysis and Prevention." In W. G. Bennis, K. D. Benne, and R. Chin (Eds.), "The Planning of Change," reading in *Applied Behavioral Sciences.* New York: Holt, Rinehart, 1962.

## Chapter 9    Placing and Pricing the Program

BUCHANAN, BARRY. "Building Organizational Commitment: The Social-Managers in a Work Organization." *Administrative Science Quarterly,* December 1974, pp. 533–546.

BUCHANAN, JAMES M. *Public Finance in the Democratic Process.* Chapel Hill: The University of North Carolina Press, 1967.

———. *The Demand and Supply of Public Goods.* New York: Rand McNally, 1968.

*Cost Finding for Community Mental Health Centers: An Annotated Bibliography.* Rockville, Md.: National Institute of Mental Health, Community Mental Health Branch, 1970.

CULLEY, JAMES P., BARBARA H. SUTTLES, and JUDITH B. VAN NAME. *Understanding and Measuring the Cost of Foster Care.* Newark: The University of Delaware, 1975.

DUNNETT, MARVIN (Ed.). *Handbook of Industrial and Organizational Psychology.* Chicago: Rand McNally, 1976.

GOODMAN, NATHANIEL. "Fee Charging." In Robert Morris (Ed.), *Encyclopedia of Social Work* (16th ed.). New York: National Association of Social Workers, 1971.

GROSS, MALVERN J. *Financial and Accounting Guide for Non-Profit Organizations.* New York: Ronald Press, 1972.

HILL, JOHN G. and RALPH ORMSKY. *Cost Analysis Method for Casework Agencies.* Philadelphia: Family Service Agency of Philadelphia, 1953.

LOHMANN, ROGER A. *Breaking Even: Financial Management in Human Service Organizations.* Philadelphia: Temple University Press, 1980.

———. "Break Even Analysis." *Social Work,* Vol. 21, July 1976, pp. 300–308.

MASLOW, ABRAHAM. *Toward a Theory of Being.* New York: Van Nostrand, 1968.

STAW, BARRY and GERALD SALANCIK (Eds.). *New Directions in Organizational Behavior.* Chicago: St. Clare, 1977.

STIGLER, GEORGE. *The Theory of Price.* New York: Macmillan, 1952.

STIGUM, MARCIA L. *Problems in Micro-Economics.* Homewood, Ill.: Richard C. Irwin, 1975.

SORENSEN, JAMES E., et al. *Cost-finding and Rate Setting for Community Mental Health Centers.* Rockville, Md.: National Institute of Mental Health, 1972.

VINTER, ROBERT and REAH KISH. *Budgeting for Not-for-Profit Organizations.* New York: The Free Press, 1984.

## Chapter 10 Budgeting the Program

*Budgeting: A Guide for United Ways and Not-For-Profit Human Service Organizations.* Arlington, Va.: United Way of America, 1975.

Family Service Association of America. *Budget Presentation: Some Guides for Family Service Agencies.* New York: Family Service Association of America, 1969.

GOLEMBIEWSKI, ROBERT J. (Ed.). *Public Budgeting and Finance.* Itasca, Ill.: F. E. Peacock Publishers, 1968.

GROSS, LAVERN J. *Financial and Accounting Guide for Non-Profit Organizations.* New York: Ronald Press, 1974.

HALL, MARY. *Developing Skills in Proposal Writing.* 2d Ed. Corvallis, Ore.: Continuing Education Publishers, 1981, chap. 12.

JONES, REGINALD and GEORGE TRENTIN. *Budgeting: Key to Planning and Control.* Washington, D.C.: American Management, 1971.

KIRITZ, NORMAN J. "Program Planning and Proposal Writing." *The Grantsmanship Center News*, Vol. 34, May-June 1978.

LAUFFER, ARMAND. *Grantsmanship and Fundraising.* Beverly Hills: Sage Publications, 1984.

VINTER, ROBERT D. and REAH KISH. *Budgeting for Not-for-Profit Organizations.* New York: The Free Press, 1984.

WILSON, RICHARD M. S. *Financial Control: A Systems Approach.* London: McGraw-Hill, 1974.

## Chapter 11 Getting on the Charts

BRODY, RALPH. *Problem Solving: Concepts and Methods for Community Organizations.* New York: Human Sciences Press, 1982, Chap. 9.

CRAIG, DOROTHY. *A Hip Pocket Guide to Planning and Evaluation.* Austin, Texas: Learning Concepts Publications, 1976.

HOFFER, JOE R. *A Programmed Introduction to PERT for Planning Large Projects in Social Welfare.* Columbus, Ohio: National Conference on Social Welfare, 1971.

_____. "PERT: a Tool for Managers of Human Service Programs." In Fred M. Cox, John L. Erlich, Jack Rothman, and John E. Tropman (Eds.), *Tactics and Techniques for Community Practice.* 2d Ed. Itasca, Ill.: F. E. Peacock, 1983.

KRUECKENBERG, DONALD A. and ARTHUR L. SILVERS. *Urban Planning Analysis: Methods and Models*. New York: Wiley, 1977.

LAUFFER, ARMAND. *Social Planning at the Community Level*. Englewood Cliffs, N.J.: Prentice-Hall, 1978, Chap. 9.

LEFFERTS, ROBERT. *How to Prepare Charts and Graphs for Effective Reports*. New York: Harper and Row, 1981.

MACDICKEN, ROBERT, et al. *Toward More Effective Management*. Washington, D.C.: Administration on Aging, 1975.

Policy Management Systems, Inc. *A Programmed Course of Instructions in PERT*. Washington, D.C.: Office of Economic Opportunities, 1969.

VINTER, ROBERT D. and REAH KISH. *Budgeting for Not-for-Profit Organizations*. New York: The Free Press, 1984.

## Chapter 12 Evaluating Program Outcomes

AUSTIN, MICHAEL, J., et al. *Evaluating Your Agency's Programs*. Beverly Hills: Sage Publications, 1982.

BRODY, RALPH. *Problem Solving*. New York: Human Sciences Press, 1982, Chap. 11

EPSTEIN, IRWIN and TONY TRIPODI. *Research Techniques For Program Planning, Monitoring and Evaluation*. New York: Columbia University Press, 1977.

FAST, DOROTHY. "A New Approach to Quantifying Training Program Effectiveness." *Training and Development Journal*, September 1974, pp. 8–14.

KIRESUK, THOMAS and GEOFFREY GARWICK. "Basic Goal Attainment Scaling Procedures." In Beulah Compton and Burt Galawick, *Social Work Processes*. Homewood, Ill.: Dorsey Press, 1975, pp. 388–400.

PERKINS, D. N. T. "Evaluating Social Interventions: A Conceptual Schema." *Evaluation Quarterly*, Vol. 1, No. 4, November 1977, pp. 639–656. (Reprinted in Ralph M. Kramer and Harry Specht (Eds.), *Readings in Community Organization Practice*. 3d Ed. Englewood Cliffs, N.J.: Prentice-Hall, 1983.

ROSSI, PETER H. and HOWARD E. FREEMAN. *Evaluation: A Systematic Approach*. 2d Ed. Beverly Hills: Sage, 1982.

RUTMAN, LEONARD. *Understanding Program Evaluation*. Beverly Hills: Sage Publications, 1983.

———— (Ed.). *Evaluation Research Methods: A Basic Guide*. Beverly Hills: Sage Publications, 1977.

## Chapter 13 The Profitable Way to Raise Money

*Bibliography of Fundraising and Philanthropy*. National Catholic Development Conference, 130 E. 40th St., New York, N.Y. 10016, "Special Fund Raising Events."

CREAMER, R. *Fundraising and Local Community Organization*. Chicago: Midwest Academy, 1974.

DAVIS, KING. *Fundraising in the Black Community*. Metuchen, N.J.: Scarecrow Press, 1975.

DERMER, JOSEPH (Ed.). *America's Most Successful Fundraising Letters*. New York: The Public Service Materials Center, 1978.

FISHER, JOHN. *How to Manage a Nonprofit Organization*. Toronto, Ontario: Management and Fund Raising Centre, 1978.

FLANAGAN, J. *The Grass Roots Fundraising Book*. Chicago: Contemporary Books, 1982.

FRIANT, RAY J., JR. *Preparing Effective Presentations*. Pilot Industries, 347 Fifth Avenue, New York, N.Y. 10016, 1971.

"Fundraising Letters" and "Organizing Your Way to Dollars." Fundraising Centre, 287 McPherson Avenue, Toronto, Ontario M4V 1A4.

*Fundraising Management*. Journal published by Hoke Communications, 224 7th St., Garden City, New York.

GURIN, MAURICE G. *What Volunteers Should Know for Successful Fundraising*. New York: Stein and Day, 1981.

KELLER, MITCHELL (Ed.). *The KRC Guide to Direct Mail Fundraising*. KRC Development Council, 212 Elm Street, New Canaan, Conn. 06840, 1979.

LEIBERT, EDWIN R. and BERNICE SHELDON. *Handbook of Special Events for Non-Profit Organizations*. New York: Association Press, 1972.

MIRKIN, HOWARD R. *The Complete Fundraising Guide*. New York: The Public Service Materials Center, 1975.

MUSSELMAN, VIRGINIA W. *Money Raising Events for Community Groups*. New York: Association Press, 1969.

NEWMAN, EDWIN S. and LEO J. MARGOLIN. *Fundraising Made Easy*. New York: Oceana Publications, 1954.

PULLING, LISA. *The KRC Desk Book for Fund Raisers: With Model Forms and Records*. New Canaan, Conn.: The KRC Development Council, 1980.

SCHNEPPER, JEFF A. *How to Pay Zero Taxes*. Reading, Mass.: Addison-Wesley, 1982.

SEYMOUR, HAROLD J. *Designs for Fund Raising: Principles, Patterns and Techniques*. New York: McGraw-Hill, 1966.

SHEPPARD, WILLIAM E. *Annual Giving Idea Book*. Plymouth Meeting, Pa.: The Fund Raising Institute, 1979. (Also get the Institute's *Monthly Portfolio*.)

STEIN, LOUIS (Ed.). *Building a Successful Campaign*. New York: Council of Jewish Welfare Federations, 1979.

TATUM, LISTON. *The KRC Computer Book for Fund Raisers*. New Canaan, Conn.: The KRC Development Council, 1978.

UTECH, INGRID. *Stalking the Large Green Giant*. Washington, D.C.: National Youth Alternatives Project, 1976.

WARNER, IRVING. *The Art of Fundraising*. New York: Harper and Row, 1975.

## Chapter 14    Increasing Your Grants, Contracts, and Allocations Power

*Annual Register of Grant Support.* Academic Media, 32 Lincoln Avenue, Orange, NJ 07050.

*Annual Register of Grant Support.* Chicago: Marquis Academic Media.

*Corporate Foundation Directory.* Washington, D.C.: Taft Corporation, 1977.

*Corporate Foundation Profiles.* New York: Foundation Center, 1980.

DERMER, JOSEPH. *Where America's Large Foundations Make Their Grants.* New York: Public Service Materials Center, 1977.

————. *How to Get Your Fair Share of Foundation Grants.* New York: Public Service Materials Center, 1973.

————. *How to Raise Funds From Foundations.* New York: Public Service Materials Center, 1977.

————. *How to Write Successful Foundation Presentations.* New York: Public Service Materials Center, 1975.

DESMARAIS, PHILLIP. *How to Get Government Grants.* New York: Public Service Materials Center, 1977.

*Directory of Research Philanthropy.* San Francisco: Public Management Institute, annually.

*Directory of Research Grants.* Phoenix: Oryx Press, 1977.

ECKSTEIN, BURTON. *Handicapped Funding Directory.* Oceanside, New York: Research Grant Guides, 1978.

*Federal Register.* Published daily by the federal government.

*Federal Grants and Contracts Weekly.* Capitol Publications, Suite G-12, 2430 Pennsylvania Ave., N.W., Washington, DC 20037.

FLANAGAN, JOAN. *Grass Roots Fundraising Book.* Chicago: Swallow Press, 1977.

*Forbes "Market 500."* Published in May in *Forbes Magazine*, Forbes, 500 Fifth Avenue, New York, NY, 10010.

*Fortune "Double 500 Directory."* Fortune Magazine. 541 North Fairbanks Court, Chicago, IL 60611.

*Fortune "Double 500 Directory."* Fortune Magazine, P.O. Box 40, Trenton, NJ 08007.

*Foundation Center National Data Book.* New York: Foundation Center.

*Foundation Center Source Book Profiles.* New York: Foundation Center, periodic updates.

*Foundation Directory.* (8th Ed.). New York: Foundation Center, 1982.

*Foundation Grants Index.* New York: Foundation Center (annually).

*Foundation Grants to Individuals.* New York: Foundation Center.

*Foundation News.* New York: Council on Foundations, bimonthly.

*Foundations That Send Their Annual Reports.* New York: Public Service Materials Center, 1976.

*Foundations Today.* New York: Foundation Center, 1980.

*Funding in Aging.* Garden City: Adelphi Press, 1979.

*Grantsmanship Center News.* Los Angeles: Grantsmanship Center, eight times a year.

*Grantsmanship Money and How to Get It.* Chicago: Marquis Academic Media, 1978.

*Guide to Corporate Giving in the Arts.* New York: American Council for the Arts, 1981.

HALL, MARY. *Developing Skills in Proposal Writing.* 2d Ed. Corvallis, Ore.: Continuing Education Publications, 1981.

*Health Grants and Contracts Weekly.* Capitol Publications, Inc., Suite G-12, 2430 Pennsylvania Ave., N.W., Washington, DC 20037.

*How to Get Money for Arts and Humanities, Drugs and Alcohol Abuse and Health.* Human Resources Network, Radnor, Pa.: Chilton Book Co., 1979.

*How to Get Money for Conservation and Community Development.* Human Resources Network, Radnor, Pa.: Chilton Book Co., 1975.

*How to Get Money for Youth, the Elderly, the Handicapped, Women and Civil Liberties.* Radnor, Pa.: Chilton Book Co., 1975.

KIRTIZ, NORTON J. *Program Planning and Proposal Writing.* Los Angeles: The Grantsmanship Center, 1980.

KURZIG, CAROL M. *Foundation Fundamentals: A Guide for Grantseekers.* New York: The Foundation Center, 1980.

LAUFFER, ARMAND. *Grantsmanship.* 2d Ed. Beverly Hills: Sage Publications, 1984.

LEFFERTS, ROBERT. *Getting a Grant: How to Write Successful Grant Proposals.* Englewood Cliffs, N.J.: Prentice-Hall, 1978.

*Private Funding for Rural Programs.* Washington, D.C.: National Rural Center, 1978.

*The Proposal Writer's Swipe File II.* Washington, D.C.: National Rural Center, 1976.

*Register of Corporations and Register of Directors and Executives.* Standard and Poor's Publications, 345 Hudson Street, New York, NY 10014.

*Register of Directors and Executives.* Standard and Poor's Publications, 345 Hudson Street, New York, NY 10014.

SMITH, CRAIG. *Getting Grants.* New York: Harper & Row, 1980.

STRUCKHOFF, E. C. *The Handbook for Community Foundations: Their Formation, Development and Operation.* Washington, D.C.: Council on Foundations, 1977.

U.S. Department of the Treasury, Internal Revenue Service. *Statistics of Income, 1974–78, Private Foundations.* Government Printing Office, updated annually.

U.S. Executive Office of the President. *Catalogue of Federal Domestic Assistance.* Washington, D.C., U.S. Government Printing Office, updated annually.

WHITE, VIRGINIA. *Grants: How to Find Out About Them and What to Do Next.* New York: Plenum Press, 1975.

## Chapter 15    Promotions: A Strategic Communications Approach

ANDERSON, N. and F. D. ROSA. *How to Use the Media Effectively*. Milford, Conn.: New England Environmental Network, 1978.

ARONSON, J. *Deadline for the Media: Today's Challenges to Press, TV and Radio*. Indianapolis: Bobbs-Merrill, 1972.

BALLENGER, B. *Playing the Media Game*. Chicago: Midwest Academy, 1978.

BEACH, M. *Editing Your Newspaper: A Guide to Writing, Design and Production*. Portland, Ore.: Coast to Coast Books, 1980.

BRAWLEY, EDWARD A.' *Social Work and the Mass Media*. Beverly Hills: Sage Publications, 1983.

CHURCH, D. *It's Time to Tell: A Media Handbook for Human Services Personnel*. Washington, D.C.: U.S. Department of Health and Human Services, 1980, Preface.

Connecticut Education Association. *Public Relations Handbook*. Hartford: Connecticut Education Association (no date).

CREIGHTON, J. L. *The Public Involvement Manual*. Cambridge, Mass.: Abt Books, 1981.

DELOACHE, W. F. "Public Relations: A State of Mind." *Social Casework*, Vol. 57, No. 7, 1976, pp. 432–7.

GOLDMAN, M. W. "Radio: A Medium for the Presentation of Social Work." *Social Work*, Vol. 5, No. 2, 1960, pp. 84–90.

GORDON R. *We Interrupt This Program: A Citizen's Guide to Using the Media for Social Change*. Amherst, Mass.: Citizen Involvement Training Project, 1978.

JOSLYN-SCHERER, MARCIA. *Communication in the Human Services: A Guide to Therapeutic Journalism*. Beverly Hills: Sage Publications, 1980.

KLEIN, T. and F. DANZIG. *How to Be Heard: Making the Media Work for You*. New York: Macmillan, 1974.

League of Women Voters. *Getting Into Print*. Washington, D.C.: League of Women Voters (no date).

_____. *Speaking Out: Setting Up a Speaker's Bureau*. Washington, D.C.: League of Women Voters, 1977.

_____. *Breaking Into Broadcasting*. Washington, D.C.: League of Women Voters, 1978.

MARTINEZ, B. and R. WEINER. *Guide to Public Relations for Non-Profit Organizations and Public Agencies*. Los Angeles: The Grantmanship Center, 1979.

National Citizen Committee for Broadcasting. *The Why's and How's of Public Service Announcements*. Washington, D.C.: National Citizens Committee for Broadcasting, 1976.

National Association of Broadcasters. *If You Want Air Time: A Publicity Handbook*. Washington, D.C.: National Association of Broadcasters, 1979.

Prentice-Hall Editorial Staff. *How to Use the Telephone Effectively*. Englewood Cliffs, N.J.: Prentice-Hall (no date).

Public Media Center. *A Handbook on Free Access to the Media for Public Service Advertising*. San Francisco: The Public Media Center (no date).

SCHMIDT, F. *Using Publicity to Best Advantage.* New York: Public Relations Society of America, 1977.

United Way of America. *Public Relations for Human Services.* Alexandria, Va.: United Way of America (no date).

## Chapter 16 The Marketing Audit

HASENFELD, YEHESKEL. "Program Development." In F. M. Cox, John L. Ehrlich, Jack Rothman, and John E. Tropman (Eds.), *Strategies of Community Organization.* Itasca, Ill.: F. E. Peacock, 1979.

KOTLER, PHILIP. "Marketing Methods." In *Marketing for Non-Profit Organizations.* (2d Ed.). Englewood Cliffs, N.J.: Prentice-Hall, 1982, chap. 4.

LORSCH, J. W. and JOHN L. MORSE. *Organizations and Their Members: A Contingency Approach.* New York: Harper and Row, 1974.

MOURSEND, JOHN P. *Evaluation: An Introduction to Research Design.* Belmont, Calif.: Brooks/Cole Publishing Co., 1973.

SUCHMAN, EDWARD A. "Action For What? A Critique of Evaluation Research." In R. O'Toole (Ed.), *The Organization, Management, and Tactics of Social Research.* Cambridge, Mass.: Schenkman Publishing Co., 1970.

TRIPODI, TONY, PHILLIP FELLIN, and IRWIN EPSTEIN. *Differential Social Program Evaluation.* Itasca, Ill.: F. E. Peacock, 1978.

WASHINGTON, R. "Alternative Frameworks For Program Evaluation." In Fred M. Cox, John L. Ehrlich, Jack Rothman, and John E. Tropman (Eds.), *Tactics and Techniques of Community Practice.* 2d Ed. Itasca, Ill.: F. E. Peacock, 1983.

WEISS, CAROLE H. *Evaluation Research: Methods for Assessing Program Effectiveness.* Englewood Cliffs, N.J.: Prentice-Hall, 1972.

WEISS, ROBERT S. and MARTIN REIN. "The Evaluation of Broad-Aim Programs: A Cautionary Case and a Moral." *Annals of the American Academy of Political and Social Science*, Vol. 385, September 1969, pp. 118–132.

## Appendix

BELL, D. C. "Simulation Games: Three Research Paradigms." *Simulations and Games*, Vol. 6, 1975, pp. 271–278.

BELL, ROBERT and JOHN COPLANS. *Decisions, Decisions: Game Theory and You.* New York: Norton, 1976.

CARLSON, JOHN G. and MICHAEL J. MISSHAUK. *Introduction to Gaming: Management Decision Simulations.* New York: Wiley, 1972.

COLEMAN, JAMES S. "Game Models of Economic and Political Systems." In Samuel Z. Klausner (Ed.), *The Study of Total Societies.* New York: Doubleday, Anchor Books, 1967.

DUKE, RICHARD. *Gaming, the Future's Language.* Beverly Hills: Sage Publications, 1975.

GILLESPIE, PHILIP H. *Learning Through Simulation Games.* Paramus, N.J.: Paulist-Newman Publishing, 1974.

GREENBLATT, CATHY and RICHARD R. DUKE. *The Principles and Practices of Gaming-Simulation.* Beverly Hills: Sage Publications, 1981.

HORN, ROBERT E. *The Guide to Simulations and Games.* 4th Ed. Beverly Hills: Sage Publications, 1981.

LAUFFER, ARMAND. *The Aim of the Game.* New York: Gamed Simulations, Inc., 1973.

TAYLOR, JAMES R. and R. WALFORD. *Learning and the Simulation Game.* Beverly Hills: Sage Publications, 1979.


*Other Versions of COMPACTS*

Lauffer, Armand. *COMPACTS.* New York: Gamed Simulations, Inc., 1973.

_____. "The Intra-Agency Cooperation Game." In *Social Planning at the Community Level.* Englewood Cliffs, N.J.: Prentice-Hall, 1978, chap. 17.

_____. "LINK" Locating Informational Network Kinetics. In *Assessment Tools.* Beverly Hills: Sage Publications, 1982, chap. 7.

_____. "R.F.P." In *Resources for Child Placement.* Beverly Hills: Sage Publications, 1980, chap. 8.

LAUFFER, ARMAND and THOMAS MORTON. *Turn-On.* Washington, D.C.: Administration on Aging, 1974.

# INDEX

—